The Role of Values in Psychology and Human Development

William M. Kurtines
Margarita Azmitia
Jacob L. Gewirtz

Editors

John Wiley & Sons, Inc.
A Wiley-Interscience Publication
New York • Chichester • Brisbane • Toronto • Singapore

Library of Congress Cataloging-in-Publication Data

The Role of values in psychology and human development / editors,
    William M. Kurtines, Margarita Azmitia, and Jacob L. Gewirtz.
        p.   cm.
    Includes bibliographical references.
    ISBN 0-471-53945-7 (alk. paper)
    1. Psychology—Moral and ethical aspects.   2. Developmental
psychology—Moral and ethical aspects.   3. Values—Psychological
aspects.   4. Moral development.   I. Kurtines, William M.
II. Azmitia, Margarita.   III. Gewirtz, Jacob L., 1924–_____   .
BF76.4.R65   1992
150'.1'3—dc20   91-18870

Printed in the United States of America

10 9 8 7 6 5 4 3 2 1

Printed and bound by Courier Companies, Inc.

Contributors

Mildred Alvarez is an Assistant Professor of Psychology at San Jose State University. She received her doctorate in developmental psychology from Boston University. In addition to the metatheoretical foundations of science and psychology, her interests include moral development, the socialization effects of television, and gender differences.

Margarita Azmitia is an Assistant Professor of Psychology at the University of California, Santa Cruz. She received her doctorate in developmental psychology from the University of Minnesota. Her interests include the role of peer interaction in children's cognitive development, the social foundations of knowledge, and the metatheoretical foundations of science and psychology.

Diana Baumrind is a Research Psychologist in the Institute of Human Development of the University of California, Berkeley, and Director of the Family Socialization and Developmental Competence Project—a longitudinal program of research. Her main research interest is parents' contribution to developmental competence and dysfunctional behavior throughout childhood and adolescence. In addition, she has been a leading advocate of ethical treatment of human subjects and has developed a rule-utilitarian justification for opposition to the use of deception.

Lyn Mikel Brown is Assistant Professor and Co-Chair of the Education Department at Colby College, Waterville, Maine. She is also a Research Associate affiliated with the Project on the Psychology of Women and the Development of Girls at the Harvard Graduate School of Education. She received her doctorate in Human Development and Psychology from Harvard University. Her research interests focus on female personality, social, and moral development, the psychology of women, the relationship between gender and culture, and interpretive research methods.

Nicholas Emler is Professor of Social Psychology at the University of Dundee. He received his doctorate in social psychology from the London School of Economics in 1976. His interests are in crime and delinquency, the relation between morality and politics, the psychology of reputation, and the development of social knowledge. He is currently chief editor of the *European Journal of Social Psychology.*

Donelson R. Forsyth is a Professor of Psychology at Virginia Commonwealth University. He received his doctorate in social psychology from the University of Florida. His current investigations are concentrated in several related areas of social psychology, but his two major interests are affective and attributional reactions in interpersonal, educational, and clinical settings and individual differences in ethical ideology. He is the author of numerous journal articles, as well as several books dealing with social psychology, group processes, and health.

Jacob L. Gewirtz is a Professor of Psychology at Florida International University and a Professor of Pediatrics and Psychiatry at the University of Miami Medical School. He received his doctorate in developmental and experimental psychology from the University of Iowa. Dr. Gewirtz's theoretical and research contributions have been on the topics of social learning and development, including attachment acquisition and loss, imitation/identification, parent–child interaction and directions of influence, and the behavioral effects of shifts in maintaining environments. He co-edited (with W. Kurtines) *The Handbook of Moral Behavior and Development: Theory, Research, and Application* (Vols. 1–3).

John C. Gibbs is an Associate Professor of Psychology at The Ohio State University. He received his doctorate in social psychology from Harvard University. His recent work has included assessment methods for, theory of, and interventions with conduct-disordered adolescents. His is the author of *Social Intelligence: Measuring the Development of Sociomoral Reflection.*

Robert Hogan is the McFarlin Professor of Psychology at the University of Tulsa, Chair of the Department of Psychology, and Director of Research at the Tulsa Psychiatric Center. He received his doctorate in personality psychology from the University of California at Berkeley. The author of over 60 articles, chapters, and books, he has been a life-long student of how the development of character impacts personality and society.

Howard H. Kendler is a Professor of Psychology at the University of California, Santa Barbara. He received his doctorate in experimental psychology for the University of Iowa. His primary areas of scholarship have been learning theory and cognitive development. He currently is involved with a methodological–historical analysis of psychology. In addition to publishing numerous articles in professional journals and books,

Kendler has authored *Basic Psychology, Historical Foundations of Modern Psychology,* and *Psychology: A Science in Conflict,* and co-edited *Essays in Neobehaviorism: A Memorial Volume to Kenneth W. Spence.*

William M. Kurtines is a Professor of Psychology and Director of Graduate Studies in the Department of Psychology at Florida International University. He is also Research Professor of Psychiatry in the School of Medicine at the University of Miami. He received his doctorate in psychology from The Johns Hopkins University. His current areas of interest include social, personality, moral, and family development. He co-edited (with J. L. Gewirtz) *Intersections with Attachment* and co-authored (with J. Szapocznik) *Breakthroughs in Family Therapy with Drug Abusing and Problem Youth.*

John A. Meacham is a Professor of Psychology and Associate Vice Provost for Undergraduate Education at the State University of New York at Buffalo. He received his training in general psychology at Stanford University and in developmental psychology at the University of Michigan, where he received his doctorate in 1972. His interests are in life-course developmental psychology, memory, moral development, issues of diversity, and the environment, topics on which he has published numerous articles and book chapters. He has edited five books, the most recent of which is *Interpersonal Relations: Family, Peers, and Friends,* and from 1978 to 1987, was editor of the journal *Human Development.* He is currently the president-elect of the Jean Piaget Society: Society for the Study of Knowledge and Development.

Martin J. Packer is an Assistant Professor in the Educational Studies Program at the University of Michigan. He received his doctorate in developmental psychology from the University of California, Berkeley. His research interests include social and moral development, with a focus on the role of peer and adult–child interaction, and classroom interaction. He is co-editor (with Richard B. Addison) of *Entering the Circle: Hermeneutic Investigation in Psychology,* and the author of *The Structure of Moral Action: A Hermeneutic Study of Moral Conflict.*

Mark B. Tappan is Assistant Professor and Co-Chair of the Education Department at Colby College, Waterville, Maine. He received his doctorate in Human Development and Psychology from Harvard University. His research interests focus on moral development, narrative, gender differences in social and personality development and interpretive research methods. He has published articles in *Human Development* and the *Developmental Review.*

Alan S. Waterman is Professor of Psychology at Trenton State University. He received his doctorate from the State University of New York at Buffalo.

He is author of *The Psychology of Individualism* and numerous articles in the areas of personality development and philosophical psychology. His research interests include identity formation during the span from adolescence to adulthood and the nature of optimal psychological functioning.

Robert H. Wozniak is Professor and Chair, Department of Human Development, Bryn Mawr College. He received his doctorate in psychology from the University of Michigan in 1971. His research interests are in developmental theory and the study of the effect of contextual factors (cultural and physical) on the development of knowledge and values. His theoretical work has involved the elaboration of a general developmental model of the co-construction of experience, symbol formation, and action as a joint transaction between person and environment. Most recently, his empirical research has focused on the development of interpersonal beliefs systems in children and families as a function of gender and subculture, and on gender and power as exemplified in family interactional patterns.

James Youniss is Professor of Psychology and Director of the Life Cycle Institute at the Catholic University of America. He has published recent articles on the social–cultural roots of the discipline of developmental psychology. He is also the author of two books on the role of particular relationships in psychological development: *Parents and Peers in Social Development* and *Adolescent Relations with Mothers, Fathers, and Friends* (with co-author Jacqueline Smollar).

Preface

The metatheoretical foundations of science have undergone dramatic transformation over the past several decades. The critique of positivism has been pushed to the point where it is no longer clear what the foundations of science are or how they can be justified. These developments have had a profound impact on the behavioral and social sciences. Thus, despite the appearance of progress in some areas, behavioral and social scientists have been persistently troubled by a vague but pervasive sense of uneasiness concerning the foundations of valid knowledge. As a consequence, they have found themselves faced with the challenge of redefining the metatheoretical foundations of the behavioral and social sciences. Metatheoretical issues concern substantive presuppositions (e.g., epistemological, ontological, normative) that are part of the shared background that makes consensual scientific activity possible. As such, metatheoretical issues are not ordinarily part of scientific discourse. Rather, normative, ontological, and epistemological issues make up the core of scientific metatheoretical discourse. The literature on metatheoretical issues has grown enormously over the last several decades as scholars and researchers have undertaken what has emerged as one of the most difficult yet decisive tasks of the postpositivist period of the history of science: defining the foundations of the behavioral and social sciences.

The aim of the scholars and researchers in this book is to contribute to this undertaking by addressing, from a variety of perspectives, an issue that has proved particularly problematic: the role of values in psychology and human development. Each chapter addresses this issue from a distinct perspective. The perspectives represented in the book are diverse and, in our view, faithfully mirror the degree to which the question of values cuts across the discipline and the enormous difficulty of the challenge that confronts the field.

The issue of the role of values in science has been central to scientific metatheoretical discourse. Historically, debate over the role of values has focused on the question of whether values should play a role in science. In the past several decades, however, there has been a growing consensus that values play an *inevitable* role in science. Consequently, the question of *how* values influence scientific practice has emerged as the issue.

The issue of the role of values in science provides the broad framework for this book. Against this background, the volume focuses on the impact of values on psychology and human development. The book seeks to move debate forward by drawing on the strengths of a number of its contributors in the field of developmental psychology by focusing on the specific issue of how values influence theory and research on human development. However, the volume goes beyond the developmental literature to provide the reader with a broader framework that addresses the impact of values on psychology and science. In this frame, the book aims to advance our understanding of the metatheoretical foundations of science, psychology, and human development by providing a variety of perspectives on central conceptual and analytic issues in the debate over the role of values.

This volume also draws on the extensive debate on normative assumptions that has taken place over the past several decades in the moral development literature. Theory and research on moral behavior and development has increased enormously over the last three decades, and the psychological study of moral phenomena has become a substantial area of scientific research. The extensive debate over the central role that value assumptions play in this literature has provided a rich source of perspectives on theoretical and empirical issues that arise in the discussion of the role of values in the scientific study of moral phenomena. All the chapters in this book touch on perspectives and issues derived from this literature, either directly or indirectly.

This collection thus brings together a representative set of writings by a knowledgeable group of contemporary scholars and researchers with specialized interests in the role of values in psychology and human development. It comprises three parts: Part I, Historical Perspectives, provides the reader with an overview of and introduction to central issues from a historical perspective. Part II, Implications for Theory and Research, provides a broad perspective on the role of values in psychology and human development, and focuses on the implications of values for theory and research in psychology and human development. Part III, Implications for the Scientific Study of Moral Phenomena, focuses on the role of values in the scientific study of moral phenomena. The extensive debate over normative issues that has taken place in this literature provides a rich source of perspectives on the influence of values on theoretical and empirical issues.

This volume would not have been possible without the collaboration and cooperation of the contributors; their effort and energy made it what it is. We also wish to thank friends and colleagues who provided support and encouragement, the editorial staff of John Wiley & Sons, and others whose contributions at various stages were instrumental in its successful completion.

William M. Kurtines
Margarita Azmitia
Jacob L. Gewirtz

Contents

Part I
Historical Perspectives

Part II
Implications for Theory and Research

Part I

Historical Perspectives

Chapter 1 ■

Science, Values, and Rationality: Philosophy of Science from a Critical Co-Constructivist Perspective ■

WILLIAM M. KURTINES
Florida International University

MARGARITA AZMITIA
University of California, Santa Cruz

MILDRED ALVAREZ
San Jose State University

The question of the role of values in psychology and human development has had a significant impact on debate in the psychological and developmental literatures. The question of values, however, extends beyond psychology and the study of human development; it touches on the very nature of the metatheoretical foundations of science. The issue of the role of values reflects a more fundamental state of uncertainty in contemporary philosophy of science. The widespread and persistent character of this uncertainty suggests that an essential first step toward a more adequate formulation of the metatheoretical foundations of science involves moving beyond the "philosophy" of science itself. Any attempt to formulate a conceptualization of the metatheoretical foundations of science must be, at the very least, grounded in a broader framework than can be provided by any particular "philosophy" of science—it must be grounded in the nature of rationality itself. In this chapter we will outline a view of nature of rationality, rooted in a critical co-constructivist perspective, that provides a framework for a broadened conceptualization of the metatheoretical foundations of science. The construction of such a broadened view of rationality is an essential first step in the development of not only an understanding of the issue of science and values, but a more adequate understanding of the nature of the metatheoretical foundations of science itself.

HISTORICAL BACKGROUND

The twentieth century has been a revolutionary period in the philosophy of science. For the first half of the century, philosophy of science was defined predominately by the positivist tradition. Although this tradition made a major contribution to the evolution of the philosophy of science, by mid-century, the philosophy of science literature was in the midst of a dramatic transformation. Thomas Kuhn (1970), in a work considered by many to have had a pivotal impact in the second half of the twentieth century, challenged the most basic metatheoretical assumptions of the positivist tradition, including the view that scientific theory is tested against mind-independent (i.e., objective) data. During the 1960s and 1970s, the emergence of *paradigmatic relativism,* as represented by the works of writers such as Kuhn (1970), Hanson (1958), and Toulmin (1953, 1961), revolutionized the philosophy of science. The paradigmatic relativists, in contrast to the positivists, argued that reality is mind dependent and that all data are theory ladened. What counts as a "fact" depends on one's theoretical perspective or orientation. More importantly, paradigmatic relativism views science as a sociohistorical institution, and scientific theories as part of larger shared world views (i.e., paradigms) that emerge within the scientific community. Not only are facts theory ladened, but theory itself is meta-theory ladened. According to this view, paradigmatic shifts (i.e., scientific revolutions) are subject to influences from both within and outside the scientific community.

Thus, according to the paradigmatic relativist, not only does theory influence what counts as fact, but theoretical categories are influenced by a broader array of shared paradigmatic constraints and conventions. The paradigmatic relativist tradition in contemporary philosophy of science is thus *relativistic* in that the scientific community is viewed as generating its own criteria for truth and that the criteria for truth are ultimately part of the shared understanding that makes up a particular scientific paradigm.

Contemporary realist philosophies of science have also challenged many of the ontological and epistemological assumptions of the positivist tradition.

Current realist philosophy of science, represented by the works Bhaskar (1975, 1979), Cook and Campbell (1979), Wozniak (Chapter 4, this volume), Harré (1970, 1972), Manicas and Secord (1983), and McMullin (1983, 1984), rejects the paradigmatic relativists' view that truth is ultimately relative to the criteria generated by the scientific community. Like the positivists, contemporary realists assume the existence of an independent reality against which scientific theories are tested. Unlike the positivists, however, they reject "strict realism." Although a variety of realist positions are represented in the current literature, a theme common to all these modified versions of realism is that although reality imposes broad constraints on scientific theories and paradigms, there exists no direct test of the truth of a theory against preinterpreted data. As Manicas and Secord (1983) pointed out:

> It is precisely the task of science to invent theories that aim to represent the world. Thus, in the spirit of Kuhn . . . the practices of the sciences generate their own *rational* criteria in terms of which a theory is accepted or rejected. The crucial point is that it is possible for these criteria to be rational precisely because on realist terms, there is a world that exists independently of cognizing experience. Since our theories are constitutive of the known world but *not* of the *world*, we may always be wrong, but *not* anything goes. (p. 401)

Contemporary realist philosophy of science thus rejects the paradigmatic relativist view that truth is ultimately relative to the criteria generated by the scientific community in favor of the view that the truth of a scientific theory is subject to the broad constraints of reality. Contemporary realist philosophy of science, however, agrees with the paradigmatic relativist in rejecting the view of data as theory neutral. As Howard (1985) noted, "one can never choose between competing theories by simply looking toward the 'brute facts' and 'allowing the facts to speak for themselves,' as the standard positivist view has held" (p. 257).

The twentieth century has thus been a revolutionary period for the philosophy of science. Perspectives on the nature of the metatheoretical foundations of science have undergone an extended period of dramatic transformation without any clear-cut resolution. Beginning with Kuhn's work, the ontological and epistemological assumptions underlying the positivist tradition were effectively challenged. However, although the difficulties associated with the assumptions came to be widely recognized, no broadly or generally accepted alternative emerged. The metatheoretical foundations of science are thus at this point subject to considerable uncertainty. In fact, as we approach the end of the century, a good case can be made that the nature of the metatheoretical foundations of science is less clear *now* than it was at the beginning of the century under the influence of positivism. Moreover, this uncertainty about the metatheoretical foundations of science has had a persistent and pervasive impact on the social sciences (Campbell, 1988; Fiske & Shweder, 1986; Hogan, 1988; Kurtines, Alvarez, & Azmitia, 1990). Concerns about the rate of progress and how progress should be evaluated have been central contributors to this uneasiness.

In discussing the state of uncertainty that characterizes the current philosophy of science literature, our aim has not been to argue in favor of the paradigmatic relativist's rejection of the positivist's ontological and epistemological assumptions or the contemporary realist's modification of these assumptions. On the contrary, the purpose of this discussion has been to lay the groundwork for a more radical undertaking. Rather than argue in favor of any particular philosophy of science, we argue that the understanding of the nature of the metatheoretical foundations of science cannot be grounded adequately in any "philosophy" of science. We argue that the historical developments in the philosophy of science that we have discussed point to critical limitations imposed by viewing questions concerning the metatheoretical foundation of science as "philosophic" questions. The current state of uncertainty in the philosophy of science, in our view, strongly suggests that an essential first step toward a more adequate formulation of the nature of the metatheoretical foundations of science involves moving beyond the philosophy of science itself.

In this frame, the impact of Kuhn's work can be viewed as illustrating the limitation of conceptualizing the foundations of science as philosophical. It is particularly telling that the person responsible for the work that has probably had the greatest influence in shaping the philosophy of science literature over the last three decades is *not* a philosopher, and that the work itself is *not* a philosophic work. Kuhn's book, *The Structure of Scientific Revolution* (1970), is a historical work (a history of science, to be sure, but a historical rather than philosophical work nonetheless). Thus, developments in the philosophy of science literature over the past three decades suggest that progress toward a clarification of the metatheoretical foundations of science requires that the issue be framed more broadly. More precisely, we argue that what is needed is to move beyond the philosophy of science to consider a conceptualization in which the philosophy of science as well as science itself can be grounded.

In making this claim, we recognize that its extremely broad and general nature raises a number of difficult issues, not all of which we can address in this chapter. Nevertheless, in this chapter, we address what we consider to be a central consideration in any attempt to formulate a conceptualization of the metatheoretical foundations of science, namely that such a conceptualization must be, at the very least, grounded in a broader framework than can be provided by any particular philosophy of science—it must be grounded in the nature of rationality itself. We also propose to pursue a more complex and difficult undertaking—to outline a view of the nature of rationality that provides a framework for a broadened conceptualization of the metatheoretical foundations of science.

In seeking to move beyond the philosophy of science, we recognize that our position is open to debate. However, we view such a move as an essential first step in the development of not only an understanding of the issue of science and values, but a more adequate understanding of the nature of the metatheoretical foundations of science itself.

Although we have drawn on a wide variety of philosophical and theoretical traditions, we view the critical co-constructivist framework that we outline in this chapter as basically rooted in the social constructivist (Berger & Luckman, 1976; Gergen, 1985; Habermas, 1979) and socioevolutionary (Campbell, 1975; Erikson, 1950; Hogan, 1974; Waddington, 1967) traditions. The next part of the chapter examines the broader historical antecedents of the current crisis of reason and rationality (see Chapter 2 by Packer for a more detailed discussion of the historical events leading to what has been called the failure of the Enlightenment project). In the second part, we outline a view of the nature of rationality from a critical co-constructivist perspective and consider some of the implications of such a perspective for the metatheoretical foundations of science and psychology.

THE NATURE OF RATIONALITY

The Crisis of Reason

The nature of rationality has been a central and persistent theme in Western intellectual history. Sociohistorical developments over the past several centuries, however, have made the issue of the nature of rationality more central to the modern age than any other. Indeed, it has been described as the most central issue in modern Western intellectual history. As Aiken (1956) noted:

> From one point of view, the whole history of ideas in the modern age may be regarded as a history of the progressive breakdown of the medieval Christian synthesis which has been most powerfully articulated in the *Summa* of Thomas Aquinas and most powerfully and persuasively expressed in Dante's *Divine Comedy*. [The Western world is undergoing a] prolonged crisis of reason more profound than any that [has] occurred in Western culture since the original collision of paganism with primitive Christianity. (p. 26)

What is the nature of this crisis? What makes rationality so problematic for our age? The roots of this crisis extend back to classical antiquity. Throughout the classical period, reason served as the Western world's principal method for obtaining knowledge of the world. For classical thinkers such as Socrates, Plato, and Aristotle, "pure" reason—that is, reasoning not dependent upon sense experience (e.g., logical and mathematical reasoning)—provided the paradigm for rational understanding. For the classical thinker and philosopher, pure reason was the chief source of dependable knowledge about the world.

The changes that followed the end of the classical age in the fifth century AD resulted in a significant transformation in the role of reason in human understanding. During the Middle Ages, reason—the cornerstone of rational understanding in the ancient world—was largely replaced by faith. For the thousand-year period between the fifth and the fifteenth centuries, faith in the truth of the Christian revelation served as the Western world's principal source of knowledge about the world (Fremantle, 1954). However, although it was viewed as subordinate to faith, reason was not entirely abandoned. Medieval philosophers such as Augustine and Aquinas, for example, considered both faith and reason (i.e., logic) as capable of revealing God's divine truths about the world.

The modern period of Western intellectual history began in the seventeenth century. With the end of the medieval interval, Western conceptions of rationality underwent another transformation. The Renaissance that occurred in the fifteenth and sixteenth centuries was a period of transition from the medieval to the modern world. As the sixteenth century drew to a close, reason replaced faith as the cornerstone of Western knowledge. By the seventeenth century, Descartes declared philosophy independent of medieval theology, marking the beginning of modern philosophy. Descartes's aim was to provide a rational foundation for knowledge independent of, but not necessarily in conflict with, the world revealed by Christian theology. Descartes argued that through the process of reason, the knowing mind could determine certain "clear and distinct" ideas and that these ideas would provide a rational foundation for knowledge and understanding.

Reason thus replaced the medieval reliance on faith, and the modern age began with a period of Enlightenment. The period of Enlightenment, however, was more apparent than real, and the Age of Reason that followed the end of the Middle Ages was relatively short-lived. What appeared to the seventeenth and eighteenth century thinker to be the beginning of the final stage in the Enlightenment of the whole of humankind was actually the first step in the breakdown of the medieval synthesis. Reason, in the sense of logical reasoning, had replaced faith as the cornerstone of Western knowledge, thus finalizing the break with the medieval past, but the power of "pure" reason was soon challenged by a number of sociohistorical changes that took place during the modern age.

Descartes's philosophy had continued the rationalist tradition in Western philosophy that was rooted in the works of classical philosophers such as Plato and Aristotle. Descartes's rationalist philosophy played a central role in shaping modern philosophy during the Age of Enlightenment. One hundred years later, however, Kant, in his *Critique of Pure Reason*, undertook what he considered to be a necessary critique of the excessive metaphysical speculation that had characterized rationalist philosophers since Descartes. Kant's critique, which was aimed at clarifying the role of positive sense experience in knowledge, severely limited the role of pure reason in understanding.

Science and Rationality

Kant's critique was intended to limit the role of pure reason in the area of knowledge known as metaphysics. Other events, including the rise of modern science, contributed to limiting the role of pure reason in the acquisition of knowledge about the natural world. With the historical emergence of scientific–technological institutions, one of the most significant trends in Western thought (at least since the time of Galileo) has been the gradual assumption by the specialized sciences of areas of knowledge that had formerly been the province of philosophy and metaphysics. The first to be so assumed were physics and the physical world. After Newton, philosophic speculation on the nature of the physical universe was effectively ruled out. Grand rationalist speculations on the nature of the universe in the Aristotelian tradition were challenged by the functional utility of the Newtonian mechanistic world view. Then came Darwin and modern biology. Finally, scientific psychology laid claim to the study of human nature itself. The rationalist and speculative tradition in philosophy, at least that part of it concerned with knowledge and understanding of the world, came to play an increasingly less significant role in the modern world.

The rise of modern science thus served to limit the role of pure reason in the acquisition of knowledge about the world. The widespread acceptance by natural scientists of the use of empirical tests for resolving theoretical differences (as well as the refinement of such tests) resulted in a redefinition of the role of pure reason. One characteristic of modern science (in contrast to ancient and medieval science) is that logical truth is subordinate to empirical truth in establishing the validity of theoretical claims. In scientific discourse, the relative "truth" status of a scientific hypothesis is viewed as more dependent upon its consistency with empirical evidence than upon its logical or internal consistency. Modern science thus assigns logic a more limited and circumscribed role in the acquisition of knowledge about the world. The scientist may frequently use logical and mathematical reasoning to arrive at a hypothesis about the world, but the truth status of the hypothesis is dependent on empirical evidence.

From the beginning of the modern age, astounding scientific discoveries followed one another so that by the time of Newton, scientific knowledge had become the prototype for dependable knowledge. In the face of the decline of the rationalist tradition in Western thought *and* the impressive accomplishment of modern science in understanding the natural world, rationality increasingly came to be equated with scientific rationality. The emergence of the influential logical positivist tradition in the philosophy of science at the beginning of the twentieth century represented a culmination of this trend. As Habermas noted, with the rise of the positivist conception of science, the theory of knowledge became the philosophy of science; reason became scientific reason; and the interests of reason were either denied or equated with the technical interest in the prediction and control of objectified process (McCarthy, 1981). Theory, as a consequence, came to mean the logically integrated system of quantitatively expressed lawlike statements characteristic of the most advanced "natural" sciences. Within this frame, given a description of the relevant initial conditions, scientific laws can be used (with certain limits) to predict future states of a system. Providing that the relevant factors are manipulable, these laws can also be used to produce a desired state of affairs. Because of the historically powerful influence of this view, the practical question of what states of affairs are desirable has tended to be absorbed by the technical question of how those states of affairs can be achieved.

In his critique of positivism, Habermas (McCarthy, 1981) pointed out that the investigations into the "logic and methodology of science" carried out by the logical positivists and their successors construed science as "value free." With the aid of the distinctions between *is* and *ought* and between *values* and *facts*, they argued that the application of the scientific method required the rigorous avoidance of normative considerations. Value judgments did not admit of truth or falsity; they were not rationally (scientifically) decidable. Scientific knowledge could, of course, be brought to bear on practical matters—for example, in analyzing the preconditions and consequences of a given course of action, in weighing the economy and efficiency of alternative means to a desired end, or even in criticizing the proposed ends from the point of view of the technical feasibility. But the choice of ends—the adoption of certain interests to the exclusion of others—was ultimately a question of values and not of facts, a matter of decision and not for demonstration. Equating rationality with scientific rationality narrowly defined as technical reason thus effectively removes from the realm of rationality all normative problems (i.e., questions of values) not technologically solvable.

The crisis in reason that has characterized the modern Western world is thus, in part, a response to the recognition of the limitations of pure reason (i.e., logic) as a source of knowledge about the world. Since Kant, the rationalist tradition of speculative metaphysics has given way to a positivist conception of scientific rationality. Like theology, one traditional area of concern for metaphysics was ethics and morality. The widespread influence of the view of science as value free has done little to contribute to the resolution of the pressing moral dilemmas that confront the twentieth century. The crisis in reason is, consequently, not only a reflection of the reevaluation of the role of pure reason; it also reflects the emergence of a conception of scientific rationality narrowly defined in terms of instrumental and technical reason. In equating rationality with scientific rationality (narrowly defined as the technical control of objectified reality), modern science, which once held the bright promise of a solution to humanity's problems, has now come to play a central role in the crisis in reason. Part of the paradox of modern life is precisely this: Technical reason, which once seemed capable of solving humanity's problems, turns out to be a major contributor to our modern moral dilemma. The potential for nuclear warfare, the widespread destruction of the environment, the threat of global warming, and other symbols of our age illustrate the point. As scientific rationality increasingly came to be defined in terms of technical understanding, it lost in scope what it gained in precision. We now have within our power the technical capability of destroying the world (piece by piece or all at once) and no "rational" way for resolving not to.

Toward a Broadened Conception of Rationality

There has thus been an increased recognition of the limitation of equating rationality with the technical control of natural–physical phenomena. The result has been a growing appreciation not only of the limitation of grounding the metatheoretical foundations of science in the positivist philosophy of science, but also of the need for a broader conception of rationality, one that encompasses more than natural–physical phenomena.

Shweder (1986), for example, suggested the need for "divergent rationalities." In discussing the metatheoretical foundations of the social sciences, Shweder noted that the historical trend in the social sciences of adopting the positivist ideal of science as the technical understanding of objectified natural–physical processes has provoked two reactions from social scientists:

> Some—let us call them "hermeneuticists"—would treat social science as a humanity, hang on to human subjectivity (emotions, beliefs, desires, values, etc.) but abandon the science. Others—let us call them "positivists"—would treat social science as a physical–natural science, leave human subjectivity to the humanists, hermeneutics, and common sense, and restrict the domain of social science inquiry to those nonsubjective social phenomena . . . where automatic, lawlike connections can be discovered. (1986, pp. 176–177)

According to Shweder (1986, p. 177), neither the hermeneutic nor the positivist perspective can provide a broad enough foundation for rationality. From both perspectives, there are only two kinds of things in the world: subjectivity devoid of matter (culture) and matter devoid of subjectivity (nature). The first is the realm of the humanist; the second is the realm of the natural scientist. Thus, according to Shweder, the hermeneutic perspective is as narrowly defined as the positivist perspective, but in the opposite direction.

In contrast to the hermeneuticist and the positivist, Shweder proposed an alternative view of the social sciences, what he calls a "science of subjectivity." Basic to a science of subjectivity is the view that "we must revise our conception of ideal scientific practice and our conception of the relationship between nature and culture, objectivity and subjectivity" (p. 178). Subjective phenomena can be studied objectively, and objective phenomena are never free of a subjective perspective. Consequently, Shweder noted:

> An important implication of this deliberate blurring of the boundaries between objectivity and subjectivity is that other conceptions that rest on a neat and clean contrast between what's objective and what's subjective ought to be revised, which means, to say the least, we may have to rethink for a bit our conception of "rationality" and our conception of "meaning." A science of subjectivity [thus] requires a broadened conception of rationality. (1986, p. 178)

Habermas, in his critique of positivism, also undertook a reconstruction of the foundations of rationality (McCarthy, 1981). The problem, Habermas argued, is not technical reason as such, but its universalization, the forfeiture of a more comprehensive concept of reason in favor of the exclusive validity of scientific and technological thought. The proper response to the tendency to confuse the practical (what ought to be desired) with the technical (how desired ends are to be achieved) lies, according to Habermas, not in a radical break with technical reason (a romantic rejection of science and technology), but in properly locating it within a comprehensive theory of rationality.

Central to the development of a comprehensive theory of rationality is what Habermas called his theory of cognitive interests. One of Habermas's central theses is that "the specific view points from which we apprehend reality," the "general cognitive strategies" that guide systematic inquiry, have their "basis in the natural history of the human species." They are tied to "imperatives of the sociocultural forms of life." The basic elements of Habermas's theory of cognitive interests include the classification of the processes of inquiry into three categories distinguished by their cognitive strategies: *empirical–analytic sciences,* including the natural sciences and the social sciences insofar as they aim at producing nomological knowledge; *historical–hermeneutic sciences,* including the humanities and the historical and social sciences insofar as they aim at interpretive understanding of meaningful symbolic configurations; and the *critically oriented sciences,* including psychoanalysis and the critique of ideology (critical social theory), as well as philosophy understood as a reflective and critical discipline. For each category of inquiry, he posited a connection with a specific cognitive interest:

> The approach of the empirical–analytic sciences incorporates a technical interest, derived from an anthropologically deep-seated interest in predicting and controlling events in the natural environment; a practical interest, derived from a deep-seated interest in securing and expanding possibilities of mutual and self-understanding in the conduct of life; and an emancipatory interest, derived from a deep-seated interest in emancipation from constraints whose powers reside in their non-transparency. (McCarthy, 1981, p. 58)

One of Habermas's goals has been to locate the various modes of inquiry within a comprehensive theory of rationality. Thus, for Habermas, a comprehensive theory of rationality is one that could account for historical–hermeneutic and critical interests, as well as interests in the control of objectified natural phenomena. Habermas's view is important for our purposes because of its implications for restoring practical interests to the realm of rationality.

THE NATURE OF RATIONALITY

A Critical Co-Constructivist Perspective

Earlier we argued that historical developments in the philosophy of science during the twentieth century indicate that an adequate formulation of the metatheoretical foundations of science requires a move beyond the philosophy of science. It requires that we address the issue of the nature of rationality itself. In this section, we outline a critical co-constructivist perspective on the nature of rationality that draws on our earlier work (Kurtines et al., 1990) and the work of Shweder (1986) and Habermas (1979).

From Shweder, we adopt the notion that a comprehensive view of rationality must include both subjectivity and objectivity. However, from a critical co-constructivist perspective, a comprehensive theory of rationality must also include intersubjectivity, that is, social reality. Indeed, a comprehensive view of rationality must include each of the distinct but interrelated spheres of reality that make up human existence—the subjective experiences of the inner world of the self, the intersubjective experiences of the social world, and the objective experiences of the natural or physical world.

From Habermas, we adopt the notion that inquiry, in the form of the pursuit of understanding, is rooted in a deep-seated human interest. However, in our view, the different domains of understanding do not correspond to different cognitive interests. In contrast to Habermas, we view the pursuit of understanding in each of the domains to be grounded in the most basic and biologically deep-seated human interest or motive, namely, the maintenance, persistence, and perseverance of the self. Thus, in our view, each domain of understanding reflects the distinct spheres of reality (subjective, intersubjective, and objective) that the self confronts in the course of ontogenesis. The different modes of understanding thus are not a reflection of differing interests, but rather represent a single, common interest (that of the self) directed toward the understanding of different spheres of reality. Consequently, from a co-constructivist perspective, the imperatives of the sociocultural forms of life cannot be used to ground a comprehensive theory of rationality, but rather are to be understood as the collective expressions of more biologically deep-seated interests of the self; that is, differing institutional forms of inquiry that have historically emerged in each of the domains of understanding are to be understood as collective expressions of the more underlying interests of the individuals who comprise the institutions.

Domains of Scientific Understanding

In this section, we argue that our conception of rational understanding can be broadened to encompass all domains about which it is possible to achieve consensual validity. One defining feature of such a broadened conception of rationality is that it includes a broadened set of assumptions about both what we know (i.e., ontological assumptions about the domains of rational understanding) and how we know it (i.e., epistemological assumptions about the modes of rational inquiry). We argue that from a critical co-constructivist perspective, a comprehensive view of scientific rationality must encompass at the very least the three spheres of reality that define the limit of human experience—subjective, intersubjective, and objective. To this ontological assumption, we add the epistemological assumption that each domain of scientific understanding is defined by a distinctive mode of inquiry—empirical–analytic, historical–hermeneutic, and phenomenological–hermeneutic. The traditional divisions in modern science between natural science, social science, and psychological science roughly correspond to the three domains of understanding. These divisions form the core of our view of the domains of scientific understanding, but with a number of qualifications as outlined below.

Objective Phenomena. The first domain of understanding is encompassed by the *natural sciences* which have as their object of knowledge natural–physical (i.e., objective) reality. In modern Western science, this domain includes not only the traditional natural sciences (physics, chemistry, astronomy, etc.), but also (as Shweder pointed out) those fields of the social sciences (economics, sociology, anthropology, psychology, etc.) that restrict their domain to nonsubjective phenomena. Historically, the natural philosophy of classical and medieval thinkers and philosophers also reflects the same domain of understanding as does the natural philosophy (or its equivalent) of non-Western thinkers. The "natural" sciences, here understood to include those fields of the "social" and "psychological" sciences that restrict their domain to natural–physical phenomena, thus have as their object of knowledge an order of reality that is basically mind independent. Consequently, the view of the metatheoretical foundations of science that we are proposing here is consistent with the recent reemergence of the realist tradition in the philosophy of science, at least with respect to natural–physical phenomena.

Like Habermas, we view the basic methodology of the natural (objective) sciences to be empirical–analytic broadly conceived. Also like Habermas, we consider the historical emergence of the natural sciences to be an expression of a deep-seated interest in the prediction and control of objectified natural processes, and hence a central domain of understanding, but not the only one.

Intersubjective Phenomena. The second domain encompasses the *social sciences* and has as its objective of knowledge the reality shared with others—social reality. This domain includes those fields within the social sciences (anthropology, sociology, psychology, etc.) that systematically incorporate intersubjective phenomena. This domain also includes the humanities, linguistics, history, and those fields of philosophy that encompass intersubjective phenomena (critical theory, philosophy of science, etc.), and their counterparts in non-Western cultures. The "social" sciences, here understood to include those fields that encompass intersubjective phenomena, have as their object of knowledge a quasi-mind-independent order of reality. Social reality is that order of reality that is a product of subjective construction and intersubjective co-construction. Hence, social reality is both subjective and mind dependent *and* intersubjective and mind independent. Consequently, with respect to intersubjective phenomena, the view of the metatheoretical foundations of science that we are proposing here can be understood as quasi-realist.

Like Habermas, we consider the social (intersubjective) sciences to be the expression of a deep-seated interest in understanding the intersubjectively shared experiences of the self and others, and view the fundamental methodology of the social–intersubjective sciences to be basically historical–hermeneutic. Hermeneutics traditionally referred to the interpretation of text, particularly biblical; however, over the past several decades, hermeneutics has come to be more broadly applied to the contextual interpretation of human action and experience, from particular situations to sociohistorical context.

Subjective Phenomena.   The third domain encompasses the *psychological sciences* and has as its object of knowledge subjective reality. This domain includes those fields of the psychological and social sciences (humanistic, phenomenological, etc.) that incorporate subjective phenomena. This domain also includes those fields of philosophy that encompass subjective phenomena (e.g., the phenomenological tradition) and some forms of literary criticism. The "psychological" sciences, here understood to include those fields that encompass subjective phenomena, have as their object of knowledge precisely that order of reality that *is* mind dependent. Consequently, with respect to subjective phenomena, the view of the metatheoretical foundations of science we are proposing here can be understood as subjectivist (i.e., "non"-realist). The fundamental method of the psychological (subjective) sciences is phenomenological–hermeneutic, which involves the hermeneutic interpretation of subjective experience, broadly conceived.

In outlining the domains of scientific understanding thus far, our aim has been to draw on previous work to point to a possible direction for the development of a more comprehensive view of rationality. Consensually valid knowledge, within the framework of the domains of scientific understanding proposed here, need not be restricted to objective phenomena. Consensually valid knowledge is also possible within the domains of subjective and intersubjective phenomena.

In outlining this framework for the domains of scientific understanding, we recognize that, although the basic division between the natural, social, and psychological sciences is common in modern Western science, our classification of fields within disciplines as representing differing types of scientific inquiry[1] is less commonly used.[2] Moreover, it has been pointed out that Western thinkers' tendency to use natural–physical phenomena and processes as a model for human social and psychological phenomena and processes is no more "rational" than the divergent tendencies of other cultures. As Shweder (1986) noted:

In some non-Western cultures . . . the social order or human order is taken as a model for the natural order. . . . It is noteworthy that in our culture the term "natural" has come to be restricted to those disciplines that study physical things devoid of subjectivity. At least in the West, Mother Nature has lost her animus, and at least in recent times, aniministic or, more accurately, human or subjective properties such as intentionality, belief, desire, meaning, feeling, self-awareness, value, and purpose have been actively driven out of the nature studied by those "natural sciences" from which many social sciences have drawn their ideas about what kinds of things are real and really out there, and how to go about finding them. Today, in the received view, what "is" has nothing to do with what "ought to be." Matters of fact are unrelated to matters of value. Particles in motion do not think, feel, or have intentions. (pp. 175–176)

The aim of our effort to outline a framework for a broadened conception of rationality has been to suggest ways in which it is possible to include a full range of phenomena (subjective, intersubjective, and objective) within the domain of rational understanding.[3] In our view, there appears to be *no* justification for excluding subjective and intersubjective phenomena from the realm of rational understanding.[4] Quite the contrary, as the history of ideas over the last several centuries indicates, any attempt to develop a comprehensive view of rationality will have to include subjective and intersubjective human phenomena as well as objective natural–physical phenomena.

The positivists' investigation into the methodology of science, as we noted earlier, distinguished between objective and subjective phenomena and between facts and values, and excluded values (and other subjective and intersubjective phenomena) from the realm of consensually valid knowledge. Much of the early history of the philosophy of science in this century has been predicated on the view that the aim of science is the determination of truth with respect to matters of fact about natural–physical (i.e., objective) phenomena, and the methodology of science (at least as interpreted by philosophers in the positivist tradition) is directed toward the resolution of conflicting claims with respect to such matters of "fact." Because matters of value were relegated to the realm of the irrational or nonrational, the issue of the resolution of competing claims concerning values was historically neglected. The restoration of subjective and intersubjective phenomena (including normative phenomena, such as values, norms, standards, principles) to the domain of rational understanding yields a broadened conception of rationality, but it also raises the issue of how a rational resolution of matters of values (as opposed to matters of fact) is possible.

In the next section, we discuss in detail Habermas's claim that practical or normative issues, like theoretical issues, are open to rational resolution. Drawing on his work in the area of communication (Habermas, 1979), we outline his view of the role that discourse plays in the resolution of conflicting or competing theoretical (factual) claims and practical (normative) claims.

The Role of Discourse in the Resolution of Theoretical and Practical Claims

In his work on communication, Habermas (McCarthy, 1981) distinguished between two types of discourse: theoretical and practical. Theoretical discourse involves the discursive redemption of competing, conflicting, or problematic claims to truth; practical discourse involves the discursive redemption of competing, conflicting, or problematic rightness (i.e., normative) claims. In theoretical discourse, the truth claims of descriptive statements are subjected to question and argumentation. Practical discourse, in contrast, subjects the rightness claims of normative statements to question and argumentation. By means of this distinction, Habermas attempted to draw a parallel between the type of communication that occurs in theoretical discourse (e.g., the type of discourse that occurs in the scientific community) and practical discourse (e.g., the type of discourse that occurs in sociomoral–political communities).

Theoretical Discourse.   Theoretical discourse has as its aim the determination of truth. At issue is the question of how we determine if statements, propositions, or assertions are true. A theory of truth is a theory of how truth can be determined. In the history of philosophy, there have been numerous theories of truth. The correspondence theory of truth holds that statements are true to the degree to which they "correspond" to reality. Positivist philosophers of science, for example, argued that scientific propositions (hypotheses) are true or false to the degree to which they correspond to scientific facts. The coherence theory of truth, on the other hand, holds that statements are true or false to the degree to which they are part of a coherent system of ideas. The rationalist tradition in Western philosophy has maintained that the truth of statements is to be determined not by the correspondence of such statements to reality, but by the coherence and internal consistency of the system of thought within which the statements are embedded and derived.

A historical concern of theories of truth has been to define criteria by which truth can be objectively determined. Although theories such as the correspondence and coherence theories of truth seek to establish "objective" criteria for truth, they are open to a number of objections, and have been challenged on a variety of grounds. The correspondence theory of truth, for example, is grounded on a fundamental presupposition that the truth of statements can be tested against a mind-independent reality, that is, that the truth of statements can be tested against the "facts." Facts are objective, and the truth status of empirically testable propositions or hypotheses (and ultimately, the theories from which they are derived) can therefore be objectively determined. However, facts are never simply facts;

they are facts only from the perspective of some particular form of understanding (i.e., even the most basic facts are theory ladened). Thus, there are, according to this view, no mind-independent facts. If there is no mind-independent reality against which propositions and theories can be tested, there is no "objective" way to determine the truth of the propositions and theories. The coherence theory of truth, in contrast, faces an even more difficult challenge: defining what coherence, as a criteria for truth, means.

Theories of truth, however, do not necessarily have to seek to define objective criteria for truth. An alternative view is that truth cannot be objectively determined, that is, that truth is in some sense relative to the individual, situation, or context. The pragmatic theory of truth, for example, holds that statements are true to the degree to which they represent satisfactory solutions to problematic situations. Charles Sanders Peirce, the founder of pragmatism, defined truth as the set of beliefs that would be held by the community of inquirers in the long run—after an indefinitely long series of inquiries. Truth, Peirce held, is the outcome of inquiry. John Dewey, extending the pragmatic tradition, argued that the quest for certainty that has characterized Western philosophy is an illusion and, like Peirce, related truth to inquiry. He extended Peirce's argument, however, by linking inquiry to problem solving. Because in Dewey's view, the goal of inquiry is to transform situations rather than to achieve abstract truth, Dewey substituted for such terms as *truth* and *knowledge* the phrase *warranted assertibility*. Relativistic theories of truth such as the pragmatic theory of truth, like objectivistic theories of truth, are open to a variety of objections, not the least of which is that, from such a perspective, truth appears to be contingent if not ultimately arbitrary.

In this frame, Habermas's work on theoretical discourse can be understood, in part, as an attempt to formulate a rational foundation for truth. More specifically, he wanted to argue that the truth value of an assertion can be rationally determined (i.e., that the truth of an assertion is not arbitrary), but to argue in such a way as to not be open to the objections that have been historically raised against objectivist theories of truth. To do so, he drew on the work of the pragmatic philosophers Peirce and Dewey, and argued that we must distinguish between the truth of the content of a statement (i.e., its propositional content) and the act of declaring the statement to be true. In the first case, we are concerned with the conditions under which the statement can be determined true, whereas in the second case, we are concerned with the conditions under which we are justified in claiming the statement to be true. This distinction separates for purposes of analyses the criteria for truth from the criteria by which a truth claim can be justified. A statement may be true, for example, but if one can provide no justification for his or her belief in the truth of the statement, the statement is an unwarranted assertion. The distinction between what is true and what is a justifiable claim to truth is useful in that it serves to shift the focus of analysis to the conditions by which truth claims can be warranted, for it is precisely these conditions with which Habermas was concerned in the analysis of the structure of theoretical discourse. An understanding of the structure of discourse is important because, Habermas argued, in the end there can be no separation of the criteria of truth from the justification of a truth claim. In the final analysis, the question of under what conditions a statement is true is inseparable from the question of under what conditions a statement can be justified.

Thus, Habermas concluded that the logic of truth must include a logic of theoretical discourse. For Habermas, this meant an examination of the conditions of the possibility of achieving rational consensus with respect to truth through discourse. Habermas is in effect proposing a consensus theory of truth—that is, that there is (or can be) a rational (i.e., argumentatively grounded) consensus that a statement is true. Consensus theories of truth are themselves open to objection. Perhaps the most serious criticism is that consensus theories of truth imply that if a consensus is reached with respect to the truth of an assertion, then the assertion is true. If we can reach an agreement that the world is flat, then the implication is that it is true that the world is flat. Clearly, not *any* agreement can pass as true. The problem for a consensus theory of truth, then, is to define those conditions when we are warranted in accepting a consensus as true. This requires an examination of the conditions under which the consensus was reached. How can we distinguish between a "true" and a "false" consensus? How can we distinguish between a rationally motivated consensus and one that merely appears to be rational? The main thrust of Habermas's work on theoretical discourse was to define the properties of a rationally motivated consensus.

The notion that critical discussion (discourse) provides the context for a shared mutual resolution to problematic issues of truth presupposes certain conditions that can lead to a genuine consensus as opposed to a false or forced consensus. The notion of a genuine consensus presupposes that the outcome of the critical discussion will be (or at least can be) the result simply of the forces of the better argument and not of accidental or systematic constraints on communication. Habermas argued (cited in McCarthy, 1981, p. 306) that communication is free from constraint only when for all participants there is a symmetrical distribution of chances to select and employ speech acts, that is, when there is an effective equality of opportunity for the assumption of dialogue roles. From this general symmetry requirement, there follow particular requirements for each basic mode of communication. In addition to having the same chance to speak at all (to initiate and perpetuate communication), participants must have the same chance to employ constative speech acts, that is, to put forward or call into question, to ground or refute statements, explanations, and so on, so that *in the long run no assertion is exempted from critical examination.* In addition, communication must be free from distorting influences, whether open domination, conscious strategic behavior, or more subtle barriers to communication deriving from self-deception. Habermas referred to this condition as constituting the "ideal speech situation" (McCarthy, 1981, p. 306).

The concept of an ideal speech situation is counterfactual. In real life, the conditions of speech rarely, if ever, approximate those of the ideal speech situation. The social, psychological, and physical limitations and constraints on human interactions effectively serve to rule out the perfect realization of the ideal speech situation. Nonetheless, this does not of itself render the ideal illegitimate. The ideal can be more or less adequately realized in reality, and the ideal can serve as a guide for the institutionalization of discourse and as a critical standard against which never actually achieved consensus can be measured:

"The ideal speech situation is neither an empirical phenomena nor a mere construct, but rather an unavoidable supposition reciprocally made in discourse. This supposition can, but need not be, counterfactual; but even if it is made counterfactually, it is a fiction that is operatively effective in the process of communication. Therefore I prefer to speak of an anticipation of an ideal speech situation." (Habermas, quoted in McCarthy, 1981, p. 310)

Thus, Habermas did not consider the ideal speech situation as "ideal" in the sense of either "not real" or "unrealistic," but rather as an ideal in the normative sense—that is, a criterion, standard, or value against which communication can be evaluated. More importantly for our purposes, it is a standard that is applicable to all communication, including the institutionalized communication patterns that define the structure of discourse communities. The notion of an ideal speech situation thus provides a link between abstract theories of truth and the concrete reality of a community of truth seekers. From such a perspective, discourse communities can be conceptualized as more or less closely approximating the features of the ideal speech situation.

In this frame, modern science, as a sociohistorical institution, is not unique in its pursuit of truth. Other institutions (e.g., religious), encompassing other cultural traditions and other historical epochs, have been defined by a value on the pursuit of truth. In our view, the feature of the scientific community that distinguishes it from other communities of truth seekers is *the degree to which it has institutionalized a value on critical modes of thinking and communication,* that is, the degree to which theoretical discourse approximates *in practice* the conditions of the ideal speech situation. To the degree to which the truth claims of scientists, for example, are open to critical discussion, and individual scientists have equal opportunity to assume dialogue roles and to put forward and challenge claims, then science approximates the feature of an ideal speech situation. Scientific truth is thus not "objective" truth; it is contingent truth. The relative truth status of any scientific hypothesis or theory is always contingent, open to critical examination and revision. However, to the degree to which the consensus reached by the scientific community is the result of conditions that approximate the ideal speech situation, then consensus reached by the scientific community represents the closest approximation to truth about the factual matters that can be achieved.

Practical Discourse.   Thus far, we have only discussed the nature of rational consensus in theoretical discourse. The view that scientific understanding can be expanded beyond the domain of objective natural–physical phenomena raises the question of how a rational consensus is possible with respect to subjective and intersubjective phenomena such as norms, values, principles, and so forth. Habermas argued in some detail that practical questions (i.e., questions of what is good, right, desirable, etc.) can also be decided rationally. His position was that the small differences that exist between the logic of theoretical discourse and practical discourse are less important than the similarities that exist between them. The structure of both theoretical and practical discourse, he suggests, are essentially the same. He said (quoted in McCarthy, 1981):

"If rightness as well as truth can qualify as discursively redeemable validity claims, it follows that right norms must be capable of being grounded in a way similar to true statements. In the philosophical tradition two views (among others) stand opposed. One was developed in classical natural law theory and says that normative statements admit of truth *in the same sense* as descriptive statements; the other has with nominalism and empiricism become the dominant view of today and says that normative statements do not admit of truth at all. In my view, the assumptions underlying both views are false. I suspect that the justification of validity claims contained in recommendations of norms of action and of evaluation can be just as discursively tested as the justification of validity claims implied in assertions. Of course the grounding of right commands and evaluations differs in the structure of argumentation from the ground of true statements; the logical conditions under which a rational motivated consensus can be attained in practical discourse are different than in theoretical discourse." (p. 311)

In practical discourse, an action or speech act takes place against a background of recognized values and norms, roles and institutions, and rules and conventions (McCarthy, 1981, pp. 311–312). In this context, it is possible for any speech act to fail or be challenged on the ground that is "wrong" or "inappropriate" when measured against accepted norms. Actions can be further justified within the established normative framework. If the questioning of validity claims continues to persist and the legitimacy of the norm is called into question, communication can either break off, switch over to strategic communication, or continue and enter into practical discourse in an attempt to achieve a consensual basis for rational agreement.

In practical discourse, "theoretical justifications" for problematic norms are advanced and justified. The backing that is required for such claims is not necessarily the type of observation and experimental evidence used to support hypothetical general laws. The relevant evidence is first and foremost the consequences and side-effects that the application of a proposed norm can be expected to have in regard to the satisfaction or nonsatisfaction of generally accepted needs and wants. In theoretical discourse, the logical gap between evidence and hypothesis is bridged by various canons of induction. The corresponding function in practical discourse is filled by the principles of universalizability: "Only those norms are permitted which can find general recognition in their domain of application. The principle serves to exclude, as not admitting of consensus, all norms whose content and range of validity are particular" (McCarthy, 1981, p. 313).

Habermas thus argued that there are two types of interests, particular interests and common or "generalizable" interests, and it is the function of practical discourse to test which interests are capable of being "communicatively shared" and admit of consensus and which interests are particular and admit at best a negotiated compromise. In the former case, if the consensus is based on an adequate knowledge of conditions and consequence and on a "truthful" perception by the participants of their "real" interests (and not deception or self-deception), then it is a rationally motivated consensus. If the motivating force behind the agreement is a nondeceptive recognition of common needs and interests in the light of existing (and effectible) conditions, likely consequences, and so forth, what grounds could there be for denying that the agreement was rational (McCarthy, 1981, p. 314)?

Habermas's analysis of the structure of theoretical and practical discourse thus indicates that it is possible to achieve rational consensus with respect to normative or practical issues as well as theoretical issues. Such a view serves to restore subjective and intersubjective phenomena, such as values, norms, standards, and so forth, to the realm of rational understanding.

Rational Understanding

We thus far have raised the issue of the meaning of rational understanding. We have argued that from the perspective of critical co-constructivism, our conception of rational understanding can be broadened to encompass all domains about which it is possible to achieve consensual validity. Such a broadened conception of rationality includes a broad set of assumptions about both what we know (i.e., ontological assumptions about the domains of rational understanding—subjective, intersubjective, and objective) and how we know it (epistemological assumptions about the modes of rational inquiry—empirical–analytic, historical–hermeneutic, and phenomenological–hermeneutic). Theoretical *and* practical questions, we argued, arise in all three domains and involve all three modes of inquiry. As Habermas noted, the true and the good are inextricably linked in real life.

A broadened conception of rationality, such as the critical co-constructivist perspective outlined here, raises what in our view has become one of the most important methodological tasks for the "rational" sciences, however construed. Such a conception of rationality raises methodological questions that move beyond the issue of the methods of the natural sciences in resolving factual disputes to the broader issue of the construction and co-construction of criteria for resolving truth *and* rightness claims in *all* areas. This shift, in our view, presents an enormous challenge and will be central in determining new directions as modern science enters the twenty-first century.

Scientific Methodology

The view that rational understanding can be expanded beyond the domain of objective natural–physical phenomena has, we argue, a number of significant methodological implications. One consequence of the historical emphasis on objective phenomena to the exclusion of subjective and intersubjective phenomena was that the positivists significantly misconstrued the role of methodology in modern science. Much of the history of the philosophy of science in this century, we noted, has been predicated on the assumption that the aim of science is the determination of the truth with respect to matters of fact about natural–physical phenomena. In the face of the impressive accomplishments of the natural–physical sciences, the result was a misplaced emphasis on the role of methodology in science. More specifically, science was viewed as defined by its methodology, and the methodology of the natural–physical sciences was viewed as *the* scientific method. Thus, "modern science" came to be viewed as defined by its method, and *the* scientific method (frequently defined with varying degrees of elaboration) was essentially interpreted as observation and experimentation, the methodology that has characterized much of the natural–physical sciences.

In contrast to the positivist tradition, from a critical co-constructivist perspective on rationality, modern science is *not* defined by a particular methodology. Indeed, not only is modern science not defined by a particular methodology, it is not defined by its methodology at all. In our view, empirical–analytic methods such as observation and experimentation can be more usefully conceptualized as methods for resolving theoretical debate about conflicting validity claims concerning natural–physical phenomena. In this frame, the use of empirical analytic methods is not a defining feature of modern science; it is a defining feature of those sciences that have as their object of knowledge the rational understanding of natural–physical reality. Empirical–analytic methods have come to play a central role in the natural–objective sciences, in our view, because they are methods for resolving conflicting claims with respect to natural–physical phenomena that can withstand critical examination. Thus, we do not view empirical–analytic methods such as observation and experimentation to constitute *the* scientific method; rather, we view them as *a* method that has proved to be particularly useful in generating consensually valid knowledge in one domain of scientific understanding.

Such a perspective has important implications for the development of a view of scientific methodology consistent with a broadened conception of scientific rationality, such as the one outlined in this chapter. Because it does not limit scientific understanding to either a particular domain (natural–physical) or a particular method (empirical–analytic), such a view facilitates the emergence of alternative methodologies. Thus, for example, the historical emergence of observation and experimentation as consensually agreed upon empirical–analytic methods for resolving conflicting or competing theoretical claims about objective natural–physical phenomena does not rule out the emergence of similar consensually agreed upon methods for resolving conflicting or competing theoretical claims with respect to intersubjective and subjective phenomena. On the contrary, as a number of the authors in this volume indicate (see Packer, Chapter 2; Tappan & Brown, Chapter 5; Youniss, Chapter 8), substantial interest has emerged in the use of both historical–hermeneutic and phenomenological–hermeneutic methods. As Campbell (1986) noted, hermeneutic principles, such as the hermeneutic circle (cycle, spiral), part–whole iteration, the principle of charity (assumption of the text producer's corationality), contextual coherence, extension of context, thick description, contrast indexicality, and so forth, have emerged from communities of scholars and have achieved what they regard as improved interpretations of texts. Hermeneutic methodology thus offers the potential for enhancing the consensual validity of knowledge in the domains of subjective and intersubjective phenomena.[5]

The positivists, as we noted, equated the scientific method with a method that had proven particularly useful in enhancing consensually valid knowledge in the domain of objective phenomena. In arguing that hermeneutic (i.e., interpretive) methodology appears to be useful in enhancing the consensual validity of knowledge in the area of subjective and intersubjective phenomena, we do not mean to rule out the potential utility of empirical analytic methods, such as observation and experimentation, in enhancing the validity of knowledge in these domains. Indeed, we do not even mean to rule out the possibility of the historical emergence of methodologies beyond those that are empirical–analytic in the sphere of objective phenomena or methodologies beyond hermeneutics in the sphere of subjective and intersubjective phenomena. In fact, the historical evolution of methodologies for resolving conflicting claims that are capable of withstanding critical examination has been, in our view, one of the central factors in fostering the rapid advances in the theoretical understanding of the natural–physical world that has taken place over the past several centuries. Thus, the view that scientific rationality can be expanded beyond the domain of natural–physical phenomena has significant implications for understanding the role of methodology in science.

Positivism, as we noted, argued that science was defined by its methodology and that methodology was construed as experimental methodology, a view that has been subject to extensive critique. We, however, do not consider it problematic that science has been viewed as defined by "experimental" methodology; we consider it problematic that science has come to be viewed as defined by *any* methodology (however construed). This is part of what we view as the problem of the misplaced emphasis on the role of methodology. Although methodology plays an unquestionably central role in science, the scientific method is not what makes modern science unique as a sociohistorical institution. If the emphasis on the scientific method has been misplaced, what is the defining feature of modern science? What is it that makes modern science unique? What the last half-century of debate over the role of values makes clear is that modern science is not defined by its methodology; it is defined by its morality. That is, *modern science is defined by its values.*

One central value that defined the historical emergence of modern science was the institutionalization of a value on critical modes of thought and discussion, that is, the degree to which scientific discourse approximates *in practice* the conditions of the ideal speech situation. The conditions of the ideal speech situation requires, for all participants, an effective equality of opportunity for participation in dialogue roles, and ensures that in the long run no claim is exempt from critical examination. Theoretical understanding of the natural world has progressed over the last several centuries because scientific discourse takes place within a community in which all can participate and no claim goes unexamined. No theory, no fact, no method (no matter how broadly accepted or consensually agreed upon) is exempt from critical examination by either the most senior or the most junior member of the scientific community, at least in principle. This "ideal"—the willingness to question, to challenge, and to criticize—has been the quintessence of the "scientific spirit" since the transition from medieval science to modern science in the sixteenth and seventeenth centuries. Clearly, the actual practices of the scientific community only *approximate* this ideal. However, it is also clear that this ideal—this value—is realized *no* more closely in practice in *any* other major social institution in the modern world than it is in the scientific community. Modern science has thus been (and continues to be) defined by its values, not its method.

CONCLUSION

The starting point for this chapter is the growing recognition that the development of a more adequate understanding of the metatheoretical foundations of science requires a move beyond the philosophy of science. The crisis in reason that has characterized the modern age, we argue, has its historical roots in the decline of the rationalistic tradition in Western philosophy *and* the rise of a positivist tradition in the philosophy of science. We argue for an expanded conception of rationality that seeks to restore matters of value to the realm of rationality. The tendency to equate rationality with scientific rationality and scientific rationality with technical interest in the prediction and control of objective physical–natural phenomena, we argue, excluded subjective and intersubjective phenomena (including values, principles, standards, norms, etc.) from the realm of rationality. The perspective outlined in this chapter, in contrast, aims to restore such phenomena to the realm of rational understanding. In undertaking a reevaluation and reconceptualization of the metatheoretical foundations of science, this chapter seeks to move beyond the philosophy of science by outlining a critical co-constructivist perspective on the nature of rationality that provides a framework for a broadened conceptualization of science itself.

NOTES

1. As described above, for example, the disciplines of anthropology, psychology, and sociology each has fields that would be classified as representing what we have called the natural (objective) sciences, the social (intersubjective) sciences, *and* the psychological (subjective) sciences.

2. There has, however, been a growing recognition of the fact that fields within disciplines display considerable variability in terms of how the disciplines are construed (see D'Andrade, 1986).

3. In briefly outlining the domains of scientific understanding, we recognize that it is far beyond the scope of this chapter to develop fully the implications that such

a view has for each of the specialized sciences. Nor do we feel it necessary to do so. Little would be gained at this point, for example, by further pursuing to what extent it would be necessary to reexamine and reevaluate the foundations for the natural (objective) sciences from within such a broadened conception of scientific rationality. Similarly, little would be gained at this point by examining in detail the foundation for the social (intersubjective) and the psychological (subjective) sciences within such a framework.

4. In this frame, the growing recognition of problems associated with adopting the "natural" sciences as a model has raised a critical metatheoretical issue for the social and psychological sciences, namely the development of alternative models. In our theoretical work, we have adopted the view of psychosocial theory as a nomotic science. *Nomotics* is the science of human rules and rule systems (Hogan & Henley, 1970). Our efforts in formulating a metatheoretical foundation for the nomotic sciences has, at least at one level, been rooted in a recognition of this issue. We would note that we consider our theoretical framework, psychosocial role theory (understood as a nomotic science), and our research (understood as nomotic research) to span the domains of the social (intersubjective) sciences and the psychological (subjective) sciences (see Kurtines, 1987). The focus of our co-constructive research falls within the domain of the former, whereas our reconstructive research falls within the domain of the latter.

5. Not all hermeneutics emphasize the validity-enhancing potential of hermeneutics. There is a tradition of hermeneutic relativism that emphasizes the changing historical, contextual, presumptive, and interpretive frame of each generation of interpreters (see Campbell, 1986 for a discussion of this issue).

REFERENCES

Aiken, H. (1956). *The age of ideology.* New York: New American Library.

Berger, P. L., & Luckman, T. (1967). *The social construction of reality.* New York: Anchor Books.

Bhaskar, R. (1975). *A realist theory of science.* Leeds, England: Leeds Books.

Bhaskar, R. (1979). *The possibility of naturalism.* Brighton, Great Britain: Harvester Press.

Campbell, D. T. (1986). Science's social system of validity-enhancing collective belief change and the problems of the social sciences. In D. W. Fiske & R. A. Shweder (Eds.), *Metatheory in social science* (pp. 108–135). Chicago: University of Chicago Press.

Campbell, D. T. (1988). *Methodology and epistemology for social sciences: Selected papers.* Chicago: University of Chicago Press.

Cook, T. D., & Campbell, D. T. (1979). *Quasi-experimentation: Design & analysis issues for field settings.* Chicago: Rand McNally.

D'Andrade, R. (1986). Three scientific world views and the covering law model. In D. W. Fisk & R. A. Shweder (Eds.), *Metatheory in social science* (pp. 19–41). Chicago: University of Chicago Press.

Fiske, D. W., & Shweder, R. A. (1986). *Metatheory in social science.* Chicago: University of Chicago Press.

Fremantle, A. (1954). *The age of belief.* New York: New American Library.

Gergen, K. J. (1985). The social constructionist movement in modern psychology. *American Psychologist, 40,* 266–275.

Habermas, J. (1979). *Communication and the evolution of society.* Boston: Beacon.

Hanson, N. R. (1958). *Patterns of discovery.* Cambridge, England: Cambridge University Press.

Harré, R. (1970). *The principles of scientific thinking.* Chicago: University of Chicago Press.

Harré, R. (1972). *Philosophies of science.* Oxford: Oxford University Press.

Hogan, R. (1974). Dialectical aspects of moral development. *Human development, 17,* 107–117.

Hogan, R. (1988). Positivism is history. *Contemporary Psychology, 33,* 9–10.

Hogan, R., & Henley, N. (1970). Nomotics: The science of human rule systems. *Law and Society Review, 15,* 135–146.

Howard, G. S. (1985). The role of value in the science of psychology. *American Psychologist, 40,* 255–265.

Kuhn, T. (1970). *The structure of scientific revolutions* (2nd ed.). Chicago: University of Chicago Press.

Kurtines, W. (1987). Psychosocial theory as a nomotic science. In W. Kurtines & J. L. Gewirtz (Eds.), *Moral development through social interaction.* New York: Wiley.

Kurtines, W., Alvarez, M., & Azmitia, M. (1990). Science and morality: The role of theoretical and meta-theoretical discourse in the psychological study of moral phenomena. *Psychological Bulletin, 107,* 283–295.

Manicas, P. T., & Secord, P. F. (1983). Implications for psychology of the new philosophy of science. *American Psychologist, 38,* 399–413.

McCarthy, T. (1981). *The critical theory of Jurgen Habermas.* Cambridge, MA: MIT Press.

McMullin, E. (1983). Values in science. In P. D. Asquith & T. Nickles (Eds.), *Proceedings of the 1982 Philosophy of Science Association* (Vol. 2, pp. 3–23). East Lansing, MI: Philosophy of Science Association.

McMullin, E. (1984). A case for scientific realism. In J. J. Leplin (Ed.), *Essays on scientific realism* (pp. 53–71). Berkeley: University of California Press.

Shweder, R. A. (1986). Divergent rationalities. In D. W. Fiske & R. A. Shweder (Eds.), *Metatheory in social science: Pluralisms and subjectivities* (pp. 163–196). Chicago: University of Chicago Press.

Toulmin, S. (1953). *The philosophy of science.* New York: Harper & Row.

Toulmin, S. (1961). *Foresight and understanding.* New York: Harper & Row.

Waddington, C. H. (1967). *The ethical animal.* Chicago, IL: University of Chicago Press.

Chapter 2 ■

Toward a Postmodern Psychology of Moral Action and Moral Development ■

MARTIN J. PACKER*
University of Michigan

In the past decade, radical changes have occurred in our understanding of the character of moral beliefs, precepts, and prescriptions, and how these are or can be justified. Profound changes have also taken place in our view of the nature of scientific inquiry, particularly in the human sciences, and how scientific knowledge claims can be justified. These changes reflect a larger transition between two very different ways of comprehending ourselves and our world: the modern and postmodern epochs. A book such as this can play a role in deciding the direction that psychology takes in this time of transition, through reflection upon the framework to which we have become accustomed. An appreciation of the need for such reflection in the sciences of humanity can be seen in the growing frequency of metatheoretical analysis (e.g., Fiske & Shweder, 1986; Stam, Rogers, & Gergen, 1987).

* The author wishes to acknowledge the support of the Office of Education Research and Improvement, Department of Education, under OERI Contract 400-86-0009 to the Far West Laboratory for Educational Research and Development, San Francisco, California. The opinions expressed herein do not necessarily reflect the position or policy of OERI, and no official endorsement by OERI or the Department of Education should be inferred. Thanks are also due to the teachers and principals of Bountiful and Knowlton Elementary Schools, and Bonnie Middleton of the Davis County School District, Utah. The name "Workshop Way" is copyrighted and owned by The Workshop Way, Inc.

Such metatheoretical discourse considers how we have come to ask the questions we ask in our consideration of psychological phenomena; what background assumptions we take for granted in our inquiry and what, on the other hand, is overlooked; what persistent problems hamper our investigations; and what are the likely results of modifying our course of inquiry.

These are the kinds of question I try to answer in this chapter. My intention is to question central assumptions we have about the way moral values are sanctioned, or warranted, or justified as reasonable. I shall try to show that even positions as generally opposed as social learning theory and cognitive–developmentalism take it for granted that moral values can be justified only by appeal to some fixed characteristics of human nature, such as the supposedly fixed and universal characteristics of human reasoning. It is further presumed that only a single, universal morality can receive this kind of objective justification, and that if such a justification proves impossible, then moral relativism or nihilism is the consequence. My thesis is that these assumptions about morality and its justification are false, and that they hinder our progress in psychology. They were first adopted in the Enlightenment, the social, political, and intellectual project initiated in the 1600s, which created what was until recently an unquestioned way of understanding the world and our place in it: the "modern" view. The Enlightenment involved a project of ethical justification that defined the terms in which morality has been understood and investigated for the past 300 years.

The first section of this chapter outlines this project of ethical justification. Because assumptions about morality went hand in hand with assumptions about human nature, reason, the relationship between facts and values, and the character of legitimate scientific knowledge, we must consider these as well. Thus, we must pay some attention to classical and medieval ethics, and to the Enlightenment's second project, that of justifying scientific knowledge claims. The argument I review is that the project of ethical justification proved to be impossible, not because of any lack of skill or agility on the part of those engaged in it, but because the character of morality, and the role it has traditionally played in human affairs and human conduct, is such that the kind of justification that was sought proves, on reflection, impossible. The very terms in which the Enlightenment's ethical project was framed made its downfall inevitable.

The second section of the chapter concerns the way two major approaches to the psychology of moral development—social learning theory and cognitive–developmentalism—have accepted the Enlightenment's definition of morality. Each assumes that either morality has an objective foundation, or it has no justification at all. The difference is that cognitive–developmentalists claim to have identified such a foundation, whereas social learning theorists treat morality as having no objective foundation, and thus nothing more than the expression of subjective preferences.

What are the consequences of the failure of the Enlightenment's ethical project? The apparent absence of any objective foundation to ethics has had profound consequences, both intellectual and social. We have been left with a misunderstanding of the kind of being we are, and of the kinds of life we should live. But these consequences are not inevitable. In fact, they follow from continued acceptance of the original assumptions that lay behind the Enlightenment project. This being so, we must try to reshape the perspective from which we comprehend morality, and the terms in which we conceive it. When we do this, the outlines of a different kind of ethical justification become apparent, one that legitimates multiple objective moralities rather than a universal moral system. In the final section, I briefly consider what is being done along these lines by contemporary philosophers of ethics, in the context of some suggestions about the shape a postmodern approach to psychological inquiry might take, once inappropriate foundational assumptions have been relinquished.

THE ENLIGHTENMENT PROJECTS

The historical period that came to be called the Enlightenment was a time of rebellion against the authority of church and state. Scientific developments, first in astronomy and then in mechanics, were throwing doubt on centuries of teaching. Political uprisings and dissent were frequent, despite the repression with which they were met. Traditional doctrines and values were subjected to harsh, unsympathetic scrutiny. In particular, theological modes of inquiry were rejected in favor of emphases on empirical science as a model form of inquiry, on the systematic use of reason, and on the individual as a valid seeker of knowledge and as the proper focus of the social and political orders. Each of these new views contrasted in key respects with the classical and medieval counterparts. A new view of reason and inquiry was developing, pitting empirically informed reason against scholastic speculation, causal explanation against teleological metaphysics, and the natural dignity and capacities of the individual against a theological hierarchy that placed man higher than beasts but lower than angels.

New Views of Empirical Science

During the seventeenth century, people witnessed startling and revolutionary successes in novel forms of empirical inquiry. Galileo was one among many who were strikingly successful at explaining both earthly and celestial phenomena in ways totally at odds with the Catholic Church's teaching. The Church had been promulgating a view of the universe, based on biblical exegesis and classical Greek texts, that emphasized a fundamental distinction between earthly and celestial phenomena. It also employed teleological explanations of natural movements, these too taken from classical Greek philosophy.

According to Aristotle's physics, all entities on the earth are composed of four fundamental elements: earth, air, fire, and water (Cohen, 1985; Evans, 1964). Each element has a natural place in the sphere beneath the moon: earth at the center, water in a sphere surrounding the earth, air surrounding water, and fire as another concentric sphere below the moon. In the absence of external influence, each element returns to its natural place. Accordingly, the proportion of the elements in a body determines whether it is heavy or light, so every object has a natural motion, an intrinsic tendency to move to its natural position. Heavy objects move toward the center of the earth; light objects move upward. Stones drop to the ground; rain falls to earth; gas bubbles up in a lake; flames leap upward. In each case, the natural motion of a terrestrial body is a straight line. Unnatural or "violent" motions can be imposed on a body by the application of a force, but linear motion reappears when the force is removed. Physics is the systematic study of natural motions; the unnatural motions brought about by efficient causes, by pushes and pulls, are not amenable to scientific explanation. Physics deals only with the natural order of things.

In this classical account, there is a second realm: that of heavenly objects. These are made from a fifth element, the "aether." The natural motion of such objects is circular, so the heavenly bodies move around the earth in circles. The aether is a perfect and unchanging material; the planets, sun, and moon are like eternal diamonds. In contrast, terrestrial objects and their elements are corruptible, marked by constant alteration and change.

The classical Greek texts in which this physics was articulated had been lost when the Roman empire collapsed, around the fifth century. In the twelfth century, the texts were rediscovered in Arabic translation and re-translated into Latin. The Catholic Church soon incorporated Aristotelian notions into the teaching it had been conducting around biblical exegesis. St. Thomas Aquinas is the most famous systematizer and unifier of these two traditions, the classical and the Christian. Scholastic physics (along with a classical ethics I shall consider shortly) became central to the curriculum of the new European universities. Aristotle's two-sphere model of the universe was adopted and adapted. In the Thomist version, the earth is the center of the universe, surrounded by the spheres of the moon, sun, and other planets. In addition, Paradise lies beyond the sphere of the stars, while the circles of Hell lie inside the earth; this portrayal had clearly taken on a symbolic Christian meaning: "The universe of spheres mirrors both man's hope and his fate. Both physically and spiritually man occupies a crucial intermediate position in this universe" (Kuhn, 1957, p. 112).

Many elements of Thomist physics were rejected by proponents of the seventeenth-century's new science, most famously the heliocentric model of planetary motion. The Church's claims that earthly and celestial realms contained different kinds of matter, manifested different natural motions, and thus were governed by different laws, proved no longer tenable. The new astronomy was able to show, for example, that the earth and the heavens have remarkable similarities. Through his telescope, Galileo saw craters on the moon, proving it is not a perfect sphere, as both Aristotle's physics and the Thomist account had claimed. Newton was able to show that local and planetary phenomena could be described in terms of the same laws of motion and gravitational attraction. Thus, general laws based on empirical observation, not on metaphysical speculation, became the norm.

The Systematic Use of Reason

Enlightenment philosophers also rejected the view of the character and aims of reason that the Catholic Church had adopted from Aristotle. In the Thomist system, events had final causes that could be identified by reason alone, rather than by empirical inquiry. The Enlightenment thinkers disagreed strongly. Reason, they argued, cannot supply genuine knowledge about powers and essences, about the final causes and the final ends of physical motion. All these are speculative metaphysical notions, neither identifiable through reflection nor accessible to empirical observation. Metaphysical speculation should be swept away for all time. Reason, informed by observation, can only identify proximal causes. Reason is calculative, dealing with matters of fact and with mathematical relations.

With these changes, the scope of reason became smaller. Many of our beliefs turn out (in this account) not to be rationally justifiable, but based merely on custom or habit. Causal relationships, for example, are merely repetitive associations of successive events (Hume's famous skeptical argument). With the rejection of Scholasticism, reason became more specialized and more powerful, but more limited in its range of application.

Emphasis on the Individual

It is not an exaggeration to say that in the seventeenth century the "individual" was invented ("a new social and cultural artifact" along with the parasol, suggests MacIntyre, 1988, p. 339). For the first time, man (woman was still generally excluded) was considered to have an existence and characteristics prior to and separate from particular social roles. The new science itself seemed to be an activity where individuals were making discoveries through their own observation and reasoning, with no reference to tradition or faith. Indeed, what they discovered disclosed prejudice and dogma in centuries of instruction by the Church. In this early science, a new view of knowledge took roots, one that placed central emphasis on the power and validity of individual reasoning and observation. For the first time, accounts of knowledge, human nature, and morality centered on the individual, distinct from the context of a culture or tradition, or a super-human deity. The individual was now considered a legitimate source of knowledge, distinct from and superior to the authority of the church and the monarchy. The individual modern self, so the account went, had been liberated from theological faith and confused teleological thinking into a proper autonomy of reflection and empirical investigation.

SCIENTIFIC AND MORAL JUSTIFICATION

The Enlightenment intellectuals defined for themselves and their succes-sors two projects, one dealing with scientific reason and knowledge of the material world, the second with practical reason and knowledge of the social and moral world. To fully understand the way we, at the end of the twentieth century, view both science and ethics—and the relationship between these two—we need to look closely at the character and history of these projects. In each case, the aim was to identify an objective foundation that would justify claims to valid knowledge or values, respectively, with-out reference to divine ordinance or speculative metaphysics.

The Rational Justification of Scientific Knowledge

The first project called for examination of the method of scientific inquiry and an account of its essential features, to characterize the manner of inquiry appropriate to matters of fact. More precisely, the aim was to iden-tify the means by which an individual can achieve valid and justified knowledge of the physical universe and its material objects, and thereby to provide a rational foundation on which to ground scientific knowledge claims. The story of the ultimately unsuccessful efforts to achieve this foundation is beyond the scope of this paper, but a brief overview will help outline the parallels between this project and the second one, and will provide background to the later discussion of alternative interpretations of the proper character of a scientific psychology.

Efforts to provide a rational justification for the new science of individual empirical investigation took the tack of trying to identify an interpretation-free origin to which all kinds of valid scientific knowledge could be traced. Two main candidates were proposed: basic sensory elements or brute facts that could be observed in a manner independent of prior theory (Locke, Hume), and self-evident principles that would frame the content of scientific theories (Descartes, Kant). In our own century, the assumption that valid scientific knowledge rests on a twin foundation of objective facts and axiomatic principles motivated the Vienna Circle's logical positivism, and it continues to the present day in "cognitive empiricist" programs (Toulmin's phrase) in psychology. In the positivist account of proper scientific investigation, modern logic provides formal rewriting rules that operate on value-neutral and interpretation-free observation statements. Validity is guaranteed by the consistency and completeness of the logical syntax and the objectivity of the observational data. Unfortunately, logic may be neither consistent nor complete (Nagel & Newman, 1958), and regardless, it is arbitrary and conventional. Also, the observations making up the empirical component turn out to be theory laden and organized by our human technological concerns (Kuhn, 1970).

In cognitive science, the digital computer today provides a root metaphor for human action and cognition, one that still reflects the view that knowledge is founded in logic and facts. Bits of information are input, stored, and transformed by algorithmic procedures that implement basic logical operations. Neither data items nor programs involve interpretation. If such a scheme were to successfully model a nontrivial aspect of human functioning, this would be strong support for the Enlightenment's epistemology. Present evidence gives no sign that this is likely.

The Rational Justification of Moral Knowledge

For the Enlightenment thinkers, science and philosophy dealt with moral issues as much as with epistemological ones. The second project called for justification of the forms of practical reasoning that guide action, a justification parallel to that sought for scientific knowledge. The aim was to provide a rational account of the character and status of moral norms and rules, one that would rest no longer on religious authority or claims of a divinely revealed truth, but would reflect the power of the individual's capacity for reasoning.

The Enlightenment philosophers shared a sense of the kind of moral justification they were seeking. It would characterize some key feature(s) of human nature, and then lay out the rational considerations that would be universally compelling to a being with such a nature, that is, the precepts of action that one would expect such a being to accept (MacIntyre, 1984). The certification of moral beliefs, claims, values, and injunctions was to take the form of principles that were binding because they were rationally inescapable, given the nature of our constitution. The elements central to the task were, then, a view of reason, an account of human nature, and an understanding of the moral precepts that were to be justified.

There was surprising agreement about the content of the morality to be justified. All the contributors to the project (Kierkegaard, Kant, Diderot, Hume, Smith, and the rest) considered that the precepts constituting genuine morality involved marriage and the family, promise keeping and justice, respect for life and property. All these were taken over uncritically from a shared Christian past. Thus, the *content* of their various ethical theories remained an unquestioned conservative individualism, despite the disparate ways of justifying it (MacIntyre, 1984, p. 47). The radical aspect of the project lay not in its content, but in its seeking a rational, rather than theological, certification for the moral order. To abandon theological justification, however, there was a move away from reference to the ends of action and of human life, just as teleological accounts of natural phenomena were rejected as speculative and unscientific. Although the Enlightenment moral scheme retained much of the content of Thomist ethics, it excluded the teleological structure that had been appropriated from Aristotle. This proved to be anything but a minor modification. The teleological features of classical ethics were not a chance matter; they reveal the social and educational role ethics played in classical Greek times.

Classical Ethics

Aristotle held that "Every craft and every inquiry, and similarly every action and project, seems to aim at some good; hence the good has been well defined as that at which everything aims."[1] Just as he described objects as having a natural place that they sought out in their motion, so he described men as having final ends that they endeavored to achieve through their action. This account reflected the social reality of his time. The Greek city states were small, close-knit communities within which there was consensus about the character and purpose of social roles such as citizen, warrior, philosopher, and slave. Accordingly, Aristotle's ethics is a teleological one: A man is virtuous when he adequately fulfills the requirements of the role into which he was born. For the flute player, playing tunefully is the final end; for the shoemaker, it is making shoes that are strong and comfortable; for the warrior, it is fearlessness in battle; for the slave, obedience to the master. And man, too, has a final end, a *telos*. "Man" is what we would now call a functional concept: He is a being with an essential nature and an essential purpose or function. What is uniquely human, distinguishing man from the animals, is *logos*. Logos has generally been translated as "reason" (although we shall see that another translation may be more appropriate). The right and appropriate exercise of logos leads man to the proper end toward which, as human being, he is directed (and from this, we should note, woman was excluded, along with the slave and the barbarian).

Just as Aristotle's description of objects moving to their natural resting places seems a puzzling kind of physics to anyone accustomed to modern mechanics, until recently his ethics has also seemed an anachronism. Thomas Kuhn described his struggle to comprehend the apparent absurdities in Aristotle's accounts of the behavior of bodies, and his sudden realization that Aristotle's subject "was changed-of-quality in general, including both the fall of a stone and the growth of a child to adulthood" (Kuhn, 1977, p. xi). The primary ontological entities were not material bodies, but the elements and other "qualities which, when imposed on some portion of omnipresent neutral matter, constituted an individual body or substance. Position . . . was . . . a quality in Aristotle's physics, and a body that changed its position therefore remained the same body only in the problematic sense that the child is the individual it becomes" (p. xii). In the same way, Aristotle's ethics had a focus unlike that of most contemporary ethical inquiries. Aristotle's teleological account of human life was tied directly to the hierarchical structure and roles of the Greek *polis*. Classical ethics was not a detached, theoretical kind of inquiry; it was the discipline that enabled a person to know how to become what he could, and should, be, to fulfill his place in the polis. Ethics had political import; it showed how to correct, improve, and educate the citizens. Central to Aristotle's ethics was the notion of "virtue," something that has until recently seemed an antiquated moral concept. Virtues such as courage, temperance, liberality, magnificence, pride, good temper, truthfulness, ready wit, friendliness, modesty, and righteous indignation are states of character that make a man good, and make him do his own work well (Aristotle, 1980, p. 37).

At the same time, natural virtue and virtue in the strict sense are distinct, and it is here that the developmental and educational function of ethics appears. Children may have the natural disposition for moral qualities, but without logos, their expression can be "evidently hurtful" (Aristotle, p. 157). Moral precepts are needed to encourage the virtues and discourage the vices, to order and educate the desires and emotions, and to cultivate appropriate habits of action. "It is not possible to be good in the strict sense without practical wisdom, or practically wise without moral virtue" (p. 158). Practical wisdom involves knowledge of the generally accepted rules of morality and an intelligent understanding of their reasons. A moral education, guided by the authority of just law, is essential:

> It is difficult to get from youth up a right training for virtue if one has not been brought up under right laws; for to live temperately and hardily is not pleasant to most people, especially when they are young. For this reason their nurture and occupations should be fixed by law; for they will not be painful when they have become customary. (p. 271)

The good life made no sense out of the setting of society and its laws:

> If (as we have said) the man who is to be good must be well trained and
> habituated, and go on to spend his time in worthy occupations and neither
> willingly nor unwillingly do bad actions, and if this can be brought about if
> men live in accordance with a sort of reason and right order, provided this has
> force . . . the law has compulsive power, while it is at the same time a rule
> proceeding from a sort of practical wisdom and reason. (p. 272)

This ethical scheme had three interconnecting elements: a view of human nature in its natural, untutored form, with its natural virtues and its faculties and passions; an understanding of the right moral precepts and laws; and a view of the moral end, that is, the "states of character" that characterize a good man. The latter comprises the human telos. As Kuhn discovered, change, including the moral changes required in "the growth of a child to adulthood," was the central subject in Aristotle's philosophy.

Medieval Christianity changed the details but retained the basic structure of Aristotelian ethics: an account of human nature, an understanding of the precepts of rational ethics, and an ethical–developmental telos. Divinely ordained law was tacked onto the ethical precepts, and Aristotle's list of virtues was elaborated to include Christian virtues such as faith, hope, and charity. Conceptions of the telos varied, but the assumption of a proper end to human life was maintained. Aristotle's accounts of virtue and of the human telos were reinterpreted in terms of Christian "natural law": there are norms of human nature as such, but they reflect Adam's original sin, and we are far from realizing human nature as it ought to be. Later in the Middle Ages, the view of the telos altered again; uniquely Christian notions of revelation and salvation were introduced. For Aquinas, for example, the end of human action and the point of moral rules was to achieve goods, to obtain what satisfies our desire. But this was not simple eudaimonism, for "God is good," so that good action aimed to a unity with god. The achievement of human nature as it ought to be was postponed to an afterlife.

The understanding of morality changed radically with the Enlightenment. The "philosophes" (Gay, 1977) had rejected the teleological component of classical physics on the grounds that it was metaphysical and unscientific. In a parallel fashion, they considered classical teleological accounts of human nature to be flawed and unscientific. Just as they considered an appeal to the natural ends of physical motion to be idle speculation, when it came to human activity, they maintained that while human reasoning could identify the *means* appropriate to a certain course of practical action, it had nothing to say about the *ends* toward which action—or life—should be directed. What they failed to see was that this rejection of a human telos undermined the classical purpose and function of ethics. What remained of the three-part scheme of Aristotelian ethics was a view of untutored human nature and a set of moral injunctions that had been stripped of their teleological context. The moral injunctions, both classical and Christian, far from being logically derivable from facts about human nature, had been designed, as we have seen, to bring about *changes* in that nature. Far from being dictates that all humans could be expected to find rationally compelling, they were prescriptions likely to run counter to human impulses. "The injunctions of morality, thus understood, are likely to be ones that human nature, thus understood, has strong tendencies to disobey" (MacIntyre, 1984, p. 55). The Enlightenment modifications to Thomist ethics were of such a kind that the task of demonstrating how moral injunctions could rationally appeal to human nature was from the outset an impossible one. Nonetheless, such a demonstration was seen as central to the project the Enlightenment philosophers undertook. Unwittingly, they initiated ethics' decline from a discipline of practical and educational consequence to one of merely abstract, theoretical academic interest.

Thus, like its sister project for a foundational justification of scientific knowledge, the project of ethical justification ran into insurmountable problems. A succession of brilliant moral philosophers struggled to achieve its goals. Increasingly, they complained of the impossibility of their task, and they argued explicitly that a rational justification of morality is simply not possible. Although they came to appreciate that their task was an impossible one, they drew the wrong conclusions. Instead of questioning the wisdom of an appeal to an objective rational foundation to justify moral precepts, one that rested on facts about a fixed human nature, they concluded that *no* reasonable ethical justification was possible. With growing frequency, they interpreted morality as rooted instead in whim, preference, or subjective value.

The concerns that found their expression in the Enlightenment projects were noble ones. The political aim to create a new kind of social order in which individuals could improve themselves and participate equally has undoubtedly been powerful and important. With the benefits of hindsight, however, as inheritors of the two projects' conceptual and social progeny, we can appreciate difficulties that the torchbearers of each project failed to anticipate.

PSYCHOLOGY AND THE FAILURE OF THE ENLIGHTENMENT PROJECTS

The psychological study of moral phenomena has lessons to learn from an examination of the Enlightenment's two projects. The first is an appreciation that many of our research programs still adopt unthinkingly the terms in which these projects were conceived. Although they share the terms, they differ in their understanding of where the projects have left us. On the one hand are conceptions of moral action and moral development that not only accept the Enlightenment perspective, but assume that the moral project has been successfully completed. Kohlberg's cognitive–developmental study of moral development is one of these. On the other hand are those programs that tacitly acknowledge the moral project's failure, but fail to see that this means we must rethink our understanding of reason, rather than conclude that morality is entirely a matter of opinion and that everything is relative. Social learning theory is one of these. It is left to the reader to judge what stand other views on moral development, including those presented in this book, take on the success or failure of the Enlightenment's project of ethical justification.

Kohlberg's Cognitive-Developmental Theory

Kohlberg's (1971/1981) account of morality has elements very similar to those found in accounts by Locke, Hume, and other moral philosophers engaged in the ethical project. The first element is a largely unquestioned content to morality, this time in the form of universal moral principles. The second is a view of a universal human nature, this time the Piagetian one of an individual who constructs cognitive structures through interaction with the environment, through universal psychological processes of assimilation and accommodation. The third common element is the effort to link these two by means of a rational justification.

Kohlberg claimed that there is wide, perhaps universal, agreement on the content of moral principles. He described empirical evidence that "there is a universal set of moral principles held by people in various cultures, Stage 6" (p. 127) and furthermore "these principles . . . would logically and consistently be held by all people in all societies." Even "the more generalized and consistently held content 'principles' of conventional morality [i.e., Stages 3 and 4] are also universal" (p. 128). Those principles characteristic of Stages 5 or 6 are prudence and respect for authority, society, or people (Stage 5 only); welfare of others; justice; and benevolence (Stage 6 only) (p. 174).

As Harré pointed out, cognitive–developmentalism adopts the morality and politics of individualism. Piaget and Kohlberg presented democratic individualism as though it was a universal empirical truth, an objective statement of the ends of human nature: "Piaget assumes that his own Cartesian logicism is the highest form of human cognition. In similar vein, Kohlberg builds on the assumption that North American colonial democracy is the most advanced form of human association" (Harré, 1984, p. 231). Harré's conclusion is one I am happy to endorse: "This suggests taking morally relevant discourse as a text in need of interpretative analysis rather than something for which a literal reading is always available through some supposed shared commonsense understanding" (p. 232).

It might seem that Kohlberg's account of human "nature" differed significantly from most versions of the Enlightenment project. Isn't there a telos involved in Kohlberg's account, an end to human development, just the kind of thing Locke and Hume were determined to avoid? Kohlberg wrote, after all, of the need to move "From Is to Ought." This is true, but the end is one that an Enlightenment philosopher would have happily sanctioned. The individual becomes a scientist–philosopher, that is, objective, able to consider all factors in their various combinations in a value-neutral manner. He becomes principled, constructing and applying universal and logical ethical principles. The end of development is the autonomous individual that the Enlightenment philosophers invented, and that they claimed we have been all along. The autonomous individual, a seventeenth-century social fiction that had been proclaimed an objective fact about human nature, a construction that has become a social reality of dubious merit in contemporary culture, one that is diagnosed as a uniquely modern malaise (e.g., Durkheim's state of anomie), becomes in Kohlberg's stage model the highest form of morality, an inevitable ethical development. "'Ethical principles' are the end point of sequential 'natural' development in social functioning and thinking" (Kohlberg, 1971/1981, p. 106). Moral development has here all the inevitability of a syllogism. There is a "**logical order** among the stages" (p. 137); each implies the previous stage but not the succeeding one. "Movement in moral thought is usually irreversibly forward in direction" (p. 137). Education is unnecessary for construction of formal operational intelligence (Piaget claimed not to understand the "American question"); nor is ethical instruction or guidance needed for an individual to reach Stage 6. This is a technological teleology, not an Aristotelian one.

To the extent that Kohlberg claimed to have given a clear account of stages of moral development, he claimed also to have provided a rational justification of ethics. Kohlberg's description of what is accomplished in moral development is exactly what the Enlightenment ethical thinkers were trying to create: a moral system that is binding for every individual, but that makes no reference to external authorities and is independent of the individual's personal situation and interests. "With each stage, the obligation to preserve human life becomes more categorical, more independent of the aims of the actor, of the commands or opinions of others" (Kohlberg, 1971/1981, p. 171). How are the universal principles and the constructivist nature brought together? According to Kohlberg, by the individual himself. A major impetus for an individual's transition from one moral stage to the next is a rational recognition of the inadequacies of the current stage. A search for cognitive consistency drives development, and the cognitive consistency of a moral system is essentially a rational justification of that system. Kohlberg acknowledged that "my psychological theory as to why moral development is upward and sequential is broadly the same as **my philosophical** justification for claiming that a higher stage is more adequate or more moral than a lower stage" (p. 131). What makes the higher stages better? The criteria of structural adequacy in the cognitive–developmental scheme of things are formal ones: increased differentiation and integration. However, morality is "an autonomous domain, with its own criteria of adequacy or rationality," although these are parallel to the cognitive criteria. A moral reason has formal characteristics of "impersonality, ideality, universalizability, preemptiveness and so on" (p. 170). In other words, a fully adequate moral judgment is binding for all. The individual who reaches Stage 6 has finally constructed what the Enlightenment thinkers were trying to find: a morality that is "universal, inclusive, consistent, and grounded on objective, impersonal, or ideal grounds" (p. 170).

Social Learning Theory

If Kohlberg assumed that the Enlightenment project of ethical justification was successful, and proposed that it is recapitulated anew by every individual, social learning theorists assume that the project has failed, and that all moral values and beliefs are relative. Moral action can be studied only as a matter of empirical fact, and moral development is, in truly eudaimonist fashion, a matter of avoiding negative consequences and seeking pleasurable ones.

Social learning theory had its beginnings in twentieth-century positivism, which expressed the stark reality the failed projects seemed to have revealed: reason is logic, facts are neutral data, values are mere preference and opinion. Once values had become considered subjective and ungrounded, ethical relativism was inevitable. And since in this view, moral judgments simply express preferences, moral development has no rational direction beyond the arbitrary norms of one's social group. People can reinforce any kind of behavior they wish. As Liebert (1984) put it: "Evaluation invariably involves preference, and preference is invariably relative." Liebert, like Hare (1952/1964), saw no possibility for *rational* evaluation in moral judgment. The pursuit of self-interest, for the social learning theorist, as for Nietzsche, is all that remains, and such a pursuit results in the development of cunning, not principle.

TOWARD A POSTMODERN PSYCHOLOGY OF MORALITY

If it is to genuinely move beyond false foundational assumptions, the psychological study of moral phenomena must allow itself to be affected in a double way by the failure to identify objective, interpretation-free foundations upon which to ground scientific and moral knowledge. A science of moral phenomena must rethink both its status as science and the character of its domain of inquiry. Neither of these two is quite what we have assumed it to be. Thomas Kuhn and others have given us a new sense of what science is, free from a foundational metaphysics. They have reinterpreted science in postmodern terms. Scientific research turns out to involve paradigms of inquiry outside which no interpretation of phenomena can take place. However, the science of psychology presents special interpretive problems. Because those parts of psychology that involve the study of human phenomena will never become "normal science" in Kuhn's (1970) sense, their practitioners must stay constantly aware of the role that perspectives and concerns play in constituting the entities being studied. A science that cannot appeal to the apparently interpretation-free data that a paradigm provides to its scientific practitioners must instead explicitly recognize and come to terms with the unavoidable part that interpretation plays in even the identification of what counts as evidence. A postmodern psychology must have a central hermeneutic component (Packer & Addison, 1989).

A variety of candidates have been proposed for a nonpositivist psychology: humanistic, phenomenological, constructionist, narrative. One way to assess these psychologies is to consider to what extent the Enlightenment framework still holds sway. Does the search continue for a foundation underlying knowledge claims? Or is it assumed instead that no rational justification is possible and that anything goes, that all interpretations are equal, and that selection among competing explanatory accounts is arbitrary?

The interpretive or hermeneutic approach I have outlined elsewhere (Packer, 1985) attempts a radical break with the Enlightenment projects for science and morality. Its domain of inquiry is neither an external realm of objective phenomena nor an internal cognitive realm of mental structures, but everyday practical activity. The source of knowledge is not taken to be interpretation-free facts about the world, observed with detachment, or cognitive principles self-evident to reflection. Inquiry has its starting place in our human understanding of each other, although this is always a partial, perspectival, and incomplete kind of understanding. Furthermore, this understanding is inevitably "projective": We comprehend new phenomena in terms of our practical engagement in the world. We understand the new *not* in terms of what we already know, but in terms of who we already are. The possible shapes of our understanding are, at least initially, those into which we have been thrown by our history and culture. Interpretive investigation entails a recognition that a projective framework is always at work, but that with effort it can be extended and altered, to bring fresh understanding.

The kind of explanation sought in hermeneutic inquiry is neither a theory made up of general laws that reflect statistically significant regularities among events, nor a rational reconstruction of some portion of a decontextualized cognitive competence. It is instead a narrative account, an interpretation, that articulates and lays out our practical understanding of a phenomenon, organized by the concerns of a particular practical engagement, a task that psychological activity seeks to further and move forward. Interpretive inquiry focuses on human activity, situated in context, and the products of activity, including institutions, histories, and texts. Human understanding traffics in "thick concepts" (Williams, 1985) that meld fact and value; an explanatory account of human action, finding its starting place in understanding, aims to articulate these concepts to a practical end.

This, in brief, is one account of the kind of science psychology can become. What, now, is the appropriate way to approach and understand the phenomena of morality? A hermeneutic approach to moral phenomena introduces changes in both the emphasis and practice of research into morality. First, we must study moral action embedded in the context of social practices. The sources of moral development lie not within the individual (in the mind, or in human nature) or even in the socializing parent–child dyad, but in the social practices within which individuals act. Tradition and culture perpetuate themselves in these practices, but they are also shaped by contemporary material circumstances. Second, moral reasoning is not usually a matter of applying moral principles, analogous to solving math or logical problems: It takes the shape of deliberation about concrete moral issues. Third, if researchers can never be detached onlookers, the relationship between researcher and people studied needs to be reexamined. Let us consider each of these three in more detail, together with some examples of interpretive research that has broken fresh ground in each area.

The Practical Grounds of Morality

Moral acts are not objects that can be simply coded or measured; they must be interpreted. An act may be foolishness or heroism, cowardice or caution, depending on the setting against which it is placed and on the circumstances of both agent and researcher. Oliver North has been described as destroyer of the Constitution, and as heroic defender of democracy. The U.S. Air Force's shooting down of two Libyan fighters was equally subject to contrasting interpretations. The ambiguity of each of these events has been striking. In what moral category should we place them? It seems that the psychologist's task is to try to understand the various ways in which such acts are interpreted. Different social practices set up their own facts; each provides an interpretive framework within which acts of right and wrong show up. As psychologists, we should not study these moral facts alone; we must study their framework, and their relation to it. At the same time, the ontological framework we work in, as scientists, shapes what we study: There is a doubly projective structure here.

From the hermeneutic perspective, the sources of morality to which the individual can lay claim, lie neither internal to that individual, as potential cognitive constructions, nor external to the individual, as social norms that must be internalized with the encouragement of authoritarian carrots and sticks. These sources, shall we say, precede and surround the individual, as social practices in which he or she can participate, and as possibilities that the individual can make his or her own. It is by becoming engaged in particular activities that children acquire and change their self-conceptions, goals, and understanding of behavior and action. Moral cognition is not general, decontextualized, and disembodied; moral thinking and moral development are practical accomplishments inherently linked with the particularities of routine, everyday experience. Engagement in everyday practical activity structures and gives meaning to thought, including thought about moral issues. Practices can be local to a particular institutional setting, or as broad as a cultural tradition. Institutions and the practices they embody provide the context for moral development. Families, workplaces, and schools all embody ways of acting that require study in their own right.

For instance, Mergendoller and I (Packer & Mergendoller, 1989) studied classroom practices set up in a novel elementary school curriculum. This study was an effort to examine the details of the social interchanges among children and among children and adults, and their interpretations of these interchanges, in a classroom setting. Teachers in several elementary schools in Utah used an instructional approach known as Workshop Way; we examined how the curriculum worked on a daily basis, by observing classes in Grades 1, 2, and 5 in two of the schools, and interviewing in some depth three teachers and perhaps one-third of their students. Interviews with the students took place on three occasions, in the fall, winter, and spring of one school year.

Social practices in this case were local ones. A workshop comprising up to 20 tasks, in fixed order, was the major academic work that students attempted each day, with the number and complexity of the tasks increasing with grade. All the tasks were taught at the start of the school year, and their labels and instructions were pinned on a "task board" on the wall. Each afternoon after the children had left, the teacher changed the content of each task for the next day, thus ensuring that it was not the teacher who "bosses" the children, but the task board. Emphasis was placed on the pleasure of working and getting work done rather than on correct answers. Students worked at their own pace, moving independently about the classroom and interacting freely with peers, but they had to maintain a reasonable noise level and not stop working altogether. We noted that teachers interacted with their students to draw them into a set of practical social activities in the classroom. These activities reflected valued forms of social interaction and engagement, including helping others and seeking help from them, being tolerant of others' faults and errors, taking academic and social risks, and working industriously. Each of these activities simultaneously encompassed an immediate practical aim and a developmental telos. First, each involved an end or purpose that was socially and personally meritorious or virtuous, for instance, providing another child with assistance in a workshop task. Second, each activity was designed to help the other children develop a "skill" that entailed conduct or concern that one would consider virtuous, for instance, sincere interest in others' learning and academic progress in class.

We also noted that the teachers worked so that they were not the "reason" the children were doing these things; instead, the teachers used a common interpretive framework that ascribed responsibility for the practices to the students in a way that emphasized their effectiveness, their initiative, and their worth as individuals. But children differed in the extent to which they took up this perspective on their own agency, and in the extent to which they accepted the classroom activities as legitimate and meaningful. Thus, they also differed in the manner in which they engaged in the activities, and in the kinds of account they gave of them.

In short, the teachers' organization of the social and instructional structure of their classes, and the detailed character of their interaction with students, accomplished three goals. First, the students became engaged in the academic and social activities of the classroom. Second, many of the children began to adopt a new way of understanding and talking about their ability, their own successes and failures, and their own academic and personal worth. Third, at least some students began to discover an intrinsic value in these classroom activities, coming to understand them as legitimate and holding themselves responsible for carrying on the activities.

In this study, we interviewed children not about hypothetical moral dilemmas, but about their daily participation in classroom activities, and about what they understood to be the meanings and purposes of these activities. We then drew conclusions about the manner in which they engaged in the activities, in particular whether they considered them legitimate.

What other kinds of study of morality in practice would be of interest? The practices in the Workshop Way classes were designed to be coherent and consistent, but this is not always the case. MacIntyre has proposed that modes of thought and practice in contemporary society have become fragmented and ineffective. This claim is worthy of empirical study. MacIntyre's (1984) argument is that the Enlightenment project not only has led to a philosophical dead end, but is also responsible for social, political, and psychological difficulties that face us now. We live in a culture shaped by social and political changes initiated by the Enlightenment and, according to both MacIntyre and Heidegger, these radical changes have led us to anomie and alienation. Our society embodies at the practical level the same oppositions that have hopelessly tangled ethical philosophy. Psychologists have tended to assume a moral homogeneity; if in actuality the moral injunctions of Western society are splintered and contradictory, we need to become sensitive to this in our empirical investigation. We can hardly expect moral development to be continuous and sequential if the practices that ground it are fragmented and contradictory.

Consider, for example, the debates over abortion. Although adherents to the pro-choice and pro-life positions are satisfied that they have made the correct moral judgment, there seems to be no basis for a reasoned debate between the two positions. Each side makes assumptions the other does not share, and conversation degenerates rapidly into name-calling and mudslinging. We all have witnessed the paradoxical outcome: Proponents of a moral position that advocates universal rights to life throw firebombs at the offices of those who disagree. The failure of rational persuasion leaves violence the only apparent option. A study of dialogues between these positions would be valuable, and would advance both theory and practice.

MacIntyre (1988) suggests that the Enlightenment's liberal individualism, intended to supplant tradition, has ironically become a tradition itself, a tradition of interminable debates over principles of rationality. Our lives have become split into compartmentalized spheres, each with its own kinds of goods and its own kind of evaluation (see Berger, Berger, & Kellner, 1973). We are expected to be mobile selves, able to slip quickly from one sphere to the next—from private to public life, from being a consumer of goods to producing them—all the while keeping our attitudes compartmentalized. These attitudes have been reduced to the status of subjective opinion, matters of personal preference about which we may be polled and interviewed, but which we are not expected to be able to defend rationally, simply because no one can say what a reasoned justification of preferences might be.

It is difficult not to agree with MacIntyre's (1988) claim that emotivism has become characteristic of our society. The night before the presidential election in 1988, the "MacNeil–Lehrer News Hour" interviewed people around the country, asking them whether they preferred Bush or Dukakis and how each man appealed to them. Political issues were scarcely mentioned; the interviewer took for granted that the only basis for choice between the candidates was personal preference. Voting has become the mere summing of preferences of individuals around the country; substantive debate among candidates has been reduced to strategies such as "soundbites" selected to have the greatest impact on public opinion. In televised commentary following the debates between the two presidential candidates, the men were evaluated almost entirely in terms of style and image, with no attention paid to the quality of argument about issues confronting the country. We were told, approvingly, that Bush used the word "values" six times in his opening remarks, but that he did not appear as relaxed as in his address to the Republican convention. We seek, presumably, a candidate whose demeanor and vocabulary, whose rhetoric, can beguile us, rather than one whose policies convince us. As citizens, we are expected to choose between rival political ideologies on grounds that seem aesthetic rather than rational. Politicians appeal not to our capacity for reason, but to our presumed tendency to maximize our pleasures through the pursuit of immediate gratifications. As MacIntyre (1988) said:

> The defense of rival moral and political standpoints is interpreted within the liberal order as the expression of preferences by those individuals who engage in such defenses . . . . The culture of individualism transforms expressions of opinion into what its political and moral theory had already said they were. (p. 343)

Research employing an interpretive approach to these and other phenomena of modern political practices would be of interest to a psychology of morality.

Heidegger has also considered modern society distorted in its practices. His analysis has centered on what he called the "truth of Being." This is "the way a historical people settles into an understanding of the world, of the gods, and of themselves." It is "the constellation of arts, science, and political arrangements within which they live out their lives" (Caputo, 1987, p. 236), and "the historical mode of Being-in-the-world to which each of us is assigned by the movement of Being itself, and the demands which each historical existence puts upon us" (p. 246). This level is more fundamental than that of ethical analysis; it is the level that moral philosophy presupposes and rests upon. Our current way of living is dominated by the persistent, acquisitive effort to manipulate and control. We have come to think nothing of, as Francis Bacon put it, torturing mother earth, twisting the lion's tail. Human existence provides the raw material for bioengineering, social control, and behavioral manipulation. In Heidegger's (1962) terms, we have by and large fallen into an inauthentic mode of being, where we view ourselves in terms more applicable to the objects with which we deal (computers are central today). The view that we are ourselves objects with fixed "natural" properties is one manifestation of this.

Ethical relativism, the yuppie pursuit of personal gain, and interminable emotivist moral debates, however, are not inevitable consequences of the failure to locate an objective ethical foundation. They seem inescapable only to those who still unwittingly share the assumptions that launched the Enlightenment projects. Once we escape the supposition that justification of an ethical position must take the form of an objective foundation, then other possibilities are revealed. Reconsidering the perspective from which we understand morality and the terms in which we conceive it exposes a way of moving beyond objectivism and relativism (Bernstein, 1983). Reason, viewed in Enlightenment terms, has not provided the ethical and scientific justification that was desired, but it does not follow—counter Nietzsche and Feyerabend—that these two areas are irrational, that anything goes. It makes better sense to conclude that our modern interpretation of reason, shaped over the past 300 years, is faulty. In the same way, morality has not dissolved because the Enlightenment effort to identify objective ethical principles has failed; it remains possible that moral prescriptions can have quite a different kind of justification. We can appeal to the rationality that every tradition contains within itself. With this in view, we can fruitfully study the circumstances in which people resist relativism, and those in which they fall prey to it.

My point in this section is that, at the level of practices, morality in our culture is currently problematic. The lack of consensus over fundamental issues of individual rights and political obligation (to name but two areas of frequent debate) is understandable in light of the history of efforts at moral justification, but it is disturbing nonetheless. Because psychologists have viewed the development of morality as a logical rather than a social phenomenon, they have constructed an idealized progression through universal stages. It is time to examine the moral development of children in diverse settings, with different moral practices. We should expect to find that as morality develops, it is often confused and contradictory, and that our culture presents young adults with unique moral conflicts and problems, which they may or may not resolve. One would expect this to be particularly the case for groups, such as women and minorities, faced with particularly conflicting practices and roles. An interpretive psychology can usefully seek to determine the loci of these problems, and the ways in which people interact when moral incommensurability strikes and reasoned argument proves impossible. To what extent and in what kinds of setting do people recognize this incommensurability, and how do they respond?

Moral Reasoning

I suggested earlier that moral reasoning is not a matter of applying moral principles, analogous to the way we usually think of solving math or logical problems, but that it involves deliberation about concrete moral issues. If moral reasoning is not algorithmic, calculative cognition, then the way in which we study it needs to be altered. But first, how did this interpretation come to be taken seriously? How did such a limited and distorted interpretation of the character of human reasoning arise?

The Enlightenment suffered from a characteristic malaise: the tendency to give priority to a detached, contemplative examination of phenomena (the "present-at-hand" mode of engagement) and to diminish the importance of involved, concerned engagement in practical activities (the "ready-to-hand" mode). (See Dreyfus, 1991, and Packer, 1985, for discussion of models of engagement.) Those involved in the Enlightenment understood themselves to be liberating the individual from the power of external, often corrupt authority, through an appreciation of man's intrinsic essential nature and an appeal to the uniquely human capacity for reason. But reason was viewed as something crucially different from Aristotle's logos. By the time of the project's collapse in the early decades of this century, reason had become narrowly construed as logical thinking, and was contrasted with blind emotion, subjective preference, and personal opinion. In other words, any form of reasoning that was not logical had to be faulty and subjective. Heidegger argued that the view that calculative reason is the essence of human being is a profound misinterpretation. Furthermore, this "thinking" by individual selves was a *construction* of the Enlightenment, not a preexisting natural process or law, which had finally been liberated:

> The shattering of the sole dominance of the church in legislating knowledge and action is understood as a liberation of man to himself. But what man is as himself, wherein his being a self should consist is determined only in his liberation and by the definitely oriented history of this liberation. Human "thinking," which here means the forming powers of man, becomes the fundamental law of things themselves. (Heidegger, 1985, p. 31)

Changes in the way reason was viewed were parallel in the scientific and moral projects. The new science seemed to involve an attitude of value neutrality that was best achieved through withdrawal from everyday concerns. Scientific observation appeared to involve only recording material objects' real properties. Everyday perception became interpreted the same way, as passive gaping, as a mechanical impinging of sensory input whereby the "primary qualities" of bodies (position, form) caused "ideas" in the mind. Scientific reasoning was interpreted as logical deduction from axiomatic principles. A mathematical criterion was applied to thinking: an ultimate and absolutely certain foundation must be found, in the form of knowledge that would be unquestionable. From this foundation, valid reasoning could proceed through either inductive logic (comparing and contrasting simple, irreducible ideas, for Locke) or deductive logic (as in Descartes's efforts to identify an indubitable starting place from which to reconstruct all valid knowledge). Soon everyday judgment was also considered this way. Thinking had become dominant over being: "this thinking understands itself as the court of judgment over Being" (Heidegger, 1985, p. 32).

The elevation of calculative, deductive reasoning to the central component of inquiry in both science and philosophy accompanied the denial, already described, of any essential human telos. A telos expresses a shared sense of the proper ends of human action, one that stems from the communal practices and consensual values that make up a tradition. Once tradition became suspect, knowledge claims apparently independent of any tradition seemed the superior ones. And in the social and historical circumstances when tradition became questioned, there was an absence of consensus about the proper ends to human action. Rational justification of moral choices without reference to apparently contingent social and cultural particularities was considered a desirable alternative to the appeal to a tradition that was one among many, and that seemed repressive and sterile.

Cares and concerns were understood not as teloi intrinsic to human action, but as subjective, personal matters that could not ground an ethical philosophy, and that should be avoided in any scientific and philosophical investigation. Concerned practical engagement was judged secondary and inferior, and the teloi of practical projects were shrugged off in the search for genuine objective knowledge. The goals of practice were seen as subjective individual preferences, tied only to the desire for pleasure. Action was considered a realm where the passions are at play, where we are at their whim. Human growth—moral development—would come only insofar as we were able to cultivate detached reason, and this is best accomplished if we rid ourselves of passions, concerns, and involvements.

The priority of detached reason over concerned engagement can be seen clearly in Hume's ethics, even in the way Hume placed emphasis on the way that reason is subordinate to the passions. Hume's ethics, like his epistemology, was a product of the present-at-hand orientation. A dualist opposition of reason and emotion, and of mind and world, was taken for granted. Action was considered essentially mechanical, not intentional, and the passions mental states linked mechanically to action. With this picture, Hume was confident he could apply Newtonian forms of explanation to psychological phenomena. At root, human life was simply the search for pleasure and avoidance of pain; there was no goal to life beyond the pleasant accumulation of wealth. When individual human judgment was not the result of calculative reasoning, it was simply a matter of taste and opinion.

The same considerations led twentieth-century thinkers, including Kohlberg, to focus their analysis on the *form* of moral judgments, not their *content*. This decision reflected the way that reason had been by design reduced, especially by Whitehead and Russell (1910), to an analytic, content-free logic. We have come to take for granted their notion that logical rules are tautologies, that they provide a way of restating and combining propositions (or imperatives) without changing their truth values. Yet with this final move, reason was reduced to empty symbol shuffling. At the same time, empirical statements were considered objective reports of observed states of affairs, and human perception had become passive gaping.

If both reason and perception were interpretation free, they must be free of any evaluative component. It was against the background of an assumed sharp distinction between fact and value that Hare (1952/1964), for instance, could argue that a moral judgment can be divided into a portion that makes a statement about facts (the "phrastic" component, pointing something out) and a portion that expresses an imperative (the "neustic" component, recording assent or dissent). Hare rewrote the nonmoral imperative "Shut the door!" as "Your shutting the door in the immediate future, please." The moral judgment "You should not kill" would be similarly rewritten as "Your not taking another's life, please." Once the fact–value distinction had been accepted, the analytic philosopher could happily examine the logical properties of each domain separately.

It might be objected that unless reason is a matter of deduction and calculation, it is nothing but caprice. How can ethical analysis be conducted without universal moral principles? How can a person reason about a moral dilemma without invoking logical analysis? In actuality, an approach to the study and judgment of ethical issues that makes no use of general principles had been at work for centuries before the Enlightenment changed the rules of the game. Casuistry is an approach to moral decision making that makes the case, a particular moral dilemma described concretely, the basis for an ethical analysis, rather than a moral theory of general moral principles.

Jonsen and Toulmin (1988) examined the history of casuistry and considered its contemporary relevance. They proposed that casuistry has much in its favor as an approach to ethical judgment. Moral reasoning, they proposed, involves:

> accumulating many, parallel, complementary considerations, which have to do with the current circumstances of the human individuals and communities involved and lend strength to our conclusions, not like links in a chain but like strands to a rope or roots to a tree. Meanwhile on a more general level, a "cumulative" view of practical moral reasoning goes naturally with the rejection of "axiomatic" theories of moral philosophy in favor of a more complex and pragmatic view of ethical theory. (pp. 293–294)

This is an account in which the individual makes a moral judgment not by appeal to ethical principles, but by considering the particular character of the circumstances, and attending to what has been done in situations that appear similar:

> The agent faced with the decision must make a specific choice about a particular action. The detailed circumstances of the action may be unique and unrepeatable; in considering its morality the decider will look for opinions about other actions in situations as similar as possible to his own. These opinions may carry a certain "probability," based on the reputation of their

author and the intrinsic argument, but the final decision how to act must rest not on a probability but on the moral certitude of the informed conscience. (p. 334)

Jonsen and Toulmin resemble other postmodernists in seeing moral injunctions embedded in a tradition and forms of social life that express and embody forms of human care, concern, and interrelationship:

All reflective moral traditions keep it in mind that the kernel of moral wisdom consists, not in a hard-line commitment to principles which we accept without qualification, but in understanding the human needs and relations that are nurtured by a life of reflexive moral action. (pp. 342–343)

How might our research benefit from these insights? Carol Gilligan and her colleagues have been conducting work that is cognizant of these complexities. They have developed a way of reading an interview about a real-life moral conflict in such a way as to identify "voice-relevant" aspects of a person's narrative. The case account given provides the material for study of moral reasoning. Their open-ended clinical interviews yield complex narratives that "reflect situational, personal, and cultural factors, including issues of language, perspective, and the relationship between the reader's and the narrator's language and perspective" (Brown, Tappan, Gilligan, Miller, & Argyris, 1989). They approach an interviewee's description of a moral conflict as a text to be read, not coded, as a text in which different voices can be discerned, reflecting alternative moral orientations. Orientations of care and justice arise from and call attention to the fact that human relationships, both public and private, involve issues of both equality and attachment.

The narrative character of moral conflicts does not appear only when a "story" is told to the researcher; the initial comprehension of the acts involved in a moral conflict has a narrative organization (MacIntyre, 1984; Mishler, 1986; Sarbin, 1986). When people reflect upon and describe a conflict, they employ narrative strategies that convey the choice of moral orientation and the orchestration of moral voices. Narrative organization plays an intrinsic part in determining what count as the facts of the case and the kinds of concern and obligation that are pertinent.

In research such as this, an actual occasion of conflict becomes the topic of inquiry. It is not assumed that the facts of the case are self-evident, and that the researcher's task is to trace the application of moral principles to these facts. Rather, the perspective from which the person understands, interprets, and describes the conflict is the first order of business. The way the moral problem is constructed, the terms in which it is presented, and the moral concerns that are voiced or silenced all are taken to be manifestations of reasoning, and worthy of detailed study.

Research along these lines could move in a number of directions. Moral reasoning, understood this way, could be investigated with conflicts of differing kinds, in a range of social and cultural settings, with people of different ages and varying social backgrounds. The voices of care and justice could be further articulated, and other voices could be sought, for instance, the voice of openness or acceptance that is suggested by de Rivera's (1977) work. Such work will find guidance in recent interpretive reconceptualizations of the conduct and analysis of interviews (e.g., Honey, 1987; Kvale, 1983,1986; Mishler, 1986).

The Relationship Between Researcher and Research Participants

The third area where the hermeneutic perspective calls for changes in our research into morality is that of the character of the relationship a researcher forges with the people whose moral action and reasoning are studied. We can longer take it for granted that science deals with facts, and ethics with values, and that the two inhabit distinct realms. When the Enlightenment began, morality and science were viewed as linked; systematic reasoning was to provide a foundational grounding for each of them, and each had a claim to rationality. The rational basis of science was to give it greater legitimacy than the ideological claims of theology. Scientific reasoning was to replace theological accounts of the universe with rationally grounded observation and experimentation, just as it was to replace theological doctrines of sin and redemption with rational ethics. Scientific inquiry was seen to have intrinsic worth; the progress that science would bring was considered almost inevitable. However, as the Enlightenment projects played themselves out, it came to seem that a rational grounding was possible only if science was value neutral, that is, if it dealt only with statements of fact and withdrew from matters of value. Ethics (and philosophy in general) became a distinct discipline; scientific inquiry, if it was to avoid the naturalistic fallacy, had to be unbiased and impartial.

Such an interpretation of science ignores and suppresses the concerned engagement that provides the background against which entities show up. If we can no longer ignore the part played by perspective and involvement, particularly in the human sciences, and if the optimistic coupling of science and "progress" no longer seems appropriate, what more accurate perception might we adopt? The two suggestions I pursue here are that we, as psychologists, should first adopt an involved, participatory kind of relationship with the people we study, and second, engage in bringing about appropriate change in those people's activities. Only some degree of participation in the practices of those studied can provide the background understanding needed to ensure that the researcher's interpretations are not arbitrary. Furthermore, interpretation is motivated by breakdown in practice (Packer,

1985), and the evaluation of an interpretive account is best considered in terms of its power to resolve such a breakdown (Packer & Addison, 1989). In everyday life, interpretation attempts to bring about changes in practice; interpretation in psychological research can fruitfully have the same aim. In such a picture, interpretive inquiry is at its best when it becomes participatory or emancipatory research (see Farrell, Peguero, Lindsey, & White, 1989; Hall, 1979, 1981; Lather, 1986). This will involve taking a stand on matters of value.

One example must suffice. Selman, Schultz, Caplan, and Schantz (1989) combined the roles of researcher and involved participant in their study of the relations of two adolescent boys in "pair therapy." Their goal was to examine the therapeutic impact of pair therapy by delineating aspects of the ongoing social interactions among the three participants—therapist and children—thereby illuminating the developments in construction of a relationship between the two children. Selman et al. broadened their analytic focus beyond the interactions between the boys so as to acknowledge and include the therapist's crucial role. The research provided guidance to the therapist (certainly for future work, and probably during his work with the two boys studied) by explicating therapeutic practice, and it provided a language for communicating this practice to others. Therapeutic expertise ensured that the research was grounded in a practical understanding of the boys' problems and of their progress during their time together.

CONCLUSION

The central question addressed in this chapter has been, What kind of inquiry is the psychological study of morality? Enlightenment philosophers such as Hume and Locke considered themselves scientists of the mind, applying Newton's methods, even his laws (e.g., association of ideas paralleling the attraction of bodies), to mental phenomena and to human experience. This psychology began with the assumption that there is an objective human nature and set out to plumb it. At the same time, psychology was conceived as playing a part in the project of ethical justification and political theorizing. Man's nature implied the recognition of certain natural political rights. And the natural character of reason and perception were appealed to as defining the epistemological character of the scientific method.

In the centuries since then, science and ethics gradually parted, and the justificatory projects foundered. Brute facts about human nature and self-evident principles of logic have proved unable to bear the epistemological weight placed upon them. In the absence of the foundations that nature and logic were to provide, what role does a postmodern psychology play? It can no longer claim to proceed by the detached, objective description of natural phenomena; we have lost our innocence. In this chapter, I have suggested that moral prescriptions are the products of forms of social life, which require study in their own right; that research into people's concrete, practical ways of dealing with particular moral cases should take priority over research on formal ratiocination; and that the researcher needs to adopt an involved stance, one that is directed toward answering the concerns that stem from participation in practical activities.

NOTES

1. This is MacIntyre's (1966, p. 57) translation of the passage, which reads more clearly than D. Ross's classic translation: "Every art and every inquiry, and similarly every action and pursuit, is thought to aim at some good; and for this reason the good has rightly been declared to be that at which all things aim" (Aristotle, 1980, p. 1).

REFERENCES

Aristotle. (1980). *The Nicomachean ethics* (D. Ross, Trans.). Oxford: Oxford University Press.

Berger, P. L., Berger, R., & Kellner, H. (1973). *The homeless mind: Modernization and consciousness.* New York: Random House.

Bernstein, R. (1983). *Beyond objectivism and relativism: Science, hermeneutics, and praxis.* Philadelphia: University of Pennsylvania Press.

Brown, L. M., Tappan, M. B., Gilligan, C., Miller, B. A., & Argyris, D. E. (1989). Interpreting narratives of real-life moral conflict and choice. In M. J. Packer & R. B. Addison (Eds.), *Entering the circle: Hermeneutic investigation in psychology.* (pp. 141–164) Albany: State University of New York Press.

Caputo, J. D. (1987). *Radical hermeneutics: Repetition, deconstruction, and the hermeneutic project.* Bloomington: Indiana University Press.

Cohen, I. B. (1985). *The birth of a new physics.* (rev. ed.). New York: Norton.

de Rivera, J. (1977). A structural theory of the emotions. *Psychological Issues, 10* (Whole No. 40).

Dreyfus, H. L. (1991). *Being-in-the-world: A commentary on Division 1 of being and time.* Cambridge, MA: MIT Press.

Evans, M. G. (1964). *The physical philosophy of Aristotle.* Albuquerque: University of New Mexico Press.

Farrell, E., Peguero, G., Lindsey, R., & White, R. (1989). Giving voice to high school students: Pressure and boredom, ya know what I'm saying? *American Educational Research Journal, 25,* 489–502.

Fiske, D. W., & Shweder, R. A. (1986). *Metatheory in social science: Pluralisms and subjectivities.* Chicago: University of Chicago Press.

Gay, P. (1977). *The Enlightenment: An interpretation. Vol. 2. The science of freedom.* New York: Norton.

Hall, B. L. (1979). Knowledge as a commodity and participatory research. *Prospects, 9,* 393–408.

Hall, B. L. (1981). Participatory research, popular knowledge and power: A personal reflection. *Convergence, 14,* 6–17.

Hare, R. M. (1964). *The language of morals. New York: Oxford University Press. (Original work published 1952)*

Harré, R. (1984). *Personal being: A theory for individual psychology.* Cambridge, MA: Harvard University Press.

Heidegger, M. (1962). *Being and time.* (J. Macquirrie & E. Robinson, Trans.). New York: Harper & Row. (Original work published 1927)

Heidegger, M. (1985). *Schelling's treatise on the essence of human freedom* (J. Staumbaugh, Trans.). Athens: Ohio University Press.

Honey, M. A. (1987). The interview as text: Hermeneutics considered as a model for analyzing the clinically informed research interview. *Human Development, 30,* 69–82.

Jonsen, A. R., & Toulmin, S. (1988). *The abuse of casuistry: A history of moral reasoning.* Berkeley: University of California Press.

Kohlberg, L. (1981). From is to ought: How to commit the naturalistic fallacy and get away with it in the study of moral development. In L. Kohlberg (Ed.), *Essays on moral development. Vol. 1. The philosophy of moral development: Moral stages and the idea of justice* (pp. 101–189). New York: Harper & Row. (Original work published 1971)

Kuhn, T. S. (1957). *The Copernican revolution.* New York: Harvard University Press.

Kuhn, T. S. (1970). *The structure of scientific revolutions* (2nd ed.). Chicago: University of Chicago Press.

Kuhn, T. S. (1977). *The essential tension.* Chicago: University of Chicago Press.

Kvale, S. (1983). The qualitative research interview: A phenomenological and a hermeneutic mode of understanding. *Journal of Phenomenological Psychology, 37,* 171–196.

Kvale, S. (1986, May). *The question of the validity of the qualitative research interview.* Paper presented at the 5th International Human Science Conference, San Francisco.

Lather, P. (1986). Research as praxis. *Harvard Educational Review, 56,* 257–277.

Liebert, R. (1984). What develops in moral development? In W. Kurtines & J. L. Gewirtz (Eds.), *Morality, moral behavior, and moral development* (pp. 177–192). New York: Wiley.

MacIntyre, A. (1966). *A short history of moral philosophy: A history of moral philosophy from the Homeric age to the twentieth century.* New York: Macmillan.

MacIntyre, A. (1984). *After virtue: A study in moral theory* (2nd ed.). South Bend, IN: University of Notre Dame Press.

MacIntyre, A. (1988). *Whose justice? Which rationality?* South Bend, IN: University of Notre Dame Press.

Mishler, E. G. (1986). *Research interviewing: Context and narrative.* Cambridge, MA: Harvard University Press.

Nagel, E., & Newman, J. R. (1958). *Godel's proof.* New York: New York University Press.

Packer, M. J. (1985). Hermeneutic inquiry in the study of human conduct. *American Psychologist, 40,* 1081–1093.

Packer, M. J., & Addison, R. B. (Eds.). (1989). *Entering the circle: Hermeneutic investigation in psychology.* Albany: State University of New York Press.

Packer, M. J., & Mergendoller, J. R. (1989). The development of practical social understanding in elementary school–age children. In T. Winegar (Ed.), *Social interaction and the development of children's understanding.* (pp. 67–93). New Jersey: Ablex.

Sarbin, T. R. (1986). *Narrative psychology: The storied nature of human conduct.* New York: Praeger.

Selman, R. L., Schultz, L. H., Caplan, B., & Schantz, K. (1989). The development of close relationships: Implications from therapy with two early adolescents. In M. J. Packer & R. B. Addison (Eds.), *Entering the circle: Hermeneutic investigation in psychology.* (pp. 59–74) Albany: State University of New York Press.

Stam, H. J., Rogers, T. B., & Gergen, K. J. (1987). *The analysis of psychological theory: Metapsychological perspectives.* Washington, DC: Hemisphere.

Whitehead, A. N., & Russell, B. (1910). *Principia Mathematica.* Cambridge, England: Cambridge University Press.

Williams, B. (1985). *Ethics and the limits of philosophy.* Cambridge, MA: Harvard University Press.

Part II

Implications for Theory and Research

Chapter 3 ■

Values in Postpositivist Developmental Research: Communication among Researchers, Participants, and Consumers ■

JOHN A. MEACHAM
State University of New York at Buffalo

Roughly a third of a century has passed since the first serious concerns were raised regarding the logical positivist philosophy of science that was dominant in the period 1930 to 1960 (Barnes, 1985; Habermas, 1971; Kuhn, 1962; Kurtines, Alvarez, & Azmitia, 1990). In many of the natural and social science disciplines, new understandings of what constitutes a vital research program, what it means to have an explanation, and how values should play a role in scientific practice have marked the transition from positivist to postpositivist conceptions of science. Yet other disciplines, including large portions of psychology, have been reluctant to question those positivist prescriptions for research methods from which it appears that so much has been gained, and only in the past few years has the shift from positivist toward postpositivist philosophy of science begun (Bickhard, Cooper, & Mace, 1985; Fiske & Shweder, 1986; Habermas, 1984; Kitchener, 1983). Certainly, much debate will continue over what forms the new philosophy of science will take, over whether positivism is to be abandoned entirely or whether some accommodation can be constructed that takes into account the challenges of postpositivist philosophy of science (Gholson & Barker, 1985; Manicas & Secord, 1983; Outhwaite, 1987).

This chapter explicitly sets forth some implications of postpositivist philosophy of science for how investigations might be conducted with children, adolescents, and older adults and for how a valid understanding might be achieved in an area quite central to the social sciences, namely, the domain of moral phenomena (Meacham, 1975). The major issue in this chapter is self-deception: How might researchers better understand the diverse influences upon their studies of the social, cultural, and value frameworks in which they as researchers are immersed? How might researchers increase their confidence that they are not deceiving themselves by underestimating the impact of sociocultural contexts and personal values upon their research conclusions? This chapter's main thrust is that, from the standpoint of postpositivism, researchers into moral phenomena must be concerned not merely with the moral behavior and judgments of those persons who are the objects of study; they must be concerned to the same, or perhaps greater, extent with their own moral values and the values of their scientific discipline.

THE VALUE CHALLENGES OF POSTPOSITIVISM

"Logical positivism is history and the model of scientific method that we typically teach our students is inappropriate for the study of social behavior" (Hogan, 1988, p. 9). This was one point of agreement that emerged from a conference held at the University of Chicago on metatheory in social science (Fiske & Shweder, 1986). The conference participants were concerned with the apparent crisis of contemporary social sciences, reflecting that generalizations from our research are quite limited, empirical findings do not converge, policy questions do not get answered, and so forth. Hogan (1988), in reviewing the proceedings of this conference for *Contemporary Psychology*, recommended that everyone, including empirically minded psychologists, read Fiske and Shweder's book because "it contains some real surprises" (p. 9); because "this is one of the most interesting books that I have read in a long while, the topic is crucial"; and because "the essays raise fundamental issues and sooner or later every responsible researcher will have to deal with them" (p. 10).

Nevertheless, in addressing the question of whether this book will make any difference, Hogan (1988) replied, "Probably not," arguing that researchers, especially young researchers in the social sciences, have no choice but "to work on problems that can be studied the right way in a laboratory" (p. 10), that is, to conduct their research according to the prescription for research methods of logical positivism. This might be good advice to young researchers intent only on their careers. Indeed, it has been said that the only original and significant contribution of the discipline of psychology has been its research methods developed over the past century. Yet to have a good understanding of research methods is no less important from a postpositivist perspective, and perhaps even more important, for our methods stand between ourselves and that which we wish to know (Meacham, 1980, p. 245). Thus, what is needed, at least for the foreseeable future, is a framework within which one retains the strengths that positivist research methods have provided for the social sciences (see, e.g., Chapter 11 by Forsyth, and Chapter 6 by Kendler in this volume), while recognizing and attempting to respond to the challenges of postpositivist philosophy of science.

Metatheory is concerned with the conditions that make it possible for us to understand our theories and research methods and, indeed, to do social science. Among these conditions are our preconceptions and prejudices as researchers, our stance on various philosophical and epistemological issues, our personal motivations and political commitments, our vantage point within the course of life, our embeddedness within a particular social or class structure, our living within a particular segment of the stream of history, and our cultural traditions (Meacham, 1981, 1984).

From the standpoint of postpositivist philosophy of science, issues of metatheory are inseparable from how one goes about doing science. Among the many distinctions between positivist and postpositivist philosophy of science are these (Bickhard et al., 1985; Kitchener, 1983; Outhwaite, 1987):

1. Positivism is an attempt to prescribe a formal ideal of what one ought to do to have good science; postpositivism is an effort to describe what researchers actually do in their investigations.

2. Positivism holds that facts can be known from a theory-free or value-free standpoint; however, postpositivism holds that all knowing is motivated and value laden.

3. Positivism views the process of science as logical and rational; postpositivism strives to understand science as a historical and cultural product.

These tenets of postpositivist philosophy of science pose crucial challenges for traditional social science research methods, particularly when the phenomena under investigation are moral phenomena. In what sense can we achieve a valid understanding of moral phenomena if our standpoint for understanding is itself value laden? In particular, how can we achieve this understanding if we are engaged in self-deception with regard to the moral nature of our own standpoint? In what sense can moral phenomena be studied scientifically?

Distinctions such as those made in the preceding paragraph appear at first to make a rapprochement between positivist and postpositivist research methods impossible to achieve. Such a rapprochement might be possible, however, if we consider the relationship between positivism and postpositivism in developmental terms. One might do so for historical reasons alone (although other reasons also might be adduced; see, e.g., Chandler, 1987). Postpositivism might become acceptable for psychology and the social sciences if its implications can be grafted onto the stock of positivist research methods. Such a grafting, if successful, might provide some comfort for Hogan's (1988) young researchers, who have no choice but to cleave to positivism, while providing some new opportunities in our investigations of moral phenomena.

I have taken as a representation of positivist research methods the *Publication Manual of the American Psychological Association* (APA, 1983), for this manual sets forth in detail many of the criteria against which research manuscripts and grant proposals are currently evaluated. I attempt to respond as concretely as possible—in the form of three modest proposals for additions to the *Publication Manual*—to the challenges posed by postpositivist philosophy of science for our traditional research methods. In part because of the specific concern with the developmental investigation of moral phenomena, I have focused upon two major statements of ethical principles in research, the "Ethical Principles of Psychologists" (APA, 1985) and the "Ethical Standards for Research with Children" (Society for Research in Child Development, 1987). Whether a grafting of postpositivist implications upon the root of positivism might be successful is, of course, debatable and, indeed, doubtful. Nevertheless, I hope that the present chapter might serve to stimulate such a debate: Can the following proposals be found acceptable by positivist researchers? If not, why not? Do the proposals respond adequately to the challenges of postpositivism? If not, why not? The answers to these questions should sharpen the debate between researchers who are adopting either a positivist or a postpositivist perspective on research into moral phenomena.

FIRST PROPOSAL: TREAT THE RESEARCHER AS PERSON, NOT AS OBJECT

Positivist philosophy of science is suspicious of the preconceptions and prejudices of the researcher, and prescribes that these should be contained and set aside so as to have the researcher be, to the fullest extent possible, a *tabula rasa* while conducting the research. Postpositivist philosophy of science, on the other hand, accepts that issues of value cannot be contained and deems that their existence is fundamental to doing research. Without a prior framework for interpretation and understanding, researchers would find it impossible to do research at all. The research methods prescribed by the *Publication Manual* have been said to devalue or dehumanize the research participant, treating the participant not as a person but merely as an object to be manipulated. These research methods provide even less acknowledgment that the researcher is a person with a history, motivations, and values. Yet the researcher is human, after all, and cannot conduct research in an objective and value-free way, as a *tabula rasa* (Outhwaite, 1985, p. 29). The *Publication Manual* prescribes that the method section of research reports be divided into subsections describing the research participants or "subjects," the apparatus or materials, and the procedures. The subsection on participants is intended to describe who the participants were and how they were selected for the study. The manual instructs researchers to provide "major demographic characteristics such as general geographic location, type of institutional affiliation, sex, and age" (p. 26) of the participants.

My first proposal is that the *Publication Manual* be revised to prescribe that the method section of research reports also include a subsection describing the researcher:

> Give major demographic characteristics of the researcher such as race or ethnicity, religion, class, age, and sex. Specify all essential details of life history and values orientation that might bear on interpretation of the purposes and conclusions of the study.

Within this portion of the method section, the researcher could shed light on such questions as: What influenced the researcher to invest time and energy in exploring a particular hypothesis? What assumptions or simplifications have been made (e.g., about the nature of society or human nature) to make the topic amenable to research? What was the social and historical context within which the data were gathered, interpreted, and prepared for communication to the research consumers? What might be some limitations on generalizability of the interpretations and conclusions, given the researcher's embeddedness within a particular social, cultural, or class context?*

Having such information as an integral part of the research report would facilitate the interpretation of the research by the research consumers— other researchers and practitioners—who appropriately desire to know

---

* To wit: My family background is English, Protestant, and middle class. My understanding of positivist research methods derives from my training at Stanford University and the University of Michigan in the 1960s. I left graduate school for 2 years to serve in the Peace Corps. My first acquaintance with postpositivism occurred at the five dialectical psychology conferences organized by Riegel beginning in 1974 (see Meacham, 1977; Riegel, 1979), although Baumrind's (1971) article earlier had raised some doubts about research methods in psychology. My thoughts on philosophy of history and science were sharpened at Catholic University of America from 1980 to 1982. During this period, I was introduced to the work of Habermas (especially through McCarthy, 1978), which has since guided much of my thinking and writing. I am increasingly interested in issues involving civil rights and the environment.

about the context within which the research was carried out, including the values held by the researcher at that time. The methods of positivist research attempt to deny or mask the researcher's values. Historians of science then attempt, through painstaking effort, to reconstruct the values and motivations of researchers whose contributions have had an impact upon the development of knowledge in the social sciences. Not only is there scant evidence for such reconstructions, but when reconstructions are done post hoc—often after the researchers' deaths—researchers cannot assert their own values and motivations in opposition to the historians' attributions. We cannot know, for example, how G. Stanley Hall might have responded to our contemporary concerns that the work of this forefather of American psychology was racist in its substance (Muschinske, 1977), how the early intelligence testers might have responded to similar charges regarding both the substance of their work and their motivations (Gould, 1981; Samelson, 1978), and so forth.

Postpositivism acknowledges that values are inherent in the research process. Understanding a research report's significance requires knowing about the researcher's values and motivations. Gergen (1973), for example, argued not only that our theories of social psychology, which certainly address moral phenomena, are merely reflections of contemporary social conditions, but also that psychologists' values influence their methods of observation and their terms of description. Psychologists use theories and descriptive terms that tend to portray psychologists and those research participants who are of similar socioeconomic background, religion, sex, and values in a highly positive light (e.g., they refer to "high self-esteem" rather than "egotism," and "cognitive differentiation" rather than "hairsplitting"). Participants with backgrounds different from those of psychologists are portrayed in a negative light ("rigidity" rather than "stability," "social conformity" rather than "prosolidarity behavior").

According to Wertsch and Youniss (1987), early developmental psychologists in the United States were motivated in large part by an unquestioned belief that immigrant children should acquire the particular ideology and patterns of behavior of the researchers: Catholic immigrant children were to be remade into Protestant Americans. Youniss (Chapter 8, this volume; see also Youniss, 1989) has argued that North American developmental psychologists have continued to fail to understand Piaget's particularist position on moral development because this view is not consistent with the universalist conception that stems from these psychologists' social and political backgrounds. It would be enormously helpful to have these early social and developmental psychologists' own presentations of their social and value backgrounds in relation to those of their research participants. To prevent this lack in the future, our normative research methods, as prescribed by the APA's *Publication Manual*, should be revised to make explicit the obligation of researchers to set forth their positions on those issues of value that touch on the subject matter of their investigations.

What objections might be raised against this first proposal, to treat the researcher as a person, not as an object? A researcher might not be honest in describing him- or herself in the method section. If the researcher cannot be trusted to describe to the best of his or her ability the relevant personal characteristics and values, then many other questions must be raised, such as whether the procedures were carried out as described, whether the statistical analyses are correct, and so forth. Indeed, if the researcher cannot be trusted to be honest, then the credibility of the research report as a whole is seriously challenged. A related objection is that the researcher may not be able to accurately perceive his or her own values and motivations; this objection is addressed below by the third proposal. A further objection to this first proposal is that it is not yet clear what and how much information regarding the researcher's background and values should be provided. The nature and extent of this information should depend on the particular issues raised in a given research study: In some studies, very little information needs to be provided; in other studies—for example, a study of moral understanding in a population of a different ethnic background or social class from that of the researcher—a much fuller account of the researcher's own background should be provided. Certainly, expectations and procedures for implementing this first proposal could be developed and revised over time, as have other portions of the *Publication Manual*.

SECOND PROPOSAL: DO GOOD
FOR THE RESEARCH PARTICIPANTS

Generalizable, Ecologically Sound Research

One feature of the current crisis in social sciences, according to Hogan (1988, p. 9), is that the results of our research have little generalizability. A number of approaches might be pursued to determine whether research findings are generalizable to or ecologically valid in everyday contexts outside the laboratory. As Scheidt (1981) pointed out, researchers typically have approached this issue from a measurement perspective, choosing measures that appear to possess ecological face validity in the real world, and then comparing findings using these measures with findings previously obtained in the laboratory. Scheidt observed that this measurement approach to ecological validity is not a certain one, and concluded by accusing many researchers of opting for "quick, convenient 'real world' representations of tasks, stimuli, situations, and rules," and thus producing merely "ecologically cosmetic" studies.

An implication of postpositivist perspectives on research methods is that we must consider further what is meant by "generalizability." This term should bring to mind not merely the universality or external validity of one's research findings, but also the interdependence of people and institutions in the human environment. This principle of interdependence—the ecological cycle—means that any intervention by researchers has the potential to be both polluting to and enriching of the human environment. Such pollution should be guarded against, and indeed our statements of ethical principles in research (APA, 1985; SRCD, 1987) are intended to facilitate this.

The potential for enriching the human environment engenders among researchers a responsibility to strive to do so. As research in psychology moves from the laboratory to the everyday world, the researchers' responsibilities to safeguard the human environment increase, just as in genetic engineering, which in recent years is moving from laboratory to real-world experiments. Participants in traditional psychological research—for example, on memory and perception—may defend themselves against its potentially polluting impact by discounting a particular laboratory experience as not real life, not relevant, or not everyday. However, such discounting can be more difficult for participants when research is designed explicitly to mimic and provide an understanding of everyday processes as, for example, in the study of moral phenomena (see, e.g., Baumrind, 1971).

How might research on moral phenomena pollute the human environment, and thus be ecologically unsound? There are at least two possibilities. First, the traditional paradigm for research confirms a relationship of inequality in *power* between the researcher and the research participant. The researcher defines the task for the participant (e.g., Kohlberg's Heinz and the druggist dilemma; Kohlberg, Levine, & Hewer, 1983) and indeed often knows the answer, in the form of a hypothesis or derivation from theory, but withholds it from the subject in the research (Meacham, 1980). The ideology that is confirmed by this traditional paradigm for both the researcher and the research participant is that science and psychology are authoritative and powerful. The researcher is superior to the participant in controlling the problem setting, in knowing the hypothesis and likely outcome but not disclosing it, and in manipulating the research participant, as an object, into a less powerful, subordinate position. Whether the reinforcing of an ideology of power differentials in the human environment is polluting is a matter of point of view; some would argue that this is the natural state of things, in the same way in which racism, sexism, and ageism are normative. I argue strongly, however, that such pollution of the human environment should be avoided.

Enriching the Human Environment

The second way in which research methods can be ecologically unsound is in neglecting to take advantage of the opportunity to strengthen and enrich those processes that are constitutive of the human environment. Let me take as a specific example psychological research on problem solving (Meacham & Emont, 1989). The implication of perspectives such as those of Habermas (1984), Harré (1984), Vygotsky (1978), and others is that the basis of problem solving lies in its interpersonal nature, that is, in the fact that the essence of humans is their communicative abilities. If this implication is correct, then the most ecologically sound research on problem solving reinforces the tendency and the skills within the research participants to call upon interpersonal resources in problem solving, that is, to ask a friend for help. Traditional research that isolates the research participant and asks that he or she solve a problem without friends is not ecologically sound, for it inculcates in the research participant precisely the opposite of the attitude and skills that can be so important in real-life, everyday problem solving. Ecologically sound research is research that leaves the participants, at its conclusion, with a stronger set of skills for life.

In summary, having generalizable, ecologically sound research should not merely mean doing research in a "natural" environment rather than in the laboratory, or research aimed more at describing what people do rather than at testing theory. It should mean conducting research that does not pollute the human environment by further legitimizing an ideology that is actually oppressive to the research participants. Furthermore, ecologically sound research should have an emancipatory intent, having as one of its aims the strengthening of existing psychological processes and the introduction of new processes and skills for the research participants. My perspective is not inconsistent with that of Howard (1985), who called upon researchers to modify their ambitious pursuit of value-free knowledge and observed that psychologists ought "to consider what human beings might become in response to our research" (p. 262).

However, when we examine two major statements of ethics for researchers, we find no prescription for doing *good* for the research participants and the human environment. These statements of ethics, constructed primarily from the perspective of positivist research methods, are concerned primarily with the potential for doing *harm* to the research participants and with how to avoid this. The "Ethical Principles of Psychologists" (APA, 1985) calls upon the researcher to respect and have concern for the dignity and welfare of the research participants. Researchers have a responsibility to provide prompt and sufficient explanations of deception, to permit participants to withdraw from the research at any time, to protect the participants from physical and psychological harm, to protect the confidentiality of information gathered during a study, and so forth. It does not appear, however, that the "Ethical Principles" charge psychologists, as researchers, with doing good for the research participants; instead, they merely prescribe that the psychologists do no harm unless the participants have been fully informed in advance of the potential for harm and have given consent for the research to proceed or, in the case of deception, that a sufficient explanation be provided to the participants after the fact of deception.

The "Ethical Standards for Research with Children" (SRCD, 1987) is similar, although perhaps slightly more balanced. The main concern is with the potential for physical or psychological harm to children, not only in the course of study, but subsequently in reporting results, making evaluative statements, or giving advice. The one exception is Principle 18, which makes researchers responsible not merely for doing no harm to the children, but in fact for doing good: "When an experimental treatment under investigation is believed to be of benefit to children, control groups should be offered other beneficial alternative treatments, if available, instead of no treatment" (SRCD, 1987, p. 254). However, because there is no requirement that positivist research methods provide any positive benefit for the research participants receiving the experimental conditions, Principle 18 only rarely needs to be considered for implementation.

My second proposal is to revise our ethical principles and standards to include the following:

> The researcher has a responsibility to design each study so as to promote the dignity, welfare, and capabilities of the research participants. When no assurance can be provided in advance that the study will be beneficial to the participants, the researcher informs the participants of this fact.

Currently, our statements of research ethics permit the research to proceed as long as the risk–benefit ratio is no greater than 1; that is, risks must be balanced by benefits so that no net harm is done to the participants. However, when the risk–benefit ratio is set precisely at 1—typically, both the risks and the benefits are regarded as minimal, and there is either some underestimation of risk or overestimation of benefits—then it is likely that through error the research participants will be harmed. My second proposal requires that the risk–benefit ratio be less than 1, not only to provide a greater margin of safety for the participants, but also to fulfill the researcher's responsibility to provide a positive benefit for the participants. A statement of the benefit provided for the research participants should appear in the research report as a subsection of the method section.

One possible objection to this second proposal is that it is not clear what constitutes doing good. Furthermore, what the researcher considers a positive benefit might be scorned by the participants. These are precisely the reasons why the calculation of the risk–benefit ratio and the determination of whether the research participants are likely to be harmed or have their lives enriched should not be left entirely to the researcher or to a "Human Subjects Review Committee" that presumes to know what is best for the research participants. It is far better to strive to ensure that each study has some positive benefit for the participants, and that when this cannot be the case, the participants are so informed and given a free choice whether to continue with the research. Some negotiation might be required, along with an effort toward mutual understanding between researcher and participant. This process should be of considerable interest to researchers interested in moral phenomena, who might gain insight, for example, by negotiating with groups of parents over what kinds of research into moral phenomena would be permitted with their children, especially if the research also is required to provide a positive benefit for the children. It is likely that negotiations of this sort do occur with various groups that become involved in research on moral phenomena, and furthermore that such negotiations affect expectations that the participants may have about the research and thus the nature of their behavior within the research setting. It is consistent with postpositivist philosophy of science to regard these calculations of risks and responsibilities and the associated negotiations and expectations as an integral part of the research program; consequently—as has been proposed—the methods section of the research report should reflect fully what has taken place.

THIRD PROPOSAL: LISTEN TO AND LEARN FROM THE RESEARCH PARTICIPANTS

The Concept of Authorship

My third proposal for responding to the challenges of postpositivism for research on moral phenomena is grounded in the work of the Soviet literary critic Mikhail Bakhtin (Clark & Holquist, 1984; see also Meacham, 1989a), one of whose major concerns was the concept of authorship. According to Bakhtin, the task of an author is to create meaning through the interweaving of the author with the heroes who people the author's text. The meaning becomes concrete when the text is read, while the author–creator remains in the background. Once the text has been completed, the position of the author-as-person (e.g., my position as author of this chapter) is no different from that of anyone reading the text, able to see the finished product of the text, but unable to see the author–creator, the process of authorship itself. Thus, the question of who has written a text, of how much of one's self is in a particular text, is unanswerable even by the author. Furthermore, for Bakhtin, authorship of a text, as for any utterance, must be shared between self and other: "The word is a two-sided act. It is determined equally by whose word it is and for whom it is meant" (Clark & Holquist, 1984, p. 15).

This postpositivist concept of authorship advanced by Bakhtin anticipates portions of K. Gergen's (1986) argument in defense of social constructivism, an argument following upon several published commentaries, including one by Kukla (1986), raising concerns with an article that Gergen had published earlier in the *American Psychologist*. Gergen argued that, in principle, any verbal formula is compatible with any experience, and then by way of illustration proposed that Kukla's letter was indeed not authored by Kukla and, more generally, that writings are never the products of individualistic authors. Instead, Gergen (1986) proposed:

> They are products or historical conventions or participatory systems in which individuals are mere conduits of communal forms. Kukla signed his comment, but it could not have emerged independent of a complex system of scholarly interchange, of which his arguments are a part. To believe that any single individual authors an article is thus little more than a veiled expression, let us say, of individualistic values. Is this proposal any less true than to say that Kukla wrote the comment? Yet, once one has climbed inside this communal perspective, to propose that individuals actually write articles is little short of nonsense. (p. 482)

Bakhtin's conception of authorship and the construction of meaning also resembles that of Tappan and Brown (Chapter 5, this volume) and that of Ricoeur (Thompson, 1981), for whom the meaning of a text is not determined exclusively by either the author or the reader. Instead, meaning exists between two speakers, in the event of discourse itself. What must be interpreted is not what the author intends, but instead what the text itself provides. Thus, a text may yield a meaning far surpassing the meaning that had been intended by the author. Honey (1987) extended Ricoeur's conception of the text to the clinical research interview, arguing that the meaning of the research transcript "cannot be seen as the exclusive property of either the interviewer or the interviewee" (p. 81).

Who authors the text of a research study on moral phenomena? The positivist perspective is that the author of the research is that individual whose name appears as a part of the byline (e.g., Kukla or Gergen). Several individuals may be named so as to include all those who have made substantial scientific contributions to the study, including "formulating the problem or hypothesis, structuring the experimental design, organizing and conducting the statistical analysis, interpreting the results, or writing a major portion of the paper" (APA, 1983, p. 20). By such criteria for authorship, Kukla's name should not have been included in the byline of Gergen's response to Kukla's comments; by Bakhtin's criteria, the possibility of including Kukla's name deserves serious consideration, for clearly Gergen would not have, and perhaps could not have, written this particular response to his critics without Kukla's participation in the dialogue.

Whose Research Is It, Anyway?

I have not yet confronted what for Bakhtin is the major issue of authorship. Research and writing in the social science study of moral phenomena is authored not merely by the professional researcher whose name appears in the byline; it is authored through involvement within a conversation constructed between this researcher and the people—children, adolescents, adults—who are the participants within the research. This conversation—the research proper, whether it consists of an interview transcript, a protocol, or a data set from a laboratory experiment—is not constructed or owned by only one participant; it is owned equally by both. Yet from a positivist perspective, the "owner" is only the researcher who stands before us at professional meetings, or who provides his or her name for the byline of an article or chapter, and delivers his or her interpretations of the text of the research conversation.

What of the second interpretation or meaning of the conversation? Why are the other authors—the participants—not permitted or encouraged to extract their own meaning from the research text and present this at professional meetings, in articles, and in chapters? Positivism prescribes that it is the researchers who provide the interpretation of the research text, and not the research participants themselves: "Immediately after the data are collected, the investigator should clarify for the research participant any misconceptions that may have arisen. The investigator also recognizes a duty to report general findings to participants in terms appropriate to their understanding" (SRCD, 1987, p. 254). "After the data are collected, the investigator provides the participant with information about the nature of the study and attempts to remove any misconceptions that may have arisen" (APA, 1985, p. xxxi).

By limiting ourselves to consideration of only the meanings extracted from the research text by the researchers, we have limited ourselves to only half the possible meanings from the research text—the interview transcript, the data set, and so forth—that lies before us. One advantage of this positivist procedure is that it makes us feel as researchers more expert, powerful, and moral, for we have claimed for ourselves—indeed, we have arrogated to ourselves—the ability and the authority to give meaning to the text of the research and to the experiences of the participants in the research (M. Gergen, 1986; Meacham, 1980).

However, it follows that from a postpositivist perspective we ought to continue the dialogue with the research participants. A number of possibilities for doing this can be suggested. Funding agencies are willing to reimburse researchers for travel to national and international conferences to present their interpretations of research texts, and are willing to pay for publication costs (e.g., the purchase and distribution of reprints) so as to disseminate the researchers' interpretations. Certainly, these same agencies, supported through tax dollars collected from research participants, should be as willing to pay for a gathering of the research participants to discuss the initial data analysis, and for us as researchers to learn what meaning, if any, the participants extract from it.

The validity of our research must derive not merely from the fact of its presentation or publication within a prestigious forum, but also—and perhaps more importantly—from the fact that the research participants are able to construct some meaning to give to their involvement in the research. Only in this way can the research be progressive and emancipatory for the research participants. Postpositivism does not call merely for "debriefing" of the research participants, that is, reporting of the general findings and clarification of the research participants' misunderstandings. In fact, it is not at all clear that debriefing, especially following the use of deception in research, is adequate to prevent significant changes within the research participants, including increased depersonalization and distrust (Baumrind, 1971, p. 890). Traditional debriefing does not restore the balance of power between researcher and participant to what it was before the experiment.

Accordingly, my third proposal is that researchers strive to obtain the research participants' meaning or interpretation of the research text. This can be accomplished if our professional associations add to their ethical principles the following:

> Investigators should solicit from the research participants their interpretations of the general findings of the research. Furthermore, investigators should strive to clarify any misconceptions they themselves may hold about the nature of the study and/or the population from which the research participants have been drawn.

This new ethical principle might be operationalized—that is, given some force—if the discussion section of studies written in the style of the *Publication Manual* were required to include, following the introduction, method, results, and traditional discussion sections, an "interpretation and discussion of the implications of the results" (APA, 1983, p. 21) written by the research participants themselves. Such an interpretation and discussion by the research participants might be accomplished in numerous ways, including additional interviews and surveys. One simple format would be to arrange a meeting with a representative group of the participants at which the researcher would present his or her results and interpretations, followed by reactions and discussion by the participants. The transcript from this meeting could then serve as the basis for the second discussion section of the empirical study, this section to be written by the researcher (if appropriate and agreed to by the participants), by one or several of the research participants, or by a third, neutral party.

This third proposal, that researchers strive to obtain a second meaning of the research text from the research participants, would substantially strengthen the research process even when research is evaluated from a positivist perspective. Even a positivist must grant that if a more valid interpretation of the data exists, then he or she is better off having this interpretation than not having it. Consider the following example, in which the researcher's conversation with the research participants led to a substantial revision in the interpretation of the data. In an investigation of language development, P. Miller (1986) observed several instances of teasing between mothers and their young children. These teasing sequences began with the mother threatening, challenging, or mocking the child, and the child responding with a denial, a counterclaim, or a nonverbal counteraction. Are we to interpret these sequences as abusive on the part of the mother, or as intended playfulness that has become inappropriate with respect to the child's level of development and capacity to respond and defend him- or herself, or what? Fortunately, P. Miller (1986, p. 204) asked the mothers for their interpretations of various teasing sequences. From the mothers' perspective, the teasing was intended to impart to the child survival skills—strength, pride, independence, control of hurt feelings, appropriate timing of anger—that would be essential as the child grew older and moved away from the protection of the family into the world. As a second example, consider these comments by Sarah Elder (Sheffield, 1989), widely acclaimed for her documentary films on Eskimo life:

> People ask me who my primary audience is and I would have to say that it is my subjects—they must enjoy it. . . . A lot of filmmakers have asked me "don't you shortchange yourself when you give up control as a media artist?" But I find that by giving up that control I gain more depth into the subjects' lives and also make a better film.

Objections and Reply

Several objections might be raised to this third proposal. One objection is that the participants may find the research to be meaningless or, at best, trivial and, furthermore, may choose to state this in writing. I would be hurt, both personally and professionally, to have such a statement from my research participants appended to one of my empirical articles. Nevertheless, casual conversation with undergraduate students suggests that the feedback provided following their required participation in psychology experiments often leaves them without a useful understanding of the purpose of the research and unconvinced of the significance of what the researchers are doing or of their own time and effort given to the research. If this is what the research participants think and say about my research, then I should hear and read this. One of the impediments to my becoming wise in the course of my research program is the drive to accumulate sufficient expertise and power that my research is no longer questioned or challenged (Meacham, 1989b).

Undoubtedly, I could construct some defenses against the participants' criticisms (e.g., "My research is not viewed as very meaningful or significant, but it is more so than most research"). Constructing an *adequate* defense might not be easy, however. We have already granted that the interpretations of the research participants are valid and that the participants have joint ownership with the researcher of the research text, so I cannot readily defend against their criticisms by dismissing them as unreasonable or illegitimate. If I cannot construct an adequate defense, I can at least hope that the participants will be gentle in their criticisms of my research. If not, perhaps I can work toward a set of ethical standards, paralleling those now in place for the protection of research participants (noninvasion of privacy, protection from physical and psychological harm, protection of confidentiality, etc.), providing some protection from psychological or professional harm for myself as a researcher.

A second objection to the proposal that research participants be encouraged to comment on the meaning and significance of the research is that the participants may not be adequately prepared, in terms of intellectual or emotional maturity, educational training, and so forth, to understand the purposes, procedures, analyses, and implications of the research. Phrased differently, the research participants do not have the expert status presumably held by the researcher. This objection is alluded to in the carefully worded prescription of the Society for Research in Child Development that researchers report "general findings to participants in terms appropriate to their understanding" (1987, p. 254). At one level, the supposed difficulty that the research participants have in understanding can hardly be an objection against encouraging them to provide their own interpretation of the research text. If their views should be discounted because the participants have not understood the purposes, procedures, and so on, then this lack of understanding should be readily apparent from a close examination of the quality of the participants' comments. Furthermore, participants who are not prepared to understand the research in the same framework or terms as the researcher might attribute greater, not lesser, significance to the research. I am not prepared to understand current research on subatomic particles, but I am willing to grant (perhaps I shouldn't?) the importance of research aimed at understanding the nature of matter and the relationship between matter and energy. Thus, no researcher should feel seriously threatened by the proposed procedures.

At a second level, the supposed difficulty that research participants have in understanding the research imposes upon the researcher, from a postpositivist perspective, a responsibility toward facilitating and promoting the understanding of the participants. In contrast, in positivist research, too often the researcher merely "blames the victims" (Ryan, 1976) for their inability or failure to understand the research. Instead, rather than merely reporting general findings to the research participants "in terms appropriate to their understanding," the researcher ought to take at least some small steps toward educating the research participants and raising their level of understanding. As G. A. Miller (1969) noted, what psychology has to offer is "not some esoteric branch of witchcraft that must be reserved for those with Ph.D. degrees in psychology. When the ideas are made sufficiently explicit, the scientific foundations of psychology can be grasped by sixth-grade children" (p. 1073). The researcher ought to make a sincere effort toward helping the participants understand the research in those terms and in that context that the researcher finds most appropriate for clarifying the research purposes, findings, and implications. Many researchers already do this. The second proposal, to do good for the research participants, is an attempt to codify this commendable practice.

An implication in the preceding paragraph and in the "Ethical Standards" (SRCD, 1987) is that the level of understanding of the researcher in traditional research is in some way greater or more expert than that of the research participants (M. Gergen, 1986). Nevertheless, it is not at all clear that the researcher can presume an intellectual advantage, *much less a moral advantage* (e.g., in understanding or evaluating the implications of the research for social action), over the research participants. This is particularly so in research with older adults, as well as with participants from disadvantaged populations or from other cultures. Indeed, the reason that the researcher is conducting the research is that he or she does not have all the answers and so is not expert on the particular subject matter of the research. The research participants, on the other hand, might well have moral insights that would be of benefit to the researcher. The researcher might be lacking in some domains of understanding, might learn by listening to the research participants, and in particular might need assistance in becoming more sensitive to the biases, prejudices, value orientations, and ideologies within which he or she is immersed.

THE PROBLEM OF SELF-DECEPTION

How might researchers better recognize and understand the relationship between themselves as researchers and the social, cultural, and value frameworks within which they conceive and conduct their research (Meacham, 1984)? How can they become more sensitive to the biases, prejudices, and ideologies within which they may be immersed? In Baumrind's (Chapter 12, this volume) terms, what procedures can researchers follow so as to have confidence that they have determined and are acting in accord with their "true self-interest?" How can they construct descriptions of human development that are adequately sensitive to the motives and goals of the research participants? I refer to this problem, which is an essential implication of postpositivist philosophy of science, especially in the study of moral phenomena, as the problem of self-deception.

The way to solve this problem is not piecemeal, subsequent to the fact of the research, with one or another writer commenting on how at some point in the history of research on moral phenomena our paradigms or research questions have merely reflected the then-contemporary social, political, economic, or philosophical values. Such an approach permits traditional research methodology to continue unchanged, and so provides no guarantee against our research being similarly biased either now or in the future. A critical social science cannot come about through the actions of a few people on the outside, overlooking and criticizing the various disciplines and their research methods. Instead, there must be a reconstruction at the heart of the discipline, at the heart of our traditional research methodology. There must be a research methodology with built-in guarantees that researchers will become aware of their own social, cultural, and moral biases.

To construct a solution to this problem of self-deception, I again draw upon the work of Bakhtin (Clark and Holquist, 1984). Bakhtin suggested that it is difficult for the participants in a conversation to discern the authors or creators behind the text of a conversation; similarly, it is difficult for researchers to discern the influence of social, cultural, historical, political, economic, and religious values in authoring their own work. Yet these things are rather easy to see in others, for example, in the work of G. Stanley Hall (Muschinske, 1977), the early developmentalists portrayed by Wertsch and Youniss (1987; Youniss, Chapter 8, this volume), and the early intelligence testers (Gould, 1981; Samelson, 1978).

This, for Bakhtin, is the key. When I see these values in and communicate them to another, and when the other does the same for me, then we construct each other in dialogue. The researcher, during research with participants who differ in background from him- or herself, has an opportunity to discover how his or her own identity has been shaped through immersion within a particular social and cultural context. The solution to the problem of self-deception in social science research is that the research dialogue must explicitly include the research participants, especially at that point at which meaning is given to the research findings. Both meanings or interpretations—the researcher's and the participants'—are valid. In this exchange of meanings with research participants and in the subsequent construction of new meanings, the researcher becomes more aware of the dependence of his or her initial interpretations upon involvement within a particular social, cultural, and historical context.

Several changes in the history of social science research illustrate this proposed reconstruction of our research methods. The early intelligence tests are now widely recognized as having discriminated against not only minorities of color but also recent, turn-of-the-century immigrant groups, such as Italians, Jews, Poles, Irish, and Greeks. The corrective for this racism within the discipline of psychology was the entry into psychology, in the 1920s and 1930s, of members of those groups (Samelson, 1978), that is, people who were formerly in the category of research participant. Similarly, the elimination of sexist language and biases in psychological measures and in social science writing, as well as the introduction of constructs of particular interest to women (e.g., the work of Bem, 1974; and of Gilligan, 1982), has stemmed in large part from the increase in numbers of women within the discipline of psychology. In both examples, the changes reflect that the research participants were brought into a peer relationship and into dialogue with the researchers and were thus able to initiate steps toward making the discipline of psychology less racist and less sexist.

Certainly, concerns might be raised, from both the "left" and the "right," against this third proposal that researchers listen to and learn from the interpretations of the research that can be provided by research participants. From the left, one might argue that the dialogue between the researcher and the research participants ought to begin not after the data have been collected and analyzed, but rather at the beginning, as the purposes and procedures of the research are being established (M. Gergen, 1986). I do not disagree with such an argument, but I doubt that researchers into moral phenomena in the 1990s will be prepared for such a dialogue with the research participants so early in the research process. Instead, I have proposed a modest and workable modification of the interpretation and reporting of research findings.

From the right, one might be concerned that admitting as valid a variety of interpretations might become an obstacle to the goal of a social science that is coherent, systematic, and unified, as well as one that provides certain guarantees of objective truth. My brief response to this concern is that it appears to stem from a limited, history- and culture-bound philosophy of science, namely, that of positivism. Postpositivism admits a variety of philosophies of science, several of which would be consistent with the constructivist, interpretive, and hermeneutic perspective of this third proposal.

Despite these potential criticisms, we are left with the conclusion that the solution to the problem of self-deception—that is, of how to perceive the dependence of our research upon the contemporary social, cultural, and moral values within which we are immersed—is to have more open discussions with the participants in our research, listening carefully to their interpretations of the research text that is a jointly authored product of their efforts and ours. This solution to the problem of self-deception will be efficacious to the extent that researchers go out of their way to enter into dialogue with groups of research participants whose backgrounds, moral values, and world views are divergent from those of the researchers. Such a reconstruction of our research methodology can promote mutual understanding between researchers and research participants, leading to the construction of a social science that will be a better foundation both for understanding and for social action in our communities and in the broader society of humans.

CONCLUSION: RESEARCH AS COMMUNICATION

In this chapter, I have set forth three proposals for how our methods of research into moral phenomena ought to be changed in response to the challenges of postpositivist philosophy of science: to treat the researcher as person, not as object, and so to humanize the researcher; to do good for the research participants; and to listen to and learn from the participants. These three proposals serve to facilitate a number of postpositivist concerns, which are brought into even sharper focus in the case of research into moral phenomena. As noted earlier in the chapter, postpositivism, in contrast to positivism, is concerned with what researchers actually do in their investigations, with the motivated and value-laden nature of knowing, and with the social and historical nature of science.

All three of these postpositivist concerns are addressed by the first proposal—to humanize the researcher—and the third proposal—to listen to the participants. From the standpoint of postpositivism, the process of science is not essentially logical and rational, as though a machine had been programmed to engage in comparisons and make decisions. Instead, the researcher him- or herself, as a human, social, and value-laden being who can readily make mistakes, must be seen as the focal point around which all else in the scientific process revolves. To have a better science means not merely to strive to know the subject matter per se, but to strive to understand the values of the knowing agent as he or she acts upon and constructs an understanding of the subject matter. Thus, to understand the humanness of the researcher, including the researcher's motivations and moral values, as well as the social, cultural, and historical context within which the researcher lives, becomes an essential step and a continuing task in the investigation of moral phenomena.

The second postpositivist concern (the motivated and value-laden nature of knowing) and the third (the social and historical nature of science) are addressed by the second proposal—to do good for the research participants. From the standpoint of postpositivism, it is not possible for the researcher to rightfully claim a morally neutral stance with regard to the research participants. Instead, the researcher must be morally engaged with and committed to what is good for the research participants. Thus, a postpositivist perspective on research into moral phenomena implies that the researcher must be concerned not merely with morality as an object of study, but also with the morality of his or her own actions as a researcher toward the research participants.

The debate between positivist and postpositivist conceptions of research is a debate over the nature of science. Among the essences of science is the attitude that all knowledge remains potentially fallible, so that the scientist must continue to doubt and reevaluate all that he or she might hope to know (Meacham, 1989b). Just as essential is the awareness that scientific knowledge must be neither merely private nor privileged knowledge, but instead must be communicated and shared broadly and openly (see Chapter 5 by Tappan and Brown, in this volume). These two essences are complementary, for it is in the public arena that our data and interpretations can best be challenged and their fallibility, if such be the case, demonstrated. The three proposals set forth in this chapter—to humanize the researcher, to do good for the research participants, and to listen to the participants—have in common bringing into the public arena more of the who and the what of science—who scientists are and what they do in their work.

One conceptual framework for considering how the process of science takes place in the public arena is communication (Meacham, 1991). Habermas (1984; see also McCarthy, 1978; Kurtines et al., 1990; Kurtines, Azmitia, & Alvarez, Chapter 1, this volume; Tappan & Brown, Chapter 5, this volume) provided a detailed account of the validity claims that are the basis for communication in an ideal speech situation. When there is a failure of understanding in the communication process, the basis for reestablishing understanding and communication is found through a critical examination of these claims. The implicit validity claims of any speaker include the claims that what is said is a *true* representation with respect to the world, that it is a *truthful* or sincere expression of the speaker's intentions, and that it is *right* or just in the context of interpersonal and social relations. In an ideal speech situation, any and all of these validity claims must be open to critical examination. Research conducted from a positivist perspective has been concerned primarily with theoretical discourse, that is, with potential challenges to the first validity claim of truth.

In contrast, my first proposal (to humanize the researcher) and third proposal (to listen to the research participants) are directed toward discussion of the third validity claim of rightness and the second validity claim of truthfulness (i.e., the sincerely of the intentions of the researcher). The major obstacle to truthful or sincere statements by the researcher is what I have referred to in this chapter as the problem of self-deception, that is, the problem of the researcher being unable to perceive his or her own social, cultural, and historical biases. The first and third proposals provide a procedure for consciousness raising and overcoming this self-deception by the researcher (as well as for development along the lines suggested by Gibbs, Chapter 10, this volume). The second proposal (to do good for the research participants) is also directed toward the validity claim of truthfulness, but is directed more forcefully toward the third validity claim, that of rightness. The question of who is empowered to determine what is beneficial for the research participants might generate considerable discussion between researchers and participants. Taken together, the three proposals set forth in this chapter serve to strengthen practical discourse, that is, discourse directed toward the critical examination of the validity claims of truthfulness and rightness (see also Kurtines et al., Chapter 1, this volume). By thus moving the communication process of science more toward the ideal speech situation as described by Habermas (1984), the three proposals add strength to the process of science.

In his review of the chapters in the Fiske and Shweder (1986) volume, Hogan (1988, p. 9) noted several problems associated with the current crisis in the social sciences, for example, narrowly restricted generalizations and a lack of answers to social policy questions. These problems, and indeed the crisis itself, might be said to reflect a breakdown of communication between researchers, research participants, and the consumers of research, this latter group including other researchers and practitioners, policymakers, and the general public. My first proposal—to humanize the researcher—will facilitate communication between researchers and the consumers of research; the second proposal—to do good for the participants—will facilitate communication between researchers and both the research participants and the consumers; and the third proposal—to listen to the participants—will facilitate communication between researchers and research participants.

To have a strong science requires that all knowledge remains potentially fallible, that the scientist remains open to the possibility of error in what he or she knows (Meacham, 1989b). Our common experience is that it is easier to perceive the errors of another's reasoning than to perceive our own. The benefit of having the process of science take place in the public arena is that it makes the uncovering of errors much more likely than for the isolated scientist working without the benefit of the criticisms of others. Conflict within the public arena facilitates the determination of what Baumrind (Chapter 12, this volume) has termed one's "true self-interest." What is important in having a productive clash of minds in the public arena is that there be equality of power, so that the flow of ideas in the communication process proceeds not with regard to any systematic constraints on communication, such as tradition, status, or power (including the power of the researcher over the research participant), but rather from the force of the better argument (Habermas, 1984; McCarthy, 1978).

The impact of grafting these three postpositivist proposals—to humanize the researcher, to do good for the participants, and to listen to the participants—onto the root of positivism is to dethrone and make less powerful the researcher, who thus becomes more instrumental as a participant in the communication process and as a facilitator of communication between research participants, on the one hand, and the consumers of research, on the other. As G. A. Miller (1969) argued, "our responsibility is less to assume the role of experts and try to apply psychology ourselves than to give it away to the people who really need it—and that includes everyone" (p. 1071). The three proposals lead to a greater consciousness of values and to more equality of power within the research situation, between researcher, research participant, and consumer, and so strengthen the process of science. As our science becomes stronger, our research on the development of moral phenomena will become better; as our research methods become more moral, our science will become stronger.

REFERENCES

American Psychological Association. (1983). *Publication manual of the American Psychological Association* (3rd ed.). Washington, DC: Author.

American Psychological Association. (1985). Ethical principles of psychologists. In *Directory of the American Psychological Association* (pp. xxviii–xxx). Washington, DC: Author.

Barnes, B. (1985). Thomas Kuhn. In Q. Skinner (Ed.), *The return of grand theory in the human sciences* (pp. 83–100). New York: Cambridge University Press.

Baumrind, D. (1971). Principles of ethical conduct in the treatment of subjects. *American Psychologist, 26,* 887–896.

Bem, S. L. (1974). The measurement of psychological androgyny. *Journal of Consulting and Clinical Psychology, 42,* 155–162.

Bickhard, M. H., Cooper, R. G., & Mace, P. E. (1985). Vestiges of logical positivism: Critiques of stage explanations. *Human Development, 28,* 240–258.

Chandler, M. J. (1987). The Othello effect: Essay on the emergence and eclipse of skeptical doubt. *Human Development, 30,* 137–159.

Clark, K., & Holquist, M. (1984). *Mikhail Bakhtin.* Cambridge, MA: Harvard University Press.

Fiske, D. W., & Shweder, R. A. (Eds.). (1986). *Metatheory in social science: Pluralisms and subjectivities.* Chicago: University of Chicago Press.

Gergen, K. (1973). Social psychology as history. *Journal of Personality and Social Psychology, 26,* 309–320.

Gergen, K. (1986). Elaborating the constructionist thesis. *American Psychologist, 41,* 481–482.

Gergen, M. (1986, August). *Toward a feminist metatheory and methodology.* Paper presented at the meeting of the American Psychological Association, Washington, DC.

Gholson, B., & Barker, P. (1985). Kuhn, Lakatos, and Laudan: Applications in the history of physics and psychology. *American Psychologist, 40,* 755–769.

Gilligan, C. (1982). *In a different voice: Psychological theory and women's development.* Cambridge, MA: Harvard University Press.

Gould, S. J. (1981). *Mismeasure of man.* New York: Norton.

Habermas, J. (1971). *Knowledge and human interests* (J. J. Shapiro, Trans.). Boston: Beacon Press.

Habermas, J. (1984). *The theory of communicative action: Vol. 1. Reason and the rationalization of society.* (T. McCarthy, Trans.). Boston: Beacon Press.

Harré, R. (1984). *Personal being: A theory for individual psychology.* Cambridge, MA: Harvard University Press.

Hogan, R. (1988). Positivism is history [Review of *Metatheory in social science: Pluralisms and subjectivities*]. *Contemporary Psychology, 33,* 9–10.

Honey, M. (1987). The interview as text: Hermeneutics considered as a model for analyzing the clinically informed research interview. *Human Development, 30,* 69–82.

Howard, G. S. (1985). The role of values in the science of psychology. *American Psychologist, 40,* 255–265.

Kitchener, R. F. (1983). Changing conceptions of the philosophy of science and the foundations of developmental psychology. In D. Kuhn & J. A. Meacham (Eds.), *On the development of developmental psychology* (pp. 1–30). Basel: Karger.

Kohlberg, L., Levine, C., & Hewer, A. (1983). *Moral stages: A current formulation and a response to critics.* Basel: Karger.

Kuhn, T. S. (1962). *The structure of scientific revolutions.* Chicago: University of Chicago Press.

Kukla, A. (1986). On social constructionism. *American Psychologist, 41,* 480–481.

Kurtines, W. M., Alvarez, M., & Azmitia, M. (1990). Science and morality: The role of values in science and the scientific study of moral phenomena. *Psychological Bulletin, 107,* 283–295.

Manicas, P. T., & Secord, P. F. (1983). Implications for psychology of the new philosophy of science. *American Psychologist, 38,* 399–413.

McCarthy, T. (1978). *The critical theory of Jurgen Habermas.* Cambridge, MA: MIT Press.

Meacham, J. A. (1975). A dialectical approach to moral judgment and self-esteem. *Human Development, 18,* 159–170. Reprinted in M. Gorman (Ed.). (1985). *Psychology and religion* (pp. 188–198). New York: Paulist Press.

Meacham, J. A. (1977). A transactional model of remembering. In N. Datan & H. W. Reese (Eds.), *Life-span developmental psychology: Dialectical perspectives on experimental research* (pp. 261–284). New York: Academic Press.

Meacham, J. A. (1980). Research on remembering: Interrogation or conversation, monologue or dialogue? *Human Development, 23,* 236–245.

Meacham, J. A. (1981). Political values, conceptual models, and research. In R. M. Lerner & N. A. Busch-Rossnagel (Eds.), *Individuals as producers of their development* (pp. 447–474). New York: Academic Press.

Meacham, J. A. (1984). The individual as consumer and producer of historical change. In K. A. McCluskey & H. W. Reese (Eds.), *Life-span developmental psychology: Historical and generational effects* (pp. 47–72). New York: Academic Press.

Meacham, J. A. (1989a). Discovering the social-context of research: Listening to and learning from research participants. In D. A. Kramer & M. J. Bopp (Eds.), *Movement through form: Transformation in clinical and developmental psychology* (pp. 136–153). New York: Springer-Verlag.

Meacham, J. A. (1989b). The loss of wisdom. In R. J. Sternberg (Ed.), *Wisdom: Its nature, origins, and development* (pp. 181–211). Cambridge, England: Cambridge University Press.

Meacham, J. A. (1991). Theory building as communication. In P. van Geert & L. P. Mos (Eds.), *Annals of Theoretical Psychology: Vol. VI. Developmental Psychology.* New York: Plenum Press.

Meacham, J. A., & Emont, N. C. (1989). The interpersonal basis of everyday problem-solving. In J. D. Sinnott (Ed.), *Everyday problem-solving: Theory and application* (pp. 7–23). New York: Praeger.

Miller, G. A. (1969). Psychology as a means of promoting human welfare. *American Psychologist, 24,* 1063–1075.

Miller, P. (1986). Teasing as language socialization and verbal play in a white working-class community. In B. B. Schieffelin & E. Ochs (Eds.), *Language socialization across cultures.* Cambridge, England: Cambridge University Press.

Muschinske, D. (1977). The nonwhite as child: G. Stanley Hall on the education of nonwhite peoples. *Journal of the History of the Behavioral Sciences, 13,* 328–336.

Outhwaite, W. (1985). Hans-Georg Gadamer. In Q. Skinner (Ed.), *The return of grand theory in the human sciences* (pp. 21–40). Cambridge, England: Cambridge University Press.

Outhwaite, W. (1987). *New philosophies of social science: Realism, hermenuetics, and critical theory.* New York: St. Martin's Press.

Riegel, K. F. (1979). *Foundations of dialectical psychology.* New York: Academic Press.

Ryan, W. (1976). *Blaming the victim.* New York: Vintage.

Samelson, F. (1978). From "race psychology" to "studies in prejudice": Some observations on the thematic reversal in social psychology. *Journal of the History of the Behavioral Sciences, 14,* 265–278.

Scheidt, R. J. (1981). Ecologically-valid inquiry: Fait accompli? *Human Development, 24,* 225–228.

Sheffield, E. (1989, February 2). Sarah Elder: Documentary-maker joins media faculty. *Reporter* (SUNY at Buffalo), *20*(16), 5.

Society for Research in Child Development. (1987). Ethical standards for research with children. In *1987 Directory* (pp. 253–254). Chicago: Author.

Thompson, J. B. (Ed. and Trans.). (1981). *Paul Ricoeur: Hermeneutics and the human sciences.* Cambridge, England: Cambridge University Press.

Vygotsky, L. S. (1978). *Mind in society.* Cambridge, MA: Harvard University Press.

Wertsch, J. V., & Youniss, J. (1987). Contextualizing the investigator: The case of developmental psychology. *Human Development, 30,* 18–31.

Youniss, J. (1989). Cultural forces leading to scientific developmental psychology. In C. B. Fisher & W. W. Tryon (Eds.), *Ethics in applied developmental psychology.* Norwood, NJ: Ablex.

Chapter 4 ■

Co-Constructive, Intersubjective Realism: Metatheory in Developmental Psychology ■

ROBERT H. WOZNIAK
Bryn Mawr College

Over a number of years and in a variety of ways, I have found myself returning to examine the value choices and commitments implicit in psychological theory in general and in the theoretical work of Piaget (1950), Vygotsky (1978), and Gibson (1966, 1979) in particular (Wozniak, 1975a, 1975b, 1981, 1982, 1983a, 1983b, 1985, 1988; Lamb & Wozniak, 1990). My interest in this issue has been motivated by a conviction that, at the metatheoretical level, despite numerous divergent theoretical claims, the perspectives represented by Piaget, Vygotsky, and Gibson are not only fundamentally compatible, but potentially complementary.[1]

From this process of examination, I have gradually derived a co-constructive, intersubjective, realist view with a metatheoretical framework designed to support a systematic integration of Piaget, Gibson, and Vygotsky. Because this view has its roots in metatheoretical analysis, in the attempt to make explicit the epistemological and value assumptions that have generally been only implicit in the work of these theorists, it has from the outset been self-conscious about its own metatheory. For that reason, I hope that this view may serve as a useful case study in an examination of the role of values in psychology and human development.

Although metatheory is, at least on first encounter, almost unrelievedly abstract and, therefore, slow reading, it seems necessary in this context to begin with an explicit statement of some of the most important metatheoretical principles on which co-constructive, intersubjective, realist theories must be based. To bring this abstract analysis somewhat down to earth, this initial metatheoretical statement will be followed by a sketch of some of the molar theoretical principles that the metatheory is designed to support. The chapter concludes with a return to metatheory, first to a few additional principles specific to a co-constructive, intersubjective, realist view, and then to three more general issues pertaining to the role of metatheory in psychological explanation.

CO-CONSTRUCTIVE METATHEORY: PART 1

Major principles of metatheory on which any co-constructive, intersubjective, realist view must be based include at least the following:

1. Just as there are human morphogenetic universals (no one, presumably, would question the universality of the broad outlines of human form), there are human psychogenetic universals. The broad outlines of human psychological structure and function, in other words, are species general.

2. On the other hand, just as endogenous and exogenous factors interact to set the parameters that construct specific, individual morphological forms and morphogenetic processes within universal constraints, endogenous and exogenous factors also set the parameters for psychogenesis.

3. In attempting to understand how such factors interact to construct psychological structures and processes (i.e., in any attempt to develop psychology as both a descriptive and explanatory enterprise), a fundamental distinction must be drawn between two levels of psychological reality: a phenomenal level and a subphenomenal level. Although broader in its implications than distinctions that have in the past been drawn between surface structure and deep structure, performance and competence, appearance and reality, and so forth, this conception is of a similar type.

4. At the phenomenal level exist those structures and processes that are publicly (e.g., action) or privately (e.g., experience) observable; these are the psychological "phenomena" that psychologists ought to be able to explain.

5. At the subphenomenal level exist those entities and relationships (e.g., cognitive and ecological structures and processes) that are presumed to underlie, to organize, and to give form and direction to psychological phenomena. Structures and processes that exist at the subphenomenal

level are *unobservable in principle*, below the level of experience, and knowable only by inference from regularities at the phenomenal level.

6. Psychological phenomena, which are organized and streamlike, can be exhaustively classified into three mutually exclusive categories: experience, symbolic discourse, and action (I discuss these in more detail below).

7. The descriptive problem for psychology is, therefore, to provide an adequate characterization of the temporally dynamic structure of experience, symbolic discourse, and action.

8. The explanatory problem for psychology is to make use of assumed structures and processes at the subphenomenal level to account for phenomenal structure and change. Psychological theories, in other words, require the use of hypothetical constructs that posit entities and relationships below the level of the phenomena—entities and relationships that are assumed to exist, to have particular structural and functional characteristics, and to organize and direct (i.e., construct) experience, symbolic discourse, and action.

9. Because psychological phenomena are a joint function of endogenous and exogenous factors, adequate psychological explanation will require two independent but interacting sets of hypothetical constructs. One such set of constructs posits structures and processes of a knowing, meaning-creating, interpreting mind. The other set posits structures and processes of a psychologically relevant (ecological) physical and social world. Together, mental and ecological structures and processes are presumed to co-construct experience, symbolic discourse, and action.

CO-CONSTRUCTIVISM AND THE PSYCHOLOGICAL SYSTEM

Although there are five additional metatheoretical principles, which I list later, it may be helpful first to clarify and elaborate the implications of this initial metatheoretical statement for an understanding of the nature of psychological theory by summarizing some of the implications for theoretical analysis of the psychological system that emerge from this metatheory. For any reader who is interested, this analysis is presented in more detail in Wozniak (1985).

Most psychologists no longer consider it controversial to claim that to experience a mailbox as something useful for posting a letter, we must know something about the existence of a postal system that picks up, sorts, and delivers mail; or that to understand our native language, we must know the syntactic rules that govern its production; or that to drink from a cup, we must know how to use the hand to guide the cup to the mouth. Knowledge (as structure) and knowing (as process), in other words, are now taken by most psychologists to be acceptable constructs relevant to the explanation of psychological phenomena, a perspective with which Piaget's constructivist program is fully compatible.

Although somewhat more controversial, a view derived from Gibson's (1966, 1979) ecological program has also begun to gain wider acceptance. According to this view, to experience a mailbox visually as affording letter posting, we must detect higher order structure invariant over time in the light to the eye that is informative about (bears a regular relationship to) certain properties of the mailbox, properties that are a function of the structure of the mailbox and its position in the postal system. To understand our native language as it is spoken, we must extract over time the higher order patterns informative about certain symbols that have been coded into the sound stream by the speaker. To drink from a cup, we must detect the properties of the cup that will support that action, such as its concavity (affording containment), solidity (affording grasping), and relatively small weight in relation to the force that we are able to exert with our arm (affording lifting and tilting at the mouth).

According to Gibson, in other words, physical and social structures and processes support properties of physical and social objects and events. These properties are, in turn, broadcast in the higher order invariant relationships over time that exist in patterned energy to receptor systems and are perceived by the organism as objects and events affording actions of various sorts. If one accepts this perspective, the psychologically relevant properties of physical and social structures, then, must also be taken to be acceptable constructs relevant to the explanation of psychological phenomena.

As I have suggested, for purposes of psychological explanation, we must treat our concepts of both cognitive structure and process and physical and social structure and process as hypothetical constructs (Hempel, 1966). In this usage, the term *hypothetical construct* refers to a concept of an entity or process assumed to exist and to underlie the organization and change in organization in the phenomena (experience, symbolic discourse, and action) about which we theorize.

The direct implication of this view is that neither the underlying structures of knowledge nor the mental acts of knowing, neither the underlying structures of physical and social objects and events nor the higher order invariants informative about properties supported by this structure, are directly given *in* experience. They are nonconscious in principle, known only by inference *from* experience, that is, from the experience of symbolic discourse and of action, our own and that of others, from the experience of objects and events, and from the experience of experience itself.

An extremely important corrolary of this view is that, as human beings, we do not have privileged access to our own cognitive structures and processes. The cognitive system is nonconscious *in principle*, below the level of awareness *in principle*, known only by inference. When we ask ourselves whether we know something or how our knowledge functions to organize our actions, we, like the psychologist who may be observing us, must infer to the nature and content of our own cognitive system from the nature and content of the available data, that is, our psychological phenomena.

This is not, of course, to deny that, as subjects, we draw our inferences from a wider data base than does the psychologist observing us (since we have access to our own experience and internal symbolic discourse and he or she does not, and since we possess a much wider sample of our actions and external symbolic discourse than he or she could possess). The fact remains, however, that when we want to know what we know, we, like the psychologist, are reduced to drawing inferences to the nature and content of our knowledge system and to engaging in semiotic activity to generate theoretical, symbolic discourse about that system in order to tell ourselves what it is we have found out. According to this account, the cognitive unconscious is radically different from the psychodynamic, boiling cauldron unconscious of Herbart (1824) or Freud (1920), an unconscious from which representations pop into awareness and into which they may be repressed.

In summary to this point, the explanatory problem for psychology is to develop adequate theories of knowledge and knowing and of the psychologically relevant structures and properties of the physical and social environment and to show how they interactively co-determine or co-construct experience, symbolic discourse, and action. A program of this sort is partly compatible with and partly larger than the constructivism of Piaget, the ecological approach of Gibson, and the sociohistorical perspective of Vygotsky. Next, starting with a discussion of experience, I briefly touch on the nature of each of the categories of psychological phenomena and on knowledge and environment as they are here conceived.

Experience

Suppose a 4-month-old infant, an average adult, and an ornithologist were all watching the same bird from roughly the same position in space. Although in one sense they would all be seeing the same "thing" (i.e., a bird), most of us would agree that in another sense they would not be "seeing" the same thing at all. The bird's shape, the flutter of its wings, the movements of its head, the texture of its feathers, and variations in its coloring might be presumed to be accessible to all three viewers. However, there is information in the light to the human eye that specifies much more than this.

Thus, for example, the nature of the bird's activity—whether it is eating, nest building, or watching for predators—and its general activity level— whether it hops slowly along the ground and takes wing only occasionally, or whether it flits from bough to bough, pausing only momentarily in each resting place—are potentially detectable elements of the stimulus array. We would be much slower to assume that the infant can attend to all these variables of stimulation. The average adult, however, can; and the ornithologist can detect even more: the bird's species and subspecies, its gender-specific coloration, its relative age, its relative state of health, and numerous other subtle features.

As Gibson (1966) pointed out, energy to receptor systems is rich in potential information, rich in structure that bears a regular relation to the numerous properties of that environment. That information is in the energy to and is potentially detectable by the infant, average adult, and ornithologist—yet, by itself, it is not sufficient for experience. The perceiver must also have the capacity to detect that information.

Although this is a claim with which Gibson would not generally have been in agreement, that capacity is, I have argued (Wozniak, 1985):

> best understood as a cognitive capacity, one dependent on the development of a conceptual system and processes in which information from and about the environment is actively interpreted, assimilated to appropriate concepts, and thereby given meaning. Perceiving, in other words, can be thought of as a process of the co-construction of experience in which the environment provides a *figurative* component (form), dependent on structure over time in the stimulus flux, and the mind provides a *conceptual* component (meaning), dependent on the structure of knowledge and knowing processes. (p. 46)

The mental acts or cognitive processes through which cognitive structures appropriate to incoming stimulus information are accessed or, put another way, through which that information is assimilated to the cognitive system are, in effect, acts of meaning attribution, and the cognitive system itself is a meaning-generating system.

Symbolic Discourse

In addition to experiencing the world, human beings also generate symbols—in the form of words or mental images—to stand for it. The function of symbolic discourse is representational. Symbols are entities that stand for something other than themselves, and by virtue of this representational function, they serve to bring back to awareness objects and events that are not currently present to the senses. When I reflect on the house in which I was raised, for example, I can bring the house itself and details of my childhood to awareness through words and/or mental images, even though the house itself is not presently available to my experience and my childhood is past.

Symbolic discourse, like experience, also has figurative and cognitive components. For the spoken word, the figurative component is auditory and phonemic; for the written word, it is visual and orthographic; for the non-linguistic mental image, it is modality-specific sensory content stored from past experience (stored patterns of light, sound, etc.). Symbol generation involves retrieving this figurative content and assimilating it to the conceptual structures that provide the basis for the meaning of the objects and events for which the symbol stands. Meaning, in other words, is not inherent in the form of the symbol, but is given to it, just as it is given to experience, by a mental act of assimilation.

What critically differentiates symbolic discourse from experience, however, is its uniquely individual yet transpersonal nature. When an individual engages in the semiotic act of symbol generation, both the conceptual and the figurative components of the symbol can be generated from within. By contrast, in the co-construction of experience, the conceptual component is provided by the perceiver, but the figurative component is provided by the environment. This is a simple point, but its force is far-reaching. It is, for example, the reason why human beings can formulate personal beliefs, symbolic representations about the nature of physical and interpersonal reality, that may or may not be veridical.

However, symbolic discourse is not solely or even primarily individual. Although experience, even social experience, has only a personal existence, symbolic discourse exists transpersonally. Indeed, the human infant is born into a sociocultural world defined in large part by a system of historically developed social meanings embedded in already existing forms of symbolic discourse. As Vygotsky (1956) pointed out, the child experiences the world in the context of communicative speech–action transactions.

Encountering cups in varying practical and social contexts, a young girl may be told by her mother, her father, or her siblings, "Here's a cup," "There's milk in the cup," "Don't drop the cup," "The cup will break," "The cup is empty," or "Give Mommy the cup," as the cup is handed back and forth, filled by one and emptied by the other, turned upside down by one and righted by the other, dropped by one and picked up by the other, and so forth. As I have suggested elsewhere (Wozniak, 1988):

> In Vygotsky's view, this common lexical item serves as a nexus around which the child abstracts and generalizes experience with the characteristics of sets of objects in the world. The development of abstract, categorical concepts, in other words—in fact the very transition from the sensorimotor thought of the infant to the properly conceptual thought of the preschooler—occurs, for Vygotsky, in and through the internalization of speech. (p. 229)

More importantly, however, as Vygotsky constantly stressed, the word *cup* is itself embedded in discourse that conveys cultural meaning. This discourse, in turn, depends on the fact that the lexical items that facilitate the child's synthesis of experience already preexist the child in socially developed systems of meanings and articulated beliefs held in social structures at all levels of complexity (friendship pairs, families, peer groups, schools, churches, subcultures, and societies) into which the child grows. These meaning and articulated belief systems might be called, for lack of a better term, social or cultural *ideologies*. Thus, the transition from sensorimotor to abstract thought, according to Vygotsky, is truly a process of acculturation through the internalization of a social semiotic system. As a consequence, sociality and historicity are embedded in the very core of human conceptualization (see Wozniak, 1988, for a somewhat longer discussion of this issue).

Action and Interaction

In addition to experiencing and constructing symbols that stand for objects and events in the environment, human beings are able to act on those objects and participate in those events. Action, in this context, is not reducible to movement, but refers to a system of hierarchically patterned sequences of movement organized in relation to some end. End states toward which action is organized furnish hierarchical systems of expectations against which the success of the action can be evaluated (see Reed, in press, for an interesting and generally Gibsonian analysis of this issue).

The cognitive component of action, in other words, includes the specification of end states and expectations, knowledge of the general structure or scheme for action, and some specification of the range of variation in action necessary and permissible under different environmental conditions. The figurative component of action consists of the actual physical and social support for action provided by these environmental conditions (a point perhaps first articulated by Tolman, 1932, in his description of environmental "manipulanda," and elaborated by Gibson, 1979, in his concept of "affordance").

Within the broad category of action, the class of interactions stands out as unique. Interactions differ from other actions in the nature of the expectational control that the cognitive system exerts as the interaction unfolds. When I reach to pick up a glass (an action), to act successfully, I must feed forward expectations about such things as the time required for my hand to make contact with the glass, the relative weight and solidity of the glass, the relative lack of attraction between the glass and the table, and so on. These expectations, which are part of the normal functioning of the cognitive system and are therefore not in awareness, regulate my reaching action, serving as parameters against which the results of my action are evaluated.

When I reach out to shake someone's hand, however, it can no longer be a case of acting only in terms of my own expectations. My action must now take into account my knowledge of the expectations that the other has concerning my action and, indeed, even my knowledge of the other's expectations about my expectations for my action. Interaction, in other words, to be successful, depends on a mutuality of expectation, or, on what is fundamentally intersubjectivity.

It would be a digression, at this point, to enter into an extended discussion of the nature of intersubjectivity. However, I should briefly mention that, metatheoretically, psychology must *not*, I believe, start from the typical (and Piagetian) assumption that babies are born into the world preadapted for action on objects and become socialized by learning how to interact with that special category of strangely variable and unpredictable objects called people. Instead, it should take the radically different assumption that babies are born into the world with a cognitive system preadapted to mutuality of expectation, to intersubjectivity, and to interaction, and that babies must learn that actions on objects are a special case in which one need not worry about what the objects think.

One final point needs to be made about action. In the performance of certain actions on objects and interactions with people, such as painting a house, shopping at the grocery store, or opening a door for someone loaded down with packages, action is frequently accompanied by semiotic activity that leads to the symbolic representation of an end state for the action or interaction (a painted house, a well-stocked larder, a grateful person). Although it is a natural temptation to regard this symbolic end-state representation (of which we are aware) as the goal regulating our action, according to this account, that would be seriously in error.

Regulation of action is a nonconscious, cognitive process. Goals and expectations are generated without awareness as the cognitive system functions. Most actions and interactions, such as dipping the brush into the paint, turning the key in the ignition, or returning the smile of the grateful person, are not accompanied by a symbolic end-state representation, yet they are as much under the regulatory control of expectations as those actions that are so accompanied.

The force of this claim is that the motivational structure of action is always inaccessible to awareness. Even when we think we are aware of the goals toward which we act or interact, what we are aware of is not our own motivational structure, buried as it is in the cognitive unconscious to which we have no privileged access, but rather the product of our own semiotic activity, our symbolic discourse about or our theory of our own action. That theory, like all theories, may or may not be adequate; frequently, as any psychotherapist will attest, it is not.

Although this proposal may sound radical, and in its implications it may be, it is one that many psychologists, of various theoretical leanings, have long implicitly accepted. If 16-year-old Johnny is out on Saturday afternoons in the fall throwing his body at the opposition on his high school football field and you ask him his goal, he will tell you he wants to win the game. If, on the other hand, you ask his friends in the stands why he is acting as he does, they will tell you he is trying to impress his girlfriend. Should you also inquire of his psychotherapist, she might reply that Johnny is acting out his anger. Is Johnny a privileged subject? I do not think so. His theory is one of a number of theories that might be held and that might or might not receive support from further samples of the psychological phenomena that are uniquely his.

Knowledge and Environment

Although both knowledge and environment have figured prominently in this discussion, they are complicated constructs, and much more could be said of them than I can say here. Nonetheless, I must draw one distinction concerning environment and one concerning knowledge before I return to metatheory.

Perhaps the most central distinction concerning environment is that between the physical and the social. This distinction rests on our inferences concerning the presence or absence in environmental objects and events of mental states—subjectivity. Although we have direct experience only of our own subjectivity, we seem irresistibly predisposed to attribute a subjectivity of their own to some objects, such as other people, and at least some animals in our environment. Such objects (or more properly *subjects*) and events involving those subjective objects constitute the social environment.

By contrast, there is a much larger class of objects and events to which we do not attribute subjectivity. These objects, such as chairs, and events, such as the rising of the sun, constitute the physical environment.

Knowledge, as it is used here, may be thought of as a structural mental code embodying information about the environment. Knowledge is both given in the human biological endowment and extracted from experience. With respect to knowledge so defined, one critical distinction must be drawn, that between knowledge structure and knowing process, that is, between mental structure and mental act. Although this, too, is a very complicated and theory-laden issue, at least one aspect of the issue directly relevant to the topic of this volume should be briefly discussed. From the metatheoretical standpoint being described here, experience, symbolic discourse, and action must, as I have indicated, be explained through an analysis of the interaction of mind and environment. Both mind and environment, in other words, are assumed to be active determinants of experience, symbolic discourse, and action.

On the mental side, this activity might be thought of as being constituted by at least two kinds of knowing processes or internal mental acts. One might be termed *constitutive* and the other *evaluative*. Both constitutive and evaluative mental processes consist in the referral of patterned information from the external and internal environment to underlying structural codes. In this process of referral, information is made meaningful, experience is constructed, and objects and events are identified or recognized for what they are and discriminated from other objects or events. The *objective* meaning of experience (experiencing a cup, e.g., as a china container with a handle) is given by constitutive mental acts organized in relation to knowledge about objects and events as they exist in independence of the knower.

Evaluative mental acts are also conceived as processes in which patterned stimulation provided by the environment is referred to underlying structural codes. However, evaluative processes refer this information not to concepts of objects and events in themselves, but to concepts of objects and events as they generally relate to the self, to its existence, its integrity, its social status, its commitments, and so forth.

Concepts of this sort might be termed *values*. Evaluation processes refer environmental information to value structures and yield not the identification or recognition of the object or event for what it is, but its meaning *for me*. Evaluation is, in other words, a process of appraisal of the potential of an object or event to bring me pleasure, to satisfy my needs, to insult me, to prove me wrong, to threaten me with harm, or even to kill me. Evaluation processes might be presumed to yield what is sometimes called the *subjective* meaning of experience (experiencing a cup, e.g., as something that will enable me to slake my thirst).

CO-CONSTRUCTIVE METATHEORY: PART 2

With that lengthy clarification and elaboration complete, I return to the principles of metatheory that seem to me to be necessarily implicated in co-constructive, intersubjective, realist theories:

10. Scientific psychology must assume the existence of mental events (e.g., conscious experience; purposeful action; symbolic discourse; mental acts of interpretation, symbol generation, and the organization of action). Mental events are presumed to be concomitant with a very special subset of physical events of a high order of biological complexity

(i.e., neurochemical events) and to exist with those events in a unitary psychophysical process.

11. Psychology, as a science, must also assume an organized atomic–molecular physical reality existing in independence of any observer and characterized by roughly the sort of ecological properties assumed by Gibson (1966, 1979).

12. Taken together, Principles 10 and 11 also imply assumption of a social reality existing in independence of any given observer and concomitant with those physical processes that are accompanied by the mental events of social others, taken as individuals, in interaction with one another or with the observer.

13. So central is the fact of human sociality that psychology must reject the typical assumption that babies are born into the world preadapted for action on objects and become socialized by learning how to interact with people. Instead, psychology should begin from the assumption that babies are born into the world with a cognitive system preadapted to mutuality of expectation, to intersubjectivity, and to interaction, and must learn that actions on objects are a special case.

14. Because psychological phenomena are presumed to be *co-organized* in relation to subphenomenal structures and processes of the mind and physical–social world, *regulated* by personal and intersubjectively held goals and expectations, *orderly* (in the sense that there are sequential dependencies between mental events as there are between physical events), and *concomitant with highly complex physicochemical events in the brain and nervous system,* they are in principle explicable. However, explanation is clearly exceedingly complicated, involving specification of organizing principles, goals and expectations, immediately prior events, and neuropsychological relationships.[2] Explicability is not, in this sense, based on a simplistic, rigidly mechanistic determinism, and psychological phenomena (mental events) are no more reducible to neurochemical events than neurochemical events are to psychological phenomena.

ISSUES IN THE NATURE AND FUNCTION OF METATHEORY IN PSYCHOLOGY

I conclude this chapter by raising three issues of metatheory that seem to me to be pressing. First, as should be evident from the bulk of this discussion, I am fully committed to the importance of metatheoretical analysis in science in general and in psychology in particular. Even before Hanson (1958) and Kuhn (1962), the justificationist program of logical positivism, and its twin ideals of unified science and value-free inquiry, was in trouble.

Although Kuhn's was a complex and, in many ways, appropriate message, especially for psychologists (who have always had a tendency to be overawed by the rigor of physics), the relativistic implications of his claim that the only standards of scientific truth are those criteria generated by the scientific community were seized upon by those who wished to sound the death knell for scientific realism. Indeed, among psychologists, forced as we are to accept the fact that the human being is quintessentially a maker of meaning, relativism has been read by some as implying that psychological theory can at most aspire to be good narrative text, theorizing a form of literary criticism.

Surely, however, there must be a middle-of-the-road view. It must be possible to hold to a realist ontology—to our cherished belief that the aim of science is to discover truth (although perhaps not absolute truth) about a nature that exists in independence of the perceiving scientist, that scientific theories contain empirically testable propositions, and that the truth value of any proposition depends at least in part upon its match with reality—while accepting the notion that facts are theory laden, that theories are metatheory laden, that values play a role in science, and that the "facts" of reality are accessible only by inference from experience, never as preinterpreted data.

The co-constructive and (although I haven't stressed it) developmental metatheory that I have outlined is an attempt to fashion such a middle-ground view. Whether and to what extent such an attempt can be successful is difficult to say. However, I believe that developmental psychologists, for whom the notion of cognitive development as a progressive approximation to more adequate knowledge, to deeper penetration of the mysteries of a real self and a real environment, are in an especially good position to make the attempt.

Second, if metatheory does play the critical role in scientific inquiry that we have assigned it, it follows directly that we need a better understanding of how that role is played, that is, we need more sophisticated logical and psychological analyses of the nature and function of metatheory. Although the standard definitional formulation that "metatheoretical assumptions are substantive presuppositions (e.g., logical, epistemological, ontological, normative, etc.) that are part of the shared background of scientific activity . . ." (Kurtines, Alvarez, & Azmitia, 1990, p. 283) is fine at a descriptive level, it tells us little about either the logical relations between metatheory and theory or the psychological relations between metatheorizing and theorizing.

Do observations that confirm theories also confirm the metatheories from within which the theories have been constructed? Can metatheoretical discourse that clarifies the assumptive base of theory also resolve metatheoretical differences? If metatheory is really the terminus of a conceptual system, the fons et origo from which theories derive their coherence, then on what ground could metatheoretical differences be resolved? If they are not logically resolvable, something about the theories that they engender and the match between those theories and reality must allow us to make a rational choice between metatheories, or we are once again perilously close to the morass of relativism.

Third, in attempting to understand how metatheory plays a role in scientific inquiry, we must first come to grips with the question of metatheoretical domain specificity. Are all the domains of science equally sensitive to metatheory? If the answer is yes, it may suggest a new and radically different (dare I suggest psychological?) route to a unitary conception of science as a human cognitive enterprise. If, however, the answer is no, then how can principled distinctions be drawn between those sciences that are more and those that are less metatheory sensitive?

Perhaps this is simply another way of posing the century-old question of what, in principle, differentiates the human from the natural sciences? If so, we know that historically there have been at least two very different candidates for this honor. One, which dates back at least to Dilthey (1894/1977), is that theoretical discourse in the human, but not in the natural, sciences is concerned with phenomena of meaning and symbolization, the critical distinction, therefore, being that between the natural and the semiotic sciences.

The second, the origins of which I do not know, is that theoretical discourse in the human, but not the natural, sciences is concerned with phenomena of intersubjectivity. The subject matter of a science such as psychology, for example, is exactly that—subject matter. The objects of study in psychology are not objects, as they are in physics, but are knowing, thinking, feeling subjects who are busily studying the psychologist as the psychologist studies them. Although physicists may have to put up with the fact that the behavior of subatomic particles varies as a function of their being observed, they have not yet had to wonder whether subatomic particles are looking back. In this case, the proper distinction is between the social and the natural sciences.

Given what I have said in the first part of this chapter, it should come as no surprise that I am inclined to accept both these candidates as a basis for principled distinctions among the sciences. However, to them, I would add a third and perhaps more fundamental candidate. Although the natural scientists can make do with one overarching system of hypothetical constructs—in this case coding the entities and processes of the physical atomic molecular world—human scientists and especially psychologists have no such luxury.

The failure of turn-of-the-century introspectionism, and to a certain extent Piaget's later constructivism, makes plain that theories of the mind, taken by themselves, simply will not do. Psychologists are in the unenviable position of needing both a theory of the mind and a theory of the environment and, if you will, a theory of how those respective structures interact in the co-construction of psychological phenomena. Truly, as Bergson is said to have said, "in comparison to understanding child's play, understanding the atom is child's play."

NOTES

1. I hold this conviction despite the actual (Vygotsky, 1960; Piaget, 1960) or probable disavowal of such complementarity by the theorists concerned.
2. It may be worthwhile to reinforce a point made by N. R. Hanson (1958), namely, that the term *explanation*, when it is used as it is being used here, is in no way simply synonymous with the specification of cause. In distinguishing explanation and cause, Hanson used the example of a billiard ball rolling down an inclined plane, striking a second billiard ball, and setting it in motion. He contrasted a reasonable response to the question, "What caused the second billiard ball to move?" (the first billiard ball struck it) with a reasonable response to the question, "How can we explain the movement of the second billiard ball?" The answer to the latter question involves specification of the angle of the inclined plane, the force of gravity, the relative mass of the billiard balls, and so forth. Although Newton's theory of motion in an important sense enters the explanation of the movement of the second billiard ball, it cannot properly be said to have *caused* it.

REFERENCES

Dilthey, W. (1977). Ideen uber eine beschreibende und zergliedernde Psychologie. Translated in W. Dilthey, *Descriptive psychology and historical understanding.* Hague: Nijhoff. (Original work published 1894).

Freud, S. (1920). *General introduction to psychoanalysis.* New York: Liveright.

Gibson, J. J. (1966). *The senses considered as perceptual systems.* Boston: Houghton-Mifflin.

Gibson, J. J. (1979). *The ecological approach to visual perception.* Boston: Houghton-Mifflin.

Hanson, N. R. (1958). *Patterns of discovery.* Cambridge, England: Cambridge University Press.

Hempel, C. (1966). *Philosophy of natural science.* Englewood Cliffs, NJ: Prentice-Hall.

Herbart, J. F. (1824). *Psychologie als Wissenschaft.* Königsberg, Germany: Unzer.

Kuhn, T. (1962). *The structure of scientific revolutions.* Chicago: University of Chicago Press.

Kurtines, W. M., Alvarez, M., & Azmitia, M. (1990). Science and morality: The role of values in science and the scientific study of moral phenomena. *Psychological Bulletin, 107,* 283–295.

Lamb, S., & Wozniak, R. H. (1990). Developmental co-construction: Metatheory in search of method. *Contemporary Psychology, 35,* 853–854.

Piaget, J. (1950). *The psychology of intelligence.* New York: Harcourt, Brace.

Reed, E. S. (in press). The intention to use a specific affordance: A conceptual framework for psychology. In R. H. Wozniak & K. Fischer (Eds.), *Thinking in context: The effects of specific environments.* Hillsdale, NJ: Erlbaum.

Tolman, E. C. (1932). *Purposive behavior in animals and men.* New York: Century.

Vygotsky, L. S. (1956). *Izbrannye psikhologicheskie issledovaniia* [Selected psychological investigations]. Moscow: RSFSR Akademiia pedagogicheskii nauk.

Vygotsky, L. S. (1978). *Mind in society.* Cambridge, MA: Harvard University Press.

Wozniak, R. H. (1975a). Dialecticism and structuralism: The philosophical foundations of Soviet psychology and Piagetian cognitive developmental theory. In K. F. Riegel & G. Rosenwald (Eds.), *Structure and transformation: Developmental and historical aspects* (pp. 25–45). New York: Wiley.

Wozniak, R. H. (1975b). A dialectical paradigm for psychological research: Implications drawn from the history of psychology in the Soviet Union. *Human Development, 18,* 18–34.

Wozniak, R. H. (1981). The future of constructivist psychology: Reflections on Piaget. *Teachers College Record, 83,* 197–199.

Wozniak, R. H. (1982). Metaphysics and science, reason and reality: The intellectual origins of genetic epistemology. In J. Broughton & D. J. Freeman-Moir (Eds.), *The cognitive developmental psychology of James Mark Baldwin: Current theory and research in genetic epistemology* (pp. 13–45). Norwood, NJ: Ablex.

Wozniak, R. H. (1983a). Lev Semonovich Vygotsky (1896–1934). *History of Psychology Newsletter, 15*(3), 49–55.

Wozniak, R. H. (1983b). Is a genetic epistemology of psychology possible? *Cahiers de la Fondation Archives Jean Piaget, 4,* 323–347.

Wozniak, R. H. (1985). Notes toward a co-constructive theory of the emotion/cognition relationship. In D. Bearison & H. Zimiles (Eds.), *Thought and emotion: Developmental issues* (pp. 39–64). Hillsdale, NJ: Erlbaum.

Wozniak, R. H. (1988). Developmental method, zones of development, and theories of the environment. In L. S. Liben (Ed.), *Development and learning: Conflict or congruence* (pp. 225–235). Hillsdale, NJ: Erlbaum.

Chapter 5 ■

Hermeneutics and Developmental Psychology: Toward an Ethic of Interpretation ■

MARK B. TAPPAN
Colby College

LYN MIKEL BROWN
Colby College

> An ethic of reading can begin only when we are willing to accept some readings as better than others and to say why this is so and to accept some texts as better than others and say why this is so. . . . Some judgments . . . require us to connect what is represented in the text with what we see in the world—in a manner that is ethical because it is political and political because it is ethical. This is a crucial point. The notion of textuality reminds us that we do nothing in isolation from others. We are always connected, woven together, textualized—and therefore politicized. This is why there can be no ethics of reading that is free of political concerns.

> > Robert Scholes
> > *Protocols of Reading*

It may seem somewhat incongruous to begin a chapter in a volume on the role of values in psychology and human development with an epigraph from the recent work of a well-known literary critic and theorist.

Preparation of this chapter was supported by grants from the Lilly Endowment, the Cleveland Foundation, the George Gund Foundation, and the Spencer Foundation.

105

We argue, however, that the problems we face as developmental psychologists working in the final decade of the twentieth century have problems similar to those that literary critics and theorists have been struggling with, and writing about, for many years. Foremost among these is the task of developing what we call an ethic of interpretation (what Scholes (1989) called an "ethic of reading")—an ethic that clearly articulates the moral and political values, biases, and assumptions that inform and guide the process of interpretation. As developmental psychologists, we have traditionally failed to address the problem of values, because we have tried to adopt and conform to positivist assumptions about the nature of scientific inquiry. However, in the postpositivist or postmodern age in which we now live, we have come to see not only that all knowledge is value laden (see Kurtines, Alvarez, & Azmitia, 1990; Kurtines, Azmitia, & Alvarez, Chapter 1, this volume; Meacham, Chapter 3, this volume), but that hermeneutics (i.e., the art and practice of interpretation) plays an intrinsic and inescapable role in all our efforts to understand human action and experience (see Packer, Chapter 2, this volume; Packer & Addison, 1989; Rabinow & Sullivan, 1979; Tappan, 1990; Tappan & Brown, 1989a; Taylor, 1979).

In this chapter, we are interested in exploring the role that values play in an approach to the study of human development that has an explicitly interpretive component—what we call a hermeneutic developmental psychology. Such an exploration is particularly appropriate in the case of developmental psychology because, as Bernard Kaplan (1967, 1983, 1986) has argued, the concept of development is fundamentally and inescapably value laden. It is, in other words, a *prescriptive* concept, used to refer to an *ideal progression* toward some specified goal, endpoint, or *telos* that has been imbued with value, not a *descriptive* concept, used to chart *all* changes that occur over time—for example, the ontogenetic changes that occur during the life span of a particular individual or organism: "Development, as distinct from change, has been and ought to be an axiological and normative notion. It has been, and ought to be, comprehended as 'movement toward perfection,' 'movement toward liberation,' 'movement toward the Good or God'" (Kaplan, 1983, p. 204). As a result, any *developmental interpretation* must necessarily be imbued with the ethical and political values, biases, and assumptions of the interpreter (see also Bruner, 1986; Kagan, 1984; Kessen, 1983; White, 1983).

Consequently, we argue that the process of developmental interpretation entails making what Scholes (1989) called judgments that "some texts are better than others." With his or her developmental telos in mind, the developmental psychologist makes a judgment that one "text"—capturing an aspect of the lived experience of a particular child, adolescent, or adult—is more or less advanced, mature, or developed than another.* Thus, as Kaplan (1983) suggested, while developmentalists often claim that their work entails simply "read[ing] off from the facts of history and biography a developmental progression in time . . . thereby dispens[ing] with transcendent values and norms, nonderivable from data or facts," in reality, any and all developmental interpretation is necessarily value driven: "Where individuals have claimed to find or discover values and norms in facts of history or biography, it is only because they have unwittingly sneaked them into their analyses" (p. 205). One of our goals in this chapter is to explore, in some detail, this inescapable aspect of developmental inquiry.

Another goal is to examine the process by which interpreters make the companion judgment that "some readings (or interpretations) are better than others." Historically, such concerns have been considered under the rubric of "validity": One interpretation is said to be more valid than another because it more accurately corresponds to, reflects, or captures the "reality" or "truth" of a particular aspect of human experience (e.g., a measure of intelligence, an assessment of psychopathology, a test of cognitive development). Although the problem of validity has occupied a long-standing position at the center of traditional thinking about psychological theory and research, it is also an issue of significant concern and controversy within contemporary hermeneutics. From the hermeneutic perspective, this problem is typically framed in terms of "validity in interpretation" (or "interpretive validity"), and it refers to concerns about finding and agreeing on standards against which to evaluate interpretive accounts. As such, contemporary thinking about the problem of interpretive validity also focuses on concerns about the degree to which interpretations reflect the ethical and political values, biases, and assumptions of interpreters (see Packer & Addison, 1989).

Our aim in this chapter is to explore, from these two angles, the role of values in the process of interpretation, with a specific focus on the emerging relationship between hermeneutics and developmental psychology. We consider the role of values in making *developmental* judgments that some texts

---

* A note on our use of the term *text* here and elsewhere in this chapter. In contemporary hermeneutic and literary theory, a text is essentially a work of literature, for example, a poem, a play, or a novel. One of the central arguments of hermeneutic approaches to social science, however, is that *all* human action and symbolization can best be understood as texts (or text-analogues) (see Dilthey, 1900/1976; Gergen, 1988; Honey, 1987; MacIntyre, 1981; Packer, 1985a, 1987; Ricoeur, 1979; Taylor, 1979). In recent interpretive efforts in developmental psychology, such texts have taken the form of video recordings of human social interaction (Packer, 1983, 1985b, 1987) and written transcripts of open-ended semiclinical interviews (Brown, Debold, Tappan, & Gilligan, 1991; Brown, Tappan, Gilligan, Miller, & Argyris, 1989; Gilligan, 1982; Gilligan & Attanucci, 1988; Kohlberg, 1984; Selman, Schultz, Caplan, & Schantz, 1989; Shweder & Much, 1987; Tappan, 1989, 1990; Tappan & Brown, 1989b).

are better than others, as well as the role of values in making *validity* judgments that some interpretations are better than others. Ultimately, however, we seek an ethic of interpretation that will enable us not only to make such judgments, but to make them without falling into the objectivism–relativism trap (see Bernstein, 1983). Although avoiding either pole of this traditionally messy and problematic dialectic will not be an easy task, we argue that finding an ethic that addresses the tension between them is crucial to the formulation of a full-fledged hermeneutic developmental psychology.

Two alternative positions within contemporary hermeneutic and literary theory provide the initial heuristic framework for our exploration of these issues in this chapter. The first position, exemplified by the work of E. D. Hirsch (1967, 1978), focuses squarely on the problem of "validity in interpretation." It claims that a text has one and only one determinant meaning (the author's "intended" meaning); hence, the only legitimate aim of interpretation is to attain an accurate and valid understanding of that "true" meaning. According to this view, therefore, final authority for the legitimacy of any and all interpretations rests with the text, and the values of the interpreter must not influence or interfere with his or her quest for a valid interpretation of that text.

The second position, exemplified by the work of Stanley Fish (1980, 1987), focuses on the role and authority of "interpretive communities" in determining what count as legitimate and valid interpretations of a given text. This position, in contrast to the first, holds that a text does not have one and only one true meaning, but rather that the interpreter's personal, relational, and social context—including specific ethical and political values—necessarily shapes and influences his or her interpretation of that text. According to this view, therefore, the way in which an interpreter interprets and understands a given text is fundamentally a function of the interpretive community of which he or she is a member—a community constituted around a shared set of values, biases, assumptions, and commitments.

These two positions are discussed in the first two sections of this chapter. In the final section, we outline our own ethic of interpretation, in response to the positions articulated by Hirsch and Fish and in light of our ongoing research on social, moral, and personality development. We argue, ultimately, that the process of interpretation is dialectical, in which the impulse to seek and *understand* the true or intended meaning of a text always stands in tension with the impulse to *construct* the meaning of a text, informed by the values, biases, and assumptions of the interpreter and his or her interpretive community. We also suggest that any ethic of interpretation must necessarily address the twin problems of *authority* and *power*, because, in the postmodern world in which we live, it is questions regarding authority and power in interpretation and the legitimation of knowledge that are the most pressing (see Feyerabend, 1975; Lawson, 1985; Lyotard, 1984; Steiner, 1971): On whose (or by what) authority can an interpreter claim legitimacy for his or her interpretations? Who, in fact, has the power to decide what counts as a legitimate interpretation? Who knows best what a particular human experience really means?

We believe that the most helpful response to such questions entails acknowledging that the interpreter and the text must share interpretive authority and power. In our view, therefore, the process of interpretation is fundamentally a *relational* activity, in which the interpreter and the text that he or she is reading/interpreting are, as Scholes (1989) suggested, "connected," "woven together," and thus exist in the context of a relationship that has both interpersonal and intertextual dimensions. As such, we suggest that an ethic of *care* or *responsiveness* provides a foundation upon which to construct a postpositivist, postmodern, hermeneutic developmental psychology that not only enables judgments about different texts and about different interpretations, but also gives rise to genuine understanding.

VALIDITY IN INTERPRETATION

The title of this section self-consciously evokes the title of Hirsch's (1967) influential volume, *Validity in Interpretation*, "the first full-dress treatise in general hermeneutics written in English" (Palmer, 1969, p. 60). Hirsch's work has attracted widespread attention because it represents perhaps the most sustained attempt in contemporary hermeneutic theory to achieve Wilhelm Dilthey's (1900/1976) dream of an "objectively valid interpretation." The problem of validity, as we have suggested above, is not only a key issue in traditional conceptions of psychological research and theory; it is also a problem that must be addressed in any elaboration of a hermeneutic developmental psychology. Hence, we turn to Hirsch's work in hopes of finding insight vis-à-vis this problem, in particular, as well as insight vis-à-vis the role of values in developmental interpretation, in general.

Hirsch (1967) staked his argument on the following assertion, which clearly grants legitimacy only to interpretations that can achieve "validity" (in his terms): If an interpretive discipline is to make any lasting contribution to human knowledge, it must be able to demonstrate that the understanding it offers, gained via hermeneutic techniques, is valid. "The activity of interpretation," Hirsch therefore argued, "can lay claim to intellectual respectability only if its results can lay claim to validity" (p. 164).

The key to Hirsch's view of how an objectively valid interpretation of a particular text can be achieved is to distinguish between the *meaning* of that text and its *significance*. Hirsch (1967) claimed that, by and large, in the history and practice of hermeneutics, this distinction has been obscured, leading to great difficulty in assessing the validity of any and all interpretations:

> *Meaning* is that which is represented by a text; it is what the author meant by his use of a particular sign sequence; it is what the signs represent. *Significance,* on the other hand, names a relationship between that meaning and a person, or a conception, or a situation, or indeed, anything imaginable. Authors, who like everyone else change their attitudes, feelings, opinions, and value criteria in the course of time will obviously in the course of time tend to view their own work in different contexts. Clearly what changes for them is not the meaning of the work, but rather their relationship to that meaning [i.e., their view of its significance]. Significance always implies a relationship, and one constant, unchanging pole of that relationship is what the text *means*. Failure to consider this simple and essential distinction has been the source of enormous confusion in hermeneutic theory. (p. 8)

The "enormous confusion" that Hirsch had in mind stems from the assumption (which he attempted to refute) that a text can be interpreted in different ways by different readers—an assumption that implies that a text does not have one meaning, but rather that it can have many different meanings. Ultimately, according to Hirsch, this assumption is not only confused, but it is dangerous, because it can lead to subjectivism, relativism, and even moral chaos—if the authority of the text is not acknowledged and upheld (see Crosman, 1980).

Hirsch's purpose in distinguishing between meaning and significance was to challenge those who claim that any number of different and even competing interpretations of a particular text are valid because the meaning of any text necessarily changes when the context (i.e., history, culture, ideology, personality) in which it is read changes (see, e.g., Gadamer, 1975). Hirsch argued that what changes with context is not the text's *meaning,* but its *significance:* There is one and only one *true* meaning of a text; it is stable and determined by the author. There are, however, numerous possible views of the significance of a text; they are indeterminant and depend on the values, biases, assumptions, and context of the interpreter. Thus, Hirsch offered the term *understanding* (following Dilthey's use of the term *verstehen*) to refer to the process by which an interpreter gains access to the author's meaning, and the term *judgment* to refer to the process by which an interpreter determines the significance of a particular text:

> By "understanding" . . . I mean a perception or construction of the author's verbal meaning, nothing more, nothing less. The significance of that meaning, its relation to ourselves, to history, to the author's personality, even to the author's other words can be something equally objective and is frequently

even more important. What shall we call this function by which we perceive significance?

The obvious choice is "judgment": one understands meaning; one judges significance. In the first instance, one submits to another—literally, one stands under him. In the second, one acts independently—by one's own authority—like a judge. (p. 143)

Hirsch's primary concern, then, was how a valid interpretation (i.e., understanding) of an author's intended meaning can be achieved; validity, as such, is not a concern with respect to "judgment." His fundamental claim was that, for a valid understanding to be achieved, there must be a norm or standard against which to assess the validity of any particular interpretation. That norm, he argued, is provided exclusively by the author himself:

Validity requires a norm—a meaning that is stable and determinate no matter how broad its range of implication and application. A stable and determinate meaning requires an author's determining will. . . . All valid interpretation of every sort is [therefore] founded on a re-cognition of what an author meant. (p. 126)

Thus, Hirsch's project was ultimately devoted to exploring how the interpreter can accurately and validly accomplish such "re-cognitive" interpretation. The method of "verification" that Hirsch proposed to achieve such interpretations, although too complex to be presented here, nevertheless rests on his central point that there is only one true meaning of a particular text—the original author's intended meaning. The interpreter's task, therefore, is to arrive at an accurate and valid understanding of that meaning. This is done by reconstructing the author's own subjective stance vis-à-vis the text in question: "Even though the process of verification is highly complex and difficult, the ultimate verificative principle is very simple—the imaginative reconstruction of the speaking subject" (p. 242).

At this point, we turn to the implications of Hirsch's work for our consideration of the role of values in a hermeneutic developmental psychology. Our reflections hinge on acknowledging, again, the fundamentally value-laden nature of any developmental inquiry. This view, that any developmental analysis necessarily entails making judgments informed by certain a priori ethical and political value assumptions and presuppositions, is quite similar, we would argue, to Hirsch's view of how the significance of a given text is determined. If a literary text and an interview text from a developmental study are essentially isomorphic with respect to the process of interpretation, then, from Hirsch's perspective, the aim of a *developmental* analysis and interpretation of a given text is not to explicate its meaning, but to determine its significance. In other words, because any developmental analysis is guided by a set of ethical and political value assumptions and presuppositions on the part of the researcher, it is clear that the aim of such an interpretation is, in Hirsch's terms, not understanding, but judgment—judgment against the standard provided by those values that determine what counts as developmental progress, and what does not. This is not to say that such a focus on significance and judgment is misguided; Hirsch himself believed that the significance of a text is often as important as its meaning. It is, however, to consider Hirsch's claim that such a process of judging the significance of a text is not true hermeneutics because it does not focus on achieving a valid interpretation (i.e., understanding) of the author's intended meaning.

We argue, therefore, that Hirsch's work on validity in interpretation ultimately calls into question the possibility of ever achieving a genuine hermeneutic developmental psychology. The point of Hirsch's distinction between meaning and significance was to focus attention on the proper focus of hermeneutics: understanding meaning. It was also to offer a way to think about how an objectively valid understanding of that meaning can be achieved—by "re-cognizing" the author's intended meaning—thereby avoiding the subjectivism, relativism, and anarchy that can result from different readings of the same text informed by different contexts, values, and points of view. If, however, the proper aim of a *developmental* analysis and interpretation is, by definition, to make judgments based on certain value assumptions about what constitutes progress, then it would seem, again, that such a focus is more on judging significance than on understanding meaning. As a result, although making such value-laden judgments of developmental significance may well be an important enterprise, from Hirsch's point of view it must not be confused with true hermeneutics.

Consequently, Hirsch would claim that developmental psychologists interested in hermeneutics should abandon their "developmental" interests, at least initially, and turn instead to interpreting and understanding the true meaning of the texts with which they work. This will require striving to achieve validity in interpretation using the kinds of methods, such as the process of verification, that Hirsch outlined; only when such an understanding of meaning is achieved can a focus on developmental significance begin. In other words, Hirsch's view of the relationship between meaning and significance suggests at the least a distinct two-step process: a primary focus on meaning followed by a secondary focus on significance. Again, this is because "significance always implies a relationship, and one constant, unchanging pole of that relationship is what the text *means*" (p. 8).

In sum, then, Hirsch's distinction between meaning and significance suggests that the emerging relationship between hermeneutics and developmental psychology is, at worst, incompatible, and, at best, problematic. It calls for a radical distinction between a hermeneutic focus on the meaning of a particular text and a developmental focus on the significance of that text, although it assumes that an objectively valid understanding of meaning is the unchanging foundation upon which various judgments of developmental significance must rest. It therefore grants primary authority to the text, and gives the interpreter very little leeway in terms of his or her interpretations, yet at the same time it assumes a kind of radically relativistic plurality of possible judgments of significance. As such, from Hirsch's point of view, an interpreter *can* make the judgment that some interpretations are better (i.e., more valid) than others, but he or she *cannot* make the judgment that some texts are better (i.e., more developed) than others.

In the last analysis, therefore, although Hirsch's work provides an interesting perspective on the ways in which judgments about interpretive validity might be made, we would argue that it does not provide a satisfactory foundation upon which to forge a relationship between hermeneutics and developmental psychology. This is primarily because, in radically distinguishing meaning from value, Hirsch does not allow for the kind of value-driven developmental interpretation that, as we have suggested above, is central to a hermeneutic developmental psychology.

THE AUTHORITY OF INTERPRETIVE COMMUNITIES

The title of this section again self-consciously evokes the title of an important book—in this case, the subtitle of Fish's (1980) volume, *Is There a Text in This Class?* It also captures the essence of Fish's project: Whereas Hirsch was concerned with validity in interpretation and meaning in their pure or ideal forms, Fish focused on the role and authority of what he called *interpretive communities* in constructing what count as legitimate and valid interpretations in the real world in which we live. Consequently, Fish's work not only challenges Hirsch's in fundamental ways, but it also provides a quite different perspective on the role that values play in the process of interpretation.

We address two central aspects of Fish's work. The first is his view on the determinacy of meaning. Recall that Hirsch's view is essentially a *foundational* view: because there is one and only one true meaning of a text, and it is determined by the author's original intent in producing that text, the author is granted sole and final authority in determining the meaning of his or her text. In contrast, Fish's *antifoundational* view is that there is no such thing as a fixed, stable, determinant meaning of a text that serves once and for all as the foundation or standard against which all "valid" interpretations of that text are to be compared and evaluated. Texts are inherently unstable and determinate meanings are unavailable because questions of fact, truth, accuracy, and validity cannot be answered by appealing to the authority of a fixed reality, standard, or value that somehow stands outside the contextual influences of history, culture, and personality:

> Rather, anti-foundationalism asserts, all of these matters are intelligible and debatable only within the precincts of the contexts or situations or paradigms or communities that give them their local and changeable shape. It is not just that anti-foundationalism replaces the components of the foundationalist world-picture with other components; instead it denies to those components the stability and independence and even the identity that is so necessary if they are to be thought of as grounds or anchors. Entities like the world, language, and the self can still be named; and value judgments having to do with validity, factuality, accuracy, and propriety can still be made; but in every case, these entities and values, along with the procedures by which they are identified and marshalled, will be inextricable from the social and historical circumstances in which they do their work. (Fish, 1987, pp. 67–68)

Although Fish's antifoundational attack on the view that textual meanings are fixed and determinant might be taken to entail, as Hirsch and the foundationalists fear, a radically relativistic and anarchic view of the process of interpretation, that is not the case. Rather, Fish made the paradoxical postmodern argument that although relativism is a position that can be entertained and contemplated, it is not a position that can, in fact, be *occupied*. This is not only because the claim that "all truths are relative" reflexively negates itself (see Lawson, 1985), but also because:

> no one can achieve the distance from his own beliefs and assumptions which would result in their being no more authoritative *for him* than the beliefs and assumptions held by others, or, for that matter, the beliefs and assumptions he himself used to hold. (Fish, 1980, p. 319)

Fish's attempt to stake out a position that claimed neither that meanings are determined by fixed and stable texts nor that meanings are produced by relativistic and/or solipsistic readers, led him, ultimately, to the core of his project: exploring the role and authority of interpretive communities. This is the second aspect of his work that we want to explore in some detail.

Fish began by making what might be called a radically constructivist assumption about how any given text is understood. Rather than focusing on what the text "means," Fish focused on how the reader or interpreter "responds" to that text, that is, the way in which the reader produces his or her understanding of the meaning of that text (see also Culler, 1982; Iser, 1978; Suleiman & Crosman, 1980; Tompkins, 1980). "In this formulation," therefore, "the reader's response is not *to* the meaning; it *is* the meaning, or at least the medium in which . . . the meaning comes into being" (Fish, 1980, p. 3). In other words, although skilled reading and/or interpretation is usually thought to entail discerning something that is already there, *in* the text from the start, according to Fish, skilled reading and/or interpretation is a matter of knowing how to *produce* what can thereafter be said to "be there": "Interpretation is not the art of construing but the art of constructing. Interpreters do not decode [texts]; they make them" (p. 327).

How are such constructions of meaning shaped and determined? This is where the interpretive community comes into play. The assumption that meaning is made, not found, does not lead inexorably to subjectivity and relativism, Fish argued, because the means by which meaning is made are social and conventional, and therefore limited by the institution or community of which the interpreter is a part. There is no such thing as an isolated individual working alone, on his or her own, to interpret a text in some unique and idiosyncratic manner: "We do not do these things because we could not do them, because the mental operations we can perform are limited by the institutions in which we are *already* embedded" (p. 331). In other words, the interpretive community of which a particular reader or interpreter is a member is responsible, to a large extent, both for the shape of his or her interpretive activities—Fish called these "interpretive strategies"—and for the texts those activities and strategies produce.

Consequently, it is also the interpretive community that resolves the tension (so apparent in Hirsch's work) between objectivity and subjectivity. The self is not an independent entity, free to substitute its own meanings for the meanings that authors intended texts to have; rather, it is a social construct whose operations are delimited by the systems of intelligibility that inform it. As a result, the meanings it confers on texts are not its own, but have their source in the interpretive community (or communities) in which it is embedded:

> Moreover, these meanings will be neither subjective nor objective, at least in the terms assumed by those who argue within the traditional framework: they will not be objective because they will always have been the product of a point of view rather than having been simply "read off": and they will not be subjective because that point of view will always be social or institutional. Or by the same reasoning one could say that they are *both* subjective and objective: they are subjective because they inhere in a particular point of view and are therefore not universal; and they are objective because the point of view that delivers them is public and conventional rather than individual or unique. (Fish, 1980, pp. 335–336)

In sum, then, Fish claimed that the way in which any given text is interpreted and understood is essentially a function of the interpretive community of which the interpreter is a member, and in which, therefore, the activity of interpretation takes place. Furthermore, the meaning of that text depends exclusively on the interpretive strategy the interpreter employs, the choice of which is determined and regulated (both implicitly and explicitly) by the canons of authority and acceptability that govern his or her interpretive community (see also Schweickart, 1986).

In considering the implications of Fish's work for understanding the role of values in a hermeneutic developmental psychology, we want to address three central issues. The first is simply to acknowledge the degree to which Fish's approach is compatible with the view that developmental inquiry is a fundamentally value-laden enterprise. For Hirsch, there is an inherent tension between the objective, value-free attempt to understand the (valid) meaning of a text and the inherently subjective, value-laden efforts to judge its (developmental) significance, whereas for Fish, *any* interpretation is necessarily guided and informed by the values and assumptions shared jointly by the interpreter and his or her interpretive community. In fact, it is precisely because those values and assumptions are shared jointly by the members of an interpretive community that a different, but much more productive, dialectic is sustained: the dialectic between the subjectivity that inheres in the particular point of view adopted by the interpretive community and the objectivity that obtains because that point of view is publicly acknowledged by all the members of that community. In other words, far from being a problem to be overcome in the quest for a valid interpretation of the true meaning of a particular text, according to Fish, the values and assumptions that guide and inform a developmental analysis and interpretation of that text enable the interpreter to construct and to authorize his or her understanding of the meaning of that text in the first place.

This raises a second implication of Fish's work for a hermeneutic developmental psychology: the importance of explicitly acknowledging one's membership in a particular interpretive community. Given the assumption that the way in which any text is understood is a function of both the interpretive community of which the interpreter is a member and the interpretive strategies (authorized and sanctioned by that community) that he or she employs, it follows that for the public to understand a particular developmental interpretation, the public must be aware of the interpretive community with which the interpreter is affiliated. We would argue, however, that by and large such affiliations are not made as explicit as they should be. Moreover, making such affiliations explicit must entail more than the interpreter's simply acknowledging that he or she is, for example, a Freudian or a Piagetian. Rather, it must entail a public acknowledgment of the ethical and political assumptions and presuppositions around which the interpreter and his or her community are constituted, and which therefore guide and inform his or her interpretations. Only when such an acknowledgment is made, can the public fully understand and appreciate these interpretations (see also Meacham, Chapter 3, this volume).

This brings us to the third and final implication of Fish's work for the emerging relationship between hermeneutics and developmental psychology. This issue is by far the most controversial of the three, because it calls for a radical rethinking of traditional assumptions. Simply put, this is the view that the effort to attain interpretive agreement among members of an interpretive community must come to replace the quest for objectively valid interpretations as the primary aim of developmental inquiry. If a text does not have only one true meaning, but rather its meaning is a function of the interpretive community that constructs it, then achieving *agreement* within that community is the ultimate goal: "The fact of agreement, rather than being a proof of the stability of objects, is a testimony to the power of an interpretive community to constitute the objects upon which its members (also and simultaneously constituted) can then agree" (p. 338). This suggests, furthermore, that with respect to a hermeneutic developmental psychology, "reliability" (i.e., interpretive agreement) actually holds the key to "validity" (i.e., understanding what a text "means"). Although we have neither the time nor the space to explore fully the implications of this alternative and nontraditional view of the relationship between reliability and validity in developmental research (see also Uebersax, 1988), we want to highlight the degree to which Fish's work, if taken seriously as a guide to hermeneutic developmental inquiry, calls into question a number of widely held assumptions.

Although we are intrigued by the radical perspective that Fish's work offers to a hermeneutic developmental psychology, we are concerned that perhaps it goes too far in granting primary authority and power to the interpreter and his or her interpretive community in the process of interpretation, thereby taking authority and power away from the text itself. This concern is motivated, in large part, by the fact that, as developmental psychologists, we are not working with literary texts (poems, plays, novels) that can be interpreted in different ways by different interpreters from different interpretive communities without any real harm being done. Rather, we are working with the texts of people's lives, where different interpretations may have very real—and even potentially life-threatening—consequences.

For example, how do we interpret memories of childhood sexual abuse? Freud initially interpreted such memories as memories of actual events of physical and sexual abuse. Later, as his theory developed, he changed his interpretation, claiming that such memories did not reflect real events, but rather marked memories of childhood sexual fantasies that were manifestations of the child's libido. Recently, some have criticized this interpretive change on Freud's part, based on what we now know about the high incidence of childhood sexual abuse, in both Victorian and modern times (see Masson, 1985). However, the interpretive community guided by Freud's orthodox version of psychoanalysis continues to interpret such memories as reflecting fantasies, not reality, and patients are treated on the basis of that interpretation. But what if such memories are, in fact, memories of real incidents of abuse, and not memories of fantasies? Might patients who have experienced such real abuse be helped in a different way by a more "accurate" interpretation of their experience?

Our point in raising this example is not to engage in a complicated and highly charged debate about either the history of Freud's work or the current status of psychoanalysis. Rather, it is to raise a concern that, in the context of a hermeneutic developmental psychology, we must look for ways to acknowledge the authority and power of the texts of people's lives to guide and inform, to a certain extent, the interpretations we offer regarding those texts, while at the same time recognizing that the process of interpretation is, as Fish suggests, fundamentally a process of constructing a plausible and coherent account of a text, not construing an underlying "truth" (see also Spence, 1982). As such, while we are not arguing for a return to Hirsch's emphasis on the ultimate authority of texts to determine what count as valid interpretations, we believe that we must find a way to attenuate Fish's claim that the authority and power to determine the shape of interpretations rests solely with the interpreter and his or her interpretive community.

Thus, in the end, we believe that Fish's work provides a much more helpful foundation upon which to build a hermeneutic developmental psychology than does Hirsch's. We appreciate, in particular, the insight that Fish's work offers us with respect to the ways in which developmental interpreters can—and do—make the judgments that some texts are better than others (because some texts are of more interest or more value than others to a particular interpretive community). We are concerned, however, that his work does not provide an adequate basis upon which to make the equally crucial validity judgments that some interpretations are better than others.

TOWARD AN ETHIC OF INTERPRETATION

In this section, we sketch the broad outlines of our own ethic of interpretation, in response to the positions articulated by Hirsch and Fish, and in light of our ongoing efforts to study social, moral, and personality development in childhood, adolescence, and adulthood. As such, this ethic seeks not only to enable interpreters to make judgments about different texts and about different interpretations, but also to facilitate the interpreter's genuine understanding of the texts he or she interprets. Because our work on this ethic is still in its early stages, we offer the following sketch as a starting point for further discussion, debate, clarification, and elaboration.

We begin by acknowledging that the positions articulated by Hirsch and Fish both offer important insights with respect to the process of interpretation. There are two fundamental impulses in the interpretive process: an impulse to understand the "true" or "intended" meaning of a text, and an impulse to construct the meaning of a text, informed and guided by the values, biases, and assumptions of the interpreter and his or her interpretive community. Scholes (1989) captured these two impulses well in his discussion of the two "faces" of the process of reading:

> Reading has two faces, looks in two directions. One direction is back, toward the source and original context of the signs we are deciphering. The other direction is forward, based on the textual situation of the person doing the reading. It is because reading is almost always an affair of at least two times, two places, and two consciousnesses that interpretation is the endlessly fascinating, difficult, and important matter that it is. We see this most acutely in religious, legal, and literary reading, of course, but it is part of the fabric, of the structure, of reading as a human act, whatever is being read. Most theories of reading emphasize or privilege one face or the other of this two-faced activity. Reactionary theories [such as Hirsch's] emphasize the face that looks back. They tend to seek original truth or original intent as the master protocol of readings that will be as positive and unchanging as they can be. Radical theories [such as Fish's] emphasize the face that looks forward, insisting on the freedom and creativity of the reader along with the mutability of meanings in general. (p. 7)

Scholes thus argued that reading is fundamentally a *dialectical* activity in which the impulse to *understand* a text and the impulse to *connect* that text to the reader's life experiences stand in an ongoing dynamic tension, and it is this tension that drives the interpretive process. He also emphasized, however, that both of these impulses require critical and creative skills. That is, we should not assume that the impulse to understand the intended meaning of a text entails a kind of oppressive restriction of meaning. Rather, he suggested, seeking an original, intended meaning requires an enormous amount of creative and imaginative power—power that complements that which is required to connect that text with new meanings derived from the reader's own experience:

> Reading is always, at once, the effort to comprehend and the effort to incorporate. I must invent the author, invent his or her intentions, using the evidence I can find to stimulate my creative process. . . . I must also incorporate the text I am reading in my own textual repertory—a process that is not so much like putting a book on a shelf as like wiring a new component in an electronic system, where connections must be made in the right places. (Scholes, 1989, p. 9)

In the last analysis, therefore, the dialectic becomes, in fact, a version of the "hermeneutic circle" (Dilthey, 1900/1976): To understand a text, the reader must make a creative connection between that text and the context of his or her own life experiences, yet to make such a connection, the reader must understand that text in its own terms.

It seems to us that a similar dialectic exists in any genuine relationship between two human beings. That is, one dimension of any relationship is the impulse to understand the other in his or her own terms, to try to see the world through the other's eyes, and to appreciate the truth of the other's experiences. The other dimension is the impulse to bring one's own experiences into the relationship, to share one's own perspective, and thus to respond to the other by trying to connect one's own life to his or hers. Both impulses are powerful ones, and they are not always equally balanced in any given relationship; that is, some people spend more energy trying to understand and appreciate the experiences of others than they do offering and expressing their own thoughts and feelings, whereas others spend more energy seeking connections between their experiences and the experiences of others (and incorporating the experiences of others into their own) than they do simply trying to understand the experiences of others in their own terms. In the end, however, if a relationship is authentic, genuine, and mutual, both dimensions will be manifest, and a healthy tension between them will be maintained.

We argue, therefore, that the process of interpretation is essentially a *relational activity*. The activity of relationship entails both the impulse to comprehend and the impulse to respond and connect—impulses that are central to the process of interpretation. As such, seeing the process of interpretation as a relational activity allows us to appreciate the ways in which Hirsch and Fish both contribute to our understanding of this process. Attempting to understand the intended meaning of a text, in the author's own terms—although perhaps never fully possible—*is* a crucial dimension of the process of interpretation, just as attempting to understand the other in his or her own terms is important to any relationship. Bringing the values, biases, and assumptions shared by oneself and one's interpretive community to one's interpretation of a text is also an inescapable and undeniable aspect of the process of interpretation, just as connecting one's own experiences and perspective to those of another is also an important aspect of a genuine relationship.

In addition, the traditional either/or choice between objectivism and relativism is avoided when the process of interpretation is seen as a fundamentally relational activity. That is, when interpretation is understood as entailing a relationship, there is, *at one and the same time*, both an attempt to understand the "true" meaning of another's text/experience, and a realization that such understanding will necessarily be influenced by the interpreter's standpoint and perspective, informed by his or her own values, biases, and assumptions. Thus, in contrast both to those (e.g., Hirsch) who grant the final authority to determine meaning to the text, and those (e.g., Fish) who grant the final authority to determine meaning to the interpreter and his or her interpretive community, viewing interpretation as a relational activity suggests that the interpreter and the text must *share* authority and responsibility for shaping the meaning of a given text—just as in a genuine relationship, self and other share authority and responsibility for shaping the meaning of their experiences together.

At this point, let us briefly consider the ways in which this view of the process of interpretation as a relational activity might inform a hermeneutic developmental psychology, using our own ongoing research as a model. Such a discussion also involves outlining the ethic of interpretation that this perspective entails.

Central to our research efforts has been the development of a method for reading and interpreting interview narratives of real-life moral conflict and choice for the voice of the self speaking in the narrative, and for the relational voices/moral orientations of justice and care (see Gilligan, 1982). We have called this method *A Guide to Reading Narratives of Conflict and Choice for Self and Relational Voice*, referred to hereafter as "Reading Guide" (see Brown et al., 1988; Brown et al., 1991; Brown & Gilligan, 1990a; Brown et al., 1989; Gilligan, Brown, & Rogers, 1990). The Reading Guide highlights both care and justice as voices that speak about relationships, as well as the sense of tension people often convey in their stories of lived moral experience. In other words, it is a voice-sensitive method that attempts to record the complexity of narratives of conflict and choice, and attempts to capture the personal, relational, and cultural dimensions of psychic life.

Such a method, focusing as it does on the reading process and the creation of an interpretive account of a narrative, thus raises questions both about a reader's subjectivity and perspective, and about how a reader can understand the subjectivity and perspective of the person whose narrative he or she reads. Because these issues of subjectivity and perspective highlight the relationship between the reader and the text, we have come to see the Reading Guide as a relational method. The relational nature of this method is manifest most clearly in the first two of four readings that the Reading Guide outlines for any interview text: reading for the *story*, and reading for *self* (the third and fourth readings are reading for *care* and reading for *justice*, respectively).

In the first reading, for the story, the reader is asked explicitly both to understand the story as it was experienced by the narrator, and to attend to the text in light of his or her *own* knowledge and experience—that is, to be an active reader/listener, to acknowledge the interaction or relationship between his or her own subjectivity as a reader and the text. As a function of this relationship, the reader considers seriously what similarities with the narrator might create openings and channels for connection, and what differences might inhibit understanding or a free-flowing communication.

In the second reading, for self, the reader attempts to attune his or her ear to the voice of the person speaking, that is, to open his or her eyes and ears to the words of another, taking in the story. Specifically, this exercise of directing the reader's attention to the way the narrator speaks about him- or herself is designed to highlight or amplify the terms in which the narrator sees and presents him- or herself. In this way, the reader comes into relationship with the person speaking, by paying attention to the narrator's way of seeing and speaking. Put simply, the reader listens to the other's voice and attends to the narrator's vision, and thus makes some space between the narrator's way of speaking and seeing and his or her own.

In the process of reading for self, then, the reader becomes engaged with or involved with the narrator as the teller of his or her own story, and, as the reader attends to the way in which the narrator speaks about him- or herself, the reader is likely to experience him- or herself coming into a relationship, so that the reader begins to know the narrator on his or her own terms and to respond to what the narrator is saying emotionally as well as intellectually. As the narrator's words enter the reader's psyche, a process of connection begins between the narrator's feelings and thoughts and the reader's feelings and thoughts in response to the narrator's, so that the narrator affects the reader, who begins, in fact, to learn from the narrator: about the narrator, about the reader him- or herself, and about the world they share in common—the world of relationships and its geography of moral concern.

Moreover, once the reader allows the voice of another to enter his or her psyche, the reader can no longer claim a detached, "objective" position. He or she is affected by the narrator, whose words may lead the reader to think about a variety of things and to feel sad, or happy, or jealous, or angry, or bored, or frustrated, or comforted, or hopeful. But by allowing the narrator's words to enter his or her psyche, the reader gains the sense of an entry, an opening, a way into the narrator's story in the narrator's terms. Thus, relationship or connection, rather than blurring perspective or diminishing judgment, signifies an opening of self to other that creates a channel for information, an avenue to knowledge.

Such a view of the process of interpretation as a relational activity must entail, we would argue, an ethic of interpretation that is grounded in a fundamental sense of *care* and *responsiveness* (see Gilligan, 1982; Noddings, 1984). An ethic of care and responsiveness places penultimate value on maintaining relationship and connection, attending to others and to self, listening and being listened to, responding and being responded to, loving and being loved. Thus, a "web of interdependence" is an organizing image for this ethic. Concerns about not hurting, "being there" for another, listening as a moral act, building and sustaining trust over time, being distressed or troubled by another's pain, sharing responsibility for each others' safety and welfare, knowing another well as a result of shared history, and valuing disagreement because it strengthens a secure relationship by providing evidence of listening and dependability, are all central to such an ethic. These concerns point to the need to maintain relationships on which people can depend (Brown et al., 1988).

Simply put, an interpreter engaged in a relational practice of interpretation, grounded in an ethic of care and responsiveness, attempts to enter into relationship with the author or narrator of the text he or she is interpreting. One dimension of such a relationship entails responding to the text (and its author/narrator) in its own terms, and therefore treating it with care (or caring for it). As such, the interpreter strives to let the text speak for itself, and to express its meanings as clearly and directly as possible. In this way, as Patrocinio Schweickart (1990) suggested in her reflections on the caring relation (as outlined by Nel Noddings, 1984), the interpreter responding to a text with care responds fundamentally as a good *listener*:

> We can see how easily the listener–speaker relation maps onto the caring relation: listener → one caring, and speaker → cared for. In this model the receptive subjectivity of the one caring . . . defines the role of the listener. To listen with care is to treat the text not merely in its textuality but as the expression of a subject. During the interval of care (which may be brief or extended) the speaker as subject "fills the firmament." . . . As one caring, the listener will respect the fragility of the other's speech. Rather than expecting fully formed utterances he will be attentive not only to what is written [or said] but also to what is yet to be written [or said]. He will try to discern and to bring out what the author is trying to express. . . . For her part the student/ speaker will be "confirmed." She will "grow" and "glow" under the caring attitude of the teacher/listener. (pp. 89–90)

Yet an ethic of care and responsiveness entails not only caring for and responding to the needs of the other, but also acknowledging oneself and bringing oneself fully into the relationship (see Gilligan, 1982; Lyons, 1983). As such, the other dimension of a caring relationship between an interpreter and a text entails the interpreter's feeling the obligation and responsibility to bring him- or herself into relationship with the text—that is, knowing that for the relationship to be genuine or authentic, he or she must, to the best of his or her ability, be aware of the manner in which his or her thoughts, feelings, values, biases, and assumptions, shape and inform his or her understanding of the text. When the interpreter/reader/listener enters the relationship in this way, aware and accountable, he or she can express thoughts and feelings about a text in an open and honest way—in the context of a relationship that values his or her perspective as much as it values the perspective of the author/narrator/speaker. Moreover, when care and responsiveness are extended, in this way, to cover both the interpreter and the text he or she is interpreting, it encourages a reciprocal sharing of power and authority in the context of the interpretive process.

We can now offer our final view of the dialectic that exists between the authority of the text and the authority of the interpreter. It might appear that if an interpreter were to bring his or her values, biases, and assumptions explicitly into the process of interpretation, as we have suggested above, it would lead him or her simply to invoke his or her power and authority, and to *impose* his or her interpretation, based on his or her perspective, onto the text in question. We would argue, however, that by being up-front, honest, and aware of his or her own values, biases, and assumptions, an interpreter actually attenuates his or her own power and authority in the interpretive process; that is, by making explicit what is inescapable and unavoidable in any interpretive activity—that values, biases, and assumptions necessarily shape the interpretive process—the interpreter enters into something more like a genuine relationship with the person whose text he or she is interpreting. The text, as a result, is granted reciprocal power and authority to enter into the relationship as well, and thereby to express and articulate its own meaning.

Perhaps a brief example would be helpful at this point, to illustrate this dialectic between interpreter and text. Our research group has been interviewing girls in childhood and adolescence to explore the ways in which they talk about themselves and their relationships (see Brown, 1989, 1991; Brown & Gilligan, 1990b; Gilligan, 1990; Rogers, 1990; Rogers & Gilligan, 1988; Tappan & Brown, 1989b). We have discovered that girls, at early adolescence, struggle when they encounter the conventional, stereotypical messages of our culture about how they should think, feel, and act if they want to be seen as "good girls" (and ultimately, "good women"). As a result of this struggle, some appear to *lose* their voices and the knowledge about themselves and their relationships they had in childhood to adopt these messages, whereas others appear to *resist* such a capitulation to traditional gender stereotypes. Such an interpretation, guided by the method described above, and informed by an ethic of care and responsiveness, emerges from a relationship forged between the adult women in our research group and the adolescent girls whose interview texts they have read and interpreted. In other words, this interpretation emerges from a relationship between what the girls in this study say about their thoughts, feelings, and actions in their interview texts, and the values, biases, assumptions, perspectives, and understandings of the interpreters, which arise from their experiences of living, as women, in our culture at this time in history.

In this process, interpreters necessarily make both of the judgments that have concerned us in this chapter: judgments that some texts are better (or more "developed") than others, and judgments that some interpretations are better (or more "valid") than others. The distinction between girls who resist the conventions of the culture and those who lose their voice and knowledge by capitulating to those conventions is informed by a "developmental" judgment that the resistors are, in some sense, psychologically healthier, and thus better off, than those who do not resist. The "validity" judgment that a particular interview is better interpreted as showing evidence of resistance rather than loss and capitulation is based on a careful reading of that text, and an attempt to understand the meaning of the narrator's experience in her own terms. Yet, in the context of the relationship established between the interpreter and the text, we would argue that it is ultimately impossible to distinguish between these two types of judgments: Developmental judgments about different texts must be based on an understanding of the meaning of those texts, whereas validity judgments about different interpretations must be based on the developmental significance of what those interpretations imply. In other words, when an interpreter decides that a particular text shows clear evidence of developmental advance (i.e., evidence of resistance rather than capitulation), she has also necessarily decided that such an interpretation is more *valid* than one that claims that the text shows evidence of loss, struggle, and capitulation. These decisions, furthermore, are informed, at the same time, by the narrator's representation of her thoughts, feelings, and actions, and by the interpreter's awareness of her own perspective and experience, and her understanding what it is like to be an adolescent girl growing up in this culture at this time. Once again, therefore, the hermeneutic circle is inescapable: Judgments about value are impossible without an understanding and appreciation of meaning, but an understanding of meaning must be informed and guided by judgments of value.

We would thus argue that in the context of a hermeneutic developmental psychology (in contrast to literary criticism), where the texts in question are the texts of real people's lives, when an interpreter enters into relationship with the text of another's life, informed by an ethic of interpretation based on care and responsiveness, he or she will find it impossible, in practice, to distinguish his or her developmental judgments from his or her validity judgments. Yet, because such judgments are an inescapable part of the process of interpretation, the interpreter must enter into the dynamic circularity that contains them both. Thus, the interpreter's task is to acknowledge his or her own ethical and political values, biases, and assumptions, thereby preparing to listen carefully to the meaning of the text in its own terms.

In conclusion, then, we suggest that such a relational ethic of interpretation might inform a hermeneutic developmental psychology in the following ways: Once a developmental interpreter has identified a particular text that he or she wants to interpret—a text that captures an aspect of the lived experience of a child, adolescent, or adult—his or her primary task is to enter into a caring and responsive relationship with that person and his or her text. We outlined above the method we use in our research for entering into such a relationship, but other approaches undoubtedly will serve the same purpose. In the course of establishing such a relationship with a person and his or her text, two interrelated movements occur: The first entails striving to understand the text in its own terms; the second entails making connections between the interpreter's experience and the text at hand. These two movements, furthermore, set the stage for two interrelated and fundamentally indissociable value judgments: developmental judgments about the maturity or sophistication of this text in relation to other texts (and to a predefined developmental telos), and validity judgments about the legitimacy of different (developmental) interpretations of the same text.

In the end, however, the hermeneutic developmental psychologist must acknowledge that, even in the context of a relationship with another person, in the form of a text of his or her lived experience, the temptation to violate the symmetry of that relationship and to assume ultimate power to interpret another's experience will be ever-present, by virtue of the prestige, status, and authority afforded to psychologists (and other academic researchers) in our culture at this time. What we must seek to do as readers, interpreters, researchers, and psychologists, therefore, as we come into relationships with those we study (the participants in our research projects), is to be constantly aware of our power to define the right, the good, the best, the ideal; to become accountable to the power of naming, and thus to try not to violate, unwittingly, "the immeasurable gap of quality" (Drabble, 1975, p. 347) that separates two lives.

REFERENCES

Bernstein, R. (1983). *Beyond objectivism and relativism: Science, hermeneutics, and praxis.* Philadelphia: University of Pennsylvania Press.

Brown, L. (1989). *Narratives of relationship: The development of a care voice in girls ages 7 to 16.* Unpublished doctoral dissertation, Harvard University, Cambridge, MA.

Brown, L. (1991). A problem of vision: The development of voice and relational knowledge in girls ages 7 to 16. *Women's Studies Quarterly, 19,* 52–71.

Brown, L., Argyris, D., Attanucci, J., Bardige, B., Gilligan, C., Johnston, K., Miller, B., Osborne, R., Ward, J., Wiggins, G., & Wilcox, D. (1988). *A guide to reading narratives of conflict and choice for self and relational voice* (Monograph No. 1). Cambridge, MA: Harvard Graduate School of Education, Project on the Psychology of Women and the Development of Girls.

Brown, L., Debold, E., Tappan, M., & Gilligan, C. (1991). Reading narratives of conflict and choice for self and moral voice: A relational method. In W. Kurtines

& J. Gewirtz (Eds.), *Handbook of moral behavior and development: Theory, research, and application* (pp. 25–61). Hillsdale, NJ: Erlbaum.

Brown, L., & Gilligan, C. (1990a, August). Reading for self and relational voices: A responsive/resisting reader's guide. In M. Franklin (Chair), *Literary theory as a guide to psychological analysis.* Symposium conducted at the 98th Annual Meeting of the American Psychological Association, Boston.

Brown, L., & Gilligan, C. (1990b, March). *The psychology of women and the development of girls.* Paper presented at the 1990 Biennial Meeting of the Society for Research on Adolescence, Atlanta, GA.

Brown, L., Tappan, M., Gilligan, C., Miller, B., & Argyris, D. (1989). Reading for self and moral voice: A method for interpreting narratives of real-life moral conflict and choice. In M. Packer & R. Addison (Eds.), *Entering the circle: Hermeneutic inquiry in psychology* (pp. 141–164). Albany: State University of New York Press.

Bruner, J. (1986). Value presuppositions of developmental theory. In L. Cirillo & S. Wapner (Eds.), *Value presuppositions in theories of human development* (pp. 19–28). Hillsdale, NJ: Erlbaum.

Crosman, R. (1980). Do readers make meaning? In S. Suleiman & I. Crosman (Eds.), *The reader in the text* (pp. 149–164). Princeton, NJ: Princeton University Press.

Culler, J. (1982). *On deconstruction: Theory and criticism after structuralism.* Ithaca, NY: Cornell University Press.

Dilthey, W. (1976). The development of hermeneutics. In H. Rickman (Ed. & Trans.), *Dilthey: Selected writings* (pp. 246–263). Cambridge, England: Cambridge University Press. (Original work published 1900)

Drabble, M. (1975). The gifts of war. In S. Cahill (Ed.), *Women and fiction: Short stories by and about women* (pp. 335–347). New York: New American Library.

Feyerabend, P. (1975). *Against method.* London: Humanities Press.

Fish, S. (1980). *Is there a text in this class? The authority of interpretive communities.* Cambridge, MA: Harvard University Press.

Fish, S. (1987). Anti-foundationalism, theory hope, and the teaching of composition. In C. Koelb & V. Lokke (Eds.), *The current in criticism: Essays on the present and future of literary theory* (pp. 65–79). West Lafayette, IN: Purdue University Press.

Gadamer, H. (1975). *Truth and method* (G. Barden & J. Cumming, Trans.). New York: The Seabury Press.

Gergen, K. (1988). If persons are texts. In S. Messer, L. Sass, & R. Woolfolk (Eds.), *Hermeneutics and psychological theory: Interpretive perspectives on personality, psychotherapy, and psychopathology* (pp. 28–51). New Brunswick, NJ: Rutgers University Press.

Gilligan, C. (1982). *In a different voice: Psychological theory and women's development.* Cambridge: Harvard University Press.

Gilligan, C. (1990). Joining the resistance: Psychology, politics, girls, and women. *Michigan Quarterly Review, 29,* 501–536.

Gilligan, C., & Attanucci, J. (1988). Two moral orientations: Gender differences and similarities. *Merrill-Palmer Quarterly, 34,* 223–237.

Gilligan, C., Brown, L., & Rogers, A. (1990). Psyche embedded: A place for body, relationships, and culture in personality theory. In A. Rabin, R. Zucker, R. Emmons, & S. Frank (Eds.), *Studying persons and lives* (pp. 86–147). New York: Springer-Verlag.

Hirsch, E. D. (1967). *Validity in interpretation.* New Haven, CT: Yale University Press.

Hirsch, E. D. (1978). *The aims of interpretation.* Chicago: University of Chicago Press.

Honey, M. (1987). The interview as text: Hermeneutics considered as a model for analyzing the clinically informed research interview. *Human Development, 30,* 69–82.

Iser, W. (1978). *The act of reading: A theory of aesthetic response.* Baltimore: Johns Hopkins University Press.

Kagan, J. (1984). *The nature of the child.* New York: Basic Books.

Kaplan, B. (1967). Meditations on genesis. *Human Development, 10,* 65–87.

Kaplan, B. (1983). A trio of trials. In R. Lerner (Ed.), *Developmental psychology: Historical and philosophical perspectives* (pp. 185–228). Hillsdale, NJ: Erlbaum.

Kaplan, B. (1986). Value presuppositions in theories of human development. In L. Cirillo & S. Wapner (Eds.), *Value presuppositions in theories of human development* (pp. 89–103). Hillsdale, NJ: Erlbaum.

Kessen, W. (1983). The end of the age of development. In R. Sternberg (Ed.), *Mechanisms of cognitive development* (pp. 1–17). New York: W. H. Freeman.

Kohlberg, L. (1984). *Essays on moral development. Volume II: The psychology of moral development.* San Francisco: Harper & Row.

Kurtines, W., Alvarez, M., & Azmitia, M. (1990). Science and morality: The roles of values in science and the scientific study of morality. *Psychological Bulletin, 107,* 283–295.

Lawson, H. (1985). *Reflexivity: The post-modern predicament.* La Salle, IL: Open Court.

Lyons, N. (1983). Two perspectives: On self, relationships, and morality. *Harvard Educational Review, 53,* 125–145.

Lyotard, J. F. (1984). *The postmodern condition: A report on knowledge* (G. Bennington & B. Massumi, Trans.). Minneapolis: University of Minnesota Press.

MacIntyre, A. (1981). *After virtue: A study in moral theory.* Notre Dame: University of Notre Dame Press.

Masson, J. (1985). *The assault on truth: Freud's suppression of the seduction theory.* New York: Penguin Books.

Noddings, N. (1984). *Caring: A feminine approach to ethics and moral education.* Berkeley: University of California Press.

Packer, M. (1983). Communication in infancy: Three common assumptions examined and found inadequate. *Human Development, 26,* 223–248.

Packer, M. (1985a). Hermeneutic inquiry in the study of human conduct. *American Psychologist, 40,* 1081–1093.

Packer, M. (1985b). *The structure of moral action: A hermeneutic study of moral conflict.* Basel: S. Karger.

Packer, M. (1987). Social interaction as practical activity: Implications for the study of social and moral development. In W. Kurtines & J. Gewirtz (Eds.), *Moral development through social interaction* (pp. 245–277). New York: Wiley.

Packer, M., & Addison, R. (Eds.). (1989). *Entering the circle: Hermeneutic inquiry in psychology.* Albany: State University of New York Press.

Palmer, R. (1969). *Hermeneutics: Interpretation theory in Schliermacher, Dilthey, Heidegger, and Gadamer.* Evanston, IL: Northwestern University Press.

Rabinow, P., & Sullivan, W. (Eds.). (1979). *Interpretive social science: A reader.* Berkeley: University of California Press.

Ricoeur, P. (1979). The model of the text: Meaningful action considered as a text. In P. Rabinow & W. Sullivan (Eds.), *Interpretive social science: A reader* (pp. 73–101). Berkeley: University of California Press.

Rogers, A. (1990). *The development of courage in girls and women.* Unpublished manuscript, Harvard Graduate School of Education, Cambridge, MA.

Rogers, A., & Gilligan, C. (1988). *Translating the language of adolescent girls: Themes of moral voice and stages of ego development* (Monograph No. 6). Cambridge: Harvard Graduate School of Education, Project on the Psychology of Women and the Development of Girls.

Scholes, R. (1989). *Protocols of reading.* New Haven, CT: Yale University Press.

Schweickart, P. (1986). Reading ourselves: Toward a feminist theory of reading. In E. Flynn & P. Schweickart (Eds.), *Gender and reading: Essays on readers, texts, and contexts* (pp. 31–62). Baltimore: Johns Hopkins University Press.

Schweickart, P. (1990). Reading, teaching, and the ethic of care. In S. Gabriel & I. Smithson (Eds.), *Gender in the classroom: Power and pedagogy* (pp. 78–95). Urbana, IL: University of Illinois Press.

Selman, R., Schultz, L., Caplan, B., & Schantz, K. (1989). The development of close relationships: Implications from therapy with two early adolescent boys. In M. Packer & R. Addison (Eds.), *Entering the circle: Hermeneutic inquiry in psychology* (pp. 59–93). Albany: State University of New York Press.

Shweder, R., & Much, N. (1987). Determinations of meaning: Discourse and moral socialization. In W. Kurtines & J. Gewirtz (Eds.), *Moral development through social interaction* (pp. 197–244). New York: Wiley.

Spence, D. (1982). *Narrative truth and historical truth: Meaning and interpretation in psychoanalysis.* New York: Norton.

Steiner, G. (1971). *In Bluebeard's castle.* New Haven, CT: Yale University Press.

Suleiman, S., & Crosman, I. (Eds.). (1980). *The reader in the text.* Princeton, NJ: Princeton University Press.

Tappan, M. (1989). Stories lived and stories told: The narrative structure of late adolescent moral development. *Human Development, 32,* 300–315.

Tappan, M. (1990). Hermeneutics and moral development: Interpreting narrative representations of moral experience. *Developmental Review, 10,* 239–265.

Tappan, M., & Brown, L. (1989a, April). *Hermeneutics and developmental psychology: Reflections on an emerging relationship.* Paper presented at the 1989 Biennial Meeting of the Society for Research in Child Development, Kansas City, MO.

Tappan, M., & Brown, L. (1989b). Stories told and lessons learned: Toward a narrative approach to moral development and moral education. *Harvard Educational Review, 59,* 182–205.

Taylor, C. (1979). Interpretation and the sciences of man. In P. Rabinow & W. Sullivan (Eds.), *Interpretive social science: A reader* (pp. 25–79). Berkeley: University of California Press.

Tompkins, J. (Ed.). (1980). *Reader-response criticism.* Baltimore: Johns Hopkins University Press.

Uebersax, J. (1988). Validity inferences from interobserver agreement. *Psychological Bulletin, 104,* 405–416.

White, S. (1983). The idea of development in developmental psychology. In R. Lerner (Ed.), *Developmental psychology: Historical and philosophical perspectives* (pp. 55–77). Hillsdale, NJ: Erlbaum.

Chapter 6 ■

Ethics and Science:
A Psychological Perspective ■

HOWARD H. KENDLER
University of California, Santa Barbara

This chapter is an outgrowth of a question posed to me in an informal setting by one of the editors of this book: "Can ethical decisions influence scientific knowledge?" The question demanded, at that time, no more than the curt reply, "Yes, without a doubt." But the answer left me dissatisfied because, as I soon realized, the question was too broad. The more fundamental and interesting question is, "Can scientific knowledge be completely detached from ethical considerations?" The answer is "Yes," but numerous qualifications are demanded. In elaborating on these qualifications, I try to show that the contributions psychology can make to the moral problems and ethical conflicts of our society will be determined by how *science, psychology,* and *ethics* are conceptualized.

Justifying my analysis requires a description of the epistemological framework within which I operate. I am a research psychologist who, in my later years, has become captivated by methodological and historical issues. I am not a philosopher. These identifications are offered with neither apology nor pride; they serve only to make clear the manner in which the issues will be examined.

An additional point needs to be made in the form of a confession. After completing books on the methodology and the history of psychology (Kendler, 1981, 1987), I became preoccupied, if not obsessed, with the problem of the relationship between ethics and psychology. This relationship had assumed a greater significance in my methodological–historical analysis of psychology than I anticipated. In addition, ethical conflicts are the root cause of the disunity that has infested the profession of psychology. My interests were also whetted by the fundamental and pervasive ethical conflicts (e.g., affirmative action, abortion, the nature of social responsibility) in American society. In my effort to understand the psychology of ethics, and its relationship to science and society, I began an experiment in self-education. I started a book to be entitled "Ethical Conflicts: A Psychological Perspective" with no compulsion to finish it. If the book failed to jell, at least my understanding of the psychology of ethics would be enhanced, and those nagging, insolvable questions that bothered me could be put to rest alongside the others that life poses. I began the book in secret with the intention not to share its themes with others. An invitation to contribute to this volume led me to decide, after much deliberation, that the educational benefits of sharing my initial ideas with others would outweigh the risks of exposing my limited background in the field of ethics.

Now that my participation in this volume is explained, I shift my analysis of the relationship between ethics and science from my previous defensive stance to one that might be considered offensive. To initiate this phase, I assert, without qualifications, that an analysis of ethics cannot properly be approached independently of psychological considerations. This assertion reflects Wilhelm Wundt's position that psychology is a propaedeutic science. By this, he meant that psychology is basic to all physical sciences because of its concern with sensory and perceptual experience, an essential component of the observational foundation of natural science methodology. Psychology is also basic to all the social sciences because it seeks to reveal the nature of the human mind and/or action that must be comprehended if social phenomena are to be understood. In sum, any attempt to decipher any aspect of human existence, such as ethics, demands a psychological interpretation.

THE NATURE OF PSYCHOLOGY

Insisting that the study of ethics requires a psychological perspective immediately raises the question as to how ethics and psychology interact. They do so in several different ways, but before these interactions can be discussed productively, a clarification of the term *psychology* is needed. Psychology can be conceptualized as a mental science or a behavioral science, and the manner in which it is conceptualized will determine its relationship to ethics. Throughout the history of psychology, a continuing debate has been whether *consciousness* or *behavior* is the proper subject matter for psychologists. The debate is beyond resolution, but of equal significance is the profound misunderstanding the controversy has generated. Whether consciousness or behavior is the dependent variable for psychology represents a *volitional bifurcation* (Reichenbach, 1938), a choice that leads to divergent conceptions. "Psychology is the science of consciousness" and "psychology is the science of behavior" define fundamentally different disciplines, and no rules of logic or weight of empirical evidence can tip the scales in favor of one interpretation. The preference for one subject matter over the other is some combined expression of personal taste and/or pragmatic concern.

A prevailing misunderstanding about the interpretation of psychology as either a mental or a behavioral science is caused by the failure to distinguish clearly between two fundamentally different operational meanings of *mind*, as a directly observed entity or as an inferred theoretical construct. Most early psychologists considered the first meaning to be more valid. William James (1842–1910), for instance, employed the term *introspection* to refer to the direct examination of consciousness: "Introspective observation is what the [psychologists] have to rely on first and foremost and always. The word introspection need hardly be defined—it means, of course, looking into our own minds and reporting what we there discover" (James, 1890, p. 185).

An idea not fully appreciated at that time, mainly because behaviorism had yet to appear on the psychological scene, was that the nature of the mind could be, and was, inferred from behavior. Wundt (1832–1920), the father of experimental psychology, frequently used this inferential ploy to develop his theory of the mind. For example, in his effort to understand the mental processes that controlled reaction times, he conducted experiments in which the time interval between the onset of a stimulus and the subject's reaction to it served as the basis for inferring mental processes. Later in his career, he used the same inferential tactic to develop his theory of cultural psychology from social history. Wundt never faced up to the complex methodological issue of assessing the relative value of data based on introspection versus behavior and historical evidence. He employed both in his theory of the mind, but assigned no priority to one over the other.

Harvey Carr (1873–1954), a member of the Dewey–Angell–Carr triumvirate that played a primary role in directing American psychology toward a functionalist approach to the mind, recognized more clearly than Wundt the difference between the two methods of examining mental events, but, like Wundt, did not allocate priority to one. Carr (1925) noted that "Mental acts may be subjectively or objectively observed" (p. 7). Each has advantages and disadvantages. Introspection (subjective observation) can provide "intimate . . . knowledge of mental events" that is not reflected in behavior (objective observation). For example, one cannot discern whether a person, trying to solve a puzzle, is employing words and/or images. Only introspection can provide such information. But introspective evidence is suspect: "Any verification or disproof of [introspection] is practically impossible inasmuch as [the] particular mental event can be observed only by [one] individual" (p. 8). Only behavioral data can meet the standards of objective evidence. The solution, for functionalism, was to use both kinds of data: "Psychology like the other sciences utilizes any fact that is significant for its purposes irrespective of how or where or by whom it was obtained" (Carr, 1925, p. 11). Carr's tolerance was maintained at the expense of evading the problem of the exact role *inner* and *outer* observations should play in the knowledge claims of psychology.

Although Wundt and Carr avoided judging the relative merits of the two kinds of observations—direct examination of consciousness versus that of behavior—John Watson (1878–1958), the behaviorist, confronted the task with vigor and fervor. Watson insisted that if psychology aspires to the status of a natural science, only publicly observed behavior could serve as the dependent variable, the object of inquiry. Self-observation of consciousness, because of its essential intrasubjectivity, cannot qualify as the observational foundation of a natural science discipline. Watson, however, overstated his case in his effort to promote a mentally free psychology. By failing to distinguish between mind as a directly observed entity and mind as an inferred theoretical construct, Watson essentially rejected a legitimate theoretical strategy for behaviorism: the construction of an objective model of the mind. Edward C. Tolman (1886–1959), a more sophisticated methodologist than Watson, proposed a cognitive theory of animal behavior (Tolman, 1932) that directly opposed Watson's antimentalism, without compromising methodological behaviorism.

Kurt Koffka (1886–1941), a member of the triumvirate that launched the phenomenologically oriented Gestalt psychology, expressed a theoretical strategy that essentially merged with Tolman's cognitive position of combining a model of the mind with methodological behaviorism. In a key passage that has gone unnoticed over the years, Koffka stated:

> Although psychology was reared as the science of consciousness of mind, we shall use behavior as our keystone. . . . if we start with behavior, it is easier to find a place for consciousness and mind than it is to find a place for behaviour if we start with mind or consciousness. (Koffka, 1935, p. 25)

Finally, it should be noted that the cognitive revolution in psychology was not a revolution against methodological behaviorism; it was a rejection of the strategy that proscribed the use of mentalistic processes in theorizing. The comments of Mandler, a cognitive psychologist, illuminate this point:

> We [cognitive psychologists] have not returned to the methodological confused position of the late nineteenth century, which cavalierly confused

introspection with theoretical processes and theoretical processes with conscious experience. Rather, many of us have become methodological behaviorists in order to become good cognitive psychologists. (Mandler, 1979, p. 281)

This analysis of methodological behaviorism can be easily misunderstood. I am not advancing the argument that a theory of behavior must be based on a model of a mind. Through the analysis, I intend to make clear the fundamental schism between a psychology that bases its knowledge claims on the direct examination of consciousness and one that employs behavior as its observational base. When the latter option is adopted, a choice still remains between a theoretical strategy that postulates mental processes and one that does not. A third strategy, *pragmatic behaviorism*, demands attention. It takes the guarded position that theorizing about mental processes may be fruitful for interpreting some forms of behavior, but misleading or unnecessary for other behaviors.

ETHICS AND PSYCHOLOGY

The point of this methodological analysis of psychology was to lay the groundwork for the psychological examination of ethics. As I suggested, the manner in which psychology is conceptualized determines how ethics is interpreted. Having distinguished between a purely phenomenologically based psychology that describes our interior life and a behavioristic psychology that deals with our public actions, I can proceed with dissecting the implications of each position for ethical facts and theory.

The role of values in science, when viewed from a psychological perspective, depends on whether psychology is perceived from a phenomenological or behavioral outlook. Instead of attempting to be exhaustive in conveying the meanings of *value, science, phenomenological,* and *behavioral,* I discuss each concept broadly and highlight the relationships among them.

Conscious Experience (Phenomenology) and Ethics

Phenomenology is concerned with the nature of human experience, how we come to know the mind as it appears to us. In this sense, I have been a phenomenologist as long as I can remember because my involvement with my conscious experience has been constant, and at times exhausting. At the same time, I fail to qualify as a professional phenomenologist because I do not share the goals of those serious scholars who seek to interpret human conscious experience. My repudiation of phenomenological psychology, despite its intrinsic fascination, stems from its limited potential in yielding reliable knowledge, a conclusion that history supports.

A prototypic example of the results of self-observation is the unresolved imageless thought controversy that did much to destroy confidence in introspective psychology. Investigations of thinking at the University of Würzburg, where Oswald Külpe (1860–1915) was professor, led to reports that thinking sometimes occurred in the absence of any images. Titchener rejected these claims because of their incompatibility with the generally held belief among experimental psychologists that thinking involved mental images. When thought was analyzed in Titchener's laboratory at Cornell, the introspectors always reported images, thus encouraging him to conclude that the imageless thought experiences reported by the Würzburgers were not properly analyzed; if they had been, images would have been observed. To complicate matters, Wundt rejected Külpe's and Titchener's findings because they were products of faulty methodology; one cannot observe thought while thinking. In sum, phenomenological analysis of thought, as conducted by trained introspectors, failed to yield reliable knowledge about the nature of mental events during thought. If you were trained to be an introspector at Würzburg, you might experience imageless thought; if trained at Cornell, you would always experience images while thinking; and if you accepted Wundt's methodological proscription, you would avoid observing consciousness while thinking. Thus, the content of consciousness is determined by how one is trained to observe consciousness. This conclusion underscores William James's criticism, known as the *psychologist's fallacy*, of the method of trained introspection. This objection essentially states that the observation of consciousness is determined by the observer's preconceptions; the introspector is encouraged to observe what he or she is instructed to observe. When interpreting introspective knowledge, one cannot isolate the introspective observations from the observer.

James's psychologist's fallacy was interpreted, even by James, in too restricted a fashion. Although serving as a compelling criticism of Wundtian-type introspection, it applied with equal force to all forms of self-observation, including the type James favored, which can be described as *naive phenomenology*, "the unbiased scrutiny of experience" (MacLeod, 1968, p. 68). All self-observation suffers from observational bias, a point James failed to realize. As long as consciousness can be observed by only one individual, the argument goes, it is impossible to separate the observer's preconceptions from what is observed.

Calling attention to the contaminated knowledge base of all forms of self-observation cannot justify the exclusion from psychology of knowledge gained from the direct examination of consciousness. It can serve as the source of theoretical hypotheses. And those who insist that psychology must be based on consciousness, as we experience it (Polkinghorne, 1983), have no other alternative but to directly examine conscious experience, the rock-bottom foundation of what they consider to be a truly human science. Once such a decision is made, however, one should be aware of the epistemological limitations of the knowledge base chosen to justify theoretical claims.

I have painted myself into a corner. By denying that I am a professional phenomenologist, I implicitly acknowledge a deficiency in my capacity to illuminate the relationship between phenomenological experience and ethics. Although my inadequacy cannot be denied, its significance can be attenuated. Most important in minimizing the impact of my limitations is the fact that no one method of phenomenological analysis has gained ascendancy over all others. There is no single phenomenology; instead there are many phenomenologies, each differing in some degree in how consciousness is observed, how the mind is conceptualized, and what criteria are employed to judge the fidelity of the interpretation. I am not in the position to offer the ultimate analysis of the relationship between phenomenology and ethics, but neither is anyone else. Perhaps of equal importance to the absence of authority is the point that phenomenological psychology, by its intrinsic nature, is incapable of achieving consensual agreement about the nature of consciousness. Perhaps my limitations as a phenomenologist are balanced by the limitations of phenomenology to yield reliable knowledge.

The striking feature of ethical judgments—determining *good, bad, right, wrong*—is their all-encompassing, compelling, experiential nature. In describing such experiences, I cannot avoid using the phrase *subjective reality,* despite my reluctance to blur the meaning of *reality.* The sense of repulsion generated by the terrorist act of blowing up a commercial airplane is as "real" as the rain that falls on my face. As a methodologist, I can distinguish between my intrasubjective moral judgments and my intersubjective sensations of wetness and pressure, but I cannot deny their equal *mental* status. Nor can I deny that these moral feelings are at the core of my existence, saturating all aspects of my life, including that of psychologist, both as researcher and as methodologist–historian. Although I will not offer a detailed exposé of my experiential life to justify this conclusion, I will nevertheless insist that it is impossible to disconnect my life as a psychologist from my moral experiences. From a phenomenological perspective, it appears obvious that scientific actions, scientific knowledge, and scientific applications are inextricably intertwined with the values of scientists and their societies.

The acknowledgment by my phenomenological self of the ubiquitous impact of values on science triggers the flippant comment "So what!" from my experimental psychologist self. Three reasons justify devaluing my admission of the pervasive role played by my moral commitments in my experiential existence. First, conscious experience, which may be appropriately described as the locus of our humanity, so completely dominates our existence that it appears trite to observe that a core component, moral feelings, is related to our actions as scientists.

The second reason to minimize the import of the compelling nature and unbounded influence of my moral experience is that the implication of the conclusion is limited to myself. It offers no help in unlocking the phenomenological experiences of others. To justify this statement requires traveling down the well-worn path that ends in the clarification of knowledge claims about other minds. To save time and reduce strain, Bergmann's (1956, p. 266) conclusion that "there are no interacting minds" can be endorsed. Nevertheless, this summation, although methodologically sound, does not represent the entire story. We experience the *capacity* to empathize with others despite our inability to measure exactly our success. At times, I feel that I can completely share the phenomenological world of others, but in other cases, only an incomplete picture emerges. To complete the range of possibilities, I must confess that the phenomenology of others, like the aforementioned airline terrorist, is beyond my ken. William Dilthey (1833–1911) appeared intuitively correct when he suggested that the more one knows about the social context in which a person lives, the greater the probability one has of sharing, or more properly, *appearing to share*, that person's experience. An admission of an intuitive impression of being able to share the experiences of others is supplemented by a countervailing gnawing doubt that emerges from the methodological conclusion that interacting minds are not possible. Of relevance to this discussion is the artistic conclusion contained in the blunt and eloquent comments of one of Saul Bellow's characters who strives to understand—share—the desires of his young daughter for a 10-speed bike:

> This was my kid, whom I loved, and it should have been elementary to find out what a soul in its fresh state craved with such intensity. But I couldn't do this. I tried until I broke into a sweat, humiliated, disgraced by my failure. If I couldn't know this kid's desire could I know any human being? . . . The only desires I knew were my own and those of nonexistent people like Macbeth or Prospero. Those I knew because of the insight and language of genius made them clear. (Bellow, 1975, p. 416)

The recourse to the authority of a character in a novel may seem an odd way for an experimental psychologist to make a methodological point, but it serves the purpose of highlighting the third reason for devaluing a phenomenological approach. Phenomenology, the interpretation of human consciousness, does not provide a suitable framework for reliable knowledge, and certainly not for predictive accuracy. Those who wish to assign the interpretation of conscious experience as the goal of psychology will be forced to abandon any hope for logically organized knowledge with systematic deductive empirical consequences. No methodological recipe is available to achieve consensual agreement about the mind as experienced. In addition, one might speculate that those who seek to share the experiences of others may achieve greater gratification in literature than in experiential psychology, a suggestion that some psychologists would reject, not because they consider phenomenological interpretation to be superior to a literary portrayal, but because they do not believe them to be qualitatively different. My own phenomenology rejects such an equation. Kundera, the great Czech novelist, offered a litmus test for a novel that phenomenological psychology, to my mind, cannot meet: "A novel that does not discover a hitherto unknown segment of existence is immoral. Knowledge is the novel's only morality" (Kundera, 1988, pp. 5–6). However one interprets the relationship between a phenomenological and a literary analysis of human experience, the kind of knowledge that each generates will diverge markedly from the knowledge claims of a behavioral psychology.

Behavior and Ethics

Behavior can be simply defined as the publicly observable responses of an organism. Although this definition is not free of difficulties, both empirical and theoretical, we should constantly be reminded of the relative ease with which research psychologists have investigated a wide variety of behaviors: sensory discrimination, animal learning, human memory, concept formation, social aggression, and so forth. One must not conflate the problem of defining and measuring behavior, which is simple in clear-cut empirical problems, with the task of explaining behavior, which is admittedly very difficult.

Public observations are fundamentally *intersubjective* observations; thus, conscious experience plays as much a role in the observation of behavior as it does of the mind. Although the observations of "inner" and "outer" events are equally subjective, they are qualitatively different. Because of the nature of the world and the structure of our bodies, we can reach agreement about the occurrence of outer events, but not about the occurrence of inner events, unless future scientific breakthroughs enable us to peer into the minds of others (Kendler, 1981). It is not the experience itself that distinguishes private from public observations, but the availability of the observed event to the personal scrutiny of other observers. When an event can, in principle, be observed by more than one person, socially agreed upon criteria can be adopted to encourage observational agreement.

The notion that observational agreement about outer events can be achieved implies some basis for the concurrence. The obvious candidate to serve this function is an outside reality that operates to shape agreement among independent observers. Although I have always tried to avoid getting entangled in the metaphysical issue of whether a reality exists beyond our experience of observing, I find that adopting the unprovable realist assumption serves as an effective antidote to those misguided claims that natural science methodology is exclusively a subjective process. I think of myself as a *sophisticated, naive realist* because of my refusal to get bogged down in the quicksand of metaphysics and my simultaneous acceptance of the existence of a real world that scientists seek to decipher, a strategic gambit that has great pragmatic value in countering the excessive subjectivity that has penetrated all corners of the social and behavioral sciences, and university education in general.

Having offered a public definition of behavior and having made explicit a realist assumption, I am in a position to argue that the knowledge claims of a behavioral psychology can be value free. Arriving at this conclusion demands the ready admission that a scientist's preconceptions, including his or her value commitments, will determine what he or she observes. The choice of science as a career, the selection of a given scientific discipline, the involvement with a particular scientific problem, the preference for a given theory, the interpretation of the social implications of scientific knowledge, are all direct or indirect consequences of a person's ethical commitments. Such a disclosure merely indicates that a scientist's actions are governed by the same motivational principles and social attitudes as are the actions of nonscientists. The crucial issue is not whether the scientist's behavior is free of preconceptions, but whether his or her scientific observations can be detached from those influences. Take the simple example of observing a rat at the choice point of a T-maze, a task that dominated my years as a graduate student. It seemed obvious to me then, as it does today, that—regardless of an observer's value judgments, theoretical preconceptions, social beliefs, or any other predisposition—consensual agreement about the rat's behavior will be guaranteed if a minimal commitment to natural science methodology is maintained (e.g., being honest and sober). Is the T-maze experimental paradigm representative of all possible research situations in behavioral psychology? Yes, if clear ideas are combined with precise response measures. To help justify this strong conclusion, I make reference to opposing positions within the context of experimental data.

The question about whether immaculate perceptions are possible in scientific research is fundamentally a psychological problem, and, not surprisingly, psychological research has been employed to clarify the issue. Take the case of Bruner and Postman's (1949) study of the perception of incongruous playing cards (e.g., a black four of hearts), which has been employed to support the methodological position of the inseparability of the scientific observer from what is observed (Kuhn, 1962). These incongruous playing cards were perceived more in line with the observer's preconceptions than with the cards' physical characteristics; that is, the black four of hearts was seen either as a red four of hearts or as a black four of spades, but not as a black four of hearts. The significant question about this study, which demonstrates that one's preconceptions can distort one's observations, is whether such an experiment is an appropriate model of scientific observation. The dramatic effects were obtained when the anomalous playing card was briefly exposed. Longer exposure times practically guaranteed that the incongruity would be identified. One can speculate as to what would have been the results if the experiment had been designed to reflect actual research practices. Presumably, efforts would have been made to observe the anomalous cards under optimal conditions that would have encouraged accurate identifications. If an error were made—and no doubt observational errors are more likely to occur when events are at odds with prevailing expectations—then the self-correcting procedures of good research practice, such as the use of several observers and/or the replication of the study, would uncover the observational error. In sum, although preconceptions may influence empirical observations, they do not necessarily have to, especially when precautions in the form of experimental controls are taken.

In addition to being misled by the results of Bruner and Postman's (1949) study, philosophers have interpreted the experiment from the wrong perspective. The argument that the observer, the experimenter, and the observable (the scientific observations) are inseparable suggests that Bruner and Postman would have encountered difficulty in specifying clearly the actual characteristics of their experimental material. However, this did not occur; the physical nature of the anomalous playing cards was clearly understood by the psychological community, thus supporting the notion that from *the perspective of the experimenter,* the observer and what was observed were independent.

Another way of looking at the problem of immaculate perceptions in scientific observations is to discuss it within the context of the debatable distinction between observational and theoretical terms. Those who favor such a distinction argue that a qualitative difference exists between the two kinds of terms: Observational terms represent directly perceived events, whereas theoretical terms are inferred. Those who deny the independence suggest that both observational and theoretical terms are inferential and equally unreliable. Clark and Paivio's (1989) empirical analysis of the methodological issue concluded, "that the observational–theoretical distinction parallels the concrete–abstract distinction in natural language, . . . and that natural language research supports" (p. 500) the distinction. Based on their findings, Clark and Paivio recommended, "that scientists do and ought to maintain distinct attitudes toward observational and theoretical terms when thinking about or communicating scientific ideas" (p. 510).

The arguments that have been advanced—that immaculate perceptions, in principle, are possible, and that the distinction between observational and theoretical terms is justified—converge to support the use of behavior as a dependent variable for a psychology that employs natural science methodology in its effort to produce a body of reliable knowledge and a capacity for predictive accuracy. The problem now is to determine whether behavior as a subject of inquiry carries any *intrinsic* value implications such as would justify the judgment that certain kinds of behavior are good, bad, right, or wrong. Although the intuitively appealing answer is "Yes," the epistemologically correct response is "No." Many reasons can be offered for the allure of an affirmative response, most notably the authority that might be forthcoming to demand acceptance of favored ethical principles and social policies. However, moral beliefs based upon a foundation of illusions, however compelling, will inevitably create social conflicts that would not arise if one appreciated the dichotomous relationship between facts and values. With this point in mind, it will prove useful to dismantle several common misconceptions so that a subsequent analysis of the moral conflicts that confront our society can be approached constructively.

The first common belief is that the biological world is endowed with a purpose and that the behavior of organisms serves that end. This position takes many forms, varying from the assumption that survival is the ultimate moral imperative to the transcendental view that biological organisms strive toward some ideal state. Such a belief has no basis in biology, or in behavior, which we must remember is an expression of neurophysiological processes. Richard Dawkins (1986) described the ethical barrenness of evolutionary biology:

> Natural selection, the blind, unconscious, automatic process which Darwin discovered, and which we now know is the explanation for the existence and apparently purposeful form of all life, has no purpose in mind. . . . It does not plan for the future. It has no vision, no foresight, no sight at all. (p. 5)

We cannot assign a moral value to any form of behavior, any more than we can assign an ethical judgment to the gravitational pull of the earth on an apple suspended from a tree. The only way of making such moral evaluations is to create them ourselves and project them onto behavioral and physical phenomena.

The second common belief is that facts imply value judgments and related social policies. Many would assume that if it is demonstrated that violence on television encourages social violence, then it is morally correct to restrict television violence. Such a verdict fails to recognize the dichotomous relationship between "is" and "ought"—empirical data and value judgments. Supporting a law to restrict television violence would be justified by (1) empirical evidence that indicates restrictive programming decreases social violence, and (2) the value judgment that the good resulting from the reduced violence outweighs the bad resulting from the imposed censorship. In sum, no logical bridge connects empirical data with ethical judgments. This epistemological principle is forcefully revealed in the statement that "if genetic differences in [IQ] were found between different breeding populations or ethnic groups the findings would have no direct implications for social policy" (Kendler, 1981, p. 255). From the facts alone, no logical conclusion could be drawn as to whether applicants for college admission should be accepted on the basis of IQ score, or their racial or ethnic affiliation, or some combination of both. Facts such as the genetic bases of intelligence are as ethically neutral as the law of gravity.

The third misconception springs from the intuitive trap that equates developmentally superior performance with morally good behavior. Psychologists seem to enjoy being victimized by this conceptual confusion, perhaps because Wilhelm Wundt set the precedent by being a willing dupe. He proposed that cultures evolved in a sequence of stages from tribal organization in early times to the highly structured states of the present. Consequently, societies could be ranked along a dimension of historical development with a social organization that balanced the needs of the state and its citizens representing the highest level of social organization. Wundt argued during World War I that Germany had achieved a truly balanced organic society that emphasized heroism, duty, and spiritual ideals, which was superior to British and American societies that were weighted toward the individual with excessive concerns with materialism, pragmatism, and commercialism.

Wundt's historical interpretation transparently displayed his own value system. Wundt offered an oversimplified interpretation of cultural change, with little detailed historical evidence to support it, to justify his patriotic opinion that his country had achieved the highest level of cultural development, and therefore moral virtue was on the side of the German army. Wundt's historical analysis was practically ignored, but the basic gambit that he employed to attempt to conceal his value judgments in the guise of empirical data was repeated by Abraham Maslow (1908–1970) with more effective techniques of camouflage.

Instead of interpreting the historical development of social organizations, Maslow sought to shed light on personality development. He postulated a hierarchy of inborn human needs in which the motives at the higher level do not operate until those lower down are satisfied. At the lowest level are the basic physiological goadings of hunger, thirst, and sex, while at the top level is the need for self-actualization, "the desire to become more and more what one is, to become everything that one is capable of becoming" (Maslow, 1954, p. 92).

This theory of personality development provided an opportunity, thought Maslow, to discover a scientifically valid ethical system. Maslow's reasoning appears simple: Because self-actualized people have achieved the highest level of the human potential, they are the psychologically healthiest, and therefore their ethical systems are valid. Maslow decided to reveal this psychologically valid ethical system by collecting information about a group of self-actualized people: Jefferson, Lincoln, Einstein, Eleanor Roosevelt, Jane Addams, and some of Maslow's friends and acquaintances. As a group, Maslow described them as individuals who identified with mankind and who were realistic, accepting of themselves, spontaneous, and humorous in a philosophical sense as opposed to a hostile sense (poor Grouch Marx failed to achieve self-actualization!). In addition, self-actualized people report peak experiences, feeling that they are fused into one with the rest of the world, are at the height of their power, and are living fully in the present, emancipated from the thoughts of the past and the future. From this evidence, Maslow drew his conclusions, as well as justified them:

> You can find the values by which mankind must live, and for which man has always sought, by digging into the best people in depth. I believe . . . that I can find ultimate values which are right for mankind by observing the best of mankind. . . . If under the best conditions and in the best specimens I simply stand aside and describe in a scientific way what these human values are, the old values of truth, goodness, and beauty and some additional ones as well— for instance, gaiety, justice, and joy. (Maslow, 1961, pp. 5–6)

A moment's reflection on Maslow's analysis should reveal the tautological, sleight-of-hand reasoning in which he indulged. The link between the empirical evidence and the "right" set of values is illusory. Maslow selected self-actualizers because they shared his own value system, he labeled them the "best," and thereby their ethical commitments became the "ultimate values which are right for mankind." Like Wundt, Maslow failed to logically bridge the gap between facts and values, but gave the impression he did. I also suggest that such concepts as *ideal speech situation, false consciousness,* and *authentic living,* which have been sprinkled throughout this volume, bear a striking epistemological resemblance to Maslow's concept of self-actualization, in that a value judgment, an ideological pronouncement, is offered in the guise of an empirical concept.

Another effort to interpret "superior" performance to be morally superior represents a more interesting and sophisticated attempt than those just reviewed, but, nevertheless, is equally flawed. No one can deny the importance of investigating developmental changes in moral behavior (Kohlberg, 1981), but one must be aware of two important considerations when interpreting the results. First, one must constantly be reminded that general behavioral terms, such as *morality*, have to be invented; their characteristics must be abstracted from behavior, and no rule or convention prevails to encourage agreement about their defining features. As a result, for a variety of reasons, both scientific and extrascientific, *morality*, like the concept of *intelligence*, will become controversial and ambiguous no matter how precisely some investigators define the term. The appropriate antidote to this inevitable state of disagreement is to make clear the nature of the discord and to judge the relative merits of the competing views within some pragmatic framework.

The second important consideration when interpreting the facts of moral development is to distinguish sharply between their empirical and ethical implications. "Do unto others as you would have them do unto you" is ethically more mature than the moral exhortation "An eye for an eye, and a tooth for a tooth," but is not ethically more "valid." Consider developmental changes in intelligence. Formulating a theory of relativity requires greater intelligence than tuning a piano or repairing a defective plumbing system, but it is quite another thing to say that the former is better for society than are the latter. Victims of the atomic bomb attack in Hiroshima would probably agree with this conclusion. No matter how deep our understanding of moral development becomes, including answering the important question of whether humans are preprogrammed to prefer certain moral principles over others, such information can never provide society with a psychologically valid moral code. Psychololgy has no special insight into moral principles that should govern all mankind; however, neither does any other scientific discipline, philosophical study, or artistic masterpiece. At the same time, the inability of psychology to validate moral principles should not conceal the pragmatic usefulness that the facts of moral development can contribute to social planning designed to reduce social conflict.

CRITICAL AND PRACTICAL ETHICS

I have indulged in an exercise in critical ethics, the analysis of the nature of moral arguments. I have discussed ethics within a psychological framework in an effort to focus attention on core problems that are basic to the moral conflicts humankind faces. I have distinguished between two kinds of psychology, one that bases its knowledge claims on phenomenological assertions, the other on behavioral evidence. Although intrinsically fascinating, phenomenological psychology holds no hope of offering a foundation of reliable knowledge that can be used constructively to resolve ethical conflicts. A behavioral psychology, in contrast, based on natural science methodology that assumes a real world operating on deterministic principles, promises objective evidence capable of throwing light on the acquisition, operation, and modification of moral beliefs.

However intellectually appealing an exercise in critical ethics is, or attractive the goal of a scientific understanding of moral behavior may appear, a gnawing dissatisfaction remains for those who recognize that both efforts ignore the most important ethical problems of all: providing guidance to help people act properly. Without a moral code to steer people in the right direction, society will inevitably collapse under the pressures of the conflicting needs, desires, and passions of its members. One can also suggest that the absence of an ethical commitment is destructive to individuals themselves, regardless of the moral requirements of society. Some psychologists (e.g., Frank, 1972) have argued that valuelessness—the lack of a sense of what is right and wrong, what is desirable and undesirable— represents the major psychological disturbance of our time. At one extreme, it generates a social malaise that alienates individuals from their society, while at the other extreme, it creates an irrational violence that seeks to destroy the entire society. Without purpose, individuals become demoralized and society drifts aimlessly, incapable of coping effectively with its current problems while being unable to plan for the future.

My concern at this point is not with the empirical justification of the above generalizations, but rather with the distinction between practical and critical ethics. Great moral philosophers from Aristotle on considered the problem of ethics to be of practical concern because they were interested in distinguishing right from wrong. Contemporary moral philosophers, in contrast, have for the most part been concerned with analyzing the nature of moral arguments. This critical approach has led to the conclusion that science in general, and psychology in particular, can offer no unqualified authority upon which to base an ethical system. If this critical conclusion is combined with the reasonable acknowledgment that ethical commitments profoundly influence individual behavior and the functioning of an entire society, then psychologists are caught on the horns of a disturbing dilemma: Ethical commitments are psychologically important, but moral truth is alien to the science of psychology.

In the face of such a dilemma, what can the psychologist do? One possibility is to prod individuals to adopt ethical imperatives on the basis of faith in sources outside of psychology. Such an action, it must be recognized, is consistent with the critical conclusion mentioned above, but is certainly not demanded by it. Because psychology cannot offer valid ethical imperatives and yet moral guidance is needed, it does not logically follow that psychologists should encourage people to seek values through religious faith or political fervor. Another possibility, on pragmatic grounds, is to renounce the critical conclusion that psychology cannot recommend the ethical imperatives that humanity needs; any critical conclusion, no matter how impeccable the logic may be, that counters the fundamental needs of humans and their society, must be rejected. An additional alternative is to finesse the disturbing dilemma by failing to recognize it. By uncritically insisting that psychology offers special insights into moral truth, one can serve the public interest while simultaneously enhancing one's own sense of social responsibility and self-righteousness, a ploy in which many social scientists have indulged, to the detriment of scientific progress and social responsibility.

Those who demand intellectual rigor need not abandon the field of ethics to those who do not, but they do have to contemplate the disturbing thought that their methodological stance creates a moral vacuum that could be employed to justify nihilism. Because no moral imperative is valid, all moral positions can be denied. Once this solution is accepted, an opening wedge is created, which might lead to the stark conclusion that prevailing political institutions are unjustified and therefore should be destroyed. Unfortunately, one need only point to the spread of violence and destructiveness in our recent history, and the nihilistic rationalizations of it, to justify one's worst fears about the possible side effects that are created when science fails to offer any ethical guidelines to govern human behavior.

How can one cope with this dreary consequence of the denial of the validity of moral principles? As noted, one could agree with the epistemological conclusions but, for pragmatic reasons, decide not to abide by them. The world does not offer any ultimate morality, but it needs one; therefore, it must be created by some act of faith in religion, political philosophy, or psychology. A more realistic choice, and intellectually more justified, and certainly more challenging, is to recognize that moral imperatives do not reside in nature; our demands for the ultimate values of life must go unheeded. For some, the ethical plight of humanity demonstrates that life is absurd; for others, it highlights the animalistic origins of homo sapiens. In either case, there is no escape from this moral predicament; we can only hope to adjust to it. If one takes seriously the consequence of this critical analysis, then self-deception is not a viable alternative; a rational solution remains the only possibility.

TOWARD A RATIONAL SOLUTION

It should be clear that even if we fully understood the psychology of morality, such knowledge could not automatically be implemented to relieve the moral crises, or solve the ethical conflicts, of our world. Scientific knowledge does not have any built-in application mechanism for automatically solving social problems.

Two independent obstacles confront us when solutions to ethical problems are sought: (1) incomplete knowledge about moral behavior, and (2) political mechanisms and social engineering techniques for applying scientific knowledge in a socially acceptable and constructive way. The argument has been advanced that progress in hurdling these barriers demands conceptualizing ethical processes within a behavioral framework. The philosophy of ethics illustrates the dead end to which purely mentalistic conceptions of morality ultimately lead when searching for moral knowledge that has practical social implications. To suggest, as some philosophers have done, that an experiential sense of goodness is psychologically akin to an unanalyzable sensation of yellow or to a mysterious product of intuition may be phenomenologically interesting but behaviorally empty. This conclusion does not argue against the strategy of employing a model of the mind for clarifying the nature of moral processes or for proposing a blueprint of an ethical system that might achieve wide appeal. Such efforts, the argument goes, are not to be judged as ends in themselves, but only as means for furthering our understanding of the behavioral consequences of differing ethical principles.

In addition to encouraging a behavioral approach, suggestions can be offered about large issues and circumscribed problems that must be addressed if psychology is to contribute to the solution of ethical problems of our society. We must rid ourselves of the delusion that absolute answers can be given to the psychological meanings of such moral concepts as *right, good,* and *justice,* or that any specific meaning of such concepts can become morally compelling or universally accepted. Instead, flexible and adjustable models of morality must be created that can gain wide acceptance not only because of their appeal to different ethical constituencies, but because of their capacity to be modified to cope with changing moral problems and ethical concerns. In addition, and more intimately connected to psychology's traditions, is the light that research can throw on the complex, and frequently conflicting, relationship between individual needs and communal responsibilities. To be successful, such research has to emerge not from some ideological dogma that defines the true image of man and the ideal society, but instead from a sophisticated, detached perspective that strives to understand humans with those objective methods that have proved successful in comprehending animals and machines. One must, in striving to achieve detachment, distinguish between explaining and justifying behavior as well as be guided by a realistic instead of an overly optimistic estimate of the moral potentialities of human beings.

Another suggestion, consistent with past recommendations (Kendler, 1989), is that a biopsychological approach may prove particularly fruitful in exposing what has been commonly referred to as *human nature:* What is the character and range of our genetic preprogramming, and how can such predispositions be modified by training? Of equal importance, what is the extent, in this nature–nurture relationship, of individual differences?

The major way that psychology can contribute to the resolution of ethical conflicts in a political democracy is by providing empirical evidence of the possible consequences of competing social programs so that a choice, by democratic processes, can be made. For example, what are the social consequences of the policy of abortion on demand, affirmative action programs, sex education in elementary schools, euthanasia, and so on? For many people, competing social policies about such matters do not represent any dilemma because one alternative is so morally repugnant or politically objectionable that a choice is not even entertained. For others, however, the political preference results from some pragmatic judgment as to which alternative has greater utility. For these people, relevant information would enhance the quality of the choice. For example, one person may decide to support affirmative action if it improves the educational achievements of minorities without compromising educational standards, but oppose the program if the educational system becomes less productive. Empirical evidence that would throw light on this matter could help a society reach an educated and democratic decision.

The basic question is whether the science of psychology has the technical capability to produce data that could illuminate the potential psychological consequences of controversial social policies. An affirmative reaction appears justified considering the sophisticated techniques invented to measure behavior, the analytic power of experimental designs and survey research, and the robustness of statistical analyses. One reservation, which reflects the basic issue that has dominated this paper, must be expressed. Can psychologists assume an impartial attitude in their research so that the resulting data will not be contaminated by their personal value commitments? In more general terms, can psychologists operate within the ethics of natural science methodology and not of politics? An affirmative response is again possible, but unfortunately, qualifications are also demanded. Many scientists, including many psychologists, believe that not only is it impossible to separate their values from their research, but more importantly it is their duty to promote their political ideology. Political goals, they feel, are at least as important as truth. When researchers adopt such ideological principles as the "ultimate tests [of a science] are always twofold: tests of truth and social function" (Lewontin, Rose, & Kamin, 1984, p. 33) and an "essential dialectical unity of the biological and the social, not as two distinct spheres, but as ontologically conterminous" (Lewontin et al., 1984, p. 48), they are essentially setting the stage to mold nature into a form that fits their political preconceptions. The corrupting influence of such an orientation is exhibited in the absurd empirical conclusions that are generated: "There exists no data which would lead a prudent man to accept the hypothesis that IQ scores are in any degree inheritable" (Kamin, 1974, p. 1) and the refusal to accept a genetic predisposition in the etiology of schizophrenia (Lewontin et al., 1984).

The fact that some psychologists insist on politicizing their research does not mean that others cannot operate impartially. Much good research has been done to evaluate the outcome of different social policies, and a sophisticated psychologist can distinguish value-biased research from impartial investigations. But society usually cannot make such a distinction, and as a result, psychological evidence is rejected or ignored to the mutual disadvantage of both society and psychology.

I admittedly am oversimplifying the problems of evaluation research. Evaluation research is not as simple as has been suggested, mainly because competing social policies (e.g., pro- and anti-affirmative action programs) involve many more than one independent and dependent variable. Inevitably, a research study, or even a sequence of several experiments, will overlook an empirical relationship that some people will consider important. Evaluation research must be judged not from some ideal goal of perfection, but from some reasonable goal of clarification. The underlying assumption of applied social experimentation is that a wiser decision can be made about social programs in the light of evidence, unavoidably incomplete, than in the absence of any data. In addition, evaluation research usually uncovers new information that can improve the effectiveness of a particular social program and/or suggest new ways of implementing the program while simultaneously reducing social conflict.

If nothing else, the complexity of the relationship between ethics and science in general, and psychology in particular, has been demonstrated. The argument has been advanced that the moral commitments of a scientist impacts upon the scientist's research, but *in principle*, the knowledge claims resulting can be isolated from those ethical judgments and predispositions. The differentiation between facts and values obviously becomes clearer when the researcher seeks to maintain the distinction rather than hide it. Although the validity of my methodological analysis cannot be justified by its pragmatic implications, it is worth noting that the ability to detach values from empirical phenomena can have enormous advantages for a society that is committed to democratic processes in selecting and implementing social programs. In line with this, it is worth commenting on the congruence between natural science methodology and a political democracy: common standards for judgment and freedom of individual expression. A symbiotic relationship can, and should, be established between a political democracy and psychology. The future of psychology requires that the psychology profession meet the needs of a democratic society for reliable and unbiased knowledge.

SOME FINAL THOUGHTS

It will become apparent—if it has not already—that my methodological analysis of ethics and psychology assigns me to a minority position in this volume. Although one can suggest that I am the "odd man out," such a designation would be inappropriate considering the overlapping views of Gibbs (Chapter 10). Presumably, however, the point of this book is not to identify the most popular methodological orientation for studying psychology and ethics. Instead, the primary concern is, or should be, with a detailed analysis of competing views so that an appropriate evaluation can be made. Toward this end, it will prove useful to mention two important social factors that exert powerful influences on reactions to methodological differences in contemporary psychology: *the need for change* and *social constructionism.*

A built-in need for change operates in psychology, primarily because, as already noted, psychology suffers from a lack of a clearly defined goal that precludes universally acceptable answers to its fundamental questions. No matter what successes may be achieved, failures will always remain, thus encouraging the belief, as well as the hope, that some new methodology— some new way of looking at psychology's problems—can convert past failures into future successes. The point of highlighting the built-in tendency for novelty is not to blanket all modern innovations with criticism, but instead to identify the social ploy of uncritically damning the past. The new should not replace the old simply because it is new. Ideas should be evaluated not in terms of their temporal location, but instead by their intrinsic worth. One annoying gambit, widely practiced, is to have an entire systematic view, such as behaviorism or positivism, rejected by the simple citation of negative opinion of some modern "authority" without any effort to engage the fundamental issues in dispute. Such a maneuver becomes particularly irritating when the subtle problems involved in the controversy, as well as its historical context, are ignored. One must constantly be reminded that universal assent or dissent is beyond reach in methodological controversies, and to pretend otherwise is to travel the road that ends in self-delusion.

Basic to some of the differences between my views and those of many of my colleagues in this volume is a generation gap that reflects the flight toward subjectivity initiated in the 1960s and rationalized by the popular phrase, "the myth of objectivity." This flight was encouraged, in part, by the failure of the social (behavioral) sciences to achieve a level of reliable knowledge leading to compelling theories that had been anticipated a century ago. To cope with this frustration, a variety of methodological and theoretical stratagems were created to overcome the feeling of failure and to suggest new directions for future breakthroughs.

The cause of our failure to understand the human condition and improve its state has been attributed to the pernicious effects of science in general, and of behaviorism and positivism in particular, a recognition that some psychologists celebrate as a profound insight. In contrast, those psychologists who are wedded to natural science methodology are puzzled by such a conclusion, because they reject both the notion that their methodological approach is designed to directly reveal the human condition, and the conclusion that the goal of improving the state of our lives is solely a scientific problem. The natural science psychologist also cannot understand how any confidence can be placed in any methodological orientation that fails to employ the criteria of reliable knowledge and predictive accuracy for evaluating knowledge claims. Although readily admitting that the natural science approach to psychology has not been as successful as anticipated, the setback is viewed not as a reason to abandon the orientation, but instead as a challenge for a more effective implementation.

Social constructionism refers to the obvious, but frequently overlooked point that the concepts employed in all intellectual efforts are socially created. *Gravity, gene, intelligence, aggression, fulfillment, beauty,* and *good* are constructs that have emerged from the social interactions of individuals who sought to understand the events in which these concepts are embedded. If social constructionism simply means that our everyday concepts, as well as those created in professional disciplines, are constructed within a social context, then the position is beyond criticism. However, if social constructionism implies that the sole meaning of a concept resides within the label that society assigns it, then social constructionism encourages misdirection and confusion.

The concept of *gene* illustrates the shortcomings of social constructionism as a single global approach to the meaning of concepts. Initially, the concept of gene was involved with some unspecified process that made members of successive generations of animal and plant life appear similar. Before the physical basis of this process was understood, the concept of gene was essentially a speculation, a hypothesis, that served to explain the laws of inheritance. Once the biochemical characteristics of the gene were identified, its epistemological status changed, so that it possessed a physical reality in addition to its abstract theoretical meaning. In essence, the concept of gene had its origins in social interactions, but its ultimate meaning was determined by the physical constraints responsible for the laws of genetic determination. The major thrust of this analysis is that society did not have the freedom to construct the meaning of a gene in any manner it desired; its meaning was not analogous to the social convention that dictates that a piece of food should be picked up with a fork held in the right hand.

An analogous situation prevails for the concepts of *schizophrenia* and *intelligence,* which have been socially created to refer to certain patterns of behavior that appear to share common features. One can conceptualize these two concepts in opposite ways: as a purely social distinction or as a psychophysiological reality. In the case of the former, one might suggest that the schizophrenic diagnosis has a labeling function that serves a social purpose. One possibility is that the schizophrenic pattern of behavior is offensive to an important segment of society, sometimes referred to as "the ruling class." This socially powerful group is able to remove so-called schizophrenics from the mainstream of society by stigmatizing them as being mentally ill. Similarly, the idea can be offered that creating the concept of intelligence serves a social function that justifies the assignment of discrepant social rewards to different individuals and social groups.

In contrast to such a social constructionist view is the social–realist position. Schizophrenia and intelligence are not simply social conventions, but are instead some psychophysiological realities. The evidence in support of this contention, at present, is more compelling for schizophrenia (Kendler, 1988) than for intelligence. However, contemplate the reasonable possibility that intelligence test scores, which have been geared to predict academic success, will finally be correlated, to some degree, to neurophysiological events. If this occurs, then the social acceptance of intelligence would increase because it would no longer be perceived, by many of its critics, as an arbitrarily imposed social label, but instead as an authentic behavioral characteristic based on underlying neurophysiological processes. Arguments would remain about whether intelligence tests actually measure intelligence (an irresolvable debate), but the physiological reality underlying intelligence tests would make it simpler to evaluate their genetic underpinnings and enhance their practical value.

An entirely different picture emerges when such concepts as *behaviorism* and *positivism* are analyzed. Separating them from their socially constructed roots is impossible. Disagreements about their meaning are inevitable and unavoidable. No outside reality operates to constrain their denotations. However, one can argue that their epistemological status is not completely unconstrained because they have emerged from a historical context. When examined critically, this background can help screen reasonable from absurd interpretations.

Behaviorism

Here and elsewhere (Kendler, 1981, 1985, 1987), I have tried to extract the core meaning of behaviorism from a methodological–historical analysis of psychology. The conclusion appears clear that behaviorism is a methodological orientation in psychology that considers behavior to be the dependent variable. Self-acknowledged behaviorists disagree on every significant issue—theoretical assumptions, research strategy, practical implications—except the methodological demand that psychologists choose the organism's action as the dependent variable.

Tolman's cognitive behaviorism plays a crucial role in reaching the historical conclusion that the essence of behaviorism lies in its choice of behavior as a dependent variable. Tolman's adoption of a cognitive approach, combined with the rejection of stimulus–response associationism, the law of effect, and the importance of conditioning, essentially placed him in direct opposition to such leading behaviorists as Watson, Hull, Guthrie, and Skinner, but Tolman's disagreement did not prevent him from sharing with them their abiding commitment to methodological behaviorism. Thus, it should be obvious that methodological behaviorism can incorporate cognitive processes, including the basic concept of meaning (Kendler, 1981), within a behaviorist theory as long as the formulation has publicly observable consequences. In line with the historical importance of Tolman's cognitive behaviorism, it should be noted that the Hull–Spence research program generated theoretical offshoots to account for cognitive development that anticipated information processing–type formulations (Kendler, 1987).

Although history suggests that behaviorism should be conceptualized as a methodological orientation, a rigid attitude prevails among some who insist that behaviorism be treated as a mechanistic formulation that denies mental or cognitive processes. To adopt this position would effectively deny that Tolman was a behaviorist because of his emphasis on cognition and purpose. Does such a conclusion serve any purpose but to sow confusion? At this point, it is useful to refer to Laurence Smith's (1986) insightful treatment of Tolman in his attempt to tease out the relationship between behaviorism and logical positivism, which he concluded was much less than commonly believed:

> Tolman certainly viewed himself as a behaviorist and tried to justify that self-ascription by consistently defining his elaborate system of concepts in terms of observable behavior. . . . In fact, it was Tolman's unique combination of behaviorism and cognitivism, his simultaneous emphases on observability and conceptual complexity, that forced him to pay careful attention to the constellation of issues surrounding the problem of empirical definition. Had he been less of a behaviorist, he could have let his theorizing range further from his data base of experiments in animal behavior. . . . As it turned out, his unwillingness to compromise . . . left him with the substantial task of ensuring the empirical content of his higher order quasi-mentalistic concepts. This was no mean task, but Tolman's behaviorism possessed a degree of epistemological

sophistication not evident in the classical behaviorism of Watson. The solution to the task, as proposed by Tolman in the thirties, was an operational behaviorism in which cognitive concepts were represented as intervening variables that is, variables that intervene between the independent variables of antecedent conditions and the dependent variables of consequent behavior. (pp. 69–70)

This emphasis on behaviorism as a methodological orientation that demands publicly observable behavior be employed as the dependent variable, directs attention to the fundamental methodological issue in psychology to avoid unproductive wrangling over irrelevant and/or subordinate topics. The key concern is the methodological foundation that will support the knowledge claims of psychology. And the choice of methodological behaviorism boils down to the choice of natural science methodology for psychology. Only a behavioristic psychology can meet the demands of natural science methodology. This assertion immediately raises the question as to whether natural science methodology represents a unique procedure, qualitatively different from other methods of inquiry. This question directs our attention to positivism.

Positivism

Positivism has achieved the status of a P-word, comparable to the emotion-generating power of *liberal,* the L-word during the 1988 American presidential election. In the past decade, I have been charged with being a positivist in an accusatory tone reminiscent of the insinuation, by some childhood peers, that my paternity was in doubt. I do not deny positivist leanings, but do admit to some confusion about the meaning of the indictment. Every philosophical concept has many meanings, and to understand my position about psychology and ethics requires knowledge about my interpretation of positivism.

I frankly do not know what kind of positivist I am, but if forced to select one designation, the adjective *pragmatic* would seem right. I started doing original psychological research as a junior in college with little knowledge of subtle distinctions associated with different philosophical systems. My actions as a researcher and a theorist at that young age appeared natural and were executed with confidence. Designing experiments with the proper controls to test one's hypothesis seemed to be a simple task, requiring only a reasonable amount of common sense (I learned to my amazement that some of my fellow students, and even professors, did not have very much common sense). I was fascinated with Euclidean geometry in high school and more or less assumed that its hypothetico–deductive method characterized explanations of psychological events.

The tenets of logical positivism I learned in graduate school did not appear startlingly new; rather they corroborated my intuitive notions about the nature of the scientific method. My own conception was not very sophisticated, but I seemed aware of differences between logical and factual truth, differences between empirical and theoretical concepts, the importance of deductive processes in theorizing, and the necessity of precise definitions for experimental investigations. Studying the philosophy of science expanded my understanding of the epistemological and methodological issues in psychology, but it also signaled that becoming too involved in its limitless problems could easily divert me from my research. To avoid this distraction, I decided to become involved only in those methodological issues that had a direct bearing on my efforts as a researcher and theorist. Consequently, my own brand of positivism operated as a philosophical orientation for my actions as a psychologist. Within that sphere, my positivism was essentially consistent with the thesis that "valid" psychological knowledge is based exclusively on the methods of the natural sciences.

To clarify my positivism demands attention to some common misconceptions. Positivism does not offer a blueprint that, when stringently executed, guarantees creative research and theory. I have never been able to track down the origin of this misreading, although I have heard it expressed frequently. The suggestion is clearly denied by one of the major distinctions of logical positivism: between the *context of discovery* and the *context of justification* (Reichenbach, 1938). The context of discovery refers to the form in which knowledge is subjectively created, the psychological processes that are involved with the creative act. An accurate description of a particular context of discovery would require a compelling theory of scientific creativity, an achievement well beyond our present capacity. The context of justification, in contrast, essentially states the criteria for evaluating knowledge claims. The point of the distinction is to set apart relevant and irrelevant factors in judging scientific conclusions. A theoretical assumption cannot be rejected because of factors that prevailed at the time it was formulated (e.g., the theorist was under the influence of drugs or is a bigot). The truth of a theoretical proposition should be limited to epistemological criteria that are employed to evaluate knowledge claims (e.g., supporting empirical evidence, deductive clarity).

The second feature of my positivism is that it readily acknowledges that many of the important distinctions that the logical positivists emphasized—science versus nonscience, observational versus theoretical statements, logical versus factual truth, meaningful versus meaningless statements—cannot be clearly delineated. Instead of rejecting these distinctions because of their fuzzy boundaries, the question may be raised as to whether they therefore lose all relevance for scientific practice. If some notion is not completely right, must it be completely wrong? My attitude about these distinctions is reflected in Nagel's (1971) comments about the difference between observational and theoretical statements:

> It would be idle to pretend . . . that there are no difficulties in drawing a distinction between observational and theoretical statements; and I certainly do not know how to make such a distinction precise. Nevertheless, I do not consider that this distinction is therefore otiose any more than I believe that the fact that no sharp line can be drawn to mark off day from night or living organisms from inanimate systems makes these distinctions empty or useless. (p. 19)

In essence, my positivism argues that these distinctions have pragmatic value when they serve as ideals for scientific practice. Without a precise demarcation line between science and nonscience, the scientist can either abandon the effort to maintain the distinction by operating within an anarchist framework that rejects all methodological requirements or develop some epistemological guidelines (e.g., verifiability, falsifiability, historical evaluations of research programs) that have pragmatic value for judging knowledge claims. I reject the notion that natural science methodology is indistinguishable from that employed in supernaturalism, religion, and art. My positivism favors the strategy of employing some of the epistemological distinctions of the logical positivists as goals for psychologists to approach, while recognizing that they may be beyond reach.

The third feature of my positivism demands attention because of the common tendency to equate behaviorism with Skinner's operant behaviorism. This widespread misconception is another sign of deteriorating standards of scholarship due only in part to the proliferation of journals and the overproduction of books that make it practically impossible for even the dedicated scholar to "keep up with the literature." The significant issue is that behaviorism is not wedded to a Machian philosophy of science that rejects abstract theorizing. For Ernst Mach, direct experience was the foundation of natural science. Mach stressed the observational understructure of science because he properly believed that such emphasis could help rid science of unnecessary and corrupting metaphysical influences. Skinner, with his ambiguous attack on theories (Kendler, 1987), was also trying to eliminate unscientific issues from psychology. However, both Mach and Skinner, with their emphases on the empirical component of science, mistakenly rejected the rationalist component of science—that theory is anchored, now or in the future, to public observations. The clearest concise statement of my position is expressed by Giorgio de Santillna: "The true scientist has an empiricist conscience and a rationalist imagination" (cited in Williams, 1967, p. 74).

The final point about my positivism is that it is not a world view for me as it is for some other positivists. It seemed to have permeated all aspects of the life of Auguste Comte (1798–1857), the founder of positivism. He was convinced that his philosophy represented a style of life that could lead to an ideal society. His basic assumption was that the empirical laws that governed sociological knowledge were comparable in factual status to the empirical laws of astronomy. If people agreed about the scientific laws of astronomy, they would also agree about the scientific laws of sociology. It would follow that if a government were designed on sociological principles, its citizens would automatically abide by its laws. This led Comte to conclude that sociological knowledge could free the world of the misunderstandings responsible for wars and revolutions.

From my positivist perspective, Comte's idealistic view of sociology and society is a combined product of his psychological and methodological naivete that resulted in his failure to distinguish between facts and values. Universal adoption of any particular social organization, whatever the factual basis for its acceptance, could not occur for the simple reason that the application of scientific laws involve value judgments, decisions that inevitably generate disagreements.

The point of this discussion of Comte's positivism is to distinguish between full-time and part-time positivists. I qualify for the latter category because my positivism operates primarily when I function as a psychologist, although I find it very useful for judging the knowledge claims of politicians, advertisers, salespeople, and surgeons. My positivist inclinations are usually ignored when reading a novel, criticizing a movie, discussing the meaning of life at a cocktail party, and having fun. During those activities, I could easily be mistaken for a humanist or an existentialist or even a hedonist. Once a discussion shifts to psychology, however, I rapidly don my positivist robes and insist upon evaluating knowledge claims and their implications with positivist criteria that have been described throughout this chapter.

Of course, I can be accused of having a multiple personality when it comes to my general philosophy. Although I do not deny the charge, I reject the implication of pathology. The diversity of life precludes one philosophy from serving the needs of all phases of existence. If one consistently operated as a positivist, the flavors of life would be severely narrowed. However, if one refuses to recognize the distinctive quality of science, then science itself will be destroyed by deceptive practices and fraudulent conclusions. I emphasize these points to resist the current tendency to perceive natural science methodology as being completely infiltrated with subjective bias and personal conviction to such an extent that the ideal of reliable knowledge is beyond realization. Only if the psychology of morality is approached within the admittedly imprecise confines of natural science methodology, can we ever hope to gain sufficient insights that can serve a practical purpose. Such an achievement will represent the perseverance of a positivist tradition.

REFERENCES

Bellow, S. (1975). *Humboldt's gift.* New York: Viking.

Bergmann, G. (1956). The contributions of John B. Watson. *Psychological Review, 63,* 265–276.

Bruner, J. S., & Postman, L. (1949). On the perception of incongruity: A paradigm. *Journal of Personality, 18,* 206–223.

Carr, H. (1925). *Psychology.* New York: Longmans, Green.

Clark, J. M., & Paivio, A. (1989). Observational and theoretical terms in psychology: A cognitive perspective on scientific language. *American Psychologist, 44,* 500–512.

Dawkins, R. (1986). *The blind watchmaker.* New York: Norton.

Frank, J. D. (1972). The bewildering world of psychotherapy. *Journal of Social Issues, 58,* 27–43.

James, W. (1890). *The principles of psychology* (Vol. 1). New York: Holt.

Kamin, L. J. (1974). *The science and politics of IQ.* Hillsdale, NJ: Erlbaum.

Kendler, H. H. (1981). *Psychology: A science in conflict.* New York: Oxford University Press.

Kendler, H. H. (1985). Behaviorism and psychology: An uneasy alliance. In S. Koch & D. Leary (Eds.), *A century of psychology as science* (pp. 121–134). New York: McGraw-Hill.

Kendler, H. H. (1987). *Historical foundations of modern psychology.* Pacific Grove, CA: Brooks/Cole.

Kendler, H. H. (1989) The Iowa tradition. *American Psychologist, 44,* 1124–1132.

Kendler, K. S. (1988). The genetics of schizophrenia and related disorders. In D. L. Dunner, E. S. Gershon, & J. E. Barrett (Eds.), *Relatives at risk for mental disorder* (pp. 247–263). New York: Raven Press.

Koffka, K. (1935). *Principles of Gestalt psychology.* New York: Harcourt.

Kohlberg, L. (1981). *Essays in moral development (Vol. 1): The philosophy of moral development.* New York: Harper & Row.

Kuhn, T. S. (1962). *The structure of scientific revolutions.* Chicago: University of Chicago Press.

Kundera, M. (1986). *The art of the novel.* New York: Grove Press.

Lewontin, B. C., Rose, S., & Kamin, L. (1984). *Not in our genes.* New York: Pantheon.

MacLeod, R. B. (1968). Phenomenology. In D. L. Sills (Ed.), *International encyclopedia of the social sciences* (Vol. 12, pp. 137–186). New York: Macmillan and Free Press.

Mandler, G. (1979). Emotion. In E. Hearst (Ed.), *The first century of experimental psychology.* Hillsdale, NJ: Erlbaum.

Maslow, A. H. (1954). *Motivation and personality.* New York: Harper & Row.

Maslow, A. H. (1961). Eupsychia—The good society. *Journal of Humanistic Psychology, 1*(2), 1–11.

Nagel, E. (1971). Theory and observation. In E. Nagel, S. Bromburger, & A. Grunbaum (Eds.), *Observation and theory in science.* (pp. 15–43) Baltimore: Johns Hopkins University Press.

Polkinghorne, D. (1983). *Methodology for the human sciences.* Albany: State University of New York Press.

Reichenbach, H. (1938). *Experience and prediction.* Chicago: University of Chicago Press.

Smith, L. D. (1986). *Behaviorism and logical positivism.* Stanford, CA: Stanford University Press.

Tolman, E. C. (1932). *Purposive behavior in animals and men.* New York: Century.

Williams, B. (1967). Rationalism. In P. Edwards (Ed.), *The encyclopedia of philosophy* (Vol. 7, pp. 69–75). New York: Macmillan and Free Press.

Chapter 7 ▪

The Use of Normative Metatheoretical Values in the Process of Personality Theory Development ▪

ALAN S. WATERMAN
Trenton State College

We have reached a point in the philosophy of psychology as a science at which we can no longer adequately defend the logical positivist claim that we can (or even should) treat our theoretical or empirical work as value free (Overton, 1984). A reopening of value questions in the field of psychology has occurred as a result of the abandonment of the view that science is holding a mirror up to nature (Laudan, 1984; Rorty, 1979); the work on paradigm shifts in science (Kuhn, 1970); the contributions of the social constructionists that all experiences, including scientific observations, are subject to an almost unlimited range of interpretations, with those adopted being influenced by personality, language, and cultural world views (Gergen, 1982); and the defection of many physical scientists, most notably the theoretical physicists, from the ranks of positivism (Capra, 1982). Yet we, as psychologists whose field it is to study the origins and implications of values in human functioning, have found it very awkward to examine our own value assumptions, as these may be impinging on our theories and our research endeavors. We seem to be unable to sustain a belief that we are "doing science" if we openly acknowledge that we embark on these endeavors with the baggage of a set of values.

With respect to personality theory and research, my field of particular concern within psychology, I wish to make three claims, discussed further in the following sections of this chapter. The first, and by now the least controversial, is that there are metatheoretical assumptions with normative (i.e., moral) implications underlying all theories of personality and all personality research. Indeed, I believe it is not possible to make any generalized claim about personality, even the most seemingly descriptive, that is truly value free. The second claim, and perhaps a more controversial one, is that the typical way of generating personality theories on the basis of clinical observations and/or from empirical data analyses without the explicit examination of value implications during the process of theory development has resulted in the creation of paradoxes, inconsistencies, and other problems that are uncovered only when the value assumptions implicit in the theories are eventually examined. The third claim, and the one that most directly contravenes traditional procedures for theory construction, is that we are better advised to begin our theory building and our empirical research within an explicit metatheoretical value framework. I do not mean simply that we should have an awareness of the value implications in our proposed work, but rather that in psychology and the other social sciences, our intent should be to use our value agenda both in developing our theoretical propositions and in designing our empirical investigations so as to evaluate the predictive adequacy of those propositions.

METATHEORETICAL ASSUMPTIONS AND PERSONALITY THEORIES

The rediscovery of the importance of philosophical assumptions for theory building in psychology took place within the field of developmental psychology (Overton, 1975; Reese & Overton, 1970; Riegel, 1972). Pepper's (1942) taxonomy of four philosophical world views has come to serve as a principal vehicle for contrasting psychological theories with respect to metatheoretical assumptions on ontology, epistemology, explanation, and views of persons (Johnson, Germer, Efran, & Overton, 1988). These four world views are formism, mechanism, organicism, and contextualism. Each is associated with a root metaphor that serves as a representation of its metatheoretical assumptions. For psychologists interested in theory building, different metaphors may hold appeal, thus contributing to the adoption of different sets of metatheoretical assumptions. My concern with ethical assumptions cuts across these world views, since each world view embodies a distinctive set of value assumptions.

The metatheoretical assumptions with normative implications that are typically embedded within theories of personality include (1) whether there is a capacity for human agency or volition, (2) whether teleological goals or purposes play a role in the selection of day-to-day behaviors, (3) whether human nature is considered basically destructive or creatively prosocial, (4) the extent of malleability in human nature, and (5) whether individuals can be held morally responsible for their actions. These assumptions are not independent; decisions reached on one issue in theory building will have ramifications for which other assumptions may be made.

Support for the claim that theories of personality are normative theories can also be drawn from the propositions they contain as to what constitutes psychological health or appropriate behavior as opposed to what is viewed as unhealthy or inappropriate behavior. The supposition that some behaviors are change-worthy implies a standard against which behaviors are valued or judged. That standard may be explicitly ethical or, more commonly, is implicitly value based. For example, to say that a behavior is change-worthy because it is maladaptive is to use adaptation as a moral standard for the worthiness of behavior. Defense of this standard must be made based on philosophical grounds, not on empirical observations.

PARADOXES ASSOCIATED WITH THE METATHEORETICAL ASSUMPTIONS UNDERLYING PERSONALITY THEORIES

This is not the place for a detailed discussion of the array of problems, paradoxes, and inconsistencies arising from the normative metatheoretical assumptions underlying various personality theories. Rather, I limit the discussion to three examples of the kind of paradoxes created regarding moral responsibility that follow from particular metatheoretical value assumptions. My examples are from psychoanalytic theory, social learning theory, and the Rogerian variant of humanistic theory. The paradoxes became manifest when critical analyses of the implications of those assumptions were undertaken, typically by individuals working in competing theoretical frameworks. In these instances, the paradoxes are generally recognized by the proponents of the theories, seemingly without generating any great dissonance as advocates of the respective theories go about using those theories in the course of their work in psychology, or in the course of their own lives.

Psychoanalytic Theory of Personality

Freud developed his theoretical propositions regarding personality on the basis of his clinical observations of his patients and of himself. The most significant metatheoretical assumption he made, and upon which much of his speculations about personality and therapy rest, is psychic determinism.

His view of determinism was based upon the model of mechanistic physics, and admitted of no agency on the part of the individual, although the person might well have subjective experiences that seem to offer the possibility of choice (Knight, 1946). However, Freud viewed such experiences as mere screens, arising from the unconscious to mask the true motivational forces determining behavior. Even chance was denied as a factor in psychological functioning (Freud, 1901/1960). The "discovery" of the unconscious, the recognition of the instinctive (drive) basis of motivation, and the understanding of the defense mechanisms as representing adaptive or maladaptive coping strategies for the binding and discharge of drive energy, all rest upon the cornerstone provided by the metatheoretical assumption of psychic determinism (Brenner, 1973).

The heuristic power of this assumption in psychoanalytic theory building and in the development of treatment techniques, made it easy to overlook the paradox regarding moral responsibility in human nature that was being created for the psychoanalyst in his or her dual persona of theorist and clinician (May, 1969). For the theorist, the denial of agency sets up a view of humans as mechanical automata moved by internal (drive, superego) and external (reality) forces that are far from fully recognized and are poorly understood in our conscious functioning. Even if such forces were better understood, the assumption of psychic determinism still allows no option for a true choice between alternatives in line with reasoned judgment and rational belief. Yet, for the clinician, the goal of psychoanalysis is to increase self-insight through rendering the unconscious drives conscious; through analyzing the transference, thereby increasing accuracy in perceiving reality; and through "working through" to the development of more adaptive coping strategies for the handling of instinctive energies. Psychoanalysts have no difficulty in seeing a patient approaching a successful termination of therapy as achieving more conscious control of his or her life. That, after all, is the purpose of therapy for both the patient and the therapist. Yet, while the determinants of behavior may have changed in a salutary fashion as a function of therapy, the metatheoretical assumption of psychic determinism still dictates the view that the successful client is an automaton moved by internal and external forces about which he or she has no true choice.

It has long been recognized that in the absence of possibilities for agentic choice, the concept of moral responsibility becomes either trivial or meaningless. Following the dictum of Hare (1963) that "ought implies can," we cannot hold individuals morally responsible for their actions unless it was possible for them to have chosen to act differently than they did. It appears paradoxical that psychoanalytic clinicians work diligently to increase conscious processes in the selection of behaviors without increasing the capacities for agentic functioning or the moral responsibility of their clients.

However, the paradox goes deeper, for the psychoanalytic therapist, while utilizing the assumption of psychic determinism, is not likely to emphasize to the patient the full implications arising from it. Such insight may be avoided either in the belief that an awareness of the implications of psychic determinism is antitherapeutic or because of a concern that it would drive patients from therapy. The question should also be asked as to how consistently, and with what effect, psychoanalysts view their own lives as psychically determined and without moral responsibility.

Social Learning Theory

Social learning theory, like behaviorist learning theory and psychoanalysis, also has embodied a metatheoretical assumption on the side of determinism as opposed to agency. It is thus subject to a paradox similar to that just discussed. Although insight is not stressed as an essential ingredient in therapies based on social learning theory, advances in the cognitive area have led to the recognition of the importance of conscious awareness of contingencies in affecting outcomes (Mischel, 1973).

Some of the greatest advances regarding an understanding of agency-related concepts—for example, expectancies for locus of control (Lefcourt, 1982; Rotter, 1966) and self-efficacy (Bandura, 1982)—have been made within social learning theory. Yet until recently, social learning theorists espoused the determinist assumptions employed by Skinner (1971) for behaviorist theory. To the extent that social learning theory relies exclusively on external (social) factors in explaining the origins of behavior, there is a denial of a capacity for agency, and consequently a denial of moral responsibility.

To have a generalized expectancy for an external locus of control is to see the outcomes of one's behaviors as largely a function of fate, chance, or the actions of powerful others. To have a generalized expectancy for an internal locus of control of reinforcement is to perceive the outcomes of one's activities, in terms of rewards and punishments, as being substantially a function of one's own actions. Extensive evidence indicates that favorable consequences follow from the holding of an internal locus of control expectancy (Waterman, 1984b), at least where such an expectancy is veridical. It follows that one goal of psychotherapy within a social learning framework is to foster a sense of agency through the development of internality where the conditions for it are appropriate.

Bandura (1982) took this perspective a significant step further in his discussion of the quality of self-efficacy. Self-efficacy refers to the belief that one can competently execute a particular behavior. These perceptions, veridical or not, influence our choice of behaviors, our preparation for carrying them out, and our persistence at them in the face of obstacles.

When Bandura addressed the issue of self-efficacy and agency, he was not explicit regarding whether choices based on perceptions of self-efficacy entail volitional action. Rather, he cast his presentation in terms of the traditional social learning theory paradigm that "external factors affect behavior" (Bandura, 1982, p. 123). He treated perceptions of self-efficacy as a mediational variable, determined by situational influences and, in turn, determining manifest behavior. When Bandura (1989) returned to this issue, he explicitly endorsed a concept of freedom and human agency in terms of "the exercise of self-influence" (p. 1182): "Given the same environmental conditions, persons who have developed skills for accomplishing many options and are adept at regulating their own motivation and behavior are more successful in their pursuits than those who have limited means of personal agency" (Bandura, 1989, p. 1182).

Although in his recent writing, Bandura (1989) transcended the paradox that is the focus of my concern here, the history of social learning theory is replete with locutions such as "perceived freedom" (Steiner, 1970), "the illusion of control" (Langer, 1975), and "the determinants of free will" (Easterbrook, 1978) that attempt to reconcile the language of agency with the metatheoretical assumption of determinism. The extent to which other social learning theorists will follow the lead of Bandura regarding human agency remains an open question.

Rogerian Humanistic Theory

Carl Rogers's theory of personality (Rogers, 1959) is an outgrowth of his clinical insight that if we provide a warm, accepting, supportive (nondirective) environment for children (or for adults), individuals are able to take significant steps toward becoming "fully functioning." By explicitly endorsing the agentic capacities of the individual, Rogers's theory avoids the particular paradoxes arising within the psychoanalytic and social learning theory perspectives. His theory yields its own paradoxes and problems, however, because of a metatheoretical assumption about the nature of human creative and destructive potentials.

The outcomes of the therapeutic enterprise for Rogers were typically improvements in both personal and interpersonal functioning of benefit to all concerned. In the absence of specific instructions in nondirective therapy to adopt a more socially productive orientation, it seemed reasonable to conclude that the therapeutic enterprise served to facilitate the client's natural inclinations. Thus, this theory assumed that the fundamental nature of humankind is benign, even creative and prosocial.

Given the existence of rampant destructive behavior in the world, the problem of evil takes on a special significance for Rogerian theory. If the providing of unconditional positive regard in therapy was the key to fostering prosocial action in clients, then the presumed cause for problem behaviors, including destructiveness, must lie in use of conditional positive regard earlier in the person's life. Because of the conditions of worth imposed on children by parents, teachers, and others, individuals come to lose touch with their natural inclinations. It thus seems that problem behaviors are determined by personal historical antecedents, not agentic choices individually made. We are thus relieved of our moral responsibility for any actions not in line with our naturally benign inclinations, while retaining responsibility for our more socially productive and creative activities.

Although this analysis may be greeted by some with equanimity because it affords the opportunity for accepting credit for positive outcomes while avoiding blame for outcomes deserving of censure, many will reject this stratagem as too self-serving. The concepts of credit and blame seem too thoroughly intertwined to be uncoupled as Rogers has done. The denial of agency here is more subtle than in the two cases previously discussed, but its effects are comparably disquieting. Certainly, Rogers and his followers did not set out to provide a formula for rationalizing away responsibility for morally objectionable actions, but that is what their theory has produced.

AN ALTERNATIVE APPROACH TO THEORY BUILDING

If the paradoxes and problems alluded to above are a function, in part, of the failure to fully explore the value implications of the metatheoretical assumptions being made, it follows that in theory building there should be more explicit attention devoted to metatheoretical concerns. To advocate the explicit use of values in the development of theories and in the design of studies to test hypotheses drawn from theory is in many respects a direct antithesis of conventional philosophy of science in psychology. Yet nothing in the view I advocate is inconsistent with established approaches for the evaluation of theories or their associated hypotheses. In this connection, it is useful to employ Howard's (1985) distinction between epistemic and nonepistemic values. Epistemic values "are those criteria employed by scientists for choice among competing theoretical explanations" (Howard, 1985, p. 257). They include predictive accuracy, internal coherence, external consistency, unifying power, and heuristic fertility. Simplicity has been advanced as another epistemic value, although it is less widely endorsed.

The particular values that I propose should be considered in the scientific enterprise are those nonepistemic values with normative implications. In other words, I propose that the ethical implications of theoretical propositions be thoughtfully considered at the time metatheoretical value assumptions are introduced in theory building. Furthermore, I propose that the ethical values implied in the design of research studies to evaluate theoretical propositions be openly acknowledged. However, when evaluating the adequacy of theories or tests of theories from a scientific perspective, the array of epistemic values takes precedence. A theory may be ethically laudable, but it is of no scientific utility if it lacks predictive accuracy, internal coherence, and so forth.

Perhaps the greatest concern raised by the introduction of nonepistemic normative values into theory building is that the theorist's predilections will come to serve as the principal factor in the formulation of theories, extending even to the exclusion of the epistemic values of science. There is, however, less reason for concern than might initially appear. The meta-theoretical assumptions involving normative implications are not in themselves provable, one way or the other. The controversy regarding agency and determinism is not at present amenable to an empirical resolution, and I foresee no possibility of such a resolution in the future. Therefore, scientific endeavors can proceed along paths of inquiry involving either assumption, or any variation of them, without violating the epistemic values that are the defining criteria for the scientific enterprise. As scientists, we can then evaluate the worth of the various attempts in terms of the results they yield, both substantively and in terms of the extent to which the epistemic values are upheld.

Another important concern about what I propose arises in connection with the objectivity of researchers who embark on their investigations with nonepistemic value assumptions clearly in mind. If science is not value free, then does this not raise questions as to whether an investigator's preferences will not bias the study design, the manner in which the study is conducted, and even the honesty with which the results are reported? Again, there appears less basis for concern than might at first be thought.

Those who advance the view that science is, or should be, value free, apparently believe that scientists can be free from values in the pursuit of their work. Whether in terms of psychoanalytic, sociological, or existential conceptions, it is dubious in the extreme that any individual scientist can be objective in his or her pursuit of knowledge. Following Camus, who observed that "to breathe is to judge," the selection of a research question reflects the relative value assigned by the investigator to that topic as opposed to the value of other topics that could have been chosen for study. Also, when embarking on a study, the researcher is not indifferent to the nature of the results obtained. It is plausible that virtually all scientists enjoy their research more when their results confirm their hypotheses than when the results confirm some rival perspective or when null outcomes are obtained. When statistical analyses are involved, scientists prefer significant to nonsignificant results, if only because of the difficulties encountered in publishing the latter. Thus, I am suggesting that openly acknowledging both our nonepistemic and our epistemic values at the outset of a research project does not manifestly alter the extent to which values impinge on the work being done. To the contrary, readers will be better able to evaluate a study when they are apprised of the nonepistemic values the investigator is trying to advance.

I am willing to acknowledge that researchers may design their studies to increase the likelihood that they will confirm the hypotheses with which they start, although this is unlikely to increase under my proposal compared with what is currently done. I am also willing to acknowledge that the researchers' values may lead to experimenter bias effects (Rosenthal, 1966), although I do not concede that under my proposal, such effects will be more frequent or larger than is currently the case. Whether being explicit about one's values and metatheoretical assumptions increases or decreases either design or experimenter biases is an empirical question, and I urge that it be studied.

My proposal carries an implied model for how scientific controversies over value-laden theories might most fruitfully proceed. If there are concerns that particular hypotheses are being confirmed in investigations carried out by researchers holding one particular value perspective, due either to design or experimenter biases, then it becomes important for the same hypotheses to be tested by researchers holding to a different value perspective. If tests involving seemingly identical procedures result in quite different outcomes, in each instance consistent with the values of the particular investigators conducting the research, then there is, at least prima facie, a case that value-based experimenter biases are involved. Similarly, if new designs to test a disputed hypothesis can be formulated by researchers starting with contrasting value assumptions and these lead to different conclusions, then a case can be made that design biases may be at work. In either instance, the presence of a heated controversy in the literature may well attract additional researchers to the field, drawn more by the existence of the controversy than by a commitment to one or the other value orientations. These quasi-neutral participants in the scientific debate may be in the best position to analyze discrepancies between the studies and to identify the operating variables contributing to the contrasting results.

Finally, there is no reason to believe that researchers who openly espouse their nonepistemic and epistemic value orientations at the start of an investigation will be unreliable regarding the truthfulness of the results reported. Instances of fraud in science have typically been related to the obtaining of grant funds or to the making of reputations, rather than to a need to protect one's metatheoretical assumptions.

AN EXAMPLE OF THE EXPLICIT USE OF NORMATIVE VALUES IN THE DEVELOPMENT OF PERSONALITY THEORY: A THEORY OF PSYCHOLOGICAL INDIVIDUALISM

Metatheoretical Assumptions

For the past decade, I have been working on a theory of personality pertaining to effective psychological functioning that is explicitly grounded in a normative philosophical framework (Waterman, 1981, 1984b, 1986; see also Archer & Waterman, 1988). I began this work because I was dissatisfied with the value implications of much of contemporary personality theory. Some of my objections have been presented above. Also contributing to my interest in providing an alternative metatheoretical framework for psychological theory on effective functioning was my sympathetic reading of philosophical works on eudaimonism, most notably Norton (1976) and May (1969), and on deontological conceptions of human rights (Hospers, 1982; Nozick, 1974; Thoreau, 1849/1962).

Among the normative value assumptions with which I started are the following:

1. Individuals are capable of *agentic action*. I conceive of individuals as capable of choosing among alternatives, with respect to both the teleological goals they wish to pursue and the means by which to pursue them. I recognize that the choices made with respect to both means and ends will be influenced by the person's biological nature, physical and social environment, and developmental history. I do not assume, however, that the outcome of a person's choice processes is reductively determined by such influences, such that the person could not have acted otherwise. Rather, the individual has available a relatively wide range of alternative ways of cognitively and affectively structuring the various elements of the environmental situation, biological capabilities, past learning history, and previous value-laden decisions regarding ends and means, and human agency exists in the act of choosing among them. An individual can allow his or her actions to be determined by the preferences of others or by chance (e.g., the toss of a die), but agency is nevertheless operative in the selection of the means by which action is determined (Fromm, 1941).

2. There is both a species-wide and an individual human nature resulting in *limited malleability* for each person. Specifically, the potentials for effective actions in terms of goals and means available to each person are not unlimited. Although the number of behaviors in which an individual could engage may be unlimited, not all those actions can be done well.

Therefore, trying to pressure a person into making particular choices in line with the preferences of some second party risks a reduction in the likelihood of effective functioning, when the direction of influence is toward activities not in line with the person's strongest potentials.

3. Human nature is such that each person has both *socially productive and socially destructive potentials*. Following one's natural inclinations will not necessarily result in ethical behavior. Similarly, the preferences that any second party may hold regarding one's behavior may include both socially productive and socially destructive behaviors, such that following one's socialization demands will not necessarily result in ethical behavior. The discovery of a basis for distinguishing socially productive from socially destructive inclinations is one of the primary tasks encountered in personality development.

4. Individuals are *morally responsible* for their choices. Because in any given situation, a person has a variety of possibilities for behavior, some laudable and others censurable, the concepts of credit and blame can be meaningfully applied when evaluating the intentions and the consequences of the actions taken.

This listing of metatheoretical assumptions is by no means exhaustive, and I do not claim to have worked through all their implications in the process of formulating the theoretical propositions I have advanced. Perhaps I have prepared a paradox as large as any I have encountered in other theories. Still, I believe I have made a more systematic effort to delineate the set of normative assumptions on which I base my theoretical explorations than is typically undertaken. It bears repeating that none of the assumptions made is empirically provable. The advantage of the process I have employed in setting forth my metatheoretical assumptions is that I have increased the likelihood that the testable propositions I generate are ones with which I can be comfortable both in my professional and personal life. The adequacy of my theoretical work from a scientific perspective must be evaluated in terms of the extent to which supportive empirical evidence can be generated while upholding the epistemic values of the scientific method.

Some Theoretical Propositions

The starting point for my development of a theory of psychological individualism is the concept of the *daimon* or "true self." The origins of this concept can be traced at least as far back as classic Hellenic philosophy, where it received its most notable treatment in Aristotle's (1980) *Nicomachean Ethics*. Contemporary presentations of eudaimonistic ethics are provided by Rollo

May (1969) in *Love and Will* and David Norton (1976) in *Personal Destinies*. In philosophical terms, the daimon refers to those potentialities of each person, the realization of which represents the greatest fulfillment in living of which each is capable. These include both the potentialities shared by all humans by virtue of our common specieshood and those unique potentials that distinguish each individual from all others. The daimon is an ideal in the sense of being an excellence, a perfection toward which one strives; hence, it can give direction and meaning to one's life. Eudaimonia refers to the feelings accompanying behavior in the direction of self-realization, that is, behavior consistent with one's true potentials. These are not easy pleasures to achieve, but rather require effort and discipline. The intrinsic rewards of self-realization are feelings of rightness, of strength of purpose, of competence.

According to the ethics of eudaimonism, each individual "is obliged to know and live in truth to his daimon" (Norton, 1976, p. ix). This spirit is embodied in two famous classical Greek injunctions: "Know thyself," and "Become what you are." To choose "to live freely the life that is one's own" (Norton, 1976, p. 26) is an affirmation of personal responsibility and a statement of personal integrity. It requires a commitment to both the principles by which one chooses to live and the goals toward which one's life is to be directed.

The concept of the daimon is generally unfamiliar to psychologists, although it was discussed in some depth by May (1969). On first impression, the concept may seem uncongenial to an empirical discipline. On the one hand, because it is defined in terms of potentialities rather than actualities, there would appear no means by which it can be studied. On the other, it is a concept that almost seems to invite reification. Yet it is incorrect to think of it as having any physical or tangible reality. Nevertheless, the concept of the daimon can be translated into the language of psychology, losing perhaps some of the poetry of its philosophical expression, but still offering us some revealing implications for an understanding of effective psychological functioning.

Let us think of the potentials that are the daimon in terms of talents, a concept that probably poses no particular problems for psychologists. Talents for various skill-related activities can be said to be present in varying degrees, and it is also meaningful to speak of talents as developed or undeveloped. To bridge the language of the two disciplines, undeveloped talents are as yet unrealized potentialities. Psychologists have long been willing to use a sample of current behavior as a predictor of possible future behavior that could result from exposure to appropriate education or training. Thus, as yet unrealized potentialities can indeed be empirically studied.

It follows that each of us will have greater talents, whether developed or undeveloped, in some areas than in others. In the absence of major physical disorders, the majority of our talents probably will be in the average range, slightly above or slightly below the norm. We are likely to have some talents in which our greatest potentials, even with the best of training, will be significantly below the norm, and others at which we may have the potential to succeed significantly above the norm if we have the necessary training and pursue those talents with dedicated discipline. However, the more relevant set of norms is not external, where others are the basis of comparison, but internal, where the comparison is among the potentialities of our achieving success at the myriad of goals we might pursue. In some areas, our potential accomplishments are significantly greater than in other areas. Eudaimonist philosophers speak of these areas of highest potentials as potential excellences, ideals toward which we are morally obligated to strive. Because everyone has at least some areas in which their potentials are the greatest, in terms of internal norms, the daimon is indeed universal, as are the possibility of self-realization and the attendant experience of eudaimonia.

However, talent is only one criterion for the choice of actions through which self-realization may be attained. The purposes to which any talents are directed must also be considered, and these also are aspects of the daimon. Again, we can set about the task of empirical investigations of the daimon, this time through the use of verbal reports of self-assessments of individual purpose (Crumbaugh, 1968; Frankl, 1965; Waterman, 1989).

The origins of particular purposes for an individual are difficult to identify at present, but may be assumed to include both self-generated influences and physiological and environmental factors. It is evident, however, that there are wide individual differences in the extent to which people have consciously identified their purposes in living and in the intensity or dedication with which they endeavor to realize them. To the extent that people fail to identify or to work toward the realization of their purposes in living, they can be said to be defaulting on their daimonic potentials. The reasons for such defaults are varied. Individuals may be limited by their environment to activities necessary for the satisfaction of needs (e.g., those associated with survival) that take precedence over the pursuit of self-realization. They may succumb to external social pressures directing them into other channels. They may allow themselves to be distracted by pleasures incompatible with the pursuit of their unique excellences or purposes. Also, they may turn aside from the arduous nature of tasks that they have identified as theirs to do.

At the outset of my work on psychological individualism, I recognized that there were many concepts developed by personality theorists from widely differing theoretical traditions that were relevant to my concerns. Four that I (Waterman, 1984b) could adapt readily to a eudaimonistic perspective were (1) a sense of personal identity (Erikson's ego analytic theory), (2) self-actualization (Maslow's huministic theory), (3) an internal locus of control (Rotter's social learning theory), and (4) principled moral reasoning (Kohlberg's cognitive–developmental theory). Not all these theorists would accept that their work has individualistic implications, but as I have demonstrated elsewhere (Waterman, 1984b), the fit between philosophical individualism and these constructs is remarkably close. This correspondence allowed me to use extensive bodies of existing empirical data to evaluate a wide range of hypotheses drawn from the theoretical propositions I was developing.

Hypotheses Drawn from a Theory of Psychological Individualism

In the *The Psychology Of Individualism* (Waterman, 1984b), I developed 10 hypotheses pertaining to the advantages for effective psychological functioning presumed to be associated with the individualistic personal qualities of a sense of personal identity, self-actualization, an internal locus of control, and principled moral reasoning. These hypotheses were grouped into four sets:

1. The individualistic personal qualities were expected to be positively interrelated; that is, evidence of any one should predict a higher than chance probability of functioning of each of the others. A review of the research literature revealed confirmation of this hypothesis in 15 instances and null outcomes in 26 comparisons.

2. The individualistic personal qualities were expected to be related to measures of personal well-being, including positive associations with levels of self-acceptance and self-esteem, and negative associations with debilitating affective states, including anxiety, depression, and alienation, and with various forms of psychopathology and social deviance. Of 235 tests of this set of hypotheses, the expected results were obtained in 151 instances, null outcomes in 80 instances, and results in the reverse direction in 4 cases.

3. The individualistic personal qualities were expected to be positively related to competence in functioning, including the use of the more sophisticated and efficient modes of cognitive reasoning, higher achievement motivation, and the holding of attitudes reflecting job involvement and job satisfaction. This set of hypotheses had been tested in 133 instances, with 52 outcomes in the expected direction, 78 null outcomes, and only 3 outcomes in the reverse direction.

4. The individualistic personal qualities were expected to be positively related to measures of social interdependence, including social attitudes reflecting tolerance for a diversity of social viewpoints and a nonmanipulative acceptance of other people; a willingness to cooperate with and be helpful to others; and the participation in close, mutually

supportive, and satisfying friendship and romantic love relationships. This set of hypotheses is of particular interest because it runs counter to the widely held view that individualism is antithetical to social inter-dependence. Of 165 tests of this set of hypotheses, 103 indicated the advantages of individualistic functioning, 62 null results were obtained, and none indicated a negative relationship.

Overall, this initial set of tests of hypotheses drawn from the theory of psychological individualism provided a substantial level of support for the perspective I have been developing. With respect to concerns about the objectivity with which research can be conducted when a particular nonepistemic value system is explicitly endorsed, it should be noted that the studies included in the review were, with few exceptions, conducted by other researchers whose values may very well have been quite different from my own and involved instruments not specifically developed for testing hypotheses associated with a theory of psychological individualism. If there is a concern that I may have been selective in identifying the 574 tests of the hypotheses described, the research record is available to anyone who wishes to replicate my efforts.

I have developed a range of other hypotheses pertaining to the theory of psychological individualism since the review just described (Waterman, 1984a, 1988b, 1989). Two of these hypotheses are discussed here because data are available on them. The first concerns the possibility of gender differences with respect to the qualities of psychological individualism. The second pertains to the nature of the cognitive–affective experiences accompanying efforts at self-realization.

When I developed the theory of psychological individualism, I explicitly stated that there were no theoretical grounds on which to expect gender differences in the qualities involved. When I presented the findings of the literature review in various settings, people often asked about possible gender differences in the individualistic qualities, with the expectation that psychological individualism would be more characteristic of males. Archer and Waterman (1988) reviewed the literature on the four individualistic qualities to determine whether males and females differed in their average levels of each. No consistent pattern of differences was found for any quality (although there was some indication that females might be higher on self-actualization than males) or for the four qualities combined. Of the 88 tests of gender differences reviewed, males scored significantly higher in 11 instances, females scored significantly higher in 11 instances, one comparison yielded mixed results, and the rest of the findings were nonsignificant. Furthermore, the original review of the literature on relationships of the individualistic qualities to other variables (Waterman, 1984b) revealed comparable levels of confirmation of the hypotheses when separate samples of males and females were involved. Archer and Water-man (1988) concluded that although males are conventionally thought of as individualistic in their functioning and females as functioning in a more communal fashion, neither gender typically functions in the way expected. Rather, males may better be characterized as functioning in an egocentric fashion, whereas females more often defer to the wishes of others. Thus, on average, neither gender is particularly high on the qualities of psychological individualism, but when those qualities are expressed, they are associated with more effective psychological functioning for both females and males.

Most recently, I have been concerned with the psychological concept of personal expressiveness, which I take to be the counterpart of the philosophical concept of eudaimonia (Waterman, 1990). According to eudaimonistic Hellenic philosophy, success in living in truth to one's daimon is said to be accompanied by a distinctive condition (eudaimonia) usually translated from the Greek as "happiness." However, there are excellent reasons for believing that the cognitive–affective experiences accompanying self-realization, while related to happiness in the hedonic meaning of the word, represent a distinct subjective condition. In a study involving 110 college students and adults (Waterman, 1989), measures of personal expressiveness and hedonic enjoyment of self-descriptive activities were found to be positively correlated ($r = .74$, $p < .0001$). As predicted, the measure of personal expressiveness was positively correlated with the perception that an activity provided the opportunity for the person to develop his or her best potentials ($r = .39$. $p < .001$), whereas the measure of hedonic enjoyment was not significantly correlated with this perception ($r = .15$). Furthermore, ratings of an activity as personally expressive were more highly correlated with reports that when engaged in it, the person invests a great deal of effort, feels competent, has clear goals, feels assertive, feels it is always different, feels alert, and feels good about himself or herself, than were ratings of the activity as enjoyable. In contrast, ratings of an activity as enjoyable were more highly correlated with reports that when engaged in it, the person forgot personal problems and felt relaxed, excited, content, and happy. Thus, emerging evidence is consistent with the expectation drawn from eudaimonist philosophy that efforts at self-realization are accompanied by a cognitive–affective condition related to, but distinct from, hedonic enjoyment.

CONCLUDING COMMENTS

In developing the theory of psychological individualism, I have been aware of the normative philosophical values underlying the theoretical propositions and specific hypotheses I have formulated. My value orientation has helped in setting my agenda regarding the aspects of the theory on which to focus at a given point in time. It has aided in the selection of the hypotheses that I have chosen to investigate through my own data collection activities. Perhaps most importantly, it has afforded me a sense of coherence and continuity across my professional and personal roles.

There are no inconsistencies between the nonepistemic values I endorse and the epistemic values of science that I strive to incorporate into my theoretical and research endeavors. Were I to be pursuing goals in another field of endeavor (e.g., law or the arts), I might not be concerned with the epistemic values of science, but rather consider my normative values in strictly deontological terms. However, as a psychologist involved in theory building and research, I am unwilling to consider those values on a strictly a priori basis. I believe there are important, empirically testable consequences that follow from efforts to live in accordance with one or another normative value system. As a scientist, I wish to investigate whether those consequences actually occur. If the results of my investigations were to repeatedly lead to the rejection of the hypotheses with which I started, I would conclude that the normative value system I endorse does not have the practical significance that I have attributed to it. Because my original adoption of the value system described herein was made on the basis of deontological considerations, negative research findings would not *in themselves* constitute a basis for their abandonment. Negative findings would, however, cause me to seriously reassess my normative premises.

Fortunately, my research efforts have resulted in a gratifying level of support for the hypotheses I have advanced. This support cannot be used to conclude that my normative premises are valid, because any of a variety of reasons could account for the research outcomes, some totally unrelated to the metatheoretical assumptions made. It is possible that other normative values, perhaps some quite at variance to my own, could be used to arrive at the same predictions I have made. But I think it fair to conclude that empirical findings in line with theoretical expectations provide support not only for the continued viability of the theory itself, but also for the continued viability of the metatheoretical assumptions on which it was based (Waterman, 1988a). In this manner, empirical investigations can contribute to the process of ethical inquiry, but we cannot expect that science will be able, finally, to settle philosophical disputes.

REFERENCES

Archer, S. L., & Waterman, A. S. (1988). Psychological individualism: Gender differences or gender neutrality? *Human Development, 31,* 65–81.

Aristotle. (1980). *The Nicomachean ethics.* New York: Oxford University Press.

Bandura, A. (1982). Self-efficacy mechanism in human agency. *American Psychologist, 37,* 122–147.

Bandura, A. (1989). Human agency in social cognitive theory. *American Psychologist, 44,* 1175–1184.

Brenner, C. (1973). *An elementary textbook of psychoanalysis.* New York: International Universities Press.

Capra, F. (1982). *The turning point.* New York: Simon and Schuster.

Crumbaugh, J. C. (1968). Cross-validation of Purpose-in-Life Test based on Frankl's concept. *Journal of Individual Psychology, 24,* 74–81.

Easterbrook, J. A. (1978). *The determinants of free will: A psychological analysis of responsible, adjustive behavior.* New York: Academic Press.

Frankl, V. E. (1965). *The doctor and the soul: From psychotherapy to logotherapy* (2nd ed.; R. Winston & C. Winston, Trans.). New York: Knopf.

Freud, S. (1960). *The psychopathology of everyday life.* New York: Norton. (Originally published in 1901)

Fromm, E. (1941). *Escape from freedom.* New York: Holt, Rinehart & Winston.

Gergen, K. (1982). *Toward transformation in social knowledge.* New York: Springer-Verlag.

Hare, R. M. (1963). *Freedom and reason.* Oxford: Oxford University Press.

Hospers, J. (1982). *Human conduct: Problems of ethics* (2nd ed.). New York: Harcourt Brace Jovanovich.

Howard, G. S. (1985). The role of values in the science of psychology. *American Psychologist, 40,* 255–265.

Johnson, J. A., Germer, C. K., Efran, J. S., & Overton, W. F. (1988). Personality as the basis for theoretical predilections. *Journal of Personality and Social Psychology, 55,* 824–835.

Knight, R. (1946). Determinism, freedom, and psychotherapy. *Psychiatry, 9,* 251–262.

Kuhn, T. S. (1970). *The structure of scientific revolutions* (2nd ed.). Chicago: University of Chicago Press.

Langer, E. J. (1975). The illusion of control. *Journal of Personality and Social Psychology, 32,* 311–328.

Laudan, L. (1984). *Science and values: The aims of science and their role in scientific debate.* Los Angeles: University of California Press.

Lefcourt, H. M. (1982). *Locus of control: Current trends in theory and research* (2nd ed.). Hillsdale, NJ: Erlbaum.

May, R. (1969). *Love and will.* New York: Norton.

Mischel, W. (1973). Toward a cognitive social learning reconceptualization of personality. *Psychological Review, 80,* 252–283.

Norton, D. L. (1976). *Personal destinies: A philosophy of ethical individualism.* Princeton, NJ: Princeton University Press.

Nozick, R. (1974). *Anarchy, state and utopia.* New York: Basic Books.

Overton, W. F. (1975). General systems, structure, and development. In K. F. Riegel & G. C. Rosenwald (Eds.), *Structure and transformation* (pp. 61–81). New York: Wiley.

Overton, W. F. (1984). World views and their influence on psychological theory and research: Kuhn–Lakatos–Laudan. In H. W. Reese (Ed.), *Advances in child development and behavior* (Vol. 18, pp. 191–226). New York: Academic Press.

Pepper, S. C. (1942). *World hypotheses.* Berkeley: University of California Press.

Reese, H. W., & Overton, W. R. (1970). Models of development and theories of development. In L. R. Goulet & P. B. Baltes (Eds.), *Life-span developmental psychology: Research and theory* (pp. 116–145). New York: Academic Press.

Riegel, K. F. (1972). Influence of economic and political ideologies on the development of developmental psychology. *Psychological Bulletin, 78,* 129–141.

Rogers, C. R. (1959). A theory of therapy, personality, and interpersonal relationships as developed in the client-centered framework. In S. Koch (Ed.), *Psychology: A study of a science, Vol. III. Formulations of the person and the social context* (pp. 184–256). New York: McGraw-Hill.

Rorty, R. (1979). *Philosophy and the mirror of nature.* Princeton, NJ: Princeton University Press.

Rosenthal, R. (1966). *Experimenter effects in behavior research.* New York: Appleton-Century-Crofts.

Rotter, J. D. (1966). Generalized expectancies for internal versus external control of reinforcement. *Psychological Monographs, 80* (1, Whole No. 609).

Skinner, B. F. (1971). *Beyond freedom and dignity.* New York: Knopf.

Steiner, I. D. (1970). Perceived freedom. In L. Berkowitz (Ed.), *Advances in experimental social psychology* (Vol. 5). New York: Academic Press.

Thoreau, H. D. (1962). Civil disobedience. In J. W. Krutch (Ed.), *Thoreau: Walden and other writings* (pp. 85–104). New York: Bantam. (Original work published 1849.)

Waterman, A. S. (1981). Individualism and interdependence. *American Psychologist, 36,* 762–773.

Waterman, A. S. (1984a). Identity formation: Discovery or creation? *Journal of Early Adolescence, 4,* 329–341.

Waterman, A. S. (1984b). *The psychology of individualism.* New York: Praeger.

Waterman, A. S. (1986, August). *Parameters of the self in a theory of self-realization.* Paper presented at the meeting of the American Psychological Association, Washington, DC.

Waterman, A. S. (1988a). On the uses of psychological theory and research in the process of ethical inquiry. *Psychological Bulletin, 103,* 283–298.

Waterman, A. S. (1988b). Psychological individualism and organizational functioning: A cost–benefit analysis. In K. Kolenda (Ed.), *Organizations and ethical individualism* (pp. 19–45). New York: Praeger.

Waterman, A. S. (1989, August). *Two conceptions of happiness: Research on eudaimonia and hedonic enjoyment.* Paper presented at the meeting of the American Psychological Association, New Orleans.

Waterman, A. S. (1990). Personal expressiveness: Philosophical and psychological foundations. *Journal of Mind and Behavior, 11,* 47–74.

Part III ▪ ════════════════════

Implications for the Scientific Study of Moral Phenomena ══ ▪

Chapter 8 ■

Antiparticularism in Developmental and Moral Theory ■

JAMES YOUNISS
Catholic University of America

In 1932, Piaget proposed that morality consisted in respect for persons rather than respect for rules. He explained his position in an elaborate theoretical discussion, supported it with an extensive presentation of data, and couched it in a polemical attack on the pedagogy of his day. Among other things, he sought to dismiss the Kantian view that morality did not emanate from experience, but consisted in respect for rules insofar as rules were rationally grounded. For Piaget, this view was too individualistic, asocial, and nondevelopmental. His own position was that morality consisted in respect for persons, which was engendered early in children's experiences with beneficent caretakers who provided rules for everyday life's domains of eating and sleeping to which colored pills cured which little ills. He argued further that after children developed respect for all-knowing adults, they discovered reciprocity in interactions with peers who exchange opinions, ask questions, negotiate differences, forge compromises, and co-construct ideas of right and wrong. When reciprocity became a norm, a new form of respect, founded on cooperation, emerged. It centered on persons' voluntary agreement that they should use fair procedures to guide their interactions and relationships.

Piaget's thesis has not been given a full hearing by U.S. developmental psychologists. Initially, the thesis was ignored as researchers focused on collecting empirical evidence that would operationalize concepts in behavioral terms. When Piaget's 1932 book was reintroduced into the field in the

1960s, the audience was more open to his ideas, but ready to interpret them according to a received view that emphasized Piaget's presumed cognitive outlook. "Piagetian cognition" was taken as an independent domain of development in which children constructed concepts of reality by acting, then logically reflecting on objects. Hence, for Kohlberg (1969), and others, cognitive development mediated and superseded social experience in leading to advances in moral concepts.

Another appeal of this Piagetian cognitive approach was articulated in the writings of Kohlberg, who sought grounds for a morality with universal validity and applicability. Kohlberg pointed out that the traditional socialization framework led to concepts that were experientially and culturally contingent. Kohlberg, like other scholars at the time, was still trying to understand the horrors of Nazi Germany and Stalin's USSR. Perhaps he hoped to understand whether it was possible for persons to construct a morality that went beyond the constraints of their immediate social surrounds. In this vein, Piaget's theory served to show that individuals could discover the absolute right regardless of the circumstances in which they lived. Kohlberg's understanding was that experience provided occasions for the individual to use reasoning (i.e., self-reflective thought guided by logic). Although experience could lead the individual to know the "is" of social interactions, cognition was the true grounds for rendering knowledge of the moral "ought."

Despite the compellingness of this view and its fit for the times, Piaget (1932) anticipated and explicitly dissociated himself from this interpretation. One can ask, therefore, how it came to be attributed to him as the received Piagetian interpretation. My thesis is that those who read this emphasis into Piaget wanted to escape the relativism of socialization models, which predicated moral concepts on experience, and to ground universal morality in logic. These are legitimate goals and easily justify this genre of work. Still, it remains to be explained why this interpretation of Piaget took precedence over his carefully crafted argument against a cognitive position and his effort to make social relationships the basis for a morality of human respect.

Given the clarity of Piaget's writings and their disparity from the received view, it seems worthwhile to explore the implicit theme that might have been guiding researchers. I aim in this chapter to identify one such theme that is deeply rooted in an association between morality and developmental studies of children. For at least a century in the United States, children have signified the hope of reforming society (Letchworth, 1875/1974). By housing, feeding, and educating children, reformers hoped to educate them morally and thereby strengthen the moral position of their elders and the nation in general (Brace, 1880). In the nineteenth century, this theme was often enacted by helping immigrant children sever relations with parents and ethnic groups in order to instill a new outlook that was Protestant and American in basis (Youniss, 1990). I propose that this theme has remained implicit in our thinking about children, although it is expressed in terms that reduce to the belief that children need not replicate the views and values of their families and the ethnic groups from which they come. Riesman (1950), like writers in the 1870s, argued that it was dysfunctional for parents to demand that children adopt their values, because societal norms were changing. His "other-directed" character type was encouraged to find an identity by looking outside the family. Much research since the 1950s has been devoted to specifying devices by which children can acquire concepts that take understanding beyond their specific familial experiences. Cognition, which transforms experience, is one of those devices.

I will try to demonstrate how this theme has become a metatheoretical shadow in our theories of morality and children's development. First, I establish that Piaget believed universally valid concepts of morality could be achieved through particularistic social experience. To explain why psychologists have avoided this point, I try to elaborate on the dominant countertheme that experience leads to fallible moral views and that a mature and correct moral outlook requires rising above one's personal–social experience. I show this in five ways:

1. Progressive philosophy emphasizes that moral principles do not depend on personal sentiment or on the familiarity of particularist relationships. On the contrary, universal moral principles apply to everyone; they are per force general rather than particular.
2. During the late nineteenth century, U.S. social reformers focused on children as the means to save society. They viewed childhood in a matrix of religious and patriotic ideology. Reformers hoped to switch children's loyalty from their familial heritage to the prevailing Protestant–American ethos. They justified separating children from parents, religion, and ethnic group by making identification with U.S. citizenship a personal as well as societal good.
3. Reformers were supported in their efforts by Christian theology, which made general, rather than particular, relations the ideal for which we should strive. This ideal was accepted by reformers and reappeared in the writings of G. Stanley Hall, who founded the discipline of developmental psychology.
4. During the first three decades of the present century, justification of reform through children shifted from religion to rational governmental policy. Leaders in child welfare endorsed state control over the family in managing children's lives. Among other things, they lobbied against parents' wishes for compulsory education and restrictive labor laws.

5. The foregoing events led to an interesting turn in the evolving course of this theme. As developmental psychology was forming into a discipline, the nation was changing in its multiethnic makeup and tolerance for various viewpoints. The developmental psychology of Hall, which was grounded in religious and racial suppositions, became dated. For the new scientific psychology, childhood was a natural category and functions were expressions of fundamental processes that were immune from particular experience. It took only the one further step of putting cognition into the category of natural processes to virtually eliminate any role for particular experience or relationship in children's moral development.

PIAGET'S 1932 STATEMENT

Piaget considered and rejected the "cognitive" approach in his 1932 book, *The Moral Judgment of the Child.* He identified the approach as Kantian in origin and found it inadequate. He sought, instead, to ground development in an experiential base that was social and relational. Agreeing with Kant that morality consists in a system of rules and respect for the system, Piaget consciously took a different direction and spent roughly 400 pages outlining his position.

First, he denied that moral imperatives are "inexplicable from the point of view of experience" (p. 100). Second, he shifted focus from respect for rules, as such, to respect for persons who constructed and abided by rules: "M. Bovet [and Piaget] rejects the Kantian attempt to interpret respect as an effect of rational law, and endeavours, on the contrary, to explain rational rules by respect, and respect by the empirical conditions of social relations themselves" (pp. 371–372). Third, in stressing that respect is for persons, Piaget emphasized the importance of cooperative construction: "The law is not the source of respect. It is respect for persons which causes the commands coming from these persons to acquire the force of law in the spirit that feels respect" (p. 375). Fourth, while respect for persons emanates from elders whose omniscience creates respectful awe, it is transformed into mutual respect as peers discuss, debate, and co-construct rules: "Since the rule is now subjected to the laws of reciprocity, it is these same rules, rational in their essence, that will become the true norms of morality" (p. 382). To emphasize the social character of respect, Piaget added: "Henceforward reason will be able to lay down its plan of action in so far as it remains rational . . . *i.e., in so far as the individual can adopt a perspective such that other perspectives will accord with it* " (p. 384; emphasis added). To clarify:

> As soon as A identifies himself morally with B, and thus submits his own point of view to the laws of reciprocity, the product of this mutual respect is

bound to be something new, because the norms admitted from now onwards will necessarily be contained within this very reciprocity. (p. 385)

It is evident that Piaget was trying to forge a new path that would ground morality in experience, yet permit achievement of universal concepts. He did this by founding respect on interpersonal relations and embedding reason in processes of social interaction, with emphasis on discussion and reciprocity. Only in the recent past, however, has his effort gained recognition (see Chapman, 1986; Wright, 1983; Youniss, 1978). Nevertheless, the received interpretation in the field still associates Piaget with Kant's program and denies that universal principles are achieved through social interaction. A fuller analysis of this effort can be found in the above sources. For the present, I focus on the confluence of antiparticularist sources that has shaped developmental psychology.

AMERICAN PROGRESSIVE PHILOSOPHY AND IMPERSONAL MORALITY

In a chapter on the development of moral and conventional concepts, Turiel, Killen, and Helwig (1987) used the following terminology to distinguish the conventional from the moral domain:

Conventions are part of constitutive systems and are shared behaviors . . . whose meanings are defined by the constituted system in which they are embedded. . . . Conventions are thus context-dependent and their content may vary by socially constructed meanings. . . . While morality also applies to social systems, it is not constitutive or defined by existing social arrangements . . . [P]rescriptions are . . . unconditionally obligatory, generalizable, and impersonal insofar as they stem from concepts of welfare, justice, and rights. (pp. 160–170)

Two points stand out. One is that morality is distinguished from "socially constructed meanings," and the other is an emphasis on the "impersonal" nature of morality. These points represent a widely held view in our culture. In the second presidential debate of the 1988 campaign, Bernard Shaw, the moderator, opened with a question to Governor Dukakis about whether he might change his position on the death penalty were his wife the victim of some criminal's rape or murder. The intent of the question was clear: Shaw wanted to know how much of a generalist Dukakis actually was. Dukakis answered unflinchingly that the death penalty was not justified in this or any other case because it violated a fundamental right and because it did not deter crime. This manifestation of his generalist stand proved to be costly, especially because Vice-President Bush gave a strong particularist response that stressed empathy for victims and their families.

Dukakis was, in fact, restating the view that moral principles are obligatory irrespective of personal circumstances. If it is a principle, it must be applied without regard to the individuals involved, kinship notwithstanding. Loved ones should be treated as persons in general, as should one's enemies.

A second instance appeared in the Washington *Post* on November 22, 1988, in a "Profile" on Lowell Weicker, who had just lost his U.S. Senate seat from Connecticut:

> Some people think Weicker's outspoken support of the disabled and the mentally retarded stems from his 10-year-old son, Sonny, who was born with Down syndrome—but Weicker bristles at that notion. "I really get bothered when people say that I would be motivated by a personal issue," he said, noting that his interest in the mentally retarded and the handicapped began years before Sonny was born.

Like Dukakis, Weicker holds the view that personal relationship should not be part of one's moral decision making. In "bristling" at the thought that there might be a connection, Mr. Weicker suggested that a personal motive might taint the choice to do good. If something is right, its rightness inheres in the act and does not need the prop of a personal motive, which, in fact, may detract from it.

A third case is taken from Rawls's (1971) argument regarding why individuals would freely choose a morality of fair distribution. Rawls demonstrated his argument with a device he called the "original condition," in which persons were to choose a moral position under a "veil of ignorance" as to their own standing, one to another. Choices were to be made without knowing how talents, wealth, or disabilities were distributed. Any individual might be smart or retarded, rich or poor, healthy or sickly. Rawls argued that reasonable persons in this condition would rationally select equal distribution as the core principle of justice.

Rawls's strategy is clever for bringing out the human fear that we might not be among the fortunate chosen few. Although some of us might gamble that we were members of the elect, the safe choice is to opt for equal distribution to be assured of something rather than risk getting nothing. Developmental psychologists, however, should question the applicability of this device. Moral orientations are not made "in ignorance," but are constructed through experience, which provides children with knowledge of themselves in relation to other persons. This is not to quarrel with Rawls's conclusion, but to question the premise that moral concepts arise outside interpersonal history. This may be an appropriate starting point for philosophical argumentation, but it cannot be for developmental psychology.

THE NINETEENTH-CENTURY CHILD SAVERS

There is evidence that presuppositions about religion and race were embedded in nineteenth-century concepts of childhood in the United States (Wertsch & Youniss, 1987; Youniss, 1990). By the time a discipline of developmental studies was forming, dated either by the writings of G. Stanley Hall or the founding of the Society for Research in Child Development in the mid-1920s, concepts of childhood had been framed in accord with the American culture (Kessen, 1979). From the mid-nineteenth century on, there was public interest in children's education and moral character, with a major impetus being the changing demographic distribution of the young nation's population. As non-British immigrants began to arrive in increasing numbers, the nation was becoming more "foreign." First Irish and German families came, and then, by the 1870s, eastern and southern European emigrants from Italy, Russia, Poland, and the like, were arriving (Olson, 1987). To a large extent, these immigrants were poor, spoke languages other than English, and manifested behavior patterns that were noticeably different from middle-class Protestant Americans.

In cities such as New York, the presence of these people was a cause of concern for the nation's future. It stimulated efforts on the part of reformers to make productive American citizens of the indigent immigrant masses. Lane (1932) asserted that efforts were initially focused on moral character, which entailed religious as well as patriotic features. Initial attempts were aimed at converting adults to Protestantism, but when they failed, focus was shifted to children, who were perceived as malleable. Hence, the "child saving" movement began (Platt, 1969; Tiffin, 1982), which was designed to shape the next generation of citizens who would carry on America's traditions and preserve the nation.

Reformers emphasized the importance of religious–moral character in the creation of good citizens (Brace, 1880; Campbell, 1896; Letchworth, 1875/1974). Brace is an interesting representative of this perspective. He worked for and eventually headed the Children's Aid Society (CAS) in New York. He described his activities and philosophy in his popular book, first published in 1875: *The Dangerous Classes of New York and Twenty Years Work among Them.* He defined the dangerous classes as the immigrants, mainly Irish, Italian, and Catholic, who were crowded into New York's 32,000 tenements, spent much of their lives in the streets in debauched states, and left their children unattended with license to fend for themselves. Brace believed it was necessary to intervene into these lives if the nation was to be preserved (see also Campbell, 1896).

The CAS set up numerous residential facilities where children could come off the streets for meals and bedding. They also served as educational centers for vocational training and as catchment facilities. According to Brace's plan, street children were to be enticed into the homes through tender treatment. Once their physical needs were met, their souls could be won over for Christianity and the nation:

> [We must] treat the lads as independent little dealers, and give nothing without payment, but at the same time to offer them much more for their money than they could get anywhere else. Moral, educational, and religious influences were to come in afterward. Serving them through their interests, we had permanent hold on them. (pp. 100–101)

Brace believed it was necessary to put a wedge between children and parents to break the cycle of crime and poverty; otherwise, he felt, parents would perpetuate their ill habits through their offspring. The CAS sent youngsters from New York to midwestern farm families, which took them in as their own children. Estimates are that as many as 125,000 children were shipped west between 1859 and 1929 by the CAS (Jackson, 1986; also see Bellingham, 1983). Other societies, such as the Little Wanderers in Boston, had similar programs. Many farmers needed labor, and when announcements of a coming trainload of children were made, the waiting lines were long (McOllough, 1988). The farmers got laborers, and the children received new identities that nullified their family connections. Hence, ideology merged with practicality in a growing nation.

One can see in these efforts that the welfare of children was closely tied to the nation's welfare. It is equally evident that the nation's welfare was synonymous with the American, Protestant tradition. This end justified the means of severing children from their family heritage. Reformers such as Brace saw this as necessary because adults had become degraded by the harsh circumstances they met in New York. Salvation of the children and that of the nation coincided; hence, creating loyalty to the nation, even if it meant separating children from their parents, became justified.

PROTESTANT-CHRISTIAN THEOLOGY

Smith (1957) documented how the sectarian lines that divided forms of Protestantism became increasingly blurred during the nineteenth century. He cited as evidence the popularity of religious revivals, which were held in the large cities. Itinerant preachers came to cities under the multiple sponsorship of several denominations. Their message had to be cast in nonsectarian terms to reach a large number of people and be appropriate for a wide range of beliefs. G. Stanley Hall (1904) devoted an 80-page chapter in his book, *Adolescence*, to the topic of religious conversion, and he described the revival as a campus tradition in America's elite colleges. For Hall, being born again as Christian was fundamental to the psychological nature of adolescence: "In its most fundamental sense, conversion is a natural, normal, universal, and necessary process at the stage when life pivots over an autocentric to an heterocentric basis" (p. 301).

This kind of Christianity entailed an antiparticularistic outlook. Recall that Brace and others justified removing children from their families for the sake of a broader identification as Christian Americans. This outlook can be seen as inherent in Protestant theology, which, taken in the broad a sense (Meilaender, 1981), provides insight into the tension between particularism and universalism. Meilaender approached the issue through a study of theological treatment of friendship. He showed how friendship, which is particular in the sense of being personal, stands in opposition to the Christian ideal of love, which extends to everyone, including one's enemies.

Meilaender analyzed the opposition in greater detail. Two examples illustrate his longer argument. Friendship is understood to involve reciprocity such that each friend is to return what the other has given. The rule is clear to the degree that when one friend does not reciprocate, the other is freed of obligation and the friendship is put in jeopardy. However, the Christian ideal does not require reciprocity because love is not contingent. Indeed, the ideal friend is Christ, whose voluntary death cannot be repaid by humans. A second example is loyalty, which depends on friends liking each other. However, we know that sentiment, which can form and grow, can also wane. But, the Christian ideal demands permanent loyalty in the sense that God's love of people never wavers.

In this theology, ideal love is attained in the individual's relationship with the entire Christian community. In theory, this community includes all humans in that each stands in a charitable relation to everyone else. Friendship, because it is particular, cannot be an ideal. It represents a breaking off from the community: "Every real friendship is a sort of secession, even a rebellion . . . a pocket of potential resistance" (C. S. Lewis, quoted in Meilaender, 1981, p. 79). The particularism of friendship stands in tension to the ideal of Christian love, which is universal and orients the individual to all humanity rather than to a few other specific persons.

Coser (1974) described the tension as it has applied to Christian institutions such as religious orders. Many of these institutions restrict members' contacts with their families, sever legal relations with parents, and demand vows of celibacy, which preempt formation of new family relationships.

Coser analyzed these demands in terms of the institution's desire for loyalty to it as a general entity, and viewed this desire as incompatible with dispersion of loyalty across particular relationships. This desire explains the rules of insulation and isolation that many communities impose (Kanter, 1972). The tension between love for all and affection for a few is minimized by prohibition of the latter. In Meilaender's (1981) analysis, the problem is inconstancy of personal and particular bonds that are based on sentiment. Love in Christian theology requires unconditional commitment that puts an individual in charitable relationship to all other persons.

PROGRESSIVE CHILD WELFARE

Grace Abbott (1938) and Sophonisba Breckenridge (1934) wrote histories that document the path from British common law to protective legislation for children in the United States. Although we can retrospectively see expansion of the basic position taken by nineteenth-century reformers against the family to create healthy and productive citizens, this theme was not evident to these chroniclers. Rather, they wrote with a sense that rationality and the common good gradually triumphed over ignorance with its particularistic bias. This thinking is not surprising for an era in which rational government was promoted as the antidote to special interests and the means by which the good of the whole would prevail over advantage for a select few (LaFollette, 1960).

Abbott recounted changes in child custody decisions, beginning with the extension of British common law to the new nation. Custody decisions were almost always made in favor of fathers, under the principle of "absolute paternal rights." Children were the property of their fathers, and the principle held even when fathers proved to be less than morally upright. After the Civil War, custody decisions began to move in another direction as absolute paternal rights were weighed against a new principle of "the child's best interests." Judges began to award mothers custody on the grounds that they could provide more adequate care than fathers. Abbott showed further how the new principle was extended to the next logical step: If children had interests that were different from their parents' interests, agents other than the parents might better serve them. Hence, the state could assign custody to nonparents, when parents were deemed unfit or inadequate.

Rational determination by the state was deemed a positive advance in the name of children's interests and rights. However, it also shows that during this period, a position was being adopted that the good of society took precedence over the rights of parents. According to the rational criterion of "best interests," such things as a mother's sentiment or emotional attachment became secondary to society's good. Another case is seen in the junction of laws regarding school and work. The Children's Bureau, of which Abbott was the head, sponsored numerous studies on industrial work conditions involving children. Reports focused on operators of machinery in factories, newsboys on the streets, and seasonal harvesters of farm crops. The results were instrumental in passage of restrictive and protective labor laws for children. While these laws were being framed, a complementary set was being enacted that extended the number of days per year as well as ages at which children had to attend school. The conjunction of these laws radically restructured children's lives and the family economy. Labor was removed from children's experience, being replaced by schooling, and children's contributions to family income were virtually ended.

The received view is that these laws were beneficial to society and children. Education, for example, allowed social mobility and upgraded the nation's workforce. However, it should be noted that these laws were often opposed by parents, who wanted their children to contribute to the family income as well as to enter the field of work they would hold later as adults. Abbott and Breckenridge offered the contemporary reader insight into the perspective that the parent–child relationship was not to be left to the family, but was better managed by experts. Whether nineteenth-century religious reformers or twentieth-century social scientists, these experts saw themselves as able to help children reach their ultimate development and, in the process, to strengthen the nation. By intervening into the parent–child bond, experts implied that particularism limited children and deterred children's bonding in with society. The child's identity with the family may have been important and worth cultivating, but the child's good citizenship, including being productive and moral, had priority.

DEVELOPMENTAL PSYCHOLOGY: THE SCIENCE

Smuts (1986) reported on the founding of the Society for Research in Child Development (SRCD) during the period 1925 to 1932. Documents reveal the important role played by experimental psychologists, especially Robert Woodworth of Columbia University, who served as the sponsor of SRCD through his office with the National Research Council. In helping the young society gain needed funds for its start, he advised it to avoid any interest in reform and to adopt a public posture focused strictly on scientific understanding. He suggested that SRCD should restrict "its function to research and [assure] that its scientific status was not tainted by association with child welfare or parent training activities" (quoted in Smuts, 1986, p. 112).

This advice gains significance when placed in historical context. Only a decade earlier, G. Stanley Hall had tried to form a "society of societies" that would combine scientific understanding with welfare and education (e.g., Hall, 1909). Why were Woodworth and Hall on different sides of this issue? One way to understand the difference is to recognize that Hall, the founder of the discipline of developmental psychology, belonged to two eras—the nineteenth century with its emphasis on religious and moral character, and the twentieth century with its scientific–objective outlook. Although Hall's work clearly led the way to empirical studies of children (Siegel & White, 1982), his writings were heavily laden with religious and racial views that he treated as integral to psychology. Recall the example above regarding the naturalness and necessity of adolescent religious conversion.

Hall mixed psychology, religion, and racism so thoroughly that he appears outside the boundaries of contemporary thinking. For example, in his address to the Young Men's Christian Association, Hall spoke in terms one would expect of a minister: "Full knowledge of his [Jesus's] mind would be the only complete normal psychology. His pedagogy is normative. . . . Scripture is the world's great textbook in psychology" (p. 486). Hall's racial views seem equally out of date. For instance, he considered blacks characterologically unable to control sexual impulses and unable to vote with mature judgment (Hall, 1905; cf. Muschinske, 1977; Youniss, 1990). Hall expressed these views in public forums, such as national conventions, and reprinted them in his journal, *Pedagogical Seminary.*

Hall's religious and racial categories may have been appropriate for nineteenth-century reformers, but they did not fit the tenor of the emerging twentieth-century scientific outlook. Woodworth (1910) was critical of racial categories and especially so of attempts to base them in biology. His colleague at Columbia, Edward Thorndike, was critical of Hall's use of religion to explain and justify psychology; Siegel and White (1982) quoted Thorndike's reaction to Hall's book on adolescence as "full of errors, masturbation, and Jesus" (p. 270). Surely Watson was no less ready to dismiss Hall's ideas in favor of regrounding psychology on a behavioral base. He believed that a scientific psychology could replace religion with an experimental ethics. Unlike Hall, he denied the value of explaining criminality through temperament or character (Watson, 1928).

By the 1920s and 1930s, psychologists interested in children had taken a further step against particularism as they sought to identify basic psychological processes. The categories of Irish, Italian, and Catholic children had outlived their usefulness because scientific psychology could deal with the generic child. Hartshorne and May (1928–1930), in a series of studies on morality in children, advanced the view that "situations" rather than inherent character determined children's moral behavior: "As situations became less and less alike there was found greater and greater diversity of behavior, so that one could not predict from what a person did in one situation what he would do in a different situation" (1928–1930, p. 1).

This kind of thinking was linked with the progressive movement insofar as science was the means that reformers could use to create a new society through general socialization processes. Sentiment, love, and affection between parents and children were considered by Watson and others to be irrelevant, if not counteractive to the child's and the parent's welfare. The means for directing behavior were found in general processes of acquisition and modification. Anyone could control them; the quality of the particular relation between socializers and children was not so important as the skilled employment of proper processes. Watson claimed that if parents would give him their children, he would make of them what parents wanted. He would use effective techniques to produce outcomes without regard to personal involvement or particularist bonding.

PIAGET'S 1932 THESIS REVISITED

Commentators have recently recognized the social and interpersonal basis of morality that Piaget offered in his 1932 work (Chapman, 1986; Wright, 1982; Youniss, 1980). They agree that Piaget attempted to show how children could achieve moral concepts that had universal applicability directly from interpersonal experience. As stated previously, Piaget chose this option over the position that reasoning counted more than experience and that moral concepts emanated from individual reflection rather than from social discourse. Respect for persons was founded on structures of interpersonal relations. Unilateral respect emanated from the structure of authority, but cooperation led to a more equilibrated form of mutual respect. Through these structures, children find grounds for universal concepts. For example, in a cooperative relationship, peers come to realize that to avoid stalemates, they can agree to guide the practice of reciprocity with a principle of fairness that takes account of individual differences (Youniss, 1980).

It should now be evident that Piaget's attempt to base universal concepts in the experience of close personal relationships conflicted with a perspective that has deep roots in our discipline. Children's close, particular relationships have been viewed as impediments to mature concepts of morality. This doubt is rooted in Christian theology, insofar as personal one-to-one bonds detract from general one-to-all relations. It is found in the ethos of nineteenth-century reform, which encouraged removal of children from their parents for the sake of acquiring proper Protestant upbringing. The progressive reformers forged a new approach to child welfare with techniques of education that reassigned socialization from parents to experts. The first generation of scientific developmental psychologists carried this view forward and raised it to a new plane. They hoped to find natural processes by which all children could acquire adaptive behavior. They believed that such processes were natural and could be consciously employed. Their enactment did not need the support of personal involvement or particular sentiment.

It is important to recall that a cognitive viewpoint entered psychology in the 1960s, in part because of weaknesses in the behavioral position. For cognitive theorists, that position was still too particular, because as long as children were influenced by experience, their concepts of morality were constrained by specifically observed instances of right and wrong. With reasoning as the means for constructing concepts, experience became only an occasion for the "is" to be made into a universal "ought." It is likely that Kohlberg and others who tried to get us beyond the behavioral morass of relativism, discounted the interpersonal side of Piaget as they focused on moral universals drawn from reasoning.

CONCLUSION

I agree with the efforts of Kohlberg and others who tried to answer the question of how children could construct concepts of morality that had universal validity and applicability. Indeed, Turiel et al. (1987) made a compelling case that universality is an inherent characteristic of moral, in contrast to other kinds of, concepts. I have argued, however, that Kohlberg and others operated from an intellectual tradition in which universality could not emanate from or be based in personal, particular relations. This tradition has multiple roots that can be traced back at least 100 years in the ideas of great social reformers and child savers in the United States. This effort was consonant with Protestant theology, whose idea was love for all rather than particular sentiment. The idea was maintained in the present century by progressive reformers who transferred the educative function from parents to experts.

The birth of the science of developmental psychology witnessed removal of religious and racial characterizations that applied to its predecessors. These early scientists were equally skeptical of parental relations and believed in the effectiveness of universal processes, regardless of the personal relationship between the socializing agent and recipient. Hence, when the cognitive approach took shape a few decades later, the argument against personal relations and experience did not have to be made. Theorists had only to articulate the theme that was already embedded in the discipline. By making reasoning, harnessed with interior logic, the means to construct universal moral concepts, theorists were finally able to remove the individual from all particularist interference.

My aim has been to identify a metatheoretical theme that lies deep within our tradition and to show the various guises it has had in the growth of our discipline over the past century. I have focused on Piaget's theory to illustrate how a dominant theme can block out an argument based on a different metatheory. I now want to add a final implication. In his book, *The End of Liberalism*, Theodore Lowi (1969) argued that the progressives had promised that rational procedures produce political decisions that achieve the most good for the largest number of persons. Advocates believed that this moral outcome would derive from the "blind" use of rationalism, which would no longer favor a powerful few over the welfare of the majority.

Lowi announced the "end" of that program because it had failed to deliver on its promise. Its error was in banking on rational procedures to lead to moral results. Lowi concluded that the mistake was to ignore the fact that procedures are enacted by human actors who operate for personal and particularist motives. Procedures are not inherently moral; morality depends on respect between persons who must want to act morally because they want to show respect and to be respected.

In identifying the thematic tension between particular and general relations, I hope to encourage a fresh interest in Piaget's thesis that cooperative interpersonal relationships provide the social context for universal moral concepts. In tracking the theme through the discipline's history, I hope also to encourage self-reflection that may help us join the larger debate that has been going on in other social sciences, all of which owe a debt to progressive liberalism. The ends of this philosophy are undoubtedly as legitimate today as they were a century ago; however, to reach them, we need to reflect on the weaknesses in this position and identify reasons why desired outcomes were not accomplished. Piaget's thesis provides an insight into one possible correction. Psychologists interested in children have often viewed particular relations as having limited value and as being in need of supplementation. These relationships, which are founded on reciprocity and cooperation, may be essential to mature conceptions of morality. Although they are engendered in the practice among a limited sphere of persons, they may suggest general applicability to all other persons in the developmental sense that Piaget once proposed.

REFERENCES

Abbott, G. (1938). *The child and the state.* Chicago: University of Chicago Press.

Bellingham, B. (1983). The "unspeakable blessing": Street children, reform rhetoric, and misery in early industrial capitalism. *Politics & Society, 12,* 303–330.

Brace, C. L. (1880). *The dangerous classes of New York and twenty years work among them.* New York: Wynkoop & Hallenbeck.

Breckenridge, S. P. (1934). *The family and the state.* Chicago: University of Chicago Press.

Campbell, H. (1896). *Darkness and daylight: Or light and shadows of New York life.* Hartford, CT: Hartford.

Chapman, M. J. (1986). The structure of exchange: Piaget's sociological theory. *Human Development, 29,* 181–194.

Coser, L. A. (1974). *Greedy institutions: Patterns of undivided commitment.* New York: Free Press.

Hall, G. S. (1904). *Adolescence* (Vol. 2). New York: Appleton.

Hall, G. S. (1905). The efficiency of the religious work of the Young Men's Christian Association. *Pedagogical Seminary, 12,* 478–489.

Hall, G. S. (1909). *Proceedings of the Child Conference for Research and Welfare.* New York: G. E. Stechert.

Hartshorne, H., & May, M. S. (1928–1930). *Studies in the organization of character* (Vol. 3). New York: Macmillan.

Jackson, D. D. (1986). It took trains to put street kids on the right track out of the slums. *Smithsonian, 17,* 94–103.

Kantor, R. B. (1972). *Commitment and community.* Cambridge, MA: Harvard University Press.

Kessen, W. (1979). The American child and other cultural inventions. *American Psychologist, 34,* 815–820.

Kohlberg, L. (1969). Stage and sequence: The cognitive–developmental approach to socialization. In D. A. Goslin (Ed.), *Handbook of socialization theory and research* (pp. 347–480). Chicago: Rand McNally.

LaFollette, R. M. (1960). *LaFollette's autobiography: A personal narrative of political experience.* Madison: University of Wisconsin Press.

Lane, F. E. (1932). *American charities and the child of the immigrant.* New York: Paulist Press.

Letchworth, W. P. (1974). *Homes of homeless children.* New York: Arno Press. (Original work published 1875.)

Lowi, T. J. (1969). *The end of liberalism.* New York: Norton.

McOllough, V. (1988). The orphan train comes to Clarion. *The Palimpset, 69,* 144–150.

Meilaender, G. C. (1981). *Friendship: A study in theological ethics.* Notre Dame, IN: University of Notre Dame Press.

Muschinske, D. (1977). The nonwhite as child: G. Stanley Hall on the education of nonwhite peoples. *Journal of the History of the Behavioral Sciences, 13,* 328–336.

Olson, J. S. (1987). *Catholic immigrants in America.* Chicago: Nelson-Hall.

Piaget, J. (1932). *The moral judgment of the child.* London: Kegan Paul.

Platt, A. (1969). *The child savers.* Chicago: University of Chicago Press.

Rawls, J. (1971). *A theory of justice.* Cambridge, MA: Harvard University Press.

Riesman, D. (1950). *The lonely crowd.* Garden City, NY: Doubleday.

Siegel, A. W., & White, S. H. (1982). The child study movement. In H. W. Reese (Ed.), *Advances in child development and behavior* (pp. 233–285). New York: Academic Press.

Smith, T. L. (1957). *Revivalism and social reform: American Protestantism on the eve of the Civil War.* Baltimore: Johns Hopkins University Press.

Smuts, A. B. (1986). The National Research Council Committee on Child Development and the founding of the Society for Research in Child Development, 1925–1933. In A. B. Smuts & J. W. Hagen (Eds.), History and research in child development. *Monographs of the Society for Research in Child Development, 50.*

Tiffin, S. (1982). *In whose best interest: Child welfare reform in the progressive era.* Westport, CT: Greenwood Press.

Turiel, E., Killen, M., & Helwig, C. C. (1987). Morality: Its structure, functions and vagaries. In J. Kagan & S. Lamb (Eds.), *The emergence of moral concepts in young children* (pp. 155–243). Chicago: University of Chicago Press.

Watson, J. B. (1928). *Psychological care of infant and child.* New York: Norton, pp. 155–243.

Wertsch, J. V., & Youniss, J. (1987). Contextualizing the investigator: The case of developmental psychology. *Human Development, 30,* 18–31.

Woodworth, R. S. (1910). Racial differences in mental traits. *Science, 31,* 171–186.

Wright, D. (1983). "The moral judgment of the child" revisited. In H. Weinrich-Haste & D. Locke (Eds.), *Moral judgment and moral action* (pp. 141–155). London: Wiley.

Youniss, J. (1978). Dialectical theory and Piaget on social knowledge. *Human Development, 21,* 234–247.

Youniss, J. (1980). *Parents and peers in social development.* Chicago: University of Chicago Press.

Youniss, J. (1990). Cultural forces leading to scientific developmental psychology. In C. B. Fisher & W. W. Tryon (Eds.), *Ethics in applied developmental psychology* (pp. 285–300). Norwood, NJ: Ablex.

Chapter 9 ■

Individualizing Conscience: New Thoughts on Old Issues ■

NICHOLAS EMLER
University of Dundee

ROBERT HOGAN
University of Tulsa

Outward be fair, however foul within;
sin if thou wilt, but then in secret sin.

Charles Churchill (1731–1764)

A former British prime minister observed that there is no such thing as society; there are only individuals and families. Had she fully absorbed the psychological literature on morality, she might have modified this conclusion slightly: There are only individuals. In this chapter, we argue that moral psychology has taken a course charted not by the interplay of theory and evidence alone, but by the influence upon both of a set of value assumptions. Earlier this century, Max Weber initiated a debate about the proper role of values in scientific inquiry (Weber, 1919/1946). The debate continues, but some progress has been made (Kurtines, Alvarez, & Azmitia, 1990). We now recognize that certain kinds of value commitments are not something for scientists to avoid; they are entirely proper.

However, as Kurtines et al. (1990) pointed out, the psychological analysis of morality occupies a special position in this debate because it deals with the nature and origins of value commitments. Therefore, it is all the more important to be clear about the scope of this analysis. Values that underlie research are less likely to become the objects of research, and we must ask whether they merit this immunity.

In this chapter, we develop propositions we first explored some years ago (Emler, 1983; Hogan, 1975; Hogan & Emler, 1978). Our thesis is that moral psychology has been substantially shaped and directed by the values of liberalism and individualism, which, briefly stated, reflect the position that society should be a series of freely contracted agreements between rational, equal, and autonomous individuals. These values, particularly individualism, have produced a progressive individualization and privatization of moral life, as represented in the moral psychology of this century. This is reflected in four related trends in theory and research: (1) the movement of scholarly attention in moral psychology from the processes of social control to those of individual self-control; (2) the trend from analyzing the public display of moral sentiments to examining private and internal reactions; (3) a shift in emphasis from collectively evolved moral standards to individually constructed standards; and (4) a progressive shift from seeing the individual as the source of moral danger to seeing the group as the foe of morality.

The case for reassessing the impact of individualism on moral psychology is twofold. First, individualism has significantly inhibited scientific understanding of morality and immorality, and second, the assumptions it embodies about human nature and social life are inappropriate. We propose alternative assumptions, which entail a resocialization of the conscience. We hope to convince the reader to take a new look at the old issues of social control and moral action.

To appreciate the impact of individualism on moral psychology, it is helpful first to consider moral psychology's origins in nineteenth-century social theory.

THREATS TO CIVILIZATION

The late nineteenth century was a Golden Age for social theory. Three of its greatest exponents were born within a few years of each other: Sigmund Freud in 1856 in Moravia, then part of the Austro–Hungarian empire; Emile Durkheim in 1858 in Eastern France; and Max Weber in 1864 in Prussia. In their maturity, all three were worried men, and what worried them was the survival of civilization as they knew it. It seemed to them, and to many others (see Nisbett, 1966), that the dramatic transformations in Europe in the nineteenth century would undermine all that European civilization had achieved in the preceding 200 years—the achievement was known as the Enlightenment—a progressive and rational emancipation from superstition, ignorance, and human misery, guided and supported by the equally rational and triumphant progress of science. Europe had become a humanitarian, intellectually sophisticated civilization that enjoined respect for individuals, tolerance of their individuality, and due regard for their rights. What seemed to put this civilization at risk were some of the same trends that had created it, particularly science and the secular, "disenchanted" consciousness it spawned, combined with mass urbanization and the rise of the nation state. Taken together, they spelled the loss of community.

The Loss of Community

Through the eighteenth century in Great Britain, and subsequently in continental Europe, there was a qualitative shift in the economy, a shift now popularly described as the industrial revolution. Technological innovations transformed the means of production; in particular, coal-fired steam engines made factory-style mass production economical. This industrialization also required a mass work force, and thousands of people migrated from the countryside to the industrial cities that grew up near coal fields. These new concentrations of population were not so much centers of trade and public administration as cities had been in the past, but of manufacture. Some of the *social* consequences took longer to become apparent. Ultimately, scholars concluded that not only had settlement patterns and economic activity changed, but the entire character of social life had altered, and with it the moral basis of society.

The industrial revolution not only concentrated populations on a hitherto unprecedented scale, but also physically segregated social classes as never before. For theorists such as Ferdinand Tonnies (1887/1957), the most significant consequence of this concentration of people was, in Wellman's (1979) apt phrase, "the loss of community." The economy of feudalism in Europe entailed an intimate mingling of the lives of persons from different levels of society. People had lived in small-scale communities, in which everyone knew everyone else; all transactions were between relatives, neighbors, or other acquaintances; and individuals were bound to one another by ties of loyalty based on kinship or marriage.

The solidarity of communities of this kind, Durkheim (1893/1964) argued, took a particular form that he called "mechanical"; mechanical solidarity emphasized similarities in beliefs, manners, and values and all deviance was ruthlessly condemned and punished. The proper standards were defined and promulgated by religious authorities who, in medieval Europe, wielded a degree of power that is virtually incomprehensible today. Total conformity was apparently enforceable because every detail of a person's conduct was subject to constant scrutiny by neighbors and acquaintances who were prone to envy and primed to resent any display of difference. Firm control of the populace could be maintained because their lives were directly supervised by their social and, it was assumed, moral superiors. Parishioners dwelt directly under the eyes of their priest, servants in the master's household, peasants within sight of their landlords.

No equivalent to this kind of community could be found in the new industrial cities. The inhabitants seemed submerged in a sea of strangers. It was popularly supposed, and certainly accepted by Durkheim and his contemporaries, that the new urban working class, lacking the restraint of constant supervision and physically separated from the moral leadership of the ruling class, would be literally out of control. Contained in this conclusion is an assumption so important to what followed in psychology that it needs to be set out quite explicitly: *People will be inclined to transgress when their actions are anonymous.*

Behind this conclusion lies another idea familiar to nineteenth-century scholars. It is that human nature is fundamentally self-serving; people are disposed by their makeup to be selfish and pleasure seeking. Once it was discovered that humans are animals, it seemed reasonable to conclude that, without the intervention of civilization, they would behave like animals. If religion asserted they were born as sinners, evolution seemed to suggest they were born to fight and to copulate, both socially destructive proclivities if uncontrolled.

In making sense of the social thought of this period, however, it is important to understand the interlude known as the Enlightenment, which intervened between religious and Darwinian notions of human nature. Cesare Beccaria (1738–1794) and Jeremy Bentham (1748–1832) had prompted significant judicial reforms with their secular interpretation of humans as rational beings endowed with freedom of choice. Explaining immorality was no problem for this theory: If people transgress, it is because they have made a free and rational choice based on the perception that this has greater utility for them than compliance with moral proscriptions. Prevention of crime was therefore a matter of revising the law to ensure that individuals would more often make the opposite choice. This could be done by ensuring that punishment was certain, prompt, and rationally graded according to offense. This "classical theory" had a considerable and lasting influence on legal theory. As a theory of immorality, however, little of it survived Darwin or the events of the nineteenth century. These events prompted a new "positivism" in moral theory, based initially on new views of the nonrational causes of human behavior. In Freud's view, for example, antisocial behavior is simply a biological compulsion. People are literally driven to self-serving and destructive action by their sexual and aggressive instincts. Civilization, Freud argued, depends upon rules that restrain the impulsive gratification of these instinctual desires.

Sinful Cities

Throughout history, cities were regarded as sinful places, the breeding ground of vices and wickedness. Cities were considered the venues for money lending, gambling, and prostitution, and they had been well known to be the haunts of every kind of cheat. The stereotype that country folk the world over held of city dwellers stressed the latter's venality, guile, trickery, and deception (Levine & Campbell, 1973), qualities that the special conditions of social life in the city were assumed to produce: namely, that people dealt with one another as strangers. Exchanges were believed to be, in the words of Wirth (1938), transitory, segmented, formal, and impersonal. But mass urbanization had made matters much worse, by exaggerating the anonymous and impersonal character of city life, and attracting vast numbers of simple peasants who mentally and morally were little more than children.

Events in the nineteenth century first altered and then, it appeared, amply confirmed the fears of social theorists about mass urbanization. Crime in the cities seemed out of control and ever on the increase. This could be explained in terms of the classical theory of crime: The conditions of city life obscured the identity of culprits and thus destroyed any certainty of punishment.

Back to Noble Savagery?

Events in 19th century Europe produced considerable ambivalence about the direction of civilization. William Blake's "dark satanic mills" and living conditions in the cities led some to wonder whether life in the state of nature was not such a bad thing. Others had no doubts. Rousseau in the eighteenth century and William Morris 100 years later asserted that life in cities was alienating and degrading. Urban life had robbed man of his nobility; rural existence was cleaner and more natural, and allowed a proper attachment to a place and a landscape. Paradise lost was reconstructed as a rural, and largely mythical, community. Ambivalence about civilization clearly persisted in Freud's analysis of the contemporary ills. Freud believed that civilization was bought at the price of natural spontaneity, and believed reason could be recovered only with difficulty, by emancipating the psyche through long and expensive analysis.

Durkheim's reaction was quite different. He was convinced there was no meaningful existence outside society, no such thing as noble savagery. The problem was to find a new basis for solidarity, and that meant a new basis for attachment to the collective—it could not be the village community and it should not be religion. It would have to be the nation state and its distinctive culture.

The other crucial difference between Durkheim and Freud concerned their views regarding the link between the individual and society. Freud assumed that attachment to society was the natural consequence of normal personality development, and in a sense neurosis was the normal consequence of civilization, the price of admission. Durkheim believed that solidarity would have to be arranged through the implementation of social programs, the most important of which was state education. The alternative to these programs was not simply the collapse of (French) civilization, but of human existence of any kind. This, then represents a historical dividing point between sociological and psychological analyses of moral phenomena. After Freud, the path taken by psychology became progressively dominated by the value attached to individualism.

FROM SOCIAL TO INDIVIDUAL CONTROL

The idea that changing social conditions required supplementing social control with individual self-control was familiar to nineteenth-century social and political theorists. Adam Smith's *The Wealth of Nations* (1776/1910) clearly anticipates this requirement. Moreover, it was assumed that self-control would require the moral socialization of the populace, and that in turn implied improved methods of child rearing. Modern psychology, therefore, took over an agenda whose basic terms were already well defined. Freud's contribution was to provide a theory showing how child rearing might accomplish moral socialization.

Psychoanalysis supported the liberal view that individual conduct is properly controlled by individuals themselves, and that they will do so to the extent that they have internalized an autonomous conscience. It differed from the liberal view in its conclusion that this control would be nonrational. The history of moral psychology since Freud has largely been an argument about the nature of an autonomous conscience and the conditions of its formation. Theorists disagreed not about whether normal psychological development leads to individual moral autonomy, but about how it gets there.

It is instructive here to review the methods psychology developed to measure conscience development. The classical method is a test of "resistance to temptation" (Hartshorne & May, 1928; MacKinnon, 1938). In this test, individuals are confronted with a temptation, an opportunity to do something that is intrinsically desirable or rewarding, but forbidden or morally wrong. They are also led to believe that they will be unobserved if they succumb to this temptation, that there is no possibility that their transgression will be detected or punished. In such tests, researchers must create for the individual whose conscience is being tested a compelling illusion that his or her conduct will be entirely invisible to others.

Several interesting assumptions lie behind this research method. The first is that in everyday life potential sinners have many opportunities of this kind. In other words, the experimental measures of conscience devised by Hartshorne, MacKinnon, and others re-create, under laboratory conditions, a common experience in contemporary society. Employees have opportunities to steal from their employers or to idle when they should be working; students have opportunities to cheat on tests; spouses are tempted to cheat on each other; and the purveyors of goods and services have opportunities to deceive their clients.

A second and related assumption is that public behavior is largely unproblematic. Conformity in public is overdetermined, and partly for this reason, is of no interest to moral psychology. But interest also waned because public behavior ceased to belong to the domain of the moral. From wanting to know whether individuals were sufficiently socialized to exercise self-control when they imagined themselves to be unobserved, psychology moved imperceptibly to the view that these are the *only* conditions under which conduct is moral. The morality of public action is contaminated and therefore disqualified by the operation of such motives as desire for social approval or fear of public sanction.

It is unreasonable to give all the credit to psychology for these moral assumptions. Popular literature and drama also contain many examples of secret sinners; the only witnesses to their sins are their own consciences, and we the vicarious audience. Think also of popular fictional do-gooders: the Lone Ranger, Zorro, Batman, Superman. Their civic contributions are virtuous only because their identity remains hidden. Whether psychology has merely replayed popular attitudes or whether it has shaped them, its enthusiasm for this definition of virtue is undeniable.

A third assumption of this research design is that sinners automatically conceal both their sins and their sinful character. In other words, to be unsocialized is also to be deceitful; those who behave badly also lie. Not only do they break the rules when society's back is turned, but they do not subsequently own up. It is interesting that revealing one's transgressions to others should be described as "confession," as if such revelations were tantamount to repentance; even a guilty conscience is, after all, evidence of a conscience. Because the unsocialized have no conscience, they must be caught out by the wily researcher with such indirect devices as lie scales (Hartshorne & May, 1928) and projective measures of confession (Allinsmith, 1960).

Theorists disagree about the nature of conscience. In psychoanalysis, conscience is an internalized representation of parents. For some learning theorists, it is conditioned anxiety (Eysenck, 1970); for others, it is simply a set of acquired behavioral habits. For cognitive developmentalists (Kohlberg, 1984), it is the capacity to reason about one's obligations to the requirements of justice. What these definitions of conscience share is the idea that conscience by itself can direct action. It requires no external support and, if sufficiently robust, it will resist all external pressure to behave otherwise. Fully socialized individuals are, paradoxically, completely independent of social influence or control. They act as required by their inner consciences, whether or not alone and whether or not tempted or pressured by expediency or the clamor of the mob to act in any other way.

The Privatization of Moral Reactions

Psychoanalysis brought a significant move toward the privatization of conscience in another respect; it emphasized the purely internal moral life of individuals. This can be seen in the way psychoanalysis employed the concept of guilt. Dictionary definitions of guilt emphasize the relationship between an actor and an offense; guilt depends on responsibility, culpability, or fault. In psychoanalysis, guilt refers to an internal judgment of this relationship, and then to an emotional reaction consequent upon this judgment. The conscience or superego supposedly represses wicked impulses by generating the anticipation of an intensely unpleasant emotional experience, an experience labeled as guilt. Eventually, psychological writings, whatever their theoretical orientation referred to guilt exclusively as an emotion, an internal affective state, (e.g., Aronfreed, 1968; Freedman, 1971; Gilligan, 1976; Kohlberg, 1971). Ultimately, however, it is not the experience of this emotion, but its mere anticipation, that matters.

Anthropology draws a distinction between guilt and shame cultures (Benedict, 1946; Kroeber, 1948). This distinction concerns variations in cultural interpretations of the relation between offenders and the community, and in the social mechanisms entailed in this relationship. In a guilt culture, offenders may recover their position in the community by some ritual of expiation, whether punishment or reparation. Such cultures tend to emphasize conformity and equality. Shame cultures, by contrast, are more competitive and hierarchical. Moral offenders suffer an irreversible loss of public status; they are subjected to humiliation and ridicule rather than demands for expiation.

This interpretation is consistent with the observations on which this distinction rests. However, the anthropology that proposed this distinction was heavily influenced by psychoanalytic concepts and blurred the distinction between public relationships and private experiences. A shame culture controlled its members by the threat of public humiliation; a guilt culture relied upon individuals to control themselves (Benedict, 1946). In the end, shame was also treated as an emotion; thus Kohlberg (1971) referred to fear, shame, and guilt as if they all belonged to the same class of phenomena.

Behaviorism represented, among other things, a reaction against the psychoanalytic emphasis on subjective experience. It thus seemed to retreat from the privatization of moral life by insisting that psychological research confine itself to observables. But this retreat was limited and temporary in two respects. First, although behaviorists studied actions and not private experiences, these were nonetheless treated as actions and not as communications or interactions. Indeed, behaviorists assumed that the most morally authentic actions would normally be unobserved and that some ingenuity and subterfuge would be required to observe them at all. Second, behaviorally oriented theorists found it convenient to postulate the existence of internal affective states, labeled as anxiety (Eysenck, 1970) or guilt (Aronfreed, 1968).

Cognitive–developmental theory represents another form of the privatization of moral reactions. In his early writings, Piaget (1926; see also Piaget, 1977) talked about the socialization of thought. Initially, he argued, a child's thought is highly egocentric; a child knows no point of view but his or her own. Gradually, this egocentrism is broken down as a child is continually confronted with the viewpoints of others. Other people express different points of view and impose upon the child the obligation to justify his or her own. In his early writings, Piaget described this as a social process: Children become aware of the relativity of their own viewpoints during arguments with adults and particularly peers; perspective taking and the coordination of contrasting perspectives occurs in a process of social interaction. Piaget subsequently became preoccupied with the logical structure of mental operations. His ideas about egocentrism and perspective taking were later taken up by others, but explored increasingly as individual mental capacities (see Flavell, Botkin, Fry, Wright, & Jarvis, 1968). In Kohlberg's theory of moral development, perspective-taking plays an important part in stimulating development, but research on this aspect of the theory has been limited. Several empirical studies have linked moral development to perspective-taking *abilities*, but few have linked it to perspective-taking *activity*.

Finally, consider how moral maturity is defined and assessed in Kohlberg's research. The theory is concerned with the structure of moral reasoning, in other words, with internal mental structures. The form these take in any individual can be determined by the internal mental events they generate—thoughts, beliefs, judgments. The researcher has only indirect access to these cognitions; the researcher elicits from the individual moral arguments, which are analyzed to reveal the underlying mental structures.

From Collective Conscience to Individual Reason

Although Freud and Durkheim reached different conclusions about the nature of behavioral control, they nonetheless shared important common ground concerning the standards to which moral conduct would be oriented. Both assumed that the collective was the *only* source of moral standards. Freud implied that certain standards would be embodied in all civilizations—the incest taboo, deference to elders, control of anger and violence—if only because the biological impulses of sex and aggression pose the same problems for all civilizations. Durkheim argued that the problems, the threats to civilization, are more variable, and so are the solutions. But both suggested that the solutions would be cultural.

Although it is common to refer to both Freud and Durkheim as relativists (e.g., Turiel, 1983), moral relativism owes more to social anthropology. This discipline, above all, documented the apparent cultural diversity of morals, and subsequently persuaded theorists such as Talcott Parsons that moral standards cannot be defined except in terms of a particular cultural context in which they occur. This position was particularly congenial to behaviorist psychology; it allowed behaviorists to ignore the troublesome question of what is moral and devote itself to analyzing the transmission of culturally approved habits of conduct.

The uncritical and rather extreme relativism of moral psychology in the 1940s and 1950s helped ensure the success of the inevitable reaction, when it came. Piaget (1932) laid the foundations, not so much with his critical analysis of Durkheim's work, but with his distinction between an immature "heteronomous" stage of development, and a more mature "autonomous" stage. But Piaget still acknowledged a collective basis in the generation of moral standards. Children might not assimilate cultural definitions of morality from their parents, or at least not after early childhood and not beyond a very superficial level. They would still, however, need the stimulus of other minds and the opportunity for collective deliberation to work out standards of fairness, or what rules they should follow or why they should respect these rules.

Kohlberg moved much more decisively in the direction of an individualized view of moral standards. Kohlberg (1963, 1964) examined and rejected Piaget's arguments about the role of peers in the development of moral ideas. Kohlberg (1971) elaborated a theory of individual constructivism according to which children neither absorb cultural definitions of morality from their parents nor co-construct definitions in cooperation with their peers. Rather, they spontaneously construct definitions for themselves. Ultimately, each individual might arrive at the same conclusions about the nature and basis of moral obligations, but this reflects no process of mutual influence. Instead, it occurs because the same laws of cognitive structure and the same logic of cognitive development are at work in each developing human mind.

Interestingly, even this position does not go far enough for some theorists. Turiel (1983) argued that Kohlberg was in error in assuming an intermediate stage of development in which morality is equated with convention. Turiel believes that even young children have intuitions about the nature of the moral that owe nothing to the influence of their culture. Thus, they can spontaneously distinguish between moral requirements, which are universal and admit of no exceptions, and conventional requirements or customary practices, which are not universally applicable. Turiel describes these as fundamental categories of knowledge.

Other approaches to moral socialization (e.g., Hoffman, 1963; Sears, Maccoby, & Levin, 1957) regard moral development as a social process, even if the products are not. Socialization involves a relationship in which parents seek by various means to control and discipline their children. However, as we move from natural settings to laboratory simulations of socialization, a critical social and interactive element receives progressively less attention: language. In the terminology of laboratory-based research, parents provide reinforcements which do not obviously require the medium of language. They can take the form of blows, frowns, grunts, hugs, or material inducements. Then parents became models, and the interactive element of a social process was reduced yet further. From here, it was logical to move toward an emphasis on processes occurring entirely within the individual—processes of attention, interpretation, memory, and recall—because imitative or observational learning requires no interaction. Television pictures were considered to serve as well as a relationship with a parent, and they were much more amenable to experimental control.

In the cognitive–developmental literature, parents rarely appear, and larger social forces such as class or education are rarely mentioned. Cognitive–developmental theory had defined moral socialization in terms of the cognitive equipment needed to function in any society; having taken this position, it was difficult to concede that influences peculiar to a particular society or segment of society could be consequential in the process.

The Socialization of Moral Dangers

For Freud, the threats to civilization were in the individual, more specifically in the individual's biologically derived proclivities. Sex and aggression were human appetites that had to be curbed by the community for the sake of collective harmony. However, well before Freud's main social writing, Gustav Le Bon (1896) raised concerns about the behavior of the mob and, by implication, the unsavory effect of crowds upon the individuals within them. This set the tone for the moral perspective of most subsequent social psychology. The classical folklore of social psychology is a catalogue of the moral dangers posed by the group. Asch (1951) showed that groups, merely by expressing an opinion contrary to the truth, could cause individuals to deny the evidence of their own senses and abandon the truth themselves. Latane and Darley (1970) showed that the company of others would weaken an individual's sense of moral responsibility. Wallach, Kogan, and Bem (1962) seemed to have found that individuals would make reckless and irresponsible decisions when gathered together in groups, and Janis (1972) later drew on this kind of evidence to argue for the vulnerability to moral blindness of group decisions. Finally, Zimbardo (1970) demonstrated that the group context could lead to deindividuation, causing individuals to abandon standards of decency and consideration.

In the 1950s, another version of these dangers appeared. Groups may be a threat to civilized standards, but their effects are potentially far more damaging if the group is invested with authority. For the authors of *The Authoritarian Personality* (Adorno, Frenkel-Brunswick, Levinson, & Sanford, 1950), the blame for the holocaust lay not with isolated sadistic psychopaths, but with the propensity of ordinary people to defer to the authority of the "in group." However, Adorno et al. implied that the danger would be realized only if the apparatus of the state was hijacked by men of ill will. They also allowed that obedience to authority, which would occur even when the aims of that authority were immoral, would normally be a minority reaction.

Milgram (1974) enlarged the scale of the danger with research suggesting that a majority of ordinary people will continue to defer to authority even when its demands are clearly unethical. Thus, the trend in social psychology has been to increasingly emphasize the dangers posed by the institutional and administrative apparatus of modern society.

Correspondingly, that which is threatened by compliance to authority is not group survival or collective harmony, but individual rights and interests. The status of the individual has progressively transformed from society's villain to society's victim. This reaches its logical conclusion in Kohlberg's cognitive developmental theory where all deference to authority is ultimately morally suspect; moral individuals must make independent determinations of what is right or just. Indeed, the only reliable guaranty of civilization is for each individual to become sufficiently autonomous to resist the pressures of the group or the demands of authority. Correspondingly, the group or the collective is a dangerous source of influence in the process of moral development, because its standards are arbitrary, if not actually corrupting.

Two other fields of research—that is, those concerned with justice and altruism—also promote individualism, the tendency to prioritize private interests, personal autonomy, and individual self-sufficiency. The justice field has been dominated by a discussion regarding the principles that individuals apply or regard as appropriate in the distribution of resources (see Hook & Cook, 1979; Leventhal, 1976). In analysis of distributive justice, one concept, equity, has been preeminent. As an allocation rule, equity is based on the assumptions that in any relationship, there are discrete individual contributors; that relative individual contributions can be determined; and that rewards should be allocated in proportion to individual contributions. The first two assumptions are questionable, and the third, as Deutsch (1985) argued, can actually destroy the cooperation on which group effectiveness usually depends.

The concept of altruism or helpfulness is not obviously individualistic. It implies bonds of solidarity and sympathy between people; it suggests mutual dependence. Despite this implication, the research on altruism that began to appear in the 1960s was confined largely to a special class of events—emergencies, or accidental misfortunes involving strangers. In other words, altruism was studied as it might occur outside any established or continuing relationship with the beneficiary. But the implication was also that intervention was required only because the person requiring aid had suffered some temporary, unforeseen, and unusual breakdown in self-sufficiency. In effect, this research confirmed that individual self-sufficiency is the norm.

CONTRARY VIEWS

Anyone familiar with the moral psychology literature will argue that we have told only part of the story. We would reply that it is nonetheless the major part. In what remains of the chapter, we correct some of the omissions. Our point, however, is that theorizing and research that has not fit well into this story of the progressive individualizing of conscience has, until recently, been a relatively minor part of the whole because it was inconsistent with the unifying metatheory. If ideas or observations did not map comfortably onto the value assumptions of liberal individualism, they remained relatively isolated and unconnected.

We do not try to explain the enduring popularity of individualism in moral psychology or the resurgence of what MacIntyre (1985) called "the Enlightenment project," following the temporary and ultimately superficial reverses of psychoanalysis and behaviorism. We turn instead to the following questions: What alternatives are there to individualism, and what kind of research agenda might they support?

In the last decade, some old themes have begun to reappear in the research literature. Evidence from various sources is beginning to yield a coherent alternative to the models of human nature, society, and social control that have for so long held sway. For us, the key to this alternative is recognizing that humans are a social species of a special kind. Humans live in organized groups and adapt to the environment at the level of groups, as do termites, and zebras, and baboons. Like individual termites, zebras, and baboons, individual humans cannot survive except as group members. However, a qualitative difference exists between social insects and social vertebrates; most members of insect colonies are not genetic competitors. This difference has profound consequences for the respective characters of insect and vertebrate societies. Among the former, there is no individual-level recognition, whereas among the latter, it is commonplace and perhaps universal. Humans are divided from other vertebrate species by a difference almost as profound. Humans uniquely have the capacity for symbolic communication. Precisely what consequences this has for social organization are still unclear. One might wish to argue that distinctive features of human societies—such as their complexity or their variety—have something to do with human tool making or with intellectual capacities. We cannot untangle these difficult matters here. Instead, we consider two linked consequences of being a group-living, language-using animal.

The first is that, as organizational theorists point out, all social systems require energetic input (Katz & Kahn, 1978). Individual group members must make regular and coordinated contributions to the group; if they do not, there is no group and no advantage to collective existence. The level and nature of the contributions varies widely from one economy to another, but the requirement is always present in some form. In a sense, contributions are more imperative than the abstentions, which have traditionally attracted the attentions of psychology. Lust, greed, and violence may be disruptive, but they are not necessarily fatal for the group. On the other hand, no social unit will survive if its members are unwilling to work regularly on its behalf.

From this, one might conclude that the distribution of burdens or obligations is a central issue in social life. This issue was clearly recognized by Freud, who defined justice as the equal distribution of misery. To date, however, this aspect of distributive justice remains relatively neglected by researchers (recent work by M. Lerner, Somers, Reid, & Tierney, 1989, is a notable exception), compared with the attention lavished upon the distribution of benefits.

One might also conclude that if dependence rather than self-sufficient autonomy is the natural state of humans, then altruism, helpfulness, and cooperation would be commonplace and routine rather than exceptional and episodic. We are at last beginning to see research on planned helpfulness (Amato, 1985), routine prosocial behavior (Eisenberg, Cameron, Tryon, & Dodez, 1981), and cooperation (Argyle, 1991) come into the mainstream of social and developmental psychology.

The second consequence of group living and language use of significance to our discussion is the public character of action. The contributions and noncontributions of individuals are observed and recorded by the collective. In an important respect, this is quite different from the observation of the public actions of other group-living animals. In these other groups, what each individual knows about other members—their personality and temperament, their strengths and vulnerabilities, their loyalties and hostilities, their relative position in the social structure of the group—must be based on direct personal observation. Humans are not limited in this way; language gives them access to a shared stock of experience, in effect to the accumulated experience of the entire community. Thus, what each group member can know about the others is not confined to what he or she has directly observed or experienced. To put it another way, humans uniquely can and do know one another by repute (Emler, 1990); they can and do inform themselves about others' *reputations*, those collective judgments upon the vices and virtues of individuals that only human groups can make. One can see that if the economy of the social group depends on the extent and quality of the contributions of those within it, then the group will function more successfully to the extent that it can form and disseminate judgments about contributions. It can more effectively control and sanction its members and limit the damage done by persistent offenders.

We suggest that a central tenet of moral psychology—the necessity for internalized control of conduct—is based on a false premise. The industrial revolution may have modified human communities, but it did not eliminate them. Anonymity, segmentation, and transience are relative, not absolute qualities of contemporary social life, and their significance is probably quite limited. The lives of most people continue to be embedded in communities of mutual acquaintances (Boissevain, 1974; Fischer, 1981; Litwak & Szelenyi, 1969; Wellman, 1979). Most of their encounters and exchanges occur with people they know, and who know and talk to many of the other people they know, and their actions continue to be subject to perpetual scrutiny and public comment (Emler, 1990).

Consequently, very little of what people do, whether good or bad, praiseworthy or reprehensible, foolhardy or commonsensical, is completely unobserved or anonymous, and most of it contributes to the reputations they have with their fellows. Two observations follow from this. The first is that it is unnecessary to postulate purely internal mechanisms of behavioral control, because almost all visible action of any consequence is available for social control. Even delinquent behavior is performed in public and evaluated by the delinquent community (Emler, Reicher, & Ross, 1967). The second is that social control is not infallible, and if we wish to understand immoral conduct, it may be more profitable to ask why social control does not always work than to ask how internalized control has failed.

If moral and immoral actions are public, so also are moral emotions. If guilt and shame do describe emotions, then it is not unreasonable to suppose that they will behave like other emotional reactions; they will involve overt displays (Ekman, 1971). The functional significance of emotions lies partly in what they signal or communicate to others. Thus, reactions such as remorse are important not merely as internal messages, but for their social consequences, for what they signal about the individual's relation to others and to the collective standards of the community. These emotions form a part of the individual's public performance, his or her self-presentation before the communal audience. They are part of the "accounts" people give of themselves and their actions to others.

Accounts also include the whole range of *verbal* actions people perform to promote, protect, or repair their reputations—apologies, explanations, excuses, and so forth. People do not merely have reasons for actions, or merely reason in private about what they should or should not do. They also state reasons, and give justifications. Where Kohlberg emphasized the clues that overt moral reasoning provides about underlying mental structure, we would stress the significance of overt moral reasoning as a self-presentational activity. The Kohlberg Moral Judgment Interview (see Colby, Kohlberg, et al., 1987) does not make temporarily overt what is normally a private and internal argument with the self. It only samples a widespread social activity, the activity of moral argument and debate. If we concede the social character of moral reasoning, then we might ask in more detail about the interaction process involved and the self-presentational and other social goals of this activity.

Among these goals, we believe, are the discussion, evaluation, and dissemination of moral standards. There is now extensive evidence that moral argument is used to socialize children (e.g., Hoffman, 1977). However, to acknowledge this requires reassessment of yet another central assumption of mainstream moral psychology, namely that individuals independently construct their own understanding of morality. The case for individual constructivism has been supported by a somewhat misleading caricature of the alternatives (Emler, 1987; Gibbs & Schnell, 1985). This caricature typically links the proposition that morality is socially transmitted to the additional assumptions that socially transmitted ideas are necessarily arbitrary and nonrational and that the targets of these ideas are necessarily passive participants in the process. Behind this caricature lies the distinction between universalism and relativism, but there is no empirical basis for the dichotomies implied in this caricature. On the other hand, a considerable body of evidence has accumulated about the social construction of knowledge. We know, for instance, that children can construct rational and internally consistent concepts through processes of interaction (e.g., Doise & Mugny, 1984) and that nonarbitrary knowledge can be acquired by social transmission (Emler & Glachan, 1985).

On reflection, none of this should be surprising. It is improbable that children should be able by themselves to construct a set of basic principles for the ordering of social life, and to accomplish all this within the space of 10 to 15 years. It is equally improbable that the community into which children are born should leave them alone to do this, remaining silent about everything the adult members have concluded about these questions. None of us has had to learn from scratch the principles of hygiene or how to make pottery or how to distinguish edible from poisonous plants. We have all taken advantage of the wisdom of our culture concerning these matters. Is it less likely that we will use this collective wisdom when it comes to questions about how rewards or burdens should be allocated, how culpability or punishment should be decided, or how social rules should be constructed or applied?

We are neither universalists nor relativists. Rather, we agree with MacIntyre (1985) that in matters of morality, as in matters of hygiene, diet, and pottery making, some solutions are objectively more satisfactory than others, but there is always scope for innovation and improvement. We also agree with MacIntyre that improvement is a collective process; individuals will not discover viable moral principles alone and unaided by cultural tradition. Solitary thought is an overrated activity.

Finally, we return to moral dangers. Our objection to individualism is not so much to the dangers it has emphasized, but to those it has neglected. The threat individualism has emphasized is the violation of individual rights—rights to self-determination, autonomy, noninterference, and exercise of private preferences; rights to proper rewards; rights over personal property, life, and lifestyle; and so on. However, this analysis of moral dangers obscures what we believe to be the fundamental function of morality: to preserve the social group. Hence, our emphasis is on positive as well as passive obligations, on duties of care and duties to contribute, and on requirements of noninterference in the rights and freedoms of others.

It is also worth considering those moral requirements that psychoanalysis regards as neurotic impediments to happiness or mental health, and that most other forms of psychology have simply ignored. We have in mind the various forms of self-denial that form a recurring theme in the moral teachings of world religions, particularly those related to sexual license. Despite the dissemination of psychoanalytic ideas in the twentieth century, it is still common for people to associate morals with sexual conduct. However, contemporary psychology makes no such connection. Rather than dismiss this connection in lay consciousness as a vestige of a repressive and long dead system, we might inquire more closely why sexual conduct and other human appetites fell within the moral domain in the first place. Again, the answer will concern the survival of culture.

The least satisfactory consequence of individualism in our view, however, is the contemporary analysis of hierarchy. We have discussed this in some detail elsewhere (Emler & Hogan, 1991), and will make only a few brief comments here. Abuses of power indeed constitute serious moral dangers; we would go so far as to say that the extent of these dangers has yet to be adequately appreciated. The liberal remedy for this danger—to equip individual actors with an autonomous conscience that can resist authority, in effect to eliminate subordination and thus the power differentials of social and organizational hierarchies—is not a viable solution. It is not viable because without power differentials, social organization would collapse. Rather, the solution must be the careful selection and control of power holders. To date, this remains a seriously neglected topic in psychology, a neglect we attribute to the aversion of liberal individualism to hierarchy of any kind, and thus an unwillingness to give serious attention to its proper operation.

CONCLUSION

In this chapter, we have tried to show that the analysis of morality within psychology has progressively individualized the issues. We have argued for a resocialization of conscience on the grounds that the value assumptions of liberalism and individualism are based on a faulty model of social life and human nature. We have proposed that more attention be given to the social control of conduct, and to the social function of moral emotions and moral reasoning. Also, we have emphasized the social and cultural origins of moral concepts.

Does all this mean that moral psychology should be abandoned in favor of moral sociology? Not at all. Many of the questions raised by our view are irreducibly psychological in nature. For example, moral socialization may not be primarily a matter of constructing internalized controls, but it does not follow that there is no developmental or socialization process. On the contrary, the implication of our proposals is that moral socialization involves becoming receptive to various forms of social control and capable of various forms of social participation (see Hogan & Emler, in press). Likewise, children may not construct moral concepts according to the cognitive developmental model, but they do still acquire moral insights and understandings. The processes by which individual children construct moral concepts, we suggest, depend on social interaction and social influence; what is known about these processes has come from psychological, not sociological, research.

Finally, we come to an often unfashionable concept in psychology: individual differences. In psychoanalysis, the concept is implicit but not central; the effects of childhood can to some extent be ameliorated by psychotherapy. In the cognitive–developmental perspective, individual differences are temporary and incidental; in theory, all individuals can attain the same final stage. In behaviorism, individual differences are expunged altogether. Why is liberalism so uncomfortable with the concept? Why do individual differences offend the values of individualism?

Perhaps because the concept denies the ultimate perfectibility of the individual. Perhaps also because it questions the viability of the liberal myth: a society based on contracts between free and equal individuals. If there are irreducible individual differences in character, then this implies that the state or community must intervene to guarantee an orderly society, a conclusion inimical to liberal political philosophy. Whatever the reasons, we now know that the psychoanalytic promise of perfectibility through therapy is unrealizable; that it is normal, not exceptional, for individual moral development to arrest at different levels (Colby et al., 1987); and that an account of conduct in terms of purely situational contingencies will not do (Emler, 1984).

At the heart of the moral life of any society is the reality of individual differences. If this were not so, it would be difficult to understand why individuals and groups invest so much effort in reputational inquiries. In the end, social controls work unevenly. Individuals remain incorrigibly different in their moral habits. Their differential inclinations to lie or tell the truth, to be generous or stingy, cruel or considerate, violent or placid, forgiving or vengeful, brave or cowardly, cannot be evened out by social pressures. It would be better, therefore, for a community to make accurate estimates of character and arrange opportunities accordingly.

REFERENCES

Adorno, T. W., Frenkel-Brunswik, E., Levinson, D. J., & Sanford, R. M. (1950). *The authoritarian personality.* New York: Harper.

Allinsmith, W. (1960). The learning of moral standards. In D. R. Miller & G. E. Swanson (Eds.), *Inner conflict and defense.* (pp. 141–176). New York: Holt, Rinehart & Winston.

Amato, P. R. (1985). An investigation of planned helping behavior. *Journal of Research in Personality, 19,* 232–252.

Argyle, M. (1991). *Cooperation: The basis of sociability.* London: Routledge.

Aronfreed, J. (1968). *Conduct and conscience: The socialization of internalized control over behavior.* New York: Academic Press.

Asch, S. E. (1951). Effects of group pressure on the modification and distortion of judgments. In H. Guetzkow (Ed.), *Groups, leadership and men.* (pp. 177-190). Pittsburg: Carnegie Press.

Benedict, R. (1946). *The chrysanthemum and the sword.* Boston: Houghton-Mifflin.

Boissevain, J. (1974). *Friends of friends: Networks, manipulators and coalitions.* Oxford: Blackwell.

Colby, A., Kohlberg, L., & Collaborators (1987). *The measurement of moral judgment. Volume 1: Theoretical foundations and research validation.* Cambridge, England: Cambridge University Press.

Deutsch, M. (1985). *Distributive justice: A social psychological perspective.* New Haven, CT: Yale University Press.

Doise, W., & Mugny, G. (1984). *The social development of the intellect.* Oxford: Pergamon.

Durkheim, E. (1964). *The division of labor in society* (G. Simpson, Trans.). Toronto: Collier. (Original work published 1893).

Eisenberg, N., Cameron, E., Tryon, K., & Dodez, R. (1981). Socialization of prosocial behavior in the pre-school classroom. *Developmental Psychology, 17,* 773–782.

Ekman, P. (1971). Universals and cultural differences in facial expressions of emotion. In J. K. Cole (Ed.), *Nebraska Symposium on Motivation 1971.* (pp. 207–283). Lincoln: University of Nebraska Press.

Emler, N. (1983). Morality and politics: The ideological dimension in the study of moral development. In H. Weinreich-Haste & D. Locke (Eds.), *Morality in the making: Thought, action and social context* (pp. 47–71). Chichester, England: Wiley.

Emler, N. (1984). Differential involvement in delinquency: Toward an interpretation in terms of reputation management. In B. A. Maher & W. B. Maher (Eds.), *Progress in experimental personality research* (Vol. 13, pp. 173–239). New York: Academic Press.

Emler, N. (1987). Socio-moral development from the perspective of social representations. *Journal for the Theory of Social Behaviour, 17,* 371–388.

Emler, N. (1990). A social psychology of reputation. In W. Stroebe & M. Hewstone (Eds.), *European review of social psychology* (Vol. 1, pp. 173–193). Chichester, England: Wiley.

Emler, N., & Glachan, M. (1985). L'étude experimental du developpement sociocognitif. In G. Mugny (Ed.), *Psychologie sociale du developpement de la connaissance.* (pp. 71–92). Geneva: Peter Lang.

Emler, N., & Hogan, R. (1991). Moral psychology and public policy. In W. Kurtines (Ed.), *Handbook of moral psychology* (Vol. 3, pp. 69–93). Hillsdale, NJ: Erlbaum.

Emler, N., Reicher, S., & Ross, A. (1987). The social context of delinquent conduct. *Journal of Child Psychology and Psychiatry, 28,* 99–109.

Eysenck, H. J. (1970). *Crime and personality* (2nd ed.). London: Granada.

Fischer, C. (1981). *To dwell among friends: Personal networks in town and city.* Chicago: University of Chicago Press.

Flavell, J. H., Botkin, P., Fry, C., Wright, J., & Jarvis, P. (1968). *The development of role-taking and communication skills in children.* New York: Wiley.

Freedman, J. (1971). Transgression, compliance and guilt. In J. Macauley & L. Berkowitz (Eds.), *Altruism and helping behavior.* (pp. 155–161). New York: Academic Press.

Gibbs, J., & Schnell, S. V. (1985). Moral development "versus" socialization: A critique. *American Psychologist, 40,* 1071–1080.

Gilligan, J. (1976). Beyond morality: Psychoanalytic reflections on shame, guilt and love. In T. Lickona (Ed.), *Moral development and behaviour: Theory, research and social issues.* (pp. 144–158). New York: Holt, Rinehart & Winston.

Goody, J., & Watt, I. (1963). The consequences of literacy. *Comparative Studies in Society and History, 5,* 304–326.

Hartshorne, H., & May, M. A. (1928). *Studies in the nature of character. Vol. 1: Studies in deceit.* New York: Macmillan.

Hoffman, M. L. (1963). Child rearing practices and moral development: Generalizations from empirical research. *Child Development, 34,* 295–318.

Hoffman, M. (1977). Moral internalization: Current theory and research. In L. Berkowitz (Ed.), *Advances in experimental social psychology* (Vol. 10, pp. 85–133). New York: Academic Press.

Hogan, R. (1975). Theoretical egocentrism. *American Psychologist, 30,* 533–540.

Hogan, R., & Emler, N. (1978). The biases in contemporary social psychology. *Social Research, 45,* 201–249.

Hogan, R., & Emler, N. (in preparation). Socioanalytic theory and the personological tradition in moral development. In W. Kurtines & J. Gewirtz (Eds.), *An introduction to moral development.* New York: McGraw-Hill.

Hook, J., & Cook, T. (1979). Equity theory and the cognitive ability of children. *Psychological Bulletin, 86,* 429–445.

Horton, R. (1967). African traditional thought and Western science. In M. F. D. Young (Ed.), *Knowledge and Control* (pp. 208–266). London: Collier.

Janis, I. (1972). *Victims of group-thinking.* Boston: Houghton-Mifflin.

Katz, D., & Kahn, R. L. (1978). *Social psychology of organizations* (2nd ed.). New York: Wiley.

Kohlberg, L. (1963). Moral development and identification. In H. Stevenson (Ed.), *Child psychology: 62nd Yearbook of the National Society for the Study of Education.* (pp. 277–332). Chicago: University of Chicago Press.

Kohlberg, L. (1964). Development of moral character and moral ideology. In M. L. Hoffman & L. W. Hoffman (Eds.), *Review of child development research* (Vol. 1, pp. 1–113). New York: Russell Sage Foundation.

Kohlberg, L. (1971). From is to ought: How to commit the naturalistic fallacy and get away with it in the study of moral development. In T. Mischel (Ed.), *Cognitive development and epistemology* (pp. 121–163). New York: Academic Press.

Kohlberg, L. (1984). *The psychology of moral development: Essays on moral development* (Vol. 2). San Francisco: Harper & Row.

Kroeber, A. (1948). *Anthropology.* New York: Harcourt.

Kurtines, W., Alvarez, M., & Azmitia, M. (1990). Science and morality: The role of values in science and the scientific study of moral phenomena. *Psychological Bulletin, 107,* 283–295.

Latane, B., & Darley, J. (1970). *The unresponsive bystander: Why doesn't he help?* New York: Appleton-Century-Crofts.

Le Bon, G. (1896). *The crowd: A study of the popular mind.* London: Unwin.

Lerner, D. (1958). *The passing of traditional society.* New York: Free Press.

Lerner, M., Somers, D. G., Reid, D. W., & Tierney, M. C. (1989). A social dilemma: Egocentrically based cognitions among filial caregivers. In S. Spacanpan & S.

Oskamp (Eds.), *The social psychology of aging* (pp. 73–98). Newbury Park, Ohio: Sage.

Leventhal, G. (1976). The distribution of rewards and resources in groups and organizations. In L. Berkowitz & E. Walster (Eds.), *Advances in experimental social psychology* (Vol. 9, pp. 91–131). New York: Academic Press.

Levine, R. A., & Campbell, D. T. (1973). *Ethnocentrism.* New York: Wiley.

Litwak, E., & Szelenyi, I. (1969). Primary group structures and their functions. *American Sociological Review, 35,* 465–481.

MacIntyre, A. (1985). *After virtue: A study in moral theory.* London: Duckworth.

MacKinnon, D. W. (1938). Violation of prohibitions. In H. A. Murray (Ed.), *Explorations in personality.* (pp. 491–501). New York: Oxford University Press.

Milgram, S. (1974). *Obedience to authority.* New York: Harper & Row.

Nisbet, R. A. (1966). *The sociological tradition.* New York: Basic Books.

Piaget, J. (1926). *The language and thought of the child.* London: Routledge & Kegan Paul.

Piaget, J. (1932). *The moral judgment of the child.* London: Routledge & Kegan Paul.

Piaget, J. (1977). *Etudes sociologiques.* Geneva: Droz.

Sears, R. R., Maccoby, E. E., & Levin, H. (1957). *Patterns of child rearing.* Evanston, IL: Row Peterson.

Smith, A. (1910). *The wealth of nations.* London: Dent. (Original work published 1776).

Tonnies, F. (1957). *Community and society.* New York: Harper. (Original work published 1887).

Turiel, E. (1983). *The development of social knowledge: Morality and convention.* Cambridge, England: Cambridge University Press.

Wallach, M., Kogan, N., & Bem, D. (1962). Group influence on individual risk-taking. *Journal of Abnormal Psychology, 68,* 263–274.

Weber, M. (1946). Science as a vocation. In H. H. Gerth & C. W. Mills (Eds. & Trans.), *From Max Weber: Essays in sociology* (pp. 129–156). New York: Oxford University Press. (Original work published 1919).

Wellman, B. (1979). The community question: The intimate networks of East Yorkers. *American Journal of Sociology, 84,* 1201–1231.

Wirth, L. (1938). Urbanism as a way of life. *American Journal of Sociology, 44,* 3–24.

Zimbardo, P. (1970). The human choice: Individuation, reason and order versus deindividuation, impulse and chaos. In W. J. Arnold & D. Levine (Eds.), *Nebraska Symposium on Motivation* (pp. 237–301). Lincoln: University of Nebraska Press.

Chapter 10 ■ ══════════════

Moral–Cognitive Development and the Motivation of Moral Behavior ══ ■

JOHN C. GIBBS
The Ohio State University

In Kohlberg's (1984) cognitive–developmental theory, children's morality generally progresses from a superficial to a mature level of sociomoral cognition. With cognitive development, the child penetrates through extraneous considerations to grasp or "construct" the underlying meaning of moral norms and values. A child who suggests that you should keep a promise to a friend because you never can tell when the friend might be needed to do you a favor, is evidencing an extrinsic and still immature moral orientation. According to developmental theory, the child will progress (given normal environmental opportunities) to a mature moral understanding. The child may suggest in later years, for example, that the promise should be kept to preserve the trust on which the friendship is based. Mature moral understanding applies not only to keeping promises or telling the truth, but to a broad spectrum of moral values pertaining, for example, to saving a life, helping someone, and refraining from stealing.

The general expectation in cognitive–developmental theory is that the older child's (or adult's) moral–cognitive maturity will motivate congruent conduct to some degree. The person who understands the basis in trust for keeping promises, for example, will be more likely to evidence in behavior trustworthiness and fairness. Beyond references to general cognitive structuring tendencies (see Kohlberg, 1984), however, the process whereby moral–cognitive development motivates moral behavior is not specified. Nor does the theory specify the important role of empathy and related emotions in moral motivation, or the process whereby cognition can attenuate or negate moral motivation. The revised view of moral–cognitive development presented in this chapter relates moral–cognitive development to cognitive development in general, and devotes particular attention to the clarification of cognitive and affective processes in the motivation of moral behavior.

MORAL–COGNITIVE DEVELOPMENT

Mature morality is accomplished in Kohlberg's theory through cognitive–developmental processes. I argue (citing Flavell and others) that the basic cognitive process at work is decentration, that is, the developing ability to attend to and interrelate multiple perspectives in a social situation or, in general terms, multiple features of a problem situation.

The child who does not interrelate perspectives will tend to focus on salient but superficial and extraneous features in a moral situation. The superficiality of immature moral judgment is best illustrated in terms of Stage 1, where "moral rules and labels are applied in a literal, absolute manner. . . . Characteristics of persons that determine their authority . . . or moral worth tend to be physicalistic. . . . For example, the father is the boss because he's bigger" (Kohlberg, 1984, p. 624). Similarly, one of Kohlberg's longitudinal subjects suggested that saving the life of more than one person is especially important because "one man has just one house, maybe a lot of furniture, but a whole bunch of people have an awful lot of furniture" (p. 192).

Kohlberg attributed the superficiality of Stage 1 to "naive moral realism" (an early Piagetian concept): "the moral significance of an action, its goodness or badness, is seen as a real, inherent, and unchanging quality of the act, just as color and mass are seen as inherent qualities of objects." In other words, "there is an absence of mediating concepts, such as deservingness or intentionality" (p. 624). Although Kohlberg was correct that such "mediating concepts" are not used in Stage 1 moral judgment, it was an exaggeration to imply that they are altogether "absent" in the child's thought. Piaget (1932/1965) noted that "in practice . . . children can more or less distinguish between an intentional act and an involuntary error . . . at about the age of three" (p. 144; cf. P. H. Miller & Aloise, 1989). Hence, the point is not that intentionality is "absent" in the thought of the younger child, but that intentionality tends not to be utilized "on the plane of moral reflection" (Piaget, 1932/1965, pp. 144–145; cf. Kuhn, 1988). Contemporary accounts of young children's superficial moral judgment refer not to an inability (e.g., "moral realism"), but rather to a neglect of intentions in favor of consequences—in general, to a tendency "to focus on only a single aspect of the total stimulus array" (Grueneich, 1982, p. 893; cf. Flavell, 1985; Piaget, 1975/1977). Stage 1 thinking can recognize at successive points in time different situational features or psychological perspectives, but fails to interrelate and reflect on those features to reach a deeper understanding in moral decision making— hence, the "literal," "absolute," or "physicalistic" superficiality.

Although entailing some interrelating of different features or psychological perspectives, Stage 2 morality is still too superficial or extraneous (i.e., oriented to pragmatic or instrumental considerations) to be considered mature:

> The perspective at stage 2 is pragmatic—to maximize satisfaction of one's needs and desires while minimizing negative consequences to the self. The assumption that the other is also operating from this premise leads to an emphasis on instrumental exchange. . . . For example, it is seen as important to keep promises to insure that others will keep their promises to you and do nice things for you, or it is important in order to keep them from getting mad at you. (Kohlberg, 1984, pp. 626–628)

Snarey (1985) provided five illustrations of Stage 2 instrumental thinking, each drawn from a different culture (pp. 221–222). Insofar as empathic concern for another is expressed in Stage 2 moral justification, the concern is in terms of the other person's concrete needs or desires (cf. Eisenberg, Boehnke, Schuler, & Silbereisen, 1985).

Although Kohlberg reserved moral judgment maturity until his Stages 5 and 6, in my view (Gibbs, 1977, 1979, 1991-b; Gibbs, Basinger, & Fuller, 1992), moral judgment maturity is already evident at Stages 3 and 4. At Stage 3, a child can sufficiently interrelate perspectives to enable him or her to penetrate through pragmatic or instrumental considerations to grasp the underlying meaning of interpersonal relationships:

> At Stage 3 the separate perspectives of individuals are coordinated into a third person perspective, that of mutually trusting relationships. . . . Stage 3 reciprocity . . . [allows] one to understand reciprocity as going beyond concrete notions of equal exchange to maintaining relationships, mutuality of expectations, and sentiments of gratitude and obligation. (Kohlberg, 1984, pp. 628–629)

Piaget, whose (1932/1965) study of moral judgment was seminal for Kohlberg's work, characterized this progression from instrumental exchange to a "mutuality of expectations" as a transition from "reciprocity as a fact" to "reciprocity as an ideal" or the prescription of:

behavior that admits of indefinitely sustained reciprocity. The motto "Do as you would be done by," thus comes to replace the conception of crude equality. The child sets forgiveness above revenge, not out of weakness, but because "there is no end" to revenge (a boy of 10). (pp. 323–324)

Selman (1980) provided a statement of this idea: Stage 3 indicates children's reflection on their Stage 2 construction of separate psychological perspectives, including the "ultimate futility" of an "infinite regress" in escalating acts of revenge, and the resulting construction of a "mutual and coordinated" social understanding (p. 39; cf. Feffer, 1970). Newman's (1986) argument that "mutual knowledge" does not represent "a new mental structure" (p. 141) overlooked the transformation in the nature of reciprocity involved in the emergence of Stage 3 moral judgment. In "reciprocity as a fact" (Stage 2), one evaluates whether one's perspective has been or will be matched by a reciprocal perspective; that is, one's action and its effect on another person are considered in the context of an exchange of rewards or punishments ("You scratch my back; I'll scratch yours"). In "reciprocity as an ideal" (Stage 3), one reflectively considers one's initial perspective as if it *were* the reciprocal perspective; that is, one's action and its effect on another person are hypothetically inverted and used as a guide for how one person should treat another in a relationship ("If you were to treat me that way, how would I feel? If I were to treat you that way, how would you feel?"). Mature moral reciprocity is neglected in reductionistic sociobiological (e.g., Alexander, 1987) and exchange theory (e.g., Burgess & Huston, 1979) accounts, which instead generally depict moral reciprocity in Stage 2 terms.

Stage 3 moral judgment does not fully represent moral–cognitive adequacy or maturity for individuals living in a society more complex than a face-to-face community. As adolescents or adults move beyond local communities to universities or complex work settings, they increasingly deal with anonymous individuals and relate to individuals with diverse or heterogenous values. As a result of this experience and the reflection it stimulates, their appreciation of the need for mutual trust and caring (Stage 3) expands into an appreciation of the need for commonly accepted, consistent standards and requirements (stage 4; cf. Edwards, 1975). In the words of one 18-year-old, the purpose of law is "to set up a standard of behavior for people, for society living together so that they can live peacefully and in harmony with each other" (Adelson, Green, & O'Neil, 1969, p. 328). Commonly accepted standards and requirements, then, "promote cooperation or social contribution and act as regulations designed to avoid disagreement and disorder" (Kohlberg, 1984, p. 632). As one of Kohlberg's longitudinal subjects said, "You've got to have certain understandings in things that everyone is going to abide by or else you could never get anywhere in society, never do anything" (Colby et al., 1987, p. 375). In other words, individuals in a complex society must generally understand their interdependence and accept a balance between their rights or freedoms and their responsibility to respect the rights of others as well as to contribute to society. In the absence of such commonly accepted "understandings," not only will society "never get anywhere," but (in the words of another longitudinal subject) "chaos will ensue, since each person will be following his or her own set of laws" (p. 375).

This general age trend from a superficial (literal or physicalistic, instrumental) orientation to an underlying-meaning orientation (mutual trust or caring, commonly accepted standards and other understandings) in moral judgment has been found in longitudinal (e.g., Colby, Kohlberg, Gibbs, & Lieberman, 1983), cross-cultural, and related research.[1] In a review of Kohlbergian moral judgment studies in 27 countries, Snarey (1985) concluded that Kohlberg's Stages 1 through 4 are "represented in a wide range of cultural groups" (p. 218). Stages 1 through 3 are essentially discernible in Damon's (1977) study of children's reasoning concerning fair distribution and legitimate authority, Youniss's (1980) study of friendship conceptions, Selman's (1980) broader investigation of interpersonal understanding. (Selman also described Stage 4, most clearly in children's conceptions of the peer group; cf. Adelson et al., 1969) and Eisenberg's (1982) study of prosocial reasoning.

Peterson, Peterson, and Seeto (1983) described superficial-to-underlying meaning trends in children's developing conceptions of lying. Asked "what happens" when lies are told, 80% of 5-year-olds mentioned punishment ("in which arbitrary punitive sanctions by an external authority are named, such as 'God gets angry,' 'You get sick/belted/into trouble'"; p. 1533). In contrast, only 28% of 11-year-olds mentioned punishment. Similarly, 92% of 5-year-olds responded that lying is "always" wrong, in contrast to only 28% of 11-year-olds. The trend was in the opposite direction for internally oriented responses. In responding to "what happens," only 10% of 5-year-olds referred to the loss of trust (even including marginal responses such as "people won't believe you the next time"), and none referred to guilt, having a bad feeling inside, or conscience. In contrast, the percentages of the 11-year-olds mentioning loss of trust and guilt were 48 and 22, respectively.

The basic progression is also found in other areas of social–cognitive development. The transition from physicalistic or egoistic responses to more mutualistic, or system-level responses is evident in studies of ego development (Loevinger & Wessler 1970) and development of the self-concept (e.g., Harter, 1983; Montemayor & Eisen, 1977). Similarly, children's developing understanding of gender constancy (e.g., Kohlberg, 1966; Marcus & Overton, 1978; Smetana & LeTourneau, 1984; Wehren & DeLisi, 1983) reflects a progression from judgment based on superficial, immediate appearances or actions to judgment based on underlying meaning.

Finally, the superficial-to-profound progression is discernible in physical–cognitive development. Flavell (1985) insightfully characterized the "contrast" between "perceived appearances" and "inferred reality" in physical–cognitive development during middle childhood:

> Piaget's test for conservation of liquid quantity illustrates the meaning of this and other contrasts: (1) the child first agrees that two identical glasses contain identical amounts of water; (2) the water from one glass is poured into a third, taller and thinner glass, while the child is watching; (3) the child is then asked if the two amounts of water are still identical, or whether one glass now contains more water than the other. The typical preschool nonconserver is apt to conclude, after the liquid has been poured, that the taller and thinner glass now has more water. . . . [She] is more given than the older child to make judgments on the basis of the immediate, perceived *appearances* of things. . . . The middle-childhood conserver, on the other hand, may also think that the tall glass *looks* like it contains more water because the liquid column is higher, but she goes beyond mere appearances to *infer* from the available evidence that the two quantities *are really* still the same. That is, she makes an inference about underlying reality. (pp. 93–94)

ROLE OF DECENTRATION

Flavell (1985) related this progression from superficial appearances to underlying meanings to the child's developing ability to attend to and interrelate multiple features of a situation. In terms of the conservation example:

> The preschooler is more prone to concentrate or *center* (hence *centration*) his attention exclusively on some single feature or limited portion of the stimulus array that is particularly salient and interesting to him, thereby neglecting other task-relevant features. In the present example, the difference in the heights of the two liquid columns is what captures most of his attention. . . . In contrast, the older child is likelier to achieve a more balanced, 'decentered' (hence, *decentration*) perceptual analysis of the entire display. While, of course, attending to the conspicuous height differences, just as the younger child does, he also carefully notes the correlative differences in container width. (p. 94)

In broad terms, views similar to Flavell's can be found elsewhere in the cognitive–developmental literature. Case (1985) discerned in the child's nonsocial (problem solving, exploration) and social (imitation, social conflict, social cooperation) activities a "common set" (p. 272) of decentration-like processes. The cognitive effectiveness attributable to these processes becomes more impressive as the child's working memory expands (see Pascual-Leone, 1970). A more radical position was taken by Doise and

Mugny (1984), who went beyond the point that decentration can be social as well as nonsocial to argue that decentration through *social* conflict is of preeminent importance in *physical* cognitive development. In any event, the interrelating of (social and/or physical) situational features may bring about (social and/or physical) inferential understanding. As Feffer (1970) wrote, " a stable construction of the interpersonal event depends, as in the impersonal realm, on a reconciliation of . . . complementary dimensions" (p. 206).

In a review of research on social causal reasoning, P. H. Miller and Aloise (1989) noted that "preschoolers tend not to consider motives when making moral judgments unless this information is explicit and salient" (p. 268). Miller and Aloise rejected a characterization of young children's social causal reasoning as "external," however, since young children can and do attribute much behavior to internal psychological causes. In my usage, young children's moral judgment tends to be "external" in the sense that their moral justification or problem solving tends to utilize relatively superficial considerations. Miller and Aloise themselves noted at several points the superficial, object- and action-oriented quality of young children's problem solving (see pp. 261, 271, 279). The argument I advance in this chapter is that this superficial quality dissipates as children's inferential or "decentering" ability develops. Again, Miller and Aloise themselves noted that older children "more effectively integrate multiple information about causes, . . . integrate information over time, and consider conflicting emotions" (p. 278). The older child's consideration of motives, even when they are not explicit or salient in a moral problem, may be attributable precisely to this growing ability with respect to the use of "multiple" information.

DECENTRATION, EQUALITY, AND RECIPROCITY

Decentration would seem to be characterizable in terms of certain central themes, for example, equality. In Flavell's conservation example, the equality theme is implied by the advent of a more comprehensive and "balanced" analysis of the situation, that is, the "careful" attention not only to the salient situational features, but also to the less salient ones. More evenly distributed attention may be related, in the social–cognitive realm, to the ideal of distributive justice, equal treatment, or impartiality. An ideal of impartiality is central to moral development; as Maccoby (1980) suggested, "the essence of moral maturity is giving [initially] equal weight to all moral claims" (p. 349).

The emergence of an ideal of impartiality or equality may be functionally associated with the gradual decline of egocentrism. Consider that the "feature" of the situation that is often "particularly salient and interesting" to the child may be the child's own viewpoint, needs, or desires (or those of someone similar and familiar to the child). Hence, the child's own viewpoint is likely to "capture most of [the child's] attention" (at least in the absence of an adult authority figure). Other persons' viewpoints or needs are either ignored altogether or assumed (appropriately or inappropriately) to be the same as the child's. Such an egocentric bias, allied with egoistic motives, probably accounts for the young child's unfair yet unabashed, self-serving allocations in distributive justice tasks (Damon, 1977).

Although egocentric bias may decline with decentration or cognitive development, the bias is probably never entirely eliminated. Even if egoistic motives are overcome, it remains true that "we experience our own points of view more or less directly, whereas we must always attain the other person's in more indirect manners. . . . Furthermore, we are usually unable to turn our own viewpoints off completely, when trying to infer another's" (Flavell, 1985, p. 125).

Decentration would also seem to be characterizable in terms of reciprocity. Indeed, Feffer (1970) virtually equated decentration with reciprocity, defining decentration as a "coordination and *reciprocal* correction between complementary physical [or social] dimensions" (p. 204; emphasis added). In the conservation example, one type of reciprocity involved in decentered judgment refers to the child's consideration of the "correlative" (Flavell, 1985, p. 94) or reciprocally compensating changes in height and width dimensions of the liquid quantity. Reciprocal compensation would also seem to be implied in conservers' suggestions "that the experimenter . . . merely poured the water from one container to the other . . . without *spilling* or *adding* any" (Flavell, 1985, p. 95; emphasis added). "Temporal" decentration (i.e., coordination of the present stimulus field with past and future changes) relates to "inversion" reciprocity, as when the child suggests "that the continuing equality of amounts could be proved by pouring the liquid back into its original container" (p. 95). Temporal decentration perhaps generates the older child's expanded temporal perspective not only in physical but also in social cognition.

With reference to social cognitive development, reciprocity was discerned in either instrumental and pragmatic form (Stage 2) or more hypothetical and ideal form (Stage 3; expanded to encompass society at Stage 4). Indeed, we noted that the referential terms in Piaget's work for Kohlberg's Stages 2 and 3 were, respectively, reciprocity as a fact and reciprocity as an ideal.

The equality and reciprocity features of decentered judgment, then, are manifested not only in nonsocial but also in social or sociomoral contexts. Equality and reciprocity are closely related: As the child's situational attention becomes more comprehensive, equalities among situational features or perspectives are discerned and their reciprocal relation is understood. Piaget

(1932/1965) argued that equality and reciprocity prescriptions naturally emerge as peers challenge one another's viewpoints during attempts to cooperate or discuss (cf. Youniss, 1980). Kohlberg (1984) asserted that his "moral stages represent successive forms of reciprocity" (p. 73) and that "conceptions and sentiments of justice ('giving each his due') are based on conceptions of reciprocity and equality. Reciprocity and equality are . . . cognitive as well as moral forms" (pp. 41–42).[2] Kohlberg, however, implicitly derived reciprocity and equality from general cognitive structuring tendencies; he did not specifically utilize the concept of decentration. Yet it would appear that the concept of decentration provides a plausible articulation of the cognitive structuring process (see also Gibbs, 1991-b).

DECENTRATION AND MORAL MOTIVATION

Studies of decentration imply that the equality and reciprocity prescriptions generated through decentration may contribute to the motivation of behavior. Conservation, transitivity, or other decentration-based constructions are experienced "as necessary, as something that *must* be true," rather than "as merely one of many facts that happen to be true about the world" (S. A. Miller, 1986, p. 3; see Piaget, 1971a, 1971b). Kuhn (1988, pp. 236–240) characterized cognition that leads to a sense of logical necessity as "reflective cognition" (p. 239), and argued that reflective cognition permits advances in competent judgment and decision making. The characterization of decentration-based prescriptions in terms of "necessity" connotes their compelling or obligatory—that is, motivating—quality.

In physical cognitive development, the motivational implications of decentration can be discerned in the responses of children studied in so-called countersuggestion studies. In these studies, children who make conservational or other largely logic-based judgments are confronted with (false) evidence of nonconservation (e.g., the experimenter may surreptitiously add or remove material). Although interpretations of the counter-suggestion research are controversial (S. A. Miller, 1976), studies involving "basic . . . Piagetian concepts" (S. A. Miller, 1986, p. 17) generally find that children who use logic-based judgments are surprised and upset when the experimenter confronts them with an apparent violation of "necessary" reality as they have inferred it. They seek some explanation, some logical means of accounting for or correcting, for example, an apparent nonconservation (Smedslund, 1961). In general, they act as if violations of logical reciprocity and equality "shouldn't be." The pertinent cognitive structuring of the situation motivates efforts to restore the "necessary" reciprocity or equality.

The parallel with the compelling or obligatory quality of prescriptive *moral* feelings is perhaps clear. Injustice, likewise, "shouldn't be." The cognitive structuring of a situation as unjust generates a motivation to restore the "necessary" reciprocity or equality. As Kohlberg (1984) wrote, "violation of logic and violation of justice . . . arouse . . . affects" (p. 63). The prescriptive motivation to correct a "reciprocity imbalance" (Gouldner, 1960, p. 167) in the social context may be no less cognitively based than is the corresponding motivation in the physical–cognitive context. The intimate relationship of logical with moral reciprocity is intriguingly expressed in Piaget's (1932/1965) assertion that "logic is the morality of thought just as morality is the logic of action" (p. 398). Similarly, Rest (1983) suggested that the sentiment of justice may have "a counterpart in people's sense of logical necessity derived from the application of basic logical schemas to phenomena" (p. 616).

AFFECTIVE PROCESSES IN MORAL MOTIVATION

Cognitive decentration, then, generally promotes the motivation of moral behavior. An adequate analysis of moral motivation, however, must consider the interaction of cognitive with affective processes, including the ways in which cognitive and affective processes may interact to attenuate or negate moral motivation.

First, cognition and affect are both involved in the question of whether a moral motivation results in a moral behavior. Hoffman (1983) provided the example of a child who "is excited about going to a new movie but then remembers . . . [his or her] promise to visit a sick friend" (p. 243). In this example, I would argue that there is a cognitively based moral motivation to behave in a fair and trustworthy fashion, perhaps out of Stage 3 considerations ("How would I feel if I were sick, and my friend didn't care enough to keep his promise to visit me?"). There is also an affectively based moral motive, namely, anticipatory empathy-based guilt ("My friend will feel hurt if I don't visit him, and I'd feel really bad about that") (Hoffman, 1981, 1983). Counteracting both the cognitively and affectively based moral motives, however, is an egoistic motive, namely, the desire to see the new movie. As Hoffman pointed out, moral behavior is typically accomplished only after moral motivation has overcome one or more counteracting egoistic motives.

Cognitively based moral motivation may also pertain to efforts to overcome what Hoffman (1987) termed "empathic bias." Whereas egocentric bias concerns inequality favoring self, empathic bias concerns inequality favoring those "who are familiar and similar to" oneself, or who are physically present (rather than spatially or temporally remote) (p. 67). To facilitate the reduction of empathic bias in moral motivation, Hoffman recommended:

> a moral education curriculum that stresses the common humanity of all people. . . . A positive value might be placed on spatial and temporal *impartiality*, and children . . . encouraged, insofar as possible, to give *equal* consideration to all of those who may be affected by their actions. (pp. 67–69; emphases added)

In my view, the above cited prescriptions of impartiality and equal consideration owe their motivational power at least partly to cognitive development (specifically, to the equality prescriptions of decentration as described earlier). The overcoming of empathic bias represents an interesting instance of a moral motive that, although *affectively* based (again, in empathy), must be modified by a *cognitively* based moral motive (an equality prescription) if it is to result in truly moral—that is, empathic, but also just or unbiased—behavior.

Although cognition plays an important role in the motivation to correct a perceived injustice, empathy for the distressed victim of the injustice may play a critical role in the intensity and persistence of the effort in behalf of the victim. Hoffman (1987) provided a fascinating and moving example of cognitive and affective processes in the emergence and continuation of an effort to remedy a reciprocity imbalance, in this case, between the respect someone accords others and the lack of respect—to say the least—that person receives in return. Hoffman described Coles's (1986) interview with a:

> 14-year-old Southern male 'redneck'. . . . After several weeks of joining his friends in harassing black children trying to integrate his school, this boy, a popular athlete,
>
> > . . . began to see a kid, not a nigger—a guy who knew how to smile when it was rough going, and who walked straight and tall, and was polite. I told my parents, "It's a real shame that someone like him has to pay for the trouble caused by all those federal judges."
> > Then it happened. I saw a few people cuss at him. "The dirty nigger," they kept calling him and soon they were pushing him in a corner, and it looked like trouble, bad trouble. I went over and broke it up. . . . They all looked at me as if I was crazy. . . . Before [everyone] left I spoke to the nigger . . . I didn't mean to. . . . It just came out of my mouth. I was surprised to hear the words myself: "I'm sorry" [Coles, 1986, pp. 27–28].

After this incident, he began talking to the black youth, championing him personally, while still decrying integration. Finally, he became the black youth's friend and began advocating "an end to the whole lousy business of segregation." When pressed by Coles to explain his shift, he attributed it to being in school that year and seeing "that kid behave himself, no matter what we called him, and seeing him insulted so bad, so real bad. Something in me just drew the line, and something in me began to change, I think." (p. 28) [Coles, 1986, p. 28; cited in Hoffman, 1987, pp. 56–57]

The cognitive construction of the injustice to the black youth ("It's a real shame that someone like him has to pay"; "someone like him" being someone mature enough to refrain from reciprocating insults and physical harassment) generated some motivation for the shift in behavior toward the youth, a motivation no doubt bolstered considerably by empathy for the victim's plight and by the sudden promptings of empathy-based guilt ("I was surprised to hear the words myself: 'I'm sorry'"). (Interestingly, construction of the ongoing injustice and/or empathy for the victim apparently dissipated a defensive out-group classification, as the boy "began to see a kid, not a nigger.")

Cognitive and affective processes do not always operate harmoniously to motivate moral behavior. Indeed, cognitive processes can overcome affectively based moral motivation to permit immoral behavior, as when cognitive rationalization in the service of egoistic motives neutralize guilt over harming or failing to help a victim. One may convince oneself that one was unable to help, or that helping was unwarranted because the victim somehow after all deserved to be victimized (i.e., that a reciprocity imbalance did not after all take place) (Lerner, 1980). Also (beyond empathic bias for similar and familiar persons) one may actively classify a victim as a member of an out-group (as the white youth did in the above example), and hence as not relevant to moral concern (Hoffman, 1978, p. 186). There is some evidence (Hoffman, 1970, pp. 102–103) that emotionally defensive children attempt to neutralize guilt after having committed an injustice by blaming or derogating the victim. A self-serving, defensive rationalization would seem to be evident in the retrospection of a 17-year-old delinquent with reference to victims of his burglaries: "If I started feeling bad, I'd say to myself, 'Tough rocks for him. He should have had his house locked better and the alarm on'" (Samenow, 1984, p. 115; see also Gibbs, 1991-a). Externalization of blame is also a normally occurring phenomenon in many naturalistic social conflict situations, because the ambiguity as to who "started it" permits each person to blame the other.

CONCLUSION

This chapter has concerned the relation of moral–cognitive development to the motivation of moral behavior. A revised view of Kohlberg's first four moral judgment stages depicted a progression from a relatively superficial (physicalistic, instrumental) level to a mature level of insight into the psychological meaning and functional bases of human interpersonal relationships (mutuality of expectations) and society (commonly agreed upon standards and interdependencies). This progression was related to cognitive decentration, that is, the attending to and interrelating of situational features or perspectives. Decentration is the key to cognitive motivation: The behavioral effects of certain motivating prescriptions (equality and reciprocity) are discernible across nonsocial and social contexts. In the sociomoral context, the decentration-generated prescriptions of equality and reciprocity constitute the ideal of justice. Hence, the motivation to correct a perceived injustice (i.e., a violation of equality and/or reciprocity) is cognitively based. Nonetheless, as discussed, cognitive motivation interacts with empathic motivation in the actual accomplishment of moral behavior. On the one hand, the motivation to correct an injustice is primarily cognitive insofar as the perception of the reciprocity imbalance has motivational properties. On the other hand, in a chronological sense, the motivation is primarily affective, since empathy may be a biologically rooted predisposition discernible even in infancy (Hoffman, 1978, 1981).

It is clear, then, that "both cognitive and affective sources of motivation are usually required for the accomplishment of good and fair behavior in the face of narrowly egoistic impulses" (Gibbs & Schnell, 1985, p. 1078). I have emphasized cognition in this chapter to clarify the sense in which "cognitive motivation" is a viable concept, derivable from at least a revised version of Kohlberg's cognitive–developmental theory of morality.

NOTES

1. One critic of a transition to "intrinsic" morality was Turiel (1983), who presented evidence that even young children can distinguish moral right and wrong from social conventions, and can appreciate morality's "intrinsic" character (e.g., hitting someone is always wrong, whereas addressing a teacher by a first name may or may not be wrong according to social convention). The distinction between morality and social convention is not as clear-cut as Turiel suggested, however (Rest, 1983, pp. 609–610). Furthermore, Turiel did not present evidence that young children's moral judgment is intrinsic in the sense of inferring an underlying psychological meaning (e.g., that breaking a promise is wrong because it destroys trust). Indeed, an unqualified rejection of hitting without consideration of situational circumstances (prior provocation, self-defense, absence of hostile intent, etc.) suggests possibly superficial judgment concerning the immorality of aggression. Understood as the transition from superficial appearances to inferred meanings, the external–internal transition is discernible in cognitive development generally and in moral judgment in particular.

2. Although moral development and motivation are intimately related to cognitive development, Kohlberg argued that the experiential requisites for moral–cognitive development are more complex than are those for physical–cognitive development. In developmental stage terms, Kohlberg (1984) argued (pp. 389–391) that there is a necessary but not sufficient relation between physical–cognitive and sociomoral–cognitive stages. As noted, Doise and Mugny (1984) argued that social interaction is essential even for physical–cognitive development; while not necessarily disagreeing, Kohlberg (pp. 71–79) emphasized the particular role of social interaction in making possible the attainment in the sociomoral domain of the developmental "ceiling" set by the physical–cognitive domain (but cf. Damon, 1975).

REFERENCES

Adelson, J., Green, B., & O'Neil, R. (1969). Growth of the idea of law in adolescence. *Developmental Psychology, 1,* 327–332.

Alexander, R. D. (1987). *The biology of moral systems.* New York: Aldine de Gruyter.

Burgess, R. L., & Huston, T. L. (1979). *Social exchange in developing relationships.* New York: Academic Press.

Case, R. (1985). *Intellectual development: Birth to adulthood.* New York: Academic Press.

Colby, A., Kohlberg, L., Gibbs, J. C., & Lieberman, M. (1983). A longitudinal study of moral judgment. *Monographs of the Society for Research in Child Development, 48*(1–2, Serial No. 200).

Colby, A., Kohlberg, L., Speicher, B., Hewer, A., Candee, D., Gibbs, J., & Power, C. (1987). *The measurement of moral judgment* (Vol. 2). Cambridge, England: Cambridge University Press.

Coles, R. (1986). *The moral life of children.* Boston: Atlantic Monthly Press.

Damon, W. (1975). Early conceptions of positive justice as related to the development of logical operations. *Child Development, 46,* 301–312.

Damon, W. (1977). *The social world of the child.* San Francisco: Jossey-Bass.

Doise, W., & Mugny, G. (1984). *The social development of the intellect* (A. St. James-Emler & N. Emler, Trans.). Oxford: Pergamon Press.

Edwards, C. P. (1975). Social complexity and moral development: A Kenyon study. *Ethos, 3,* 505–527.

Eisenberg, N. (1982). The development of reasoning regarding prosocial behavior. In N. Eisenberg (Ed.), *The development of prosocial behavior* (pp. 219–249). New York: Academic Press.

Eisenberg, N., Boehnke, K., Silbereisen, R. K., & Schuhler, P. (1985). The development of prosocial behavior and cognitions in German children. *Journal of Cross-Cultural Psychology, 16,* 69–82.

Feffer, M. (1970). Developmental analysis of interpersonal behavior. *Psychological Review, 77,* 197–214.

Flavell, J. H. (1985). *Cognitive development* (2nd ed.). Englewood Cliffs, NJ: Prentice-Hall.

Gibbs, J. C. (1977). Kohlberg's stages of moral judgment: A constructive critique. *Harvard Educational Review, 47,* 43–61.

Gibbs, J. C. (1979). Kohlberg's moral stage theory: A Piagetian revision. *Human Development, 22,* 89–112.

Gibbs, J. C. (1991-a). Sociomoral developmental delay and cognitive distortion: Implications for the treatment of antisocial youth. In W. M. Kurtines & J. L. Gewirtz (Eds.), *Handbook of moral behavior and development* (Vol. 1, pp. 95–110). Hillsdale, NJ: Lawrence Erlbaum Associates.

Gibbs, J. C. (1991-b). *(Toward an integration of Kohlberg's and Hoffman's theories of morality.)* In W. M. Kurtines & J. L. Gewirtz (Eds.), *Handbook of moral behavior and development* (Vol. 1, pp. 183–222), Hillsdale, NJ: Erlbaum.

Gibbs, J. C., Basinger, K. S., & Fuller, D. (1992). *Moral maturity: Measuring the development of sociomoral reflection.* Hillsdale, NJ: Erlbaum.

Gibbs, J. C., & Schnell, S. V. (1985). Moral development "versus" socialization: A critique. *American Psychologist, 40,* 1071–1080.

Gouldner, A. W. (1960). The norm of reciprocity: A preliminary statement. *American Sociological Review, 25,* 161–178.

Grueneich, R. (1982). The development of children's integration rules of making moral judgments. *Child Development, 53,* 887–894.

Harter, S. (1983). Developmental perspectives on the self-system. In J. H. Flavell & E. M. Markman (Eds.), *Handbook of child psychology* (4th ed., Vol. 3, pp. 275–386). New York: Wiley.

Hoffman, M. L. (1970). Conscience, personality, and socialization techniques. *Human Development, 13,* 90–126.

Hoffman, M. L. (1978). Empathy, its development and prosocial implications. In C. B. Keasy (Ed.), *Nebraska Symposium on Motivation* (Vol. 25, pp. 169–217). Lincoln: University of Nebraska Press.

Hoffman, M. L. (1981). Is altruism part of human nature? *Journal of Personality and Social Psychology, 40,* 121–137.

Hoffman, M. L. (1983). Affective and cognitive processes in moral internalization. In E. T. Higgins, D. N. Ruble, & W. W. Hartup (Eds.), *Social cognition and social development: A sociocultural perspective* (pp. 236–274). Cambridge, England: Cambridge University Press.

Hoffman, M. L. (1987). The contribution of empathy to justice and moral judgment. In N. Eisenberg & Janet Strayer (Eds.), *Empathy and its development* (pp. 47–80). Cambridge, England: Cambridge University Press.

Kohlberg, L. (1966). A cognitive–developmental analysis of children's sex-role concepts and attitudes. In E. Maccoby (Ed.), *The development of sex differences* (pp. 82–173). Stanford, CA: Stanford University Press.

Kohlberg, L. (1984). *The psychology of moral development: Essays on moral development* (Vol. 2). San Francisco: Harper & Row.

Kuhn, D. (1988). Cognitive development. In M. H. Bornstein & M. L. Lamb (Eds.), *Developmental psychology: An advanced textbook* (2nd ed., pp. 205–260). Hillsdale, NJ: Erlbaum.

Lerner, M. (1980). *The belief in a just world: A fundamental delusion.* New York: Plenum Press.

Loevinger, J., & Wessler, R. (1970). *Measuring ego development: 1. Construction and use of a sentence completion test.* San Francisco: Jossey-Bass.

Maccoby, E. E. (1980). *Social development: Psychosocial growth and the parent–child relationship.* New York: Harcourt Brace Jovanovich.

Marcus, D. E., & Overton, W. F. (1978). The development of cognitive gender constancy and sex role preference. *Child Development, 49,* 434–444.

Miller, P. H., & Aloise, P. A. (1989). Young children's understanding of the psychological causes of behavior: A review. *Child Development, 60,* 257–285.

Miller, S. A. (1976). Extinction of Piagetian concepts: An updating. *Merrill-Palmer Quarterly, 22,* 257–281.

Miller, S. A. (1986). Certainty and necessity in the understanding of Piagetian concepts. *Developmental Psychology, 22,* 3–18.

Montemayor, R., & Eisen, M. (1977). The development of self-conceptions from childhood to adolescence. *Developmental Psychology, 13,* 314–319.

Newman, D. (1986). The role of mutual knowledge in the development of perspective taking. *Developmental Review, 6,* 122–145.

Pascual-Leone, J. (1970). A mathematical model for the transition rule in Piaget's developmental stages. *Acta Psychologica, 32,* 301–345.

Peterson, C. C., Peterson, J. L., & Seeto, D. (1983). Developmental changes in ideas about lying. *Child Development, 54,* 1529–1535.

Piaget, J. (1965). *Moral judgment of the child* (M. Gabain, Trans.). New York: Free Press. (Original work published 1932.)

Piaget, J. (1971a). *Biology and knowledge.* Chicago: University of Chicago Press.

Piaget, J. (1971b). The theory of stages in cognitive development. In D. R. Green, M. P. Ford, & G. B. Flamer (Eds.), *Measurement and Piaget* (pp. 1–11). New York: McGraw-Hill.

Piaget, J. (1977). *The development of thought: Equilibration of cognitive structure* (A. Rosin, Trans.). New York: Viking Press. (Original work published 1975.)

Rest, J. R. (1983). Morality. In J. H. Flavell & E. M. Markman (Eds.), *Handbook of child psychology* (4th ed., Vol. 3, pp. 556–629). New York: Wiley.

Samenow, S. (1984). *Inside the criminal mind.* New York: Times Books.

Selman, R. (1980). *The growth of interpersonal understanding: Developmental and clinical analyses.* New York: Academic Press.

Smedslund, J. (1961). The acquisition of conservation of substance and weight in children: III. Extinction of conservation of weight acquired "normally and by means of empirical controls on a balance scale. *Scandinavian Journal of Psychology, 2,* 85–87.

Smetana, J. G., & LeTourneau, K. J. (1984). Development of gender constancy and children's sex-typed free play behavior. *Developmental Psychology, 20,* 691–696.

Snarey, J. (1985). The cross-cultural universality of social–moral development: A critical review of Kohlbergian research. *Psychological Bulletin, 97,* 202–232.

Turiel, E. (1983). *The development of social knowledge: Morality and convention.* Cambridge, England: Cambridge University Press.

Wehren, A., & DeLisi, R. (1983). The development of gender understanding: Judgments and explanations. *Child Development, 54,* 1568–1578.

Youniss, J. (1980). *Parents and peers in social development: A Sullivan–Piaget perspective.* Chicago: University of Chicago Press.

Chapter 11 ■

Values, Conceptions of Science, and the Social Psychological Study of Morality ■

DONELSON R. FORSYTH
Virginia Commonwealth University

In the course of human interaction, people must continually determine if the actions that others perform are morally acceptable. Because judgments of goodness and badness, rightness and wrongness, virtuousness and viciousness influence our dealings with others, moral phenomena lie at the core of many interpersonal processes. Moral judgments and cognition influence our reactions to equity and inequity (Hastie, 1983), attributions of responsibility for positive and negative outcomes (Ross & DiTecco, 1975), perceptions of altruistic (Greenberg & Frisch, 1972) and aggressive (Tedeschi, Smith, & Brown, 1974) actions, and judgments of individuals who violate social norms (Darley & Shultz, 1990; Reeder & Spores, 1983). In the behavioral realm, moral cognition has been linked to a wide range of actions, including delinquency, honesty, altruism, and conformity (Blasi, 1980; Jurkovic, 1980). Moral judgments also influence how we feel after we conform to or violate moral norms, for they play a mediating role in guilt and shame reactions (Dienstbier, Hillman, Lehnhoff, Hillman, & Valkenaar, 1975; Klass, 1978).

Psychology offers a number of theoretical models that pertain to moral processes, including cognitive–developmentalism (Kohlberg, 1983; Piaget, 1934), behaviorism (Mills, 1982; Skinner, 1974), personality models (Hogan, 1982), social learning theory (Bandura, 1990; Mischel & Mischel, 1976), and psychoanalytic theory (Freud, 1927; Gilligan, 1976). The assumptions underlying a social psychological model of morality, in contrast, have not yet been fully articulated. As Kelley (1971) noted "it is almost impossible to find moral concepts listed in the index of any social psychology textbook" (p. 293). More recently, Darley and Zanna (1982) argued that "psychology does not provide a conceptual scheme that describes the ordinary person's system of moral judgments" (p. 515). Similarly, after reviewing previous studies of distributive justice and deservingness judgments, Hastie (1983) concluded that "no generally popular logic for moral reasoning has yet been presented" (p. 533).

Why is the social psychological analysis of moral judgment and behavior relatively undeveloped? The explanation offered here highlights the impact of the field's metatheoretical assumptions on theoretical growth and empirical development. Although these assumptions are rarely made explicit, they provide an undergirding structure that guides the theories formulated and methods used by social psychologists in their analyses of moral processes. These meta-assumptions not only pertain to general beliefs about the prime causes of social behavior and the nature of human beings, but also describe the nature of science itself. These assumptions include *sociogenicism*, the supposition that the primary determinants of human behavior are exogenous and situational rather than endogenous and dispositional; *egoism*, the premise that much of human thought and action is motivated by selfish concerns; and *positivism*, the theory that scientific analyses require empiricism, objectivity, and suspension of personal values. These metatheoretical premises are examined here, and compared with several alternative assumptions that can be used to structure the social psychological study of moral processes.

ASSUMPTIONS ABOUT BEHAVIOR

Social psychology views human behavior from the unique vantage gained at the intersection of psychology and the other social sciences. In a tradition dating back to the field's founding, social psychologists focus first on exogenous causes of behavior before turning their attention to endogenous causes. Asked why an individual tells lies, why a bystander acts altruistically, or why someone harms someone else, the social psychologist's first inclination is to examine the social forces present in the situation. Intrapersonal processes are not ignored, but they are typically viewed as dependent variables or as mediators of external causes. Social psychological models tend to champion environmental determinism over biological and psychological determinism, situationism over personologism, sociogenicism over psychogenicism, and relativism over universalism.

This viewpoint arises from social psychology's roots in sociology and anthropology, but was given paradigmatic status by Hartshorne and May's (1928) early analyses of the link between personality and morality. In their classic studies, Hartshorne and May sought to discover if certain individuals, across many times and situations, tended to behave either morally or immorally. Despite their best efforts to detect individual consistencies, their investigations suggested that those who behaved morally at one time and setting were just as likely as not to behave immorally at another time and setting. Hartshorne and May summarized their findings with their doctrine of specificity: Individuals' traits—their values, attitudes, personal moral codes, and personalities—do not significantly influence their moral behavior; behavior is situation specific.

Thus, rather than searching for systematic regularities across development, psychological processes that explain individual lapses in morality, or personality correlates of individual differences in the moral arena, the social psychologist examines how interpersonal variables influence individuals' thoughts, feelings, and actions in morally toned situations. Social psychological analyses of helping behavior provide a case in point. Social psychologists continue to question the theoretical utility of trait-based models by arguing that the emergency setting, and not the bystander's personality characteristics, determines the likelihood of helping. They suggest that the true altruist—someone who consistently helps other people across a range of situations—is an anomaly. More typically, when individuals are observed in several kinds of helping situations, they behave inconsistently, sometimes helping, but sometimes not (Gergen, Gergen, & Meter, 1972). Yet, as Rushton (1981, p. 66) notes, some people are consistently more generous, helping, and kind than others. (Rushton, 1981). For example, helpful people tend to be empathic people; they have a facility for "seeing" situations from other people's perspectives (Archer, 1984; Underwood & Moore, 1982). Helpers also tend to be more deeply committed to personal moral standards and values than nonhelpers (Fogelman & Wiener, 1985; Staub, 1978). However, when various personality traits (including authoritarianism, moral development, Machiavellianism, alienation, autonomy, and trustworthiness) are correlated with helping, the correlations are usually rather paltry; they average about .30 (Rushton, 1980).

Despite the wide acceptance of social causes as primary, social psychology's sociogenicism constrains its approach to the study of moral behavior. As early as 1898, Sharp complained that his social psychological studies of moral judgment were hindered by a lack of agreement among his subjects concerning what was moral. Sharp noted that even when people with apparently similar characteristics made judgments about the same person, they sometimes reached opposite conclusions concerning the other's moral worth. More recently, Hastie (1983) reiterated this problem by arguing that a successful analysis of moral judgment must not only establish the fundamental "inference rules for moral reasoning," but also describe individual differences in the application of these inference rules.

Recognizing the limitations of a purely sociogenetic model of morality, more recent social psychological models of moral phenomena advocate a transactional view of personality and behavior. Haan (1978, 1986; Haan, Aerts, & Cooper, 1985), for example, argued that individuals' moral behavior varies because interpersonal demands vary across situations. Haan stated that moral action is "informed and influenced by variations in contexts" and by individuals' "own strategies of problem solving" when they confront a moral dilemma (Haan, 1986, p. 1282). Similarly, Kurtines (1984, 1986), by asking individuals to predict how they would behave in various social roles, found that individuals' use of principled moral reasoning varied across role settings. He concluded that "the most critical conceptual limitation of individualistic orientations is their inability to provide a theoretically meaningful account of the effects of situation-related variables on decision making" (1986, p. 790).

Forsyth (1980, 1985) offered a Person × Situation transactional model. The person side of his equation is based on individual differences in personal moral philosophies. According to this model, individuals' moral beliefs, attitudes, and values comprise an integrated conceptual system of personal ethics. This integrated system, or personal moral philosophy, provides guidelines for moral judgments, solutions to ethical dilemmas, and prescriptions for actions in morally toned situations. In describing individual differences in personal moral philosophies, Forsyth focused on two dimensions: relativism and idealism. First, individuals differ in their acceptance of universal ethical absolutes. At one end of the continuum, highly relativistic individuals espouse a personal moral philosophy based on skepticism. In contrast, people low in relativism argue that "right" actions are those that are consistent with moral principles, norms, or laws. Second, a fundamental concern for the welfare of others lies at the heart of some individuals' moral codes, but other people do not emphasize such ideals; the former individuals assume that we should avoid harming others, whereas the latter assume harm is sometimes necessary to produce good (Forsyth, 1980, 1981, 1985; Waterman, 1988).

These two dimensions, relativism and idealism, were initially identified in an exploratory study of individual differences in judgments of psychological research (Schlenker & Forsyth, 1977). They parallel, however, distinctions made by other theorists and researchers (Boyce & Jensen, 1978; Gilligan, 1982; Haan, 1978; Hogan, 1973; Kohlberg, 1983; Piaget, 1932). Hogan (1973), for example, distinguished between an "ethics of personal conscience," which is inner focused, and an "ethics of responsibility," which concentrates on societal regulatory standards that define duties. Gilligan (1982, p. 65), in her analyses of sex differences in moral thought, noted that females "hope that in morality lies a way of solving conflicts so that no one will be hurt" (concern for positive consequences), whereas males' moralities tend to stress the rational application of principles (Forsyth, Nye, & Kelley, 1988). Kohlberg (1963, 1983) concentrated on differences in principled thought, but he also noted that most moral dilemmas occur when "acts of obedience to legal–social rules or to commands of authority conflict with the human needs or welfare of other individuals" (1963, p. 12). Indeed, Kohlberg and his colleagues, recognizing the importance of variations in relativism, recently revised the scoring system for the Moral Judgment Interview (Candee & Kohlberg, 1987). The new system classifies individuals not only as to stage of development, but also as to degree of relativism within a particular stage.

Previous investigations of predictions derived from the two-dimensional model of personal moral philosophies indicated that individuals who differ in relativism and idealism divaricate when making moral judgments (Forsyth, 1985), evaluating contemporary moral issues (Forsyth, 1980), attributing responsibility after wrongdoing (Forsyth, 1981), and judging the ethics of psychological research (Forsyth & Pope, 1984; Schlenker & Forsyth, 1977). The link between moral philosophy and moral choice, however, is less certain. In one laboratory study, subjects were tempted to cheat on a difficult task when the experimenter left them alone with the answer key. Thirty-six percent of the subjects cheated, but idealism and relativism were not systematically linked to this behavior. A second attempt to test resistance to moral temptation that used a confederate who pressured the subject into cheating obtained an 83% compliance rate, but again the two dimensions failed to predict who would succumb to the temptation (Forsyth & Berger, 1982).

In explaining these results, a transactional model suggests that personal moral philosophies influence action only when these values are readily available to serve as cognitive and behavioral guides (Endler, 1982; Mischel & Peake, 1982; Snyder, 1982). At the personal level, moral values vary in clarity, prominence, and degree of internalization. At the situational level, certain environmental factors, such as the salience of moral norms or the severity of the consequences produced by actions, similarly work to increase or decrease the availability of personal moral values. As Schwartz (1968) explained:

> If a person construes a decision he faces to be a moral choice, relevant moral norms he holds are likely to be activated and to affect his behavior. When he fails to perceive that a moral decision is at stake, however, particular moral norms are unlikely to be activated. (p. 355)

This analysis was partially supported in one study of lying. As predicted, the salience of moral norms and consequences had a strong impact on moral action; only 50.0% of the subjects chose to violate a moral norm when that norm was salient and they would personally benefit by their actions; this percentage increased to 76.2% in the other conditions. Personal ethical philosophies also influenced moral choices and posttransgression reactions, for more of the idealistic subjects chose to act immorally than did the low idealists (91.66 vs. 70.83%), and subjects who were low in both idealism and relativism were less likely to transgress a moral norm if they personally would benefit. The results thus lent some support to the proposed two-dimensional model of personal moral philosophies, particularly as applied to posttransgression reactions (Forsyth & Nye, 1990).

ASSUMPTIONS ABOUT HUMAN NATURE

Psychodynamic models assume that individuals are driven by biologically based urges that can be only dimly intuited. Behaviorism considers morality to be a function of prior reinforcement history provided by one's society. Cognitive developmental models propose that individuals move through stages of growth characterized by certain issues, but that each step in development is qualitatively superior to the one that preceded it.

How, in contrast, does the social psychologist view the human being? Social psychological theorizing, in many regards, highlights humans' rationality. People are viewed as active processors of information who are constantly seeking data about themselves and others. This information guides decisions about behavior; thus, rationality often triumphs over irrationality. Although reinforcements play a major role in shaping behavior, the social psychologist adds that cognitive processes, including goal seeking and information processing systems, also must be considered. Taking a chapter from humanistic psychology, social psychologists propose that humans confront existential and moral issues and deliberate over them until they are resolved.

This image is incomplete, however, for social psychology often assumes that our ability to function as rational decision makers is muted by our unremitting egoism. The individual views the world from his or her own perspective, and the biases inherent in this limited viewpoint are never wholly escaped. This assumption, although occasionally challenged, suggests that the self is a primary psychological mechanism, and rivals the personality as the actual determinant of action and that the drive for self-promotion is stronger than the drive for other-promotion. The human is so fundamentally egocentric that social psychologists are skeptical about the inherent "goodness" of individuals, to the point that moral behaviors such as altruism are viewed as impossible (see Campbell & Specht, 1985; Kelley & Thibaut, 1985; Wispe, 1985).

Counterattitudinal advocacy studies illustrate the assumption of egoism that permeates social psychology. Studies of attitude change following counterattitudinal behavior indicate that most individuals, with very little situational pressure, willingly misrepresent their actual attitudes and beliefs on a variety of issues. Although the causes and consequences of this counterattitudinal advocacy are still debatable, a self-presentational explanation suggests that individuals lie in such settings to project an image of rationality and consistency. They realize that what they are saying is not true, but by publicly stating behavior-consistent attitudes, they present a socially attractive impression to the experimenter. Such actions are in one's best interests, even though they run counter to traditional moral norms concerning honesty (Schlenker, Forsyth, Leary, & Miller, 1981).

This assumption also informs the interpretation of the statements people make about the causes of moral or immoral behavior or justifications of moral choices. Such statements are often viewed as self-presentational devices designed to secure a particular image rather than reflections of internal moral values. Just as individuals often attribute positive outcomes to personal, internal causes, and blame negative outcomes on external, environmental factors, individuals prefer to be responsible for moral actions but not for immoral actions. Consider, for example, students' reactions following cheating on an examination. Viewed from an egoism perspective, cheating represents less of a threat to students' self-esteem if they can attribute this "immorality" to something external to themselves, such as an unfair teacher, pressure from their parents, or the persuasiveness of a fellow student. Such attributions reduce students' feelings of guilt and immorality after cheating in a classroom situation, and allow them to continue to think of themselves as moral persons who simply bent to environmental pressures. In addition, a self-serving pattern of attributions helps cheaters maintain an acceptable social image in the educational setting (Forsyth, Pope, & McMillan, 1985).

A social psychology based completely on egoism and selfishness as primary social motives is a restricted social psychology (Vitz, 1977, 1985; Wallach & Wallach, 1983). Social psychology strives to provide a cross-cultural view of human behavior, but clearly all cultures do not prize selfishness as much as the Western world does. As Hogan and Sloan (1985) asked, Is it merely coincidence that a social psychology rooted in a culture that praises independence and self-seeking strivings implicitly assumes that individuals are egoistically motivated?

Recent work on the nonselfish determinants of helping attest to the importance of considering both egoistic and altruistic determinants of action. Many years ago, William McDougall (1908) identified two possible reactions to others' distress: "sympathetic pain" and "tender emotion." According to McDougall, people who experience tenderness are more likely to help than those who experience sympathetic pain. Although it took nearly 80 years, Daniel Batson and his colleagues offered compelling support for McDougall's speculations. Like McDougall, Batson argued that two different motivations may prompt individuals to help someone in distress. First, observers may help simply to reduce their own personal distress. While watching others in need, they, too, feel upset. To erase this distress, they help. Batson describes this reason for helping as egoistic motivation, because it is self-serving; this form of helping helps the helper feel better. In contrast, the helping may be motivated by empathy, an altruistic desire to reduce the distress of the person in need. Unlike the egoistic helper, the empathic, altruistic helper is other-serving, for his or her primary goal is helping someone else through a crisis (Batson & Coke, 1981; Batson, Duncan, Ackerman, Buckley, & Birch, 1981; Batson, O'Quin, Fultz, Vanderplas, & Isen, 1983; Coke, Batson, & McDavis, 1978; Toi & Batson, 1982).

These two motivations lead to two qualitatively distinct emotional reactions. Empathic bystanders describe their feelings with such terms as concerned, softhearted, compassionate, sympathetic, and moved. Distressed bystanders, in contrast, feel alarmed, grieved, upset, worried, disturbed, or perturbed (Batson, O'Quin, et al., 1983). More importantly, people who experience empathy, rather than personal distress, tend to be more helpful. In a number of studies, Batson and his colleagues showed that bystanders who are told to "imagine how the victim feels" are more helpful than people who are told simply to "observe the situation" (Coke et al., 1978; Toi & Batson, 1982). In addition, helpful people are often higher than nonhelpers in dispositional empathy, a generalized tendency to take the perspective of other people (Archer, Diaz-Loving, Gollwitzer, Davis, & Foushee, 1981; see also Archer, 1984; Batson, Coke, & Pych, 1983). Empathy may also explain why helping behavior steadily increases with age during the first 15 years of life. Because younger children have not yet developed the cognitive skills needed to take the perspective of other people, they lack the empathic orientation needed for altruistic motivation (Bar-Tal, Sharabany, & Raviv, 1982).

ASSUMPTIONS ABOUT SCIENCE

Social psychologists' assumptions about science have undergone considerable revision in recent decades. Reacting, in part, to challenges to historical conceptions of how science works, most have abandoned a strict logical positivism in favor of a modified version, often termed *postpositivism*. This view maintains that science, as an epistemological system, relies on methods different from those of alternative epistemologies. More than other approaches to gaining knowledge, science advocates the long-term goal of increasing and systematizing our knowledge about the subject matter. It requires relating observations back to theoretical constructs that provide the framework for interpreting data and generating predictions. In addition, science insists that the test of theory be based on objective, empirical methods rather than logical claims, subjective feelings, or authorities' opinions. Science also involves a striving for consensus among members of the discipline concerning acceptable and unacceptable explanations of empirical observations. Psychological studies, if they are to be scientific, must remain within these boundaries. Hypotheses offered must be empirically testable, using methods that other scientists accept as adequate.

Other theorists, however, believe that even postpositivism provides a limited view of how science works and argue in favor of an alternative philosophy of science. These various viewpoints include sociorationalism (Gergen, 1978, 1984), hermeneutics (Alexander, 1988), dialectics (Rychlak, 1968), ethnomethodology (Garfinkel, 1967), ethogenics (Hare & Secord, 1972), realism (Manicas & Secord, 1983), and semiotics (D'Andrade, 1986). These alternatives differ from one another in a variety of ways, but most argue that social scientists must develop methods that take into account the reflexive, interpretive, constructivistic nature of human activity. Rather than assuming that facts exist, observation is a neutral process, causality is linear, and individual action can be examined in mechanistic terms, these viewpoints champion the in-depth study of behavior as it occurs in ongoing settings using ethnography and detailed interviewing, the intimate involvement of the researcher in the data collection processes, and close scrutiny of the participants' construction of the situation.

Constructivism also diverges from postpositivism with regards to the role of values in science. Although values undoubtedly play a role in determining which topics are investigated and the researcher's bias for one interpretation rather than another, positivism maintains that values should have no impact on the data collection procedures or statistical analyses. Hypotheses offered must be empirically testable, using methods that other scientists will accept as adequate. Moreover, and most importantly, the focus is on description rather than prescription. Philosophy is concerned with making prescriptive statements concerning how actions and individuals should be morally evaluated, and thus how people should make moral judgments. Social psychology, in contrast, proposes and tests theoretical formulations of how individuals make judgments and why they perform particular actions.

Psychologists are clearly not of one voice regarding this description–prescription issue (Einhorn, 1983; Haan, 1982, 1983; Kurtines, Alvarez, & Azmitia, 1990). Kohlberg's work, for example, is a case of research that defies science's mandates for value neutrality over value ladenness and description over prescription. Kohlberg's work is based on an ethical philosophy that dates back to Aristotle and finds expression in the ethics of such philosophers as Kant and Frankena. In *The Nicomachean Ethics*, Aristotle stressed the idea that the highest good is what the individual seeks "for its own sake and never for the sake of some other thing" (1953, p. 36). Morality can be achieved by becoming self-sufficient, yet at the same time conforming to the mean and avoiding activities that conflict with accepted norms. Incorporating this notion of morality into his scientific explanation of the moral development, Kohlberg assumed that autonomy and cooperation are the bases of mature morality, and that any morality based on other considerations is immoral or immature.

Critics have argued that this assumption undermines the work's scientific status, providing an example of the "ascendancy of the moral philosopher over the empirical scientist" (Simpson, 1974, p. 97). Simpson, for example, pointed out that (1) Kohlberg collapsed the oft-noted distinction between science–description and ethics–prescription, (2) the approach is not universal and content irrelevant but restricted by its typically Western morality, and (3) Kohlberg's developmental research reflects a doctrine of social evolution, ethnocentrism, and cultural bias. Simpson cited a number of Kohlberg's published statements to lend support to her indictments. These include Kohlberg's recommendation to individuals learning to score subjects' responses to his moral judgment scale that they read Frankena's (1963) book on ethics; his observation that members of preliterate societies will not be able to score better than 3 in his scheme; and his acceptance of a framework that unfairly ranks females as less morally mature than males.

Kohlberg (1971), in his chapter titled "From Is to Ought: How to Commit the Naturalistic Fallacy and Get Away with It," readily admitted many of these biases, but argued that they are only biases if one accepts the description–prescription dichotomy:

> There is a universal set of moral principles held by men in various cultures, our stage 6. (These principles, we shall argue, could logically and consistently be held by all men in all societies; they would in fact be universal to all mankind if the conditions for socio-moral development were optimal for all individuals in all cultures.) At lower levels than stages 5 or 6, morality is not held in a fully principled form. (p. 178)

> Metaethical assumptions must be compatible with, if not derived from, acceptable psychological theorizing on moral judgment. (p. 184)

Kohlberg thus admitted that his model of moral development is prescriptive, that it ranks one kind of morality over other kinds of morality. However, he felt that his claims are justified because they are based on empirical evidence attesting to the invariance of his stages and their transcultural universality.

Positivism provides no foundation for Kohlberg's view, for it argues that science and philosophy must remain distinguishable. Postpositivism, however, allows for links between science and ethics. First, science can inform moral judgment processes. For example, a political policy may be adopted based on the moral principle that human rights are sacred and should not be violated by any government. When this principle is accepted as the basis for action, information regarding how inequities in the human condition may be best reduced is required. Scientific procedures then become useful in identifying solutions to problems; the short- and long-term implications of implementing certain actions or programs designed to fulfill the standards expressed in the moral principal; and the psychological, political, sociological, and economic reactions that may accompany the implementation of the programs. Scientific research may also influence moral judgments by providing an indication of validity of factual statements made in the moral judgment process. Individuals may decide an action is moral because they feel it will have certain desirable results. A scientific analysis becomes relevant if it can provide evidence that the action being considered will or will not lead to the desired consequences. If, for example, the death penalty is deemed just only because it serves as a deterrent to violent crime, then data that speak to the validity of this claim are relevant to the moral approbation of the practice.

Second, philosophical analyses also inform scientific analyses, albeit once again in a well-defined and limited way. In many cases, philosophical arguments raise questions that psychologists feel are best answered empirically. Aristotle's model of morality, for example, argues that moral development is based on both habit formation and self-perception processes. Dienstbier et al. (1975) based their emotion-attribution model of morality on these notions. Similarly, Forsyth (1980) and Boyce and Jensen (1978) developed taxonomies of individual differences in moral thought that draw on distinctions made within moral philosophy. These philosophical distinctions, however, are used only at the theory-construction stage, and are not used as evidence attesting to the validity of the psychological theory of individual differences. In addition, although Forsyth used moral theory as a means of describing individual differences in moral thought, he did not argue that any one philosophy is more morally advanced than another. To do so would be to commit the naturalistic fallacy of moving from "This is how individuals make judgments" to "This is how individuals should make judgments."

Third, although the logical positivists argued for a view of science founded on unidirectional causality, explanation of the whole through analysis of the component parts, and an accretive research process that more and more accurately describes the world, progress in science often results from a dialectical process involving thesis, antithesis, and synthesis (Rychlak, 1968, 1977). Rather than staunchly defending a viewpoint against attack, the dialectician searches for the means to reconcile multiple, yet inconsistent, interpretations of reality. Such an approach requires taking the best from positivism and the best from constructivism, and synthesizing them in a dialectical philosophy of science.

CHANGING ASSUMPTIONS AND FUTURE DIRECTIONS

The philosopher of science, Thomas Kuhn (1970), argued that scientists working in a particular field often share a set of assumptions about the phenomena they study. His thesis was that when individuals are trained to be scientists, they learn not only the content of the science—important discoveries, general principles, facts, and so on—but also a way of looking at the world that is passed on from one scientist to another. This set of shared fundamental beliefs, exemplars, and symbolic generalizations provides researchers with a world view that determines the questions they feel are worth studying and the most appropriate methods.

The fundamental assumptions of social psychology's paradigm have served the discipline well, but they introduce serious constraints when moral processes are the focus of investigation. If one assumes that the situation and not personal qualities determine moral action, that individuals are supremely motivated only by egoistic concerns, and that social psychology must remain true to the models of the natural sciences, then advances in our understanding of moral phenomena may be a long time in coming.

REFERENCES

Alexander, J. C. (1988). The new theoretical movement. In N. J. Smelzer (Ed.), *Handbook of sociology* (pp. 77–101). Newbury Park, CA: Sage.

Archer, R. L. (1984). The farmer and the cowman should be friends: An attempt at reconciliation with Batson, Coke, and Pych. *Journal of Personality and Social Psychology, 46,* 709–711.

Archer, R. L., Diaz-Loving, R., Gollwitzer, P. M., Davis, M. H., & Foushee, H. C. (1981). The role of dispositional empathy and social evaluation in empathic mediation of helping. *Journal of Personality and Social Psychology, 40,* 786–796.

Aristotle. (1953). *The Nicomachean ethics.* (R. Thomson, Trans.). Middlesex, England: Penguin.

Bandura, A. (1990). Selective activation and disengagement of moral control. *Journal of Social Issues, 46*(1), 27–46.

Bar-Tal, D., & Raviv, A. (1982). A cognitive-learning model of helping behavior development: Possible Implications and Applications. In N. Eisenberg (Ed.), *The development of prosocial behavior.* (pp. 199–217). NY: Academic Press.

Batson, C. D., & Coke, J. S. (1981). Empathy: A source of altruistic motivation for helping? In J. P. Rushton & R. M. Sorrentino (Eds.), *Altruism and helping behavior.* (167–187). Hillsdale, NJ: Erlbaum.

Batson, C. D., Coke, J. S., & Pych, V. (1983). Limits on the two-stage model of empathic mediation of helping: A reply to Archer, Diaz-Loving, Gollwitzer, Davis, and Foushee. *Journal of Personality and Social Psychology, 45,* 895–898.

Batson, C. D., Duncan, B. D., Ackerman, P., Buckley, T., & Birch, K. (1981). Is empathic emotion a source of altruistic motivation? *Journal of Personality and Social Psychology, 40,* 290–302.

Batson, C. D., O'Quin, K., Fultz, J., Vanderplas, M., & Isen, A. M. (1983). Influence of self-reported distress and empathy on egoistic versus altruistic motivation to help. *Journal of Personality and Social Psychology, 45,* 706–718.

Blasi, A. (1980). Bridging moral cognitive and moral action: A critical review of the literature. *Psychological Bulletin, 88,* 1–45.

Boyce, W. D., & Jensen, L. C. (1978). *Moral reasoning: A psychological–philosophical integration.* Lincoln: University of Nebraska Press.

Campbell, D. T., & Specht, J. (1985). Altruism: Biology, culture, and religion. *Journal of Social and Clinical Psychology, 3,* 33–42.

Candee, D., & Kohlberg, L. (1987). Moral judgment and moral action: A reanalysis of Haan, Smith, and Block's (1968) free speech movement data. *Journal of Personality and Social Psychology, 52,* 554–564.

Coke, J. S., Batson, C. D., & McDavis, K. (1978). Empathic mediation of helping: A two-stage model. *Journal of Personality and Social Psychology, 36,* 752–766.

D'Andrade, R. (1986). Three scientific world views and the covering law model. In D. W. Fiske & R. A. Shweder (Eds.), *Metatheory in social science: Pluralisms and subjectivities* (pp. 19–41). Chicago: University of Chicago Press.

Darley, J. M., & Shultz, T. R. (1990). Moral rules: Their content and acquisition. *Annual Review of Psychology, 41,* 525–556.

Darley, J. M., & Zanna, M. P. (1982). Making moral judgments. *American Scientist, 70,* 515–521.

Dienstbier, R. A., Hillman, D., Lehnhoff, J., Hillman, J., & Valkenaar, M. C. (1975). An emotion-attribution approach to moral behavior: Interfacing cognitive and avoidance theories of moral development. *Psychology Review, 82,* 299–315.

Einhorn, J. (1983). An unequivocal "yes" for morality study. *American Psychologist, 38,* 1255–1256.

Endler, N. S. (1982). Interactionism comes of age. In M. P. Zanna, E. T. Higgins, & C. P. Herman (Eds.), *Consistency in social behavior* (Vol. 2, pp. 209–249). Hillsdale, NJ: Erlbaum.

Fogelman, E., & Wiener, V. L. (1985). The few, the brave, the noble. *Psychology Today, 19*(8), 60–65.

Forsyth, D. R. (1980). A taxonomy of ethical ideologies. *Journal of Personality and Social Psychology, 39,* 175–184.

Forsyth, D. R. (1981). Moral judgment: The influence of ethical ideology. *Personality and Social Psychology Bulletin, 7,* 218–223.

Forsyth, D. R. (1985). Individual differences in information integration during moral judgment. *Journal of Personality and Social Psychology, 49,* 264–272.

Forsyth, D. R., & Berger, R. E. (1982). The effects of ethical ideology on moral behavior. *Journal of Social Psychology, 117,* 53–56.

Forsyth, D. R., & Nye, J. L. (1990). Personal moral philosophy and moral choice. *Journal of Research in Personality, 24,* 398–414.

Forsyth, D. R., Nye, J. L., & Kelley, K. (1988). Idealism, relativism, and the ethic of caring. *Journal of Psychology, 122,* 243–248.

Forsyth, D. R., & Pope, W. R. (1984). Ethical ideology and judgments of social psychological research. *Journal of Personality and Social Psychology, 46,* 1365–1375.

Forsyth, D. R., Pope, W. R., & McMillan, J. H. (1985). Students' reactions after cheating: An attributional analysis. *Contemporary Educational Psychology, 10,* 72–82.

Frankena, W. K. (1963). *Ethics.* Englewood Cliffs, NJ: Prentice-Hall.

Freud, S. (1927). *The psychopathology of everyday life.* London: Hogarth Press.

Garfinkel, H. (1967). *Studies in ethnomethodology.* Englewood Cliffs, NJ: Prentice-Hall.

Gergen, K. J. (1978). Toward generative theory. *Journal of Personality and Social Psychology, 36,* 1344–1360.

Gergen, K. J. (1984). An introduction to historical social psychology. In K. J. Gergen (Ed.), *Historical social psychology* (pp. 3–36). Hillsdale, NJ: Erlbaum.

Gergen, K. J., Gergen, M. M., & Meter, K. (1972). Individual orientations to prosocial behavior. *Journal of Social Issues, 28,* 105–130.

Gilligan, C. (1982). *In a different voice.* Cambridge, MA: Harvard University Press.

Gillgan, J. (1976). Beyond morality: Psychoanalytic reflections on shame, guilt, and love. In T. Lickona (Ed.), *Moral development and behavior* (pp. 144–158). New York: Holt, Rinehart & Winston.

Greenberg, M. S., & Frisch, D. M. (1972). Effect of intentionality on willingness to reciprocate a favor. *Journal of Experimental Social Psychology, 8,* 99–111.

Haan, N. (1978). Two moralities in action contexts. *Journal of Personality and Social Psychology, 36,* 286–305.

Haan, N. (1982). Can research on morality be "scientific?" *American Psychologist, 37,* 1096–1104.

Haan, N. (1983). Replies to Leary, Houts, and Krasner, Waterman, and Einhorn. *American Psychologist, 38,* 1256–1258.

Haan, N. (1986). Systematic variability in the quality of moral action, as defined in two formulations. *Journal of Personality and Social Psychology, 50,* 1271–1284.

Haan, N., Aerts, E., & Coopert, B. (1985). *On moral grounds: The search for practical morality.* New York: New York University Press.

Hare, R., & Secord, P. F. (1972). *The explanation of social behavior.* Oxford: Blackwell.

Hartshorne, H., & May, M. A. (1928). *Studies in the nature of character.* New York: MacMillan.

Hastie, R. (1983). Social inference. *Annual Review of Psychology, 34,* 511–542.

Hogan, R. (1973). Moral conduct and moral character: A psychological perspective. *Psychological Bulletin, 79,* 217–232.

Hogan, R. (1982). A socioanalytic theory of personality. *Nebraska Symposium on Motivation,* 55–89.

Hogan, R., & Sloan, T. (1985). Egoism, altruism, and psychological ideology. *Journal of Social and Clinical Psychology, 3,* 15–19.

Jurkovic, G. J. (1980). The juvenile delinquent as a moral philosopher: A structural-developmental perspective. *Psychological Bulletin, 88,* 709–727.

Kelley, H. H. (1971). Moral evaluation. *American Psychologist, 26,* 293–300.

Kelley, H. H., & Thibaut, J. W. (1985). Self-interest, science, and cynicism. *Journal of Social and Clinical Psychology, 3,* 26–32.

Klass, E. T. (1978). Psychological effects of immoral actions: The experimental evidence. *Psychological Bulletin, 85,* 756–771.

Kohlberg, L. (1963). The development of children's orientations toward a moral order: I. Sequence in the development of human thought. *Vita Humana, 6,* 11–33.

Kohlberg, L. (1971). From is to ought: How to commit the naturalistic fallacy and get away with it. In T. Mischel (Ed.), *Cognitive development and epistemology,* pp. 151–235. New York: Academic Press.

Kohlberg, L. (1983). *Essays in moral development* (Vol. 2). New York: Harper & Row.

Kuhn, T. S. (1970). *The structure of scientific revolutions.* Chicago: University of Chicago Press.

Kurtines, W. M. (1984). Moral behavior as rule governed behavior: A psychological role-theoretical approach to moral behavior and development. In W. Kurtines & J. L. Gewirtz (Eds.), *Morality, moral behavior, and moral development: Basic issues in theory and research* (pp. 303–324). New York: Wiley.

Kurtines, W. M. (1986). Moral behavior as rule governed behavior: Person and situation effects on moral decision making. *Journal of Personality and Social Psychology, 50,* 784–791.

Kurtines, W. M., Alvarez, M., & Azmitia, M. (1990). Science and morality: The role of values in science and the scientific study of moral phenomena. *Psychological Bulletin, 107,* 283–295.

Manicas, P. T., & Secord, P. F. (1983). Implications for psychology of the new philosophy of science. *American Psychologist, 38,* 399–413.

McDougall, W. (1908). *Introduction to social psychology.* London: Methuen.

Mills, J. A. (1982). Purpose and conditioning: A reply to Waller. *Journal for the Theory of Social Behavior, 14,* 363–367.

Mischel, W., & Mischel, D. (1976). A social learning model of moral development. In T. Lickona (Ed.), *Moral development and behavior* (pp. 84–107). New York: Holt, Rinehart & Winston.

Mischel, W., & Peake, P. (1982). In search of consistency: Measure for measure. In M. P. Zanna, E. T. Higgins, & C. P. Herman (Eds.), *Consistency in social behavior* (Vol. 2, pp. 187–208). Hillsdale, NJ: Erlbaum.

Piaget, J. (1932). *The moral judgment of the child.* London: Kegan Paul.

Reeder, G. D., & Spores, J. M. (1983). The attribution of morality. *Journal of Personality and Social Psychology, 44,* 736–745.

Ross, M., & DiTecco, D. (1975). An attributional analysis of moral judgments. *Journal of Social Issues, 31*(3), 91–109.

Rushton, J. P. (1980). *Altruism, socialization, and society.* Englewood Cliffs, NJ: Prentice-Hall.

Rushton, J. P. (1981). The altruistic personality. In J. P. Rushton & R. M. Sorrentino (Eds.), *Altruism and helping behavior* (pp. 251–266). Hillsdale, NJ: Erlbaum.

Rychlak, J. F. (1968). *A philosophy of science for personality theory.* Boston: Houghton-Mifflin.

Rychlak, J. R. (1977). *The psychology of rigourous humanism.* New York: Wiley-Interscience.

Schlenker, B. R., & Forsyth, D. R. (1977). On the ethics of psychological research. *Journal of Experimental Social Psychology, 13,* 369–396.

Schlenker, B. R., Forsyth, D. R., Leary, M. R., & Miller, R. S. (1981). Self-presentational analysis of the effects of incentives on attitude change following counterattitudinal behavior. *Journal of Personality and Social Psychology, 39,* 553–577.

Schwartz, S. H. (1968). Awareness of consequences and the influence of moral norms on interpersonal behavior. *Sociometry, 31,* 355–369.

Sharp, F. C. (1898). An objective study of some moral judgments. *American Journal of Psychology, 9,* 198–234.

Simpson, E. L. (1974). Moral development research: A case study of scientific culture bias. *Human Development, 17,* 81–106.

Skinner, B. F. (1974). *About behaviorism.* New York: Free Press.

Snyder, M. (1982). When believing means doing: Creating links between attitudes and behavior. In M. P. Zanna, E. T. Higgins, & C. P. Herman (Eds.), *Consistency in social behavior* (Vol. 2, pp. 105–130). Hillsdale, NJ: Erlbaum.

Staub, E. (Ed.). (1978). *Positive social behavior and morality: Social and personal influences* (Vol. 1). New York: Academic Press.

Tedeschi, J. T., Smith, R. B., III, & Brown, R. C. (1974). A reinterpretation of research on aggression. *Psychological Bulletin, 81,* 540–562.

Toi, M., & Batson, C. D. (1982). More evidence that empathy is a source of altruistic motivation. *Journal of Personality and Social Psychology, 43,* 281–292.

Underwood, B., & Moore, B. S. (1982). The generality of altruism in children. In N. Eisenberg (Ed.), *The development of prosocial behavior* pp. 25–52. New York: Academic Press.

Vitz, P. C. (1985). The dilemma of narcissism. *Journal of Social and Clinical Psychology, 3,* 9–14.

Vitz, P. C. (1977). *Psychology as religion: The cult of self-worship.* Grand Rapids, MI: Eerdmans.

Wallach, M. A., & Wallach, L. (1983). *Psychology's sanction for selfishness: The error of egoism in theory and therapy.* San Francisco: W. H. Freeman.

Waterman, A. S. (1988). On the uses of psychological theory and research in the process of ethical inquiry. *Psychological Bulletin, 103,* 283–298.

Wispe, L. (1985). Selfishness, society, and sympathy: A kind of a review. *Journal of Social and Clinical Psychology, 3,* 20–25.

Chapter 12 ▪

Leading an Examined Life: The Moral Dimension of Daily Conduct ▪

DIANA BAUMRIND
University of California, Berkeley

All human action has a moral dimension. In referring to human beings as "the ethical animal," Waddington (1960) reminded us that moral reasoning is an everyday activity engaged in by the average person. One central value implicit in the ensuing argument is that the province of morality is how one ought to live. A second central value assumption of this position is that human consciousness is constituted morally to the extent that actions are determined volitionally and consciously rather than by unreflective conformity to instinct, inclination, or authority. A third central value is that the individual is not an autonomous being who belongs solely to him- or herself. Because individuals are social from inception, an individual's rights are inseparable from his or her responsibilities to the community. However worthy it may be to lead an examined life, only a life well lived is worth examining.

Human beings *are* responsible for their own lives in a way no other animal is; that is, they are required to take charge of their actions and to answer to themselves and to the community for the consequences. Degraded conditions of life or existential sloth limit human freedom, depriving individuals of what Aristotle calls our "second nature," that is, our

During the preparation of this paper, the author was supported by a Research Scientist Award (No. 1-K05-MH00485) and the William T. Grant Foundation (No. 84044973).

moral personality. Human beings in all cultures and with all degrees of intellect are required to plan their actions and implement their plans, to examine and choose among options, to eschew certain actions in favor of others, and to structure their lives by adopting congenial habits, attitudes, and rules of conduct. Morality, as construed here, is a personal and collective enterprise intended to serve the society as a whole by regulating the actions of its component individuals and subgroups to facilitate the survival and growth of the person embedded in the collective. As a personal enterprise, moral considerations regulate the activities of the individual by coordinating immediate with long-range interests. As a collective enterprise, moral considerations regulate the actions of component individuals and subgroups to achieve the common good.

Many tenets of the perspective presented here are rooted in dialectical materialism—a tradition that is rational rather than merely emotive, atheistic rather than theistic or agnostic, collectivist rather than individualistic, dialectical rather than mechanistic, and whose ideals are realizable rather than transcendent. Marxism (i.e., dialectical materialism) views morality from the perspective of how it affects and reflects the material conditions of life in particular sociocultural contexts. However, with the exception of his early, influential work on alienation, Marx did not write systematically about morality, and the perspective presented here would not be shared by all who call themselves Marxists.

Furthermore, this perspective is disequilibrated by perturbations arising from self-contained internal experiences that are asocial, impelled as much by an existential concern with the identity and self-integrity of the moral agent as with a Marxist social consciousness, that is, with the necessary fiction that I, at least, am an autonomous moral agent. Kierkegaard (1968) referred to this existential concern as Religiousness B, a sphere in which one constructs or adopts an overarching commitment that clarifies, illuminates, and integrates one's daily practice. Kohlberg's (1973) quasi-Stage 7 also grapples with what he called the ultimate religious question: "Why be moral?" The existential perspective illuminates the personal psychological motives for being moral, but fails to examine its social roots or developmental features and is, therefore, insufficient to the task of constructing a system of personal ethics. The moral dimension of daily life, then, organizes and gives meaning to our social relations and self-awareness by evaluating human conduct in particular contexts. The distinction between self-oriented and other-oriented codes of conduct that is typically used to differentiate personal from moral concerns is not observed here, because the self is conceived of as a social self, and right conduct in relations with others is understood as the primary route to self-actualization.

The position presented here developed from a rule-utilitarian meta-ethical position I used to justify my opposition to intentional deception in research with human subjects (Baumrind, 1971a, 1972, 1975a, 1975b, 1978a, 1978b, 1985). My judgment that intentional deception in the research setting is morally wrong was grounded not in act utilitarianism (which is too relativistic) or in a deontological categorical imperative (which is too dogmatic), but rather in rule utilitarianism, the view that an act is right if and only if it would be as beneficial to the common good in a particular social context to have a moral code permitting that act as to operate under a rule that would prohibit that act. Rule utilitarians grant that even actions to which we have strong moral aversions are justifiable in certain contexts. Thus, retaliative aggression may be justifiable provided it is proportionate to the grievance; killing may be justifiable if the victim is an enemy or a murderer or a fetus under 3 months; telling lies may be justifiable if intended to benefit the recipient and not the liar; hurting others may be justifiable if the agent is a dentist or surgeon. However, justifying morally aversive acts, legitimates them, and this, too, has social consequences, because harm inflicted self-righteously may appear to demand no reparation and is not self-correcting.

At least three ethical rules generally accepted in Western society proscribe deceitful research practices: (1) the right of self-determination within the law, which translates in the research setting to the right of informed consent; (2) the obligation of a fiduciary (in this case, the researcher) to protect the welfare of the beneficiary (in this case, the subject); and (3) the obligation, particularly of a fiduciary, to be trustworthy in order to provide sufficient social stability to facilitate self-determined agentic behavior. Consistent with a rule-utilitarian position, these rules were grounded teleologically by arguing that their adoption benefits modern society more than contradictory rules, thus explaining their general acceptance (Baumrind, 1985). My rationale for rejecting the use of deceptive research practices instantiates my metaethical position.

I consider five major issues in developing my approach to the investigation of moral conduct: (1) differences between cognitive judgments about morality, moral judgments, and concrete standards of right and wrong conduct; (2) universalizability as a criterion of moral adequacy; (3) the role of prudence and partiality in moral judgments; (4) bridging the gap between moral judgment and action; and (5) interpersonal morality.

JUDGMENTS ABOUT MORALITY, MORAL JUDGMENTS, AND MORAL CONDUCT

To explicate my three central values about morality—that the province of morality is how one ought to live, that moral activities must be determined volitionally and consciously, and that the individual as a social being is not an autonomous agent belonging solely to him- or herself—three meanings of the word *moral* are considered: (1) judgments about morality (justification of transcendent ideals), (2) moral judgments (realizable ideals), and (3) concrete standards of right and wrong conduct (maxims for action). Cognitive judgments about morality made from a philosophical perspective need not implicate the subject, and therefore have much to do with cognition, but little to do with morality, whereas moral judgments and normative standards of conduct do implicate the subject, and therefore have much to do with morality and are generally affect laden.

By *judgments about morality,* I refer to unrealizable ideals in the province of moral philosophy, whose criteria of adequacy are exclusively cognitive. Kohlberg's Stage 6, ideal role taking, is the prototypic example of a presumed final psychological stage of adult development that is so ideal that it virtually does not exist. In fact, Stage 6 is now used not as an empirical construct, but only as an ideal in the normative sense, in order to define the nature of the kind of development being investigated (Kohlberg, Levine, & Hewer, 1983). The psychological reality investigated by Kohlberg is dissociated from material and social events that implicate the subject. The hypothetical dilemmas in the standard moral judgment interview are intended to engage the cognitive, and not the affective and conative, faculties. Unlike concrete ethical imperatives, which implicate each individual in realizable obligations to self and society, judgments about morality are "cold" cognitive reflections on the moral behavior of hypothetical others that pertain to how one ought to evaluate a hypothetical other's options in circumstances far removed from one's own. Kohlberg's stages of moral development are judgments about morality in the Kantian tradition, because moral adequacy resides in the form rather than in the substance, and in the structure rather than in the process of action.

At a less abstract level, *moral* refers to *moral judgments,* that is, to recognizable and realizable ideals of virtue that emerge from historical cultural conditions and are adopted to provide structure and meaning to self-directed social activities. The four cardinal Aristotelian virtues are prudence, fortitude, temperance, and justice. The two cardinal Judeo–Christian virtues are justice and love, with the addition of faith and hope in Christian ethics, and of reason in Jewish ethics, whereas the emphasis is on harmony and order in Eastern morality. These moral attitudes, mores, and virtues are abstracted from social experience and, in turn, justify, and are operationalized as, maxims for action.

Concrete standards of right and wrong conduct, or maxims for action such as the Ten Commandments, state what humans are to do and what they are to avoid doing, that is, what is regarded as right and wrong conduct in a particular society. Character education is intended to generate virtue by discovering and exploring realizable ideals and normative standards of conduct that reflect real-life conditions and issues.

Judgments about morality, that is, abstract ideals derived by "pure reason," are the province of the armchair philosopher. They fail to address the moral issues crucial to human behavior, and may pertain so little to the ethical conflicts of daily life that the armchair philosopher need not feel obliged to practice them at all. Moral judgments and maxims for actions are the province of the psychologist and the citizen. As moral agents, the counterfactual–hypothetical concerns us less than how humans govern their behavior in practice. We are concerned with the volitional realization in action of personally endorsed values by agents behaving as though they have free will, or with the absence of such values and the perception of oneself as pawn rather than moral agent. Above all, both as scientists and citizens, we ought to be concerned with the sources of discrepancy between moral judgments and the moral actions they claim to govern.

Abstract moral principles (i.e., judgments about morality), then, do not deserve a more privileged status in regulating human behavior than social rules or conventions. Contextual–pragmatic factors regarded by Kantians such as Rawls (1971) and Kohlberg (1969) as premoral are in the moral province from my perspective. In fact, so-called lower level conventional reasoning, because it is situated in time and space, has clearer implications for how the respondent is to conduct his or her practical affairs than postconventional reasoning, which is directed to a hypothetical prototypic other and therefore may or may not dictate how the reasoner ought to act.

Agents acting privately, interpersonally, or as representatives of a community, assume a moral stance by asserting responsibility for making a decision and for the pragmatic and moral consequences of their actions. The scope of the action contemplated (private, interpersonal, or institutional) determines the proper locus of responsibility, which in turn determines whether moral decision making calls for introspection, consensual validation, or an appeal to authority. The appropriate locus of control of private moral events is persons themselves, of interpersonal moral events is the group, and of institutional moral events is a designated social unit, given voice by an authority or law. In making moral decisions, agents may (1) turn inward, seeking a solution that is cognitively coherent and practically appealing; (2) turn outward for social approval to obtain a consensual solution and validation; or (3) have recourse to authority and tradition represented by parental, authoritative, or social rules. There is no inherent basis for regarding one method of achieving relative certitude as more moral than another. Logical coherence of self-constructed principles, easily set aside by the stressful nature of moral conflicts in daily life, can hardly be regarded as the sole criterion by which the adequacy of moral decisions should be judged. Social sanctions and need for social approval are also firm bases for guarding against antisocial conduct and for acting prosocially. Thus, I dispute the commonly accepted notion that the mark of mature moral reasoning is rejection of extrinsic, external considerations or that such considerations are extraneous to moral cognition and conduct. These considerations are to be taken into account by the moral agent, although they are not to be internalized uncritically and intact.

Abstract principles of justice, beneficence, and respect for persons are generalized distillations of human evolutionary wisdom, whereas less abstract conventions are tailored to fit a particular society. Principles such as justice, beneficence, and respect for persons are more abstract than conventions, but both are social rules that regulate social behavior. *Justice* provides a basis for adjudicating conflicts of interest. *Distributive justice* apportions privileges, duties, and responsibilities in accord with merit, requiring from each in accord with his or her ability and giving to each in accord with his or her accomplishments. *Retributive justice* increases the good through the law of effect, providing for the containment and punishment of those who do harm as well as rewarding those who do good. *Commutative justice* demands the fulfillment of contractual obligations, without which social chaos would result. *Beneficence* leavens justice with mercy, mandating that society provide for the basic needs of all its members without regard to merit. *Respect for persons* mandates consideration of the rights and perspectives of all, especially of divergent minorities whose novel perspectives enrich the idea pool of the human species and replenish the store of socially transmittable variations available in human evolution. *Conventions* express the settled customs of a stable society and are justifiable by their regulative function to the extent that the social order is itself viewed as legitimate. Conformity or nonconformity with convention invokes moral considerations. Conformity has the metapurpose of affirming the social order. However, if a society is thought to require radical revision and designated authorities are viewed as unresponsive, antinomian acts that undermine the social order may be justified on moral grounds.

Principles, no less than conventions, have their affective and concrete aspects. An empathic response to another's distress and an inclination to "play fair" are affective components of beneficence and justice. Fear of death is contained in the principle of respect for persons, which dictates absolute regard for human life. Therefore, everyday interaction to be moral does not require the application of formal logical principles in postconventional moral reasoning, and that is fortunate, because few people use it. A prudential regard for duty, a fear of punishment, an inclination to fulfill one's obligations, empathic identification with another's distress, and a need to trust other people enable most humans to perceive their own true interests as including those of others, that is, to practice the principles philosophers reify.

UNIVERSALIZABILITY OF MORAL JUDGMENTS

Intransigent (universal) social–material realities create the need for morality in all cultures (without thereby mandating a universal hierarchy of principles). Scarcity, hierarchy, reciprocity, and indeterminacy are such social realities.

Above all, *scarcity* of goods and status creates the material conditions for the moral dimension in decision making. Those with far too little are least likely to be moral because the true interests of persons living on the edge of survival are limited to securing basic amenities. Persons with unlimited material and personal resources are also less likely to be moral than those whose goods and status are adequate but not superfluous because their homeostasis and equilibrium can be maintained without the omnipresent need to take others' interests, or even their own long-range interests, into account.

Hierarchical order acknowledges inequality in rights and responsibilities, and in the proper allocation of scarce goods. Inequalities in functionally relevant abilities legitimate the hierarchical relations that structure human economic activities. Whereas (almost) all human beings are equal in that they possess the same qualities, they are unequal in degree with regard to any given quality, including moral worth. Equality dictates that all should have the necessities and amenities appropriate to human existence and none should have so much that others (without regard to their merit) cannot be provided these necessities and amenities. Inequality dictates that within these constraints, unequals should be treated unequally in proportion to their functionally relevant competencies and deeds. Justice is served by treating persons alike insofar as they are equal, and differently insofar as they are unlike in possession of functionally relevant qualities.

The crucial principle of *reciprocity* governs all stable social systems by providing mutuality of gratification, acknowledging the "pattern of exchange through which the mutual dependence of people, brought about by the division of labor, is realized" (Gouldner, 1960, pp. 169–170). Reciprocity refers to the balance in an interactive system such that each party has both rights and duties. Within a reciprocal and interacting system, individuals produce by their actions the environmental conditions that affect their own as well as others' behavior. One person's behavior is simultaneously a response to prior environmental stimuli and a stimulus to others' responses within the interactive system of social exchange. The moral norm of reciprocity both acknowledges and places a positive value on the fact that the elements of social reality are reciprocally determined. The principle of reciprocity is central to Eastern as well as Western ethics in that Karma is held to be the sum total of the ethical consequences of a person's actions, good and bad, which then determine that individual's future.

Indeterminacy exists in all social systems, resulting in imperfect justice such that a fair balance is not achieved for each individual at each point in time. Morality thus requires (within limits) acceptance and forgiveness of human imperfection, even when oneself is the victim.

However, the existence of cross-culturally intransigent realities of scarcity, hierarchy, reciprocity, and indeterminacy does not imply a culturally invariant hierarchy of principles, and no such hierarchy exists.

In this section, I argue that generalizability, not universalizability, is a proper antidote to moral anarchy. A judgment that is merely particular is often opportunistic and expedient since it makes no claim to relevance out of the immediate context within which the judgment has been derived and to which it should apply. A particularized ad hoc decision should therefore submit to generalizable (not universalizable) rules or principles. A judgment that claims *universalizability* presumes its truth has already been secured, and cannot be negated, but merely included within a more encompassing formulation, independent of historical temporal context. A *generalizable* judgment limits the range of applications to "a given context from a given perspective," requiring therefore some particularization of the *ceteris paribus* caveat.

Societies differ greatly in how they define the good or interpret and rank such principles as harmony, enlightenment, justice, beneficence, and respect for persons. Varied understandings of what is right or wrong, good or evil, reflect diverse world views as agents act and interact within particular situational and sociocultural ecologies. Western societies elevate individual rights and personal freedoms; however, in socialist societies, subordination of individual rights to community welfare takes precedence, and in Hindu societies, harmonious relation of the parts in hierarchical subordination to the whole is the guiding principle. In Hindu society, moral virtue is unequally divided by caste, and, in theory, higher caste persons are held to higher standards and punished more severely than lower caste persons for the same infraction (Karkar, 1978; Shweder & Bourne, 1982).

Contrary to Rawls's (1971) claim, moral equality and the absolute value of life are not universally accepted first principles. The following excerpts from adult Kohlberg Moral Judgment Interviews administered to a devout Christian and a devout Buddhist demonstrate the contrasting values placed on life, death, and the human species.

The Christian: "Yes, the man should steal for his wife. I would. A life is worth that. I would penalize the druggist. Wherever there is life, there is hope. Even if it only prolonged her life, that would be something. The druggist is trespassing against a higher law than 'Thou Shalt Not Steal.' I would steal to save any human life. I was brought up to believe that the Lord gives life and He should be the only one to end it. Thou Shalt Not Kill under any circumstances. The doctor should not give her the drug (for euthanasia) whether or not the woman wanted it. For an animal, that is different. An animal is not a human. An animal is a luxury for whomever owns it. An animal is not responsible for carrying on civilization or a family."

The Buddhist: "I personally feel that death under certain circumstances and in spite of the fear it produces is not worth violating one's moral essence to avoid. The proscription against stealing is a universal truth, as is accepting one's death. If in any particular case one violates a value judgment, then the truth has no essence. I definitely would not steal for it. I would try to convince my wife to accept her death. Yes, the doctor should give her the drug, she should be able to die as she wishes. We are all part of the universe; we are not bigger and what we do is not more precious than the bird flying or the dog barking. A human life, a dog's life—it is all the same."

From my perspective presented here, what is important *morally* is that both respondents implicated themselves in their judgments and were prepared to act on these ethical values that reflected how each saw his place in the universe. The Buddhist does not believe in an independent external world that exists separate from the individual. The external world and the inner world are regarded as two sides of the same reality, inextricably bound in a net of endless, mutually conditioned relations. From the Buddhist's perspective, the value of an individual human life, which takes precedence for the Christian respondent, is subordinated to the maintenance of a proper relationship between the part and the whole. Stealing as well as killing violates the integrity of the whole, and acceptance of one's own, or a loved one's death is regarded as more important than the preservation of a particular life. Kohlberg assigned the "value of life" a preeminent place in his evaluation of moral adequacy, and would therefore consign the Buddhist respondent to a lower stage. However, by what superordinate criteria can one perspective be judged as more *moral* than the other? What is important morally is that agents implicate themselves and are prepared to act on their ethical judgments, rather than the cognitive adequacy of those judgments.

Inherent in each superordinate moral principle is its own peculiar justification for evil. We are all aware of the abuse of individual rights in pursuit of the common good in totalitarian societies and of the abuse of the common good in pursuit of individual rights in the United States. The abysmal treatment of women in India culminating in increased incidence of bride burning in the last decade could occur only in a society that values role hierarchy over equality. Each culture, then, has its peculiar hierarchy not only of virtues, but also of associated evils, which alternative societies may never tolerate.

The parochialism built into the Kohlberg system for scoring judgments about morality on logical criteria is demonstrated clearly by the high correlations between moral judgment stage scores and class-related variables, such as education. Thus, in a recent validity study, the correlations between parents' Socioeconomic Status (SES) and children's moral judgment scores were uniformly over .40, with Stage 5 present in the upper SES group but never exceeding the error cutoff in the lower SES group (Colby, Kohlberg, Gibbs, & Lieberman, 1983). Empirically, as well as theoretically, Kohlberg's stages of moral development are not generalizable to other cultures or even to other classes in this society. Moreover, in some studies, women obtain lower moral judgment stage scores (e.g., Baumrind, 1986; Holstein, 1972), although when compassion is used as the standard, women may be judged to be more moral than men (Gilligan, 1982).

The abstractness of universalizable reasoning, which excludes sentimental partiality and prudential considerations, also distances reasoning from decisive action. The universalizability of a judgment does not, in my view, enhance its moral adequacy, and in practice may even detract from it, because appeal to universalizable principles of justification may substitute a sense of certitude that is based on logical consistency for a sense of closure based on consistency between virtuous thoughts and actions.

PRUDENTIAL CONSIDERATIONS AND MORAL JUDGMENT

My third contention is that prudential, partisan considerations are a necessary ingredient of moral judgments and moral conduct. Thus, a child's justification for keeping a promise to a friend on the basis that he or she may need a favor from that friend is a less mature, but not a less moral reason than that a promise should be kept because friendship is based on mutual trust. The expression of love for that friend as a reason to not hurt him or her by breaking trust is less cognitively complex than either previous justification for keeping a promise, but is arguably the most likely to motivate congruent conduct, and, if so, by my criteria, the most moral.

The assertion by universalists, such as Rawls (1971) and Kohlberg, that the moral dimension of social cognition or conduct should exclude the practical consequences for self is to require of human beings when they behave morally that they become alienated from their own subjective natures. I regard this aspiration as immoral because it is inhumane and unrealizable. That is not to say that actions based solely on expediency and opportunism are moral. However, moral reasoning is a quintessentially human activity, so that the exclamation "I am only human" should provide the reason to coordinate one's conduct with one's values and not the excuse for failing to do so. Human insufficiencies will assure that our reach exceeds our grasp without reaching for ideals that are intrinsically unrealizable. One may not leap from "is" to "ought." But one can argue that what cannot be, in the sense of being contrary to human nature—for example, an injunction to love one's enemies as oneself—ought not to be espoused. The distinction between the merely prudential and the moral should be made on the basis of an expanded concept of the self rather than along a dimension of self-interest/disinterest.

Fundamental to moral judgment is determination of *true self-interest.* True self-interest transcends the polarization of (1) self-interest and non-self-interest implicit in traditional definitions of altruism, and of (2) prudential and moral concerns implicit in Kantian morality. In situating morality in decision making and action, I include self-interest and prudential considerations in the moral domain, contrary to typical definitions of *altruism* that polarize self-interest and concern for others. Rushton (1980) defined altruism as "behavior carried out to achieve positive outcomes for another *rather* than for the self" (p. 22; emphasis added). However, in elaborating upon his position, Rushton was unable to preserve his (false) self–other disjunction. Thus, Rushton claimed that altruism may be motivated by empathy, external consequences, or justice considerations. Empathic motivation, however, is not altruistic by Rushton's definition, because empathy is a primitive nonreflective response to one's *own* suffering, induced by emotional identification of alter's interests with one's own. Also, empathy can never be excluded from compassionate regard for another's genuine well-being. Similarly, acts induced implicitly by external consequences (what Selye, 1980, called altruistic egoism) cannot be altruistic as Rushton defined altruism, because they are not carried out to help another *rather* than oneself. Even acts induced solely by justice considerations are not altruistic as Rushton defined the term, because justice requires that the interests of self be weighed in the balance. From my perspective, acts are altruistic when they *reconcile* the interests of self and other rather than deny the just claims of self, or the probable practical consequences to self and others of one's actions.

From this perspective, impartiality is not superior morally to enlightened partiality. Partiality allows conflicts of interest to be identified, debated, and negotiated by individuals, or by the elected representatives of communities, with divergent interests. Justice, after all, is blind to the identity of who is ego and who is alter. Individuals know their own interests better than they know the interests of strangers. They also are responsible for knowing the interests of their children and, to a lesser extent, of their friends. Because they know the position of strangers less well and inevitably care less for them as persons, they are less capable of representing their interests. Therefore, the community as a whole is better served when most people represent the interests of those for whom they are responsible above those for whom they are not. The responsibilities of public servants and fiduciaries are more inclusive than of those they serve, and the scope of their partiality is correspondingly broader. However, even public servants do not serve all equally, and their partiality to their constituents is a moral failure only when carried to an extreme provincialism. Decentration should be aimed at bringing about coordination and integration of the claims of alter with ego, a realizable ideal, and not impartiality, an unrealizable ideal.

Selye's (1980) principle of altruistic egoism has much in common with what I mean by true self-interest. Selye claimed that to live in satisfying equilibration with their surroundings, human beings have a built-in survival need to work agenticly to accumulate "goodwill," which he identified as the crucial social resource. Altruistic egoism refers to the selfish hoarding of esteem, love, and respect of one's neighbors by acts of compassion, with the implicit understanding that in times of need, others will reciprocate one's goodwill. Selye's claim is compatible with my argument that individuals cannot and ought not attempt to set their interests aside to consider the interests of others. Just as enlightened self-interest includes compassionate regard for others and an inclination to behave justly, so does an enlightened sense of social obligation embrace a considered view of existential obligations to oneself. By honoring one's obligations to self, one thereby comes to understand one's obligations to others: What one claims as one's right solely by virtue of being human, one must thereby grant to all who share one's human status.

Even works of supererogation (acts in the Roman Catholic doctrine that go beyond what is required for salvation) are generally motivated by *agape* (self-giving love), rather than by justice, and these are the epitome of altruism. Such acts transcend the self–other duality rather than abnegate the self. Self-abnegation is masochistic and seldom laudable. For example, Simone Weil, in frail health and in a sanitorium in England, refused to eat more than the official wartime rations available to ordinary people in France. Her death from malnutrition saved no one. Although altruistic by Rushton's definition, because it was intended to achieve positive outcomes for others rather than for herself, her sacrifice was immoral by mine because it denied subjectivity and the probable real consequences of her actions, rather than reconciling the interests of self and others. Such immoderate selflessness may be indistinguishable from egoism. Whereas Simone Weil relinquished her life at age 33 for an ideal of justice in which self-starvation took the form of self-mortification that did not help others, Maximilian Kolbe (called the Saint of Auschwitz) *transcended* the self–other bifurcation by giving his sustenance and finally his life to preserve the life of his fellow prisoners. In relinquishing a life of agony in Auschwitz (by volunteering to die in place of another man), Kolbe believed he exchanged his temporal life for eternal life in heaven. Although he anticipated a greater reward in heaven (i.e., a long-range benefit), Kolbe's actions were altruistic by my definition because his actions greatly benefited other individuals at much cost to himself. Kolbe's actions were undertaken without regard to the merits (or demerits) of the recipient or cost to himself. Thus, they were motivated by agape, not by justice.

The question may be asked: Are justice and compassion implicit in true self-interest? My answer in the affirmative is based on the following five empirical claims: (1) Injustice and cruelty invariably create resentment and envy, and I am harmed by ill will; that is, reciprocity is a fact of social life and not merely an abstract moral principle. (2) Most human beings are empathic and have a natural desire for equity, so that I am discomfited by injury to others and inequity whether I am the perpetrator or the victim of the inequity or injustice. (3) Behaving unjustly or without compassion is internally corrosive, harming my long-range development and diminishing myself. (4) The self–other boundary is permeable, so that in poisoning my environment, I poison myself. (5) I sever my ties with my culture by breaking its rules and violating its principles or the rights of others. For these reasons, true self-interest requires that I behave justly and kindly. Moral considerations of justice and compassion, therefore, do not exclude self-interest but, on the contrary, are implicit in true self-interest.

The tension between self and other is a reflection in consciousness of the dialectical interpenetration of two contradictory realities, the self-as-entity and the self-as-process. The self-as-entity is a static hypostasis absolutely separable from the social environment with a personal and unique history, consciousness, and rights, that is, an alienated self; the self-as-process is inextricably intertwined with the environment. From the perspective of the self-as-process, the answer to the question "Why be moral?" is self-evident: The self-as-process knows that it depends for its development upon the quality of its physical environment and its social environment and therefore can afford to despoil neither. The process of becoming moral (or enlightened) is the process of decentration. To decenter is not to deny self, but rather to increase progressively the scope of self. As Marx put it poetically in the *Paris Manuscripts* (1844/1964) and later in *The Grundrisse* (1858/1971), nature, physical and social, is the human's own body: Physical nature constitutes our inorganic flesh, and the social environment our organic flesh.

BRIDGING THE GAP BETWEEN
MORAL JUDGMENT AND ACTION

In this section, I examine the relationship between moral judgment and action. This is the province of the behavioral scientist rather than the philosopher, and includes an examination of the actual conditions in which moral decision making takes place, and the personalities of those who make them. It has to do with the development of moral identity, a dimension of individual differences.

In summarizing the little we know about how moral judgments affect corresponding actions, Blasi (1980) concluded that (1) there is relatively strong evidence that delinquents differ from nondelinquents in their stage of moral reasoning; (2) at higher stages, there is greater resistance to conformity pressure; (3) the evidence concerning expectations that principled reasoners are more altruistic than preconventional reasoners is mixed but generally supportive of the hypothesis; and (4) there is little support for the expectation that postconventional reasoners resist social pressure to conform in their moral actions.

Haan (1977, 1978) claimed that because agents are subjected to the stresses of daily life, their decisions are necessarily affected by the defensive and coping strategies they have adopted to manage stress. Several empirical studies (e.g., Weiss, 1982) have confirmed the hypothesis that abstract judgments about morality are more adequate logically (i.e., they better differentiate and integrate the conflicting claims of inclination and competing obligations to others) than moral judgments made in the heat of action. Self-implication reduces the cognitive level of judgments about morality; defensive coping strategies both lower the cognitive level of moral judgments which implicate the self and induce discrepancies between moral judgments and action. Although Haan concluded that the relation between interpersonal thought and action is higher and less reactive to situational stress than the relation between formal thought and action, neither was high. Adults who habitually used strategies of intellectualization and denial had higher interview-based formal scores but did not behave more morally. In stressful, affect-laden situations constructed by Haan (1978), ego processes such as defensive doubting and cognitive coping predicted action levels, whereas levels of formal morality *or* interpersonal morality did not.

In general, verbal adherence to a norm of altruism or fairness has little or no relation to altruistic conduct (Staub, 1978) or just behavior. Social norms that control altruism are widely accepted (Krebs, 1970; Krebs & Rosenwald, 1977), but people are easily dissuaded from behaving altruistically by conditions that diffuse responsibility (Darley & Latane, 1968), allow the victim's predicament to be overlooked (Staub & Baer, 1974), or induce conflict-produced stress. Conflict-produced stress that results in a gap between ideals and conduct increases with the cost to the individual of choosing a path not entirely determined by inclination or expedient considerations. It is precisely under such conflict-arousing conditions that agents are called upon to reconcile a narrow parochial view of self-interest with their long-range interests as social beings. How well they succeed is determined by situational and characterological, as well as by cognitive, factors.

Formal reasoning improves judgment, but is only one of many faculties, cognitive and otherwise, that contributes to knowledge of true self-interest. Knowledge of true self-interest is predicated, on the one hand, upon a sense of identity, that is, of self-sameness and unity over time and situations, and, on the other hand, upon permeability to the environment. Adequate knowledge of one's true interests depends upon self-awareness, engagement in reciprocal relations, and practical intelligence. Because knowledge of one's true interests includes awareness of how others interpret theirs, social sensitivity is required. Personal virtues such as courage, compassion, self-control, integrity, and diligence enable persons to discern and act upon their own true interests. Instrumental competencies enable each person to enlarge his or her scope of action. Determination of true self-interest requires a sense of personal agency and knowledge of the material world. A sense of personal agency consists of self-awareness marked by conscience as an arbiter of conduct, and perception of oneself as a free agent able and willing to steer one's own development. Determination of true self-interest, that is, what is truly good for me, requires that I specify the conflicting claims that constitute ceteris paribus. To determine these conflicting claims (of conditions that must be equal), and to minimize unintended consequences brought on by my actions, I must aspire to full knowledge and development of material–social reality, as well as of myself.

Socialization of the child should therefore include training in construing true self-interest, and in practicing virtuous conduct—that is, in the development of prosocial, socially responsible behavior. Socialization investigators who study the development of conscience, character, and social responsibility are studying what I mean by moral development. Piaget (1932) claimed that mutuality cannot be taught through a process of parent-dominated unilateral constraints and indoctrination. He stated that naturally occurring peer groups offer children opportunities to discover that, by working together under mutually advantageous procedural rules, they can produce mutually satisfying results. Although there is little evidence other than Piaget's own on games to support his contention, there is considerable evidence to support the effectiveness of parents and other adults in promoting empathic concerns and prosocial behavior (e.g., Barnett, Howard, King, & Dino, 1980; Koestner, Franz, & Weinberger,

1990). Adults, especially parents, may assist their children to develop empathy and to behave prosocially by treating them authoritatively (Baumrind, 1971b, 1990, 1991), that is, by being responsive to their childrens' reasonable demands and requiring in turn that their children be responsive to their demands.

A unique contribution of stage/structural theory is its differentiation between preconventional and postconventional morality. In several studies, however, the political actions of preconventional and postconventional moral reasoners had more in common with each other than with those of conventional reasoners (Haan, 1975; Haan, Smith, & Block, 1968; Salzstein, Diamond, & Belenky, 1972). Thus, in situations of civil disobedience, the feelings expressed by postconventional reasoners differed from those expressed by preconventional reasoners, but their actions did not. Instead, both differed in their actions from conventional reasoners. This finding contradicts the expectation that Kohlberg stage scores should discriminate among individuals by level rather than by content of moral reasoning. Adherence to conventional versus nonconventional moral attitudes is easily predicted by a simple paper-and-pencil test of conventionality (e.g., Hogan, 1970; Hogan & Dickstein, 1972; Jessor & Jessor, 1974), and does not require the elaborate Kohlberg system to assess. If Stages 5 and 6 require philosophic sophistication, as they apparently do, they are unsuited to anchor moral judgment maturity. In that case, Kohlberg's system has been deconstructed.

Moral judgments should be directed at avoiding (at least as much as resolving) situations that create moral dilemmas, because such circumstances produce negative consequences to others, which must then be undone (negative Karma). A conflict arises in moral judgments when my desire to act or fail to act conflicts with what I, a significant other, or a generalized other (convention, law, church) believes I ought to do either to secure my long-range interests or to accommodate to the legitimate needs of others. A moral conflict exists within a person or between persons when the perceived interests of the individual or individuals are experienced as incompatible, and the agent is concerned about doing what is right rather than merely following his or her inclination. The conflict is intraindividual when only the individual's own interests are in conflict (e.g., immediate gratification of a lesser good vs. long-range gratification of a higher good), and interindividual when self-interest is perceived to conflict with the interests of others. If I regard myself as a moral agent, I will try very hard to avoid both intraindividual and interindividual moral conflicts. However, when they arise (as they must), I will try to resolve a conflict between inclination and obligation, or between apparently incompatible obligations, in such a way that I am prepared to accept fully the consequences of my decision and, if challenged, to justify by generalizable rules the bases on which I came to my decision.

My worth as a moral agent rests on the moral adequacy of my judgments and actions. The moral adequacy of my judgments rests in part on, but is not defined by, their cognitive adequacy. The *cognitive adequacy* of my judgments is based on logical criteria, such as those set forth by Kohlberg (1969), which are greater differentiation among the issues considered and integration of heretofore contradictory positions. The *moral adequacy* of my judgments is based on (1) how accurately and comprehensively I have taken into account my own true interests, and (2) how willing and able I am (a) to realize my decision in action and (b) to cope effectively with the consequences I have produced by those actions. The moral adequacy of my *action* inheres in the extent to which I hold myself responsible for that action, and this in turn is based in part on the coherence, rationality, and volitionality of my decision-making processes. It is also based on competencies that I am responsible for developing so that I may realize my good intentions. Therefore, good will does not absolve a moral agent from failure to do good well. In fact, failure to be true in action to one's professed intentions bespeaks a critical moral flaw.

INTERPERSONAL MORALITY AND "IDEAL SPEECH" CONDITIONS

A significant group of investigators, drawing on the work of Habermas (1971, 1975), MacMurray (1961), Piaget (1932), and Ricoeur (1978), have rejected Kohlberg's Kantian vision of the private subject who comes to an autonomous decision in solitary splendor, in favor of the social subject who constitutes and validates moral principles in interpersonal relations. Interpersonal moral theorists, such as Damon, Haan, and Youniss, have attempted to bridge the gap between moral judgment and action by grounding private morality in consensual validation. In place of the Kantian rational, self-contained subject, these investigators have drawn upon Habermas and Piaget to develop a social construction of moral principles redeemed by argumentative discourse. Damon (1977), Haan (1982), and Haan, Weiss, and Johnson (1982) drew upon Piaget's original formulations to locate moral development in the friendship group. Youniss (1978, 1981, 1982) and Edelstein and Noam (1982) located moral development in enlightened group processes such as "ideal speech" conditions (Habermas, 1970a, 1970b).

Ideal discourse is problematic from the perspective presented here, however, because it has the same contrafactual status in Habermas's system as Stage 6 does in Kohlberg's theory. As such, it is not a realizable ideal, but rather a normative criterion against which communication can be evaluated. For Habermas and his followers, the criteria of moral superiority are situated in ideal speech processes rather than in ideal thought processes.

Ideal speech, like Stage 6 moral reasoning, is stripped of the material constraints imposed by inequalities in personality, competence, and power, and by genuine conflicts of interests. As such, it has little relevance to real interpersonal encounters outside an academic setting. Persons engaged in communicative discourse differ in their command of linguistic skills, rationality, and personal attractiveness, and these inequalities result inevitably in differential power to persuade, even in a friendship group. If individuals are required by an experimenter to confront each other in face-to-face discussion and to argue, debate, discuss, compromise, and negotiate under conditions approaching "ideal speech," a consensus may be obtained by sharing intentions and meaning. However, the conditions that pertain in experimental studies of transactive sociomoral discussion (e.g., Berkowitz & Gibbs, 1983) are typically not present in adversarial groups comprised of interested rather than disinterested parties to the resolution of conflict. I would not expect, therefore, that individuals persuaded to engage in "ideal discourse" in contrived experimental situations would thereby choose to engage in ideal discourse in everyday life, where conditions of conflict and inequality pertain.

Four considerations persuade me that practical consensus-based decision making bears little resemblance to the "ideal speech" conditions proposed by Habermas:

1. Consensus-based decision making can take place only when the true interests of those who see themselves as adversaries are not contradictory. But characteristically, the true interests of adversaries diverge and adversarial relations divide group members. Thus, in labor–management disputes, conflicts of views reflect differences in true interests, and are not a result of failure to communicate.

2. Although the group process may aid some individuals to discover what is right, right is not determined by group consensus. The moral adequacy of a judgment is not equivalent to the level of consensual validation it can obtain. To behave morally frequently requires doing what is right against not only one's own inclination, but also in opposition to the consensual judgment of significant others. The process of seeking consensual validation is neither required by, nor always facilitative of, moral adequacy, but may serve instead to diffuse responsibility.

3. Interpersonal decisions are easily swayed by nonmoral concerns, such as the dynamics of group interaction, rather than by rational consideration of the true interests of the individuals composing the group or of the group as a whole. There is little empirical evidence that members of naturally occurring peer groups typically demonstrate mutual respect and compassionate reciprocity.

4. Although the ideal speech paradigm is feasible in mature friendship groups in which the relationship is valued for its own sake, rather than as a means to an end, most peer groups are not egalitarian friendship groups. Status inequalities generally exist among peer group members, and these differences, based on factors not related to merit such as sex and social position, generate communicative hierarchies as constraining as those produced by ascribed role hierarchies. Children's natural activity groups, far from being status blind and governed by relations of cooperation, are sensitive to task-irrelevant status considerations, which generate hierarchy and are characterized by scapegoating and bullying. Even when they wish to be fair, children are seldom scrupulous in how they divide a pie. Most young children cut their own slices a little larger than those of their friends, and when a bit older, they cut the slices for their friends a bit larger than those for the peer group who are not their friends.

Ideal discourse, as identified by Habermas (1984), requires formal training in rational argumentation, including testing of validity claims of oneself and others, and maintenance of the internal coherence of arguments. Above all, it requires motivation to find the best or fairest solution to the problem under discussion rather than to score points. It presupposes that participants, individually and jointly, want to maintain objectivity of perspective and to recognize the fallibility of their own arguments and insights as much as they do those of their intellectual adversaries. However, even in scientific discourse, a competitive partisanship generally predominates, and in my experience, this is nowhere more true than in discourse about morality; that is, the intent of the debaters is more to win the argument than to arrive at a consensually validated truth. If ideal discourse were practical, it would be used routinely to arrive at consensus in trials by jury where the participants are not directly affected by their decisions. The study of transcripts of jury deliberations could indicate to what extent features of ideal discourse are present empirically. Simulated jury deliberations that take place after adequate training in ideal discourse principles and methods would indicate whether "jurors" chose to use ideal discourse once they knew how, but were told explicitly that they could arrive at consensus by strategies of their own choosing.

When adversarial positions are based not on true differences that motivate them to be disinterested in the truth of the other's argument, but rather on misunderstandings, adversaries may be prepared to debate the matter logically and in good faith. Then ideal discourse may in fact be realizable to resolve (1) factual disagreements concerning the probable effects of a given action, or (2) differences about how a rule that disputants all affirm is applicable in a given instance, or even (3) differences in the relative weights that should be assigned to rules on which disputants all place a positive value. Some characteristics of ideal discourse, such as reasoning about the other's reasoning or taking the position of the other for the sake of argument, are used by conciliators to resolve conflicts of interest. When conflicts arise from fundamentally contradictory perspectives, as they often must, the function of a conciliator is to enable participants to decentrate from the immediacy of their own special interests and metaethical presuppositions long enough to grasp and appreciate their adversary's position so that a way through an impasse can be negotiated. However, even when expediency dictates compromise in action, seldom will the rival and divergent moral first principles and the interests they reflect be reconciled.

On the one hand, diversity of metaethical positions benefits the species as a whole by enlarging the idea pool and ought, therefore, to be encouraged. Thus, resolution of metaethical conflicts is seldom possible and not necessarily desirable. On the other hand, tolerance of diversity should not include tolerance of what one regards as truly evil. Perhaps the most difficult moral decisions are those that mandate doing harm to an adversary to preserve the common good, because that adversary is regarded not merely as wrong, but as truly evil. Under such conditions, prolonged discourse that delays decisive action may be immoral. There is probably greater agreement about what constitutes unmitigated evil than good, but little agreement about the proper recourse of a moral agent to overcome such evil.

CONCLUDING COMMENTS

In adopting a rule-utilitarian metaethics, I dispute Kohlberg's presuppositions (Kohlberg et al., 1983, pp. 66–67) that the standards of moral adequacy should be exclusively cognitive, that the ideal self is fully autonomous, that justice (individual rights) has a privileged status in defining the moral domain, and that morality must be universalizable. Although I reject the notion of culturally invariant stages, I accept the presence of predictable regularities in individual development, and of qualitative progressive transformations that bring the individual into closer conformity with cultural and/or personal ideals. I agree that advanced stages of moral *judgment* are more differentiated and hierarchically integrated than previous ones; advanced stages of moral and social development entail the ability to critique conventions and culture; and moral judgments must have a prescriptive function referring not merely to what is, but also to what ought to be.

My sociocultural perspective has in common with Hogan's socioanalytic perspective (Hogan & Busch, 1984; Hogan, Johnson, & Emler, 1978; Hogan, Chapter 10, this volume), a view of morality as a human enterprise achieved largely by means of socialization and acculturation throughout life. Both perspectives affirm that all higher functioning in the child has its origins in social life, and claim a relative moral absolutism that is justified by intransigent social realities that may, however, be manifested differently in different cultures. My perspective differs from Hogan's in that I emphasize rational and volitional rather than personality determinants, and I regard the ethics of social responsibility and the ethics of personal conscience as bidimensional rather than as bipolar (bearing close resemblance to the ubiquitous two interpersonal factors of communion and personal agency). Although I agree that personality and socialization factors generate a preference for, or an aversion to, social conformity as a basis of morality, I believe that the contradictions implicit in human social adaption require in each individual both conformance and nonconformance to social rules and, therefore, the capacities to both observe and critique conventions.

My perspective shares with the cognitive–behavioral approach a rejection of universal moral standards; an emphasis on socialization of the child by means of modeling, social persuasion, and the law of effect; and an emphasis on the *action* of the agent of inquiry. However, I find that the investigator's understanding of the subject–participants' understanding of their own behavior is essential to prediction or control of those participants' self-initiated actions. Also, I see the child as more active in the co-construction of reality, albeit with the help of adults' supportive guidance or "scaffolds." In addition, I reject the dichotomy between ego and alter presumed by the hedonic calculus and regard the behavioral laws of social reinforcement or modeling as too simplistic to explain the impulsive self-sacrificial efforts of some to save the lives of others to whom they are unrelated genetically, or of the pervasive need of many human beings to transcend their personal limitations. Indeed, as Kendler (Chapter 6, this volume) suggests, Tolman's cognitive behaviorism also rejects such simplistic behaviorist formulations. Preoccupation with the ultimate questions of why live, why be moral, or how to face death that are in the province of religion, has little to do with the law of effect. In fact, the moral maturity of an individual or of a society can be evaluated by how little his or her behavior is governed by the hedonic calculus, and is motivated instead by an overriding regard for integrating personal development as a moral agent and commitment to a realizable ideal of the common good.

Metatheoretical perspectives are adopted or generated to provide coherence and unity to the cosmos at a level of organization just beyond what can be known scientifically or consensually validated by the species as a whole. They are an effort to provide a subjective sense of certitude where none is possible objectively. With the hegemony of Kohlberg's paradigm finally over, it is possible that a synthesis of heretofore contradictory positions is in fact emerging. A shared proof structure is a social construction that binds a scientific community and allows its members to exchange and evaluate findings. However, contradictory paradigms exist side by side in the social sciences, especially in the study of moral phenomena, and the dominant paradigm shifts with the times. Each well-developed perspective uniquely grasps some aspect of reality, and misrepresents or undervalues other aspects, depending upon whether what has been grasped is the leg, the trunk, or the ear of the ethical elephant. From my perspective, what matters is that my actions authentically manifest my own convictions, and that yours do the same. Conflict, not consensus, over first principles and conceptions of justice characterize our pluralistic society. Even were we able to achieve a consensus by agreeing to conform to a particular proof structure, arrival at such consensus would not thereby validate our beliefs.

REFERENCES

Barnett, M., Howard, J., King, L., & Dino, G. (1980). Antecedents of empathy: Retrospective accounts of early socialization. *Personality and Social Psychology Bulletin, 6,* 361–365.

Baumrind, D. (1971a). Principles of ethical conduct in the treatment of subjects: Reactions to the draft report of the Committee on Ethical Standards in Psychological Research. *American Psychologist, 26,* 887–896.

Baumrind, D. (1971b). Current patterns of parental authority. *Developmental Psychology Monograph,* Vol. 4, No. I, Part 2, 1–103.

Baumrind, D. (1972). Reactions to the May 1972 draft report of the Ad Hoc Committee on Ethical Standards in Psychological Research. *American Psychologist, 27,* 1083–1086.

Baumrind, D. (1975a). It neither is nor ought to be: A reply to Wallwork. In E. C. Kennedy (Ed.), *Human rights and psychological research: A debate on psychology and ethics* (pp. 83–102). New York: Thomas Y. Crowell.

Baumrind, D. (1975b). Metaethical and normative considerations governing the treatment of human subjects in the behavioral sciences. In E. C. Kennedy (Ed.), *Human rights and psychological research: A debate on psychology and ethics* (pp. 37–68). New York: Thomas Y. Crowell.

Baumrind, D. (1978a). A dialectical materialist's perspective on knowing social reality. *New Directions for Child Development, 2,* 61–82.

Baumrind, D. (1978b). Nature and definition of informed consent in research involving deception. In the *Belmont Report, Ethical principles and guidelines for the protection of human subjects of research* (Appendix, Vol. II, (pp. 23-1–23-71); DHEW Publication No. OS 78-0014). Washington, DC: National Commission for the Protection of Human Subjects of Biomedical and Behavioral Research.

Baumrind, D. (1985). Research using intentional deception: Ethical issues revisited. *American Psychologist, 40,* 165–174.

Baumrind, D. (1986). Sex differences in moral reasoning: Response to Walker's (1984) conclusion that there are none. *Child Development, 57,* 511–521.

Baumrind, D. (1990). Parenting styles and adolescent development. In R. M. Lerner, A. C. Petersen, & V. Brooks-Gunn (Eds.), *Encyclopedia of Adolescence* (pp. 746–758). New York: Garland.

Baumrind, D. (1991). The influence of parenting style on adolescent competence and substance abuse. *Journal of Early Adolescence.* Vol. II, No. 1 (pp. 56–95).

Berkowitz, M. W., & Gibbs, J. C. (1983). Measuring the developmental features of moral discussion. *Merrill-Palmer Quarterly, 29,* 399–410.

Blasi, A. (1980). Bridging moral cognition and moral action: A critical review of the literature. *Psychological Bulletin, 88,* 1–45.

Colby, A., Kohlberg, L., Gibbs, J., & Lieberman, M. (1983). A longitudinal study of moral judgment. *Monographs of the Society for Research in Child Development,* 48(1, Serial No. 200).

Damon, W. (1977). *The social world of the child.* San Francisco: Jossey-Bass.

Darley, J. M., & Latane, B. (1968). Bystander intervention in emergencies: Diffusion of responsibility. *Journal of Personality and Social Psychology, 8,* 377–383.

Edelstein, W., & Noam, G. (1982). *Regulatory structures of the self and "postformal" stages in adulthood.* Unpublished manuscript.

Gilligan, C. (1982). *In a different voice.* Cambridge, MA: Harvard University Press.

Gouldner, A. W. (1960). The norm of reciprocity: A preliminary statement. *American Sociological Review, 25,* 161–178.

Haan, N. (1975). Hypothetical and actual moral reasoning in a situation of civil disobedience. *Journal of Personality and Social Psychology, 32,* 255–270.

Haan, N. (1977). *Coping and defending: Processes of self-environment organization.* New York: Academic Press.

Haan, N. (1978). Two moralities in action contexts: Relationships to thought, ego regulation, and development. *Journal of Personality and Social Psychology, 36,* 286–305.

Haan, N. (1982). Can research on morality be "scientific"? *American Psychologist, 37,* 1096–1104.

Haan, N., Smith, M. B., & Block, J. (1968). Moral reasoning of young adults: Political-social behavior, family background, and personality correlates. *Journal of Personality and Social Psychology, 10,* 183–201.

Haan, N., Weiss, R., & Johnson, V. (1982). The role of logic in moral reasoning and development. *Developmental Psychology, 18,* 245–256.

Habermas, J. (1970a). *Toward a rational society.* Boston: Beacon Press.

Habermas, J. (1970b). Toward a theory of communicative competence. *Inquiry, 13,* 360–375.

Habermas, J. (1971). *Knowledge and human interests.* Boston: Beacon Press.

Habermas, J. (1975). *Legitimation crisis.* Boston: Beacon Press.

Habermas, J. (1984). *Theory of communicative action: Vol. 1. Reason and rationality in society* (T. McCarthy, Trans.). Boston: Beacon Press.

Hogan, R. (1970). A dimension of moral judgment. *Journal of Consulting and Clinical Psychology, 35,* 205–212.

Hogan, R., & Busch, C. (1984). Moral conduct as auto-interpretation. In W. Kurtines & J. L. Gewirtz (Eds.), *Morality, moral behavior and moral development* (pp. 227–240). New York: Wiley.

Hogan, R., & Dickstein, E. (1972). A measure of moral values. *Journal of Consulting and Clinical Psychology, 39*, 210–214.

Hogan, R., Johnson, J. A., & Emler, N. P. (1978). A socioanalytic theory of moral development. In W. Damon (Ed.), *Moral development* (pp. 1–18). San Francisco: Jossey-Bass.

Holstein, C. B. (1972). The relation of children's moral judgment level to that of their parents, and to communication patterns in the family. In R. C. Smart & M. S. Smart (Eds.), *Readings in child development and relationships* (pp. 484–494). New York: MacMillan.

Jessor, S. L., & Jessor, R. (1974). Maternal ideology and adolescent problem behavior. *Developmental Psychology, 10*, 246–254.

Karkar, S. (1978). *The inner world: A psychoanalytic study of childhood and society in India.* Oxford: Oxford University Press.

Kierkegaard, S. (1968). *Fear and trembling, and the sickness unto death.* Princeton, NJ: Princeton University Press.

Koestner, R., Franz, C., & Weinberger, J. (1990). The family origins of empathic concern: A 26-year longitudinal study. *Journal of Personality and Social Psychology, 58*, 709–717.

Kohlberg, L. (1969). Stage and sequence: The cognitive–developmental approach to socialization. In D. Goslin (Ed.), *Handbook of socialization theory and research* (pp. 347–480). Chicago: Rand McNally.

Kohlberg, L. (1973). The claim to moral adequacy of a highest stage of moral judgment. *Journal of Philosophy, 70*, 630–646.

Kohlberg, L., Levine, C., & Hewer, A. (1983). *Moral stages: A current formulation and a response to critics.* New York: Karger.

Krebs, D. L. (1970). Altruism—An examination of the concept and a review of the literature. *Psychological Bulletin, 73*, 258–303.

Krebs, D., & Rosenwald, A. (1977). Moral reasoning and moral behavior in conventional adults. *Merrill-Palmer Quarterly, 23*, 77–87.

MacMurray, J. (1961). *Persons in relation.* London: Farber & Farber.

Marx, K. (1964). *Economic and philosophical manuscripts of 1844: Paris manuscripts.* New York: International Publishers. (Original work published 1844)

Marx, K. (1971). *The Grundrisse* (D. McLellan, Ed. and Trans.). New York: Harper & Row. (Original work published 1858)

Piaget, J. (1932). *The moral judgment of the child.* London: Routledge & Kegan Paul.

Rawls, J. (1971). *The theory of justice.* Cambridge, MA: Harvard University Press.

Ricoeur, P. (1978). The problem of the foundation of moral philosophy. *Philosophy Today, 22*, 175–192.

Rushton, J. P. (1980). *Altruism, socialization, and society.* Englewood Cliffs, NJ: Prentice-Hall.

Salzstein, H. D., Diamond, R. M., & Belenky, M. (1972). Moral judgment level and conformity behavior. *Developmental Psychology, 7,* 327–336.

Selye, H. (1980). Epilogue. In H. Selye (Ed.), *Selye's guide to stress research* (Vol I.). New York: Van Nostrand Reinhold.

Shweder, R. A., & Bourne, E. (1982). Does the concept of the person vary cross-culturally? In A. J. Marsella & G. White (Eds.), *Cultural conceptions of mental health and therapy* (pp. 97–137). London: Reidel.

Staub, E. (1978). *Positive social behavior and morality* (Vol. I.). New York: Academic Press.

Staub, E., & Baer, R. S. (1974). Stimulus characteristics of a sufferer and difficulty of escape as determinants of helping. *Journal of Personality and Social Psychology, 30,* 279–285.

Waddington, C. H. (1960). *The ethical animal.* Chicago: University of Chicago Press.

Weiss, R. (1982). Understanding moral thought: Effects on moral reasoning and decision-making. *Developmental Psychology, 18,* 852–861.

Youniss, J. (1978). Dialectical theory and Piaget on social knowledge. *Human Development, 21,* 234–247.

Youniss, J. (1981). Moral development through a theory of social construction: An analysis. *Merrill-Palmer Quarterly, 27,* 385–403.

Youniss, J. (1982). Why persons communicate on moral matters: A response to Shweder. *Merrill-Palmer Quarterly, 28,* 71–77.

Author Index

Subject Index